W9-BQX-564

STUDIES IN
SYMBOLIC INTERACTION

Volume 1 • 1978

REVIEWERS for Volume I

Charles Axelrod
Steve Brickey
William C. Cockerham
Carl J. Couch
James Cowie
Stanley Cross
Catherine Daubard
Evelyn K. Denzin
Scotty Embree
Saul Feldman
Eve Finnbogason
Elihu Gerson
Sue Gerson
Peter M. Hall
Robert Hintz

Sidney J. Kronus
James McCartney
David R. Maines
Clyde E. Martin
Ron Miller
John Money
Edward Rose
Marvin Scott
Julian Simon
Robert Stebbins
Gregory P. Stone
Anselm Strauss
Nick Tavuchis
Martin Weinberg
Joseph Zygmunt

STUDIES IN SYMBOLIC INTERACTION

An Annual Compilation of Research

Editor: NORMAN K. DENZIN
Department of Sociology
University of Illinois

Volume 1 • 1978

JAI PRESS INC.
Greenwich, Connecticut

Copyright © 1978 JAI PRESS INC.
321 Greenwich Avenue
Greenwich, Connecticut 06830
All rights reserved. No part of this publication may be reproduced, stored on a retrieval system, or transmitted, in any form or by any means, electronic, mechanical, photocopying, filming, recording or otherwise, without prior permission in writing from the publisher.

ISBN NUMBER: 0-89232-065-6

Manufactured in the United States of America

CONTENTS

FOREWORD

The essays in this annual series consist of original research and theory within the general sociological perspective known as Symbolic Interactionism. Longer than conventional journal-length articles, the essays wed micro and macro concerns within a qualitative, field-method empirical orientation. International in scope, this series draws upon the work of urban ethnographers, phenomenologists, ethnomethodologists, critical theorists, humanistic sociologists, as well as symbolic interactionists and conflict theorists. The emphasis is on new thought and research which bridge links to an emergent theory of self, socialization, interaction, social relationships, social organization and society.

The essays printed in Volume I have undergone "peer" review and the names of the reviewers who undertook this editorial function are printed on the inside title page. Their assistance is gratefully acknowledged. The use of the "peer" review technique is intended to sharpen the focus and strengths of each manuscript. It is assumed that peers, more so than anonymous editorial referees, can better assist an author when revisions are called for. Each author in Volume I submitted the names of three colleagues to me and these persons were then asked to review the manuscripts and to suggest changes.

OVERVIEW

The essays are ordered in a fashion which weaves back and forth between large-scale social organization problems, and more micro-social psychological issues. The intent is to destroy the usual distinction between macro and micro phenomena. The perspective of symbolic interactionism rejects such a distinction. The opening essay by Herbert Blumer, written during the student and war protests of the early 1970s, forcefully establishes the relevance of symbolic interactionism for the study of social unrest and collective protest. Blumer offers a conceptual bridge for the study and analysis of social unrest and in the process he notes common misunderstandings of this social process.

Edward Gross, in the first of two essays included in this volume, observes that large-scale organizations virtually dominate contemporary societies. He proposes that such organizations are inherently criminogenic—that is, they induce their members to engage in criminal activities. My essay on "Crime and the American Liquor Industry" examines Gross's hypothesis through the presentation of case-history materials on the production and distribution of whiskey in the United States since prohibition. Substantial support is found for his conclusions and the "dramaturgical" techniques employed by the industry are discussed.

Anselm Strauss extends our understanding of social worlds and indicates how their study can better illuminate the character of today's mass societies. Strauss stresses the strengths and weaknesses of the Chicago tradition, in particular that tradition's use of George Herbert Mead's interactionism. Strauss's points are extended in Harvey A. Farberman's chapter, which begins Volume 2.

The second article by Edward Gross extends symbolic interactionism into the field of learning theory, and he opens the way for a more systematic account of the childhood socialization process. His chapter anticipates Jeffrey S. Victor's paper on the social psychology of sexual activity, and both authors call for renewed attention to the conditions which affect social learning. Rita Sieden Miller examines the phenomenological events which surround the acquisition of the pregnancy identity. Social and physiological pregnancy are separated for special analysis and, like Victor, Miller attempts to show how social processes blend and combine with physiological states. The two realms are by no means easily joined.

Richard Bibbee and Julian B. Roebuck discuss the meditation movement from the critical perspective of symbolic interactionism. This movement, which purports to focus on the self, and which stresses a rejection of mind-body dualism, offers a set of directions for bringing one's mind in line with one's body. The techniques of this movement are analyzed by Bibbee and Roebuck, and they propose that C. W. Jung's concept of "synchronicity" (the simultaneous connection of seemingly unrelated events into a causal unity) offers an explanation for how the meditation process actually works. Thus, by sitting in a certain posture, chanting a certain phrase, breathing in a certain way, and by holding the proper mental attitude, the meditator believes he can change his character and the world around him. By bringing Jungian formulations into their interactionist perspective, the authors illustrate how macro-level phenomena submit to the symbolic interactionist paradigm.

David R. Maines extends this line of reasoning even further; he wishes to study bodies and identities—the meanings given bodies. Demographers persist in conceptualizing people as mere bodies. Of course, it is easier to count bodies than it is to count identities. Maines sets forth a very compelling framework for linking the study of bodies and identities to a processual view of migration and social organization. He returns social psychology (and symbolic interactionism) to the field of demography.

Miller, Weiland and Couch turn the discussion to social structure, power, and tyrannic control. The dimensions of tyrannic interaction are specified and linked to the study of social control processes at the societal level. It is a sad commentary on humanity, they note, that "the history of complex societies suggests that many of them are constructed . . . on the basis of complex tyrannic relationships." A more thorough study of such relationships, perhaps along the lines indicated by Miller, Weiland and Couch, is clearly called for.

Michal McCall applies Everett Hughes's observations on "marginal men" to an interactionist-social world account of the female artist. She examines the marginality sensed and experienced by the female in the male-dominated "art" worlds of St. Louis, itself a marginal world for all artists. Careful interviewing and field observations revealed the existence of four types of St. Louis female artists. The determinants of artistic status are discussed by McCall, as are the processes that transform "things" into artistic objects. McCall's research points in the direction of a solidly grounded sociology of art and art worlds. Such a sociology will be lodged in the actual experiences and relationships of those persons who are accorded or attempt to achieve the status of artist.

Reyes Ramos, an ethnomethodologist, criticizes most students of natural talk who only focus upon the internal structure of conversations. By introducing the technique of interviewing persons about their conversations, Ramos forces our attention to the producers of conversations. He brings the speaker back into the speech act and shows that "surface" talk often belies complex and subtle conversations persons are having with themselves, as they produce natural (recordable) conversations. This point, so evident in George Herbert Mead's theory of the self, has recently gone unnoticed in conversational studies. Ramos goes one step further by proposing that natural talk can be studied in terms of concepts taken from music theory. He views conversations as extemporaneous compositions, wherein topic changes are subject to a modulation process that leads to key changes and key shifts within the composition. He presents conversational and interview data gathered from a short conversation of two college students. Ramos's work promises to alter the field of conversational analysis, and it suggests that symbolic interactionists need to take the work of the ethnomethodologists more seriously than they have in the past.

It is hoped that readers of *Studies in Symbolic Interaction* will enjoy these research and theoretical papers. Subsequent volumes will contain studies of public, social control agencies, as well as original work on the mass media, timekeeping and calenders, surveillance and solidarity in dyads, social problems and symbolic interaction, evaluation programs and qualitative research methodology, "nested" identities, political crime, "a ritual theory of self," "Cooley's Economic Sociology," and a "dramaturgical theory of social structure." The mutual support and encouragement of symbolic interactionists throughout the world is the means and the end of this series.

Norman K. Denzin
Series Editor

SOCIAL UNREST AND COLLECTIVE PROTEST*

Herbert Blumer, UNIVERSITY OF CALIFORNIA, BERKELEY

INTRODUCTION

One of the anomalies in the study of human society is the gross neglect of the nature and role of social unrest.** This neglect is puzzling in light of the general recognition that something that is called social unrest occurs with considerable frequency in the life of human societies and that this "something" is very important. The occurrence and reoccurrence of social unrest is indicated abundantly by the frequency of references to such matters as student unrest, racial unrest, labor unrest, women's unrest, religious unrest, agrarian unrest, the unrest of youth, revolutionary un-

---

*This essay was written in 1970.

**Illustrative of this neglect is the absence of any article on social unrest in the prestigious *International Encyclopedia of the Social Sciences*. Indeed, the term "social unrest" does not even appear in the index.

Studies in Symbolic Interaction—Volume 1, 1978, pages 1–54

rest, the unrest connected with nationalist uprisings, and unrest in the case of collective hysteria and manias. The importance of social unrest is shown by the general acknowledgment that social unrest is a disturbed condition of group life marked by an unsettling of established social arrangements, a posing of alarming problems to authorities, an emergence of new and aberrant forms of behavior, and a spawning of varieties of social movements. Yet, despite the widespread recognition of the occurrence and the importance of social unrest, it has not been singled out by scholars for study and analysis. Usually, it is taken for granted, the scholar contenting himself with the mere use of the term and its dictionary definition. Occasionally, a scholar may concern himself with a particular concrete instance of social unrest, as in the case of social unrest preceding the French Revolution of 1789, or with a special type of unrest, as in the instance of contemporary student unrest. In such cases, scholars have shown little concern with any generic analysis of social unrest. Their studies of a given historical instance or type of social unrest yield scarcely any generalizable knowledge. More unfortunately, such scholars have been preoccupied predominantly with trying to find the "causes" of the given instance or type of social unrest. This concern with "causes" of social unrest is at the expense of seeing that social unrest is a distinctive process in its own right, operating in ways and leading to results that are independent of its causes.

The fixation of scholars on the causes of social unrest has been so unfortunate as to deserve some additional comments. We can note, first, that it leads to an open hunting ground for the introduction and play of widely diverse theories, doctrines, popular conceptions and concocted schemes. For example, a partial review of the literature seeking to account for contemporary student unrest (1965–1972) reveals the following welter of explanations: the presence of troublemakers; the affluence and idleness of students; the failure of families to exercise discipline over their children; the effective disappearance of the father from the modern family (the fatherless society); rebellion of students against parental figures as a result of unresolved oedipal rivalry in early childhood; an unconscious striving of students to gain, by following charismatic paranoid leaders, an emotional warmth which they lacked in childhood; a premature sophistication of youth leading them to seek power that should belong properly to adults; the inculcation of youth with insidious radical philosophies, particularly socialistic philosophies; an embracing by youth of the philosophy of democracy, leading them to seek participation in the decision-making processes that affect their future; a serious application by youth of ethical ideals, leading them to revolt against injustice and bureaucratic pettiness; the adoption of a drug culture by youth; a sudden introduction onto campuses, as a result of universal education, of large numbers of students with no understanding or appreciation of the traditions and ideals of academic life; a widening gap between generations, brought about by new technology; an inflexibility on the part of academic institutions to meet new changing conditions; a failure and weakness on the part of authorities to apply regulations and exercise control with resolute firmness; and to end this lengthy yet incomplete list, a mere matter of students' responding to numerous frustrations by engaging in aggressive attack. Obviously, enough variety of "causes" is offered to allow anyone to choose an explanation of student unrest to suit his temperament, bias, or doctrinal commitment. I am not trying to make fun of the work of scholars in their effort to explain the causes of contemporary student unrest. I am merely calling attention to what is typical in the case of scholars with their preoccupation with causal explanation of social unrest. Anyone who has plodded through the literature touching on social unrest in the case of revolutions, reform movements, labor turmoil, nationalistic upheavals, feminist movements, youth movements, and various collective manias must be vividly aware of the confused assortment of explanations advanced to account for social unrest. The perusal of such explanations yields essentially nothing to an isolation of social unrest as a generic item and to an identification of its features.

My second observation is that the preoccupation with the "causes" of social unrest carries the presumption that a knowledge of such causes suffices to explain what people do in a state of social unrest. What people do is regarded as merely an expression of what led them into the restless condition. This presumption is unwarranted. As I will seek to show, people in a state of social unrest are confronted with situations of uncertain and shifting character in which they have to develop their perspectives and to forge their lines of action. The kinds of activities in which they engage are products of meeting their situations instead of being an expression of the alleged causes of their unrest.

My third observation is similar to the second. It is that scholars err in believing that the causes underlying social unrest account for whatever emerges out of social unrest, as for example in explaining the appearance of given social movements as due to the causes that produced the social unrest out of which the movements came. This mode of explanation treats the state of social unrest as a mere medium for the expression of antecedent factors or as a mere transmission belt for conveying prior causes over into subsequent product-formations. This is a falsification of the nature of social unrest. As we shall see, social unrest is a state of agitated and uncertain action, in which people are subject to the play of divergent definitions of what they should do, in which they have to contend with various forms of opposition and repression, in which they move ahead gropingly, step by step, and in which they may be mobilized for action along alternative directions. To ignore this generative character of social unrest by assuming that the causes of social unrest produce what comes out of social unrest is poor scholarship and defective logic.

My thesis, as the foregoing remarks imply, is that social unrest deserves to be studied in its own right. It should not be seen as a mere accompaniment of social change, as a mere epiphenomenon of no particular significance, or as a mere neutral link in a chain of happenings. Instead, it should be viewed as a molding and directing process in its own right, occupying a key position in significant kinds of social change. I propose to undertake an analysis of social unrest with these points in mind. Subsequently in this essay I wish to discuss how social unrest is converted into collective protest. My presentation is based on the study of several scores of instances of social unrest and collective protest during the past four centuries.

THE NATURE OF SOCIAL UNREST

A discussion of the nature of social unrest can begin by distinguishing it from five other conditions with which it is all too frequently confused. These five conditions are social change, individual unrest, social discontent, social disruption, and crowd behavior.

It is erroneous to think that social unrest arises always when there is pronounced social change, particularly abrupt social change. Great transformations may take place in institutions, in what people strive for, and in their world perspectives with a minimum of social unrest, and on occasion without any social unrest. If new wishes and aspirations are developed quickly and unambiguously, if these wishes and aspirations are sanctioned and legitimized so that they are not looked at askance and encounter no disapproval, if means for their ready realization are at hand and are open for use, and if no opposition is exerted by one authoritative segment of the population against other segments in these efforts, vast social change may take place without social unrest. Momentous social changes of this sort have occurred frequently without noticeable social unrest—as in the mobilization of a nation for total war or in the rapid changes in ways of living among people as a result of sharing in a sudden wave of economic prosperity. It should be clear that social unrest requires a certain kind of social change—one in which there is some form of resistance to awakened wishes for a new type of social arrangement. The *balking* of awakened dispositions that seek a different scheme of life or the retention of a disappearing scheme of life is a *sine qua non* of social unrest; it sets apart the kind of social change in which social unrest occurs from those in which it does not.

It is particularly important to distinguish social unrest from individual unrest. Regrettably, most scholars confuse these two types of unrest, with consequent faulty analysis. It is not only possible but indeed very common for individual unrest to be very widespread without any accompanying social unrest. Individual unrest may be acute in the form of grave dissatisfaction with one's conditions of life, accompanied by a sense of bitter grievance and a keen feeling that things are wrong. The individual may feel greatly disturbed, at odds with himself and his social surroundings, and suffer from anguishing problems. Yet, even though this condition may exist in a vast number of individuals in a society, indeed among individuals who associate more or less constantly with one another, such individual unrest does not constitute social unrest. The distinguishing feature of social unrest is its shared character and hence its transmissibility from person to person. Social unrest arises among people sharing a common reaction to their social lot or to their life experiences and hence who are attuned sympathetically to one another's expression of this reaction. The restlessness of each carries with it a sense of communion with outside others and thus is capable of collective mobilization. This is not true of individual unrest. Individual unrest is private and highly personalized, being held and approached as a personal problem. If expressed in nervous or erratic action it is likely to repel others instead of transmitting to them the restless feeling. If unburdened orally in an attempted recital of one's woes, it does not serve to arouse a sense of indignation or a feeling of collective protest. It is unlikely to induce any contagious response. In contrast, social unrest is shareable and shared. Its expression through oral account or physical gesture touches off a sympathetic response in others who are themselves sensitized to the direction of the unrest. Thus, expressions of social unrest feed upon one another, solidifying and intensifying the unrest as it is echoed back and forth among the restless people. Social unrest is thus caught up in a form of circular interaction and emerges as a collective or shared product. This collective and contagious character is a basic mark of social unrest and must, accordingly, be fully respected in scholarly efforts to understand it. Attempts to reduce social unrest to terms of customary psychological mechanisms of the individual, such as in the use of the frustration-aggression formula, miss its essential mark of being a product of circular interaction. The same deficiency marks psychiatric explanations that seek to account for social unrest in terms of the emotional pathology of individuals. Social unrest is a collective condition.

In many ways the most defective interpretation of social unrest is to identify it with social discontent. A body of people, indeed a large population, may be marked by extensive social discontent without any sign of social unrest. The discontent may exist in the form of a group's shared dissatisfaction with their mode of life and with their social position in their social order. The members may have a keen sense of grievance, voicing to one another their complaints and experiences of mistreatment, and reinforcing each other in a common sense of suffering from injustice. Because of its shared and transmissible character, social discontent is different from individual unrest and in this respect is similar to social unrest. What, then, is the difference between social discontent and social unrest? The distinction is that social unrest signifies an aroused readiness to act against the prevailing social order (or some portion of it) whereas mere social discontent implies an acceptance of the social order; in short, a respect for the authority that undergirds the social order and hence a passive readiness to abide by it despite its harshness and unfairness. To appreciate the distinction we need only to think of underprivileged groups which, despite the disadvantages of their social position and the harshness of their mode of existence, accepted their lot as part of the order of life—such as the lower castes in India, the serfs in large parts of Czarist Russia, and the American Negroes in the antebellum South. The import of the distinction should be clear. Contrary to a belief held by many scholars, a collective life of onerous hardships and gross inequity, meeting all the requirements of "relative deprivation," need not provoke either social unrest or protest action. For social discontent to develop into social unrest the discontented people have to be brought to a different posture toward the social arrangement that is under complaint. They must come to challenge the legitimacy and propriety of the social arrangement; they must come to view the social arrangement as not merely onerous and socially wrong but as being no longer authoritative and tenable. The cloak of being an ordained part of the natural order, which shielded the going social order previously from attack, if not from criticism, must be stripped away. When this occurs the disapproval of the given social arrangement stems not only from whatever dissatisfaction it occasions but also from a belief that the social arrangement has no legitimate claim to exist. Such a belief orients the unrest into the direction of an attack on the social arrangement, in place of mere endurance and complaint about the social arrangement. The preconditions of social unrest lie less in social discontent than in the challenge to the legitimacy of the social order held accountable for the matters about which people are discontented.

The fourth common misunderstanding of social unrest is to confuse it with any unsettled condition of group life such as a disorganized state of a community suddenly subjected to a disaster such as an earthquake, flood, the panic situation of a population invaded by an enemy army, or the disturbed condition of a country caught in the throes of wild inflation or economic upheaval. In such situations, the usual routines of life are abruptly broken, people are uncertain as to what to do, they are particularly susceptible to the play of rumor and untested suggestion, and thus there is likely to be a great deal of excited and uncoordinated action. Such unsettled and crowdlike behavior may indeed occur in social unrest as a kind of adjunct. But it is necessary to distinguish clearly between the unsettled condition that arises from social disruption and the unsettled condition that is characteristic of social unrest. The difference is that, as already suggested, social unrest signifies a rejection of the authoritative character of all or some portion of the social order and hence a reaching out for a new social arrangement. In contrast, in the usual instances of social disruption people merely seek to restore the functioning of customary arrangements or to develop quickly a suitable makeshift substitute. There are absent in mere social disruption the condition of chafing under a disliked and disowned social arrangement and the groping for something new to take its place.

A fifth common source of confusion is to regard social unrest as merely a case of crowd behavior. According to this view, social unrest is a condition of excitement and unruliness that is stirred up among people who are normally orderly and without concern about their social conditions. In their condition of excitement and unruliness it is said that they become thoughtless, lose sight of normal rules and values, and become the prey of agitators and troublemakers. It is assumed that this condition is brought on by exciting happenings that momentarily unsettle people. It is asserted that agitators who have a personal spite against existing social arrangements, or who seek notoriety and power, seize on this unsettled state of people to incite and direct them to various kinds of attack on the social order. Social unrest, it is held, is to be controlled by quelling the agitators and troublemakers and by calming the people so that they can return to their normal orderly ways of living. This view of social unrest as crowd behavior is deficient in several fundamental respects. Social unrest is not a momentary arousing of feelings by exciting events or by persuasive agitation. It is rooted, instead, in vague but strong feelings of dissatisfaction and disillusionment with given social arrangements. Thus, contrary to the episodic and transitory character of crowd behavior, social unrest is deep-seated and enduring. Feelings of dissatisfaction and disillusionment exist before and persist after whatever forms of crowd behavior take place in the expression of social unrest. This last observation calls attention to a second important difference, namely, that social unrest consists of much more than a momentary condition of excited feeling and a disposition to engage in crowd activity. In the germination of social unrest there is a great deal of unexcited discussion among participants as they express their complaints to one another, analyze their common situation and identify disliked features of existing social arrangements. As social unrest takes form, such discussion may extend to inner debates, rational exchange of ideas, and deliberate planning on lines of conduct. Social unrest is oriented in the direction of progressive transformation of given social arrangements and not to an immediate change of an isolated item of momentary excitement. Consequently, while it is true that there is usually a considerable amount of crowd behavior in periods of social unrest and that such crowd behavior may be very important, it is erroneous to identify social unrest as crowd behavior. In terms of its origin, its lines of growth, and what it seeks, social unrest is basically different from crowd behavior.

The foregoing distinctions are of help in identifying more clearly the nature of social unrest. They show that social unrest has three basic ingredients: (1) a collectively induced rejection of the legitimacy or the authoritative status of a given social arrangement, (2) a collective cultivation of grievance and discontent with the social arrangement, and (3) a shared chafing in having to abide by the social arrangement. These three ingredients in combination are both the producing causes of social unrest and the central components of the collective nature of social unrest. The significance of each of these crucial ingredients needs to be explained.

1. Delegitimation.

Since the rejection of legitimacy is such a central ingredient of social unrest, there is need here to clarify the nature of legitimacy and to point out its importance in maintaining a social order. Legitimacy exists as a collective sanction that gives propriety and authority to whatever object it is attached, making mandatory the acceptance of that object. The object may be a mode of living, a practice, a custom, a belief, a principle, a doctrine, a value, a rule, an official position, a social role, an institution, a social arrangement or a style of life. When any such object acquires legitimacy it comes to be regarded as natural and in the order of life.

Legitimacy gives the object an extra quality or character that goes beyond the mere content of the object. Thus, to give random illustrations, a given marriage ceremony is not merely a means of establishing wedlock but is the means that must be respected; the principle of private property is not merely a means of allocating ownership and control of goods but is *the particular* means that must be observed; a given form of court procedure is not merely a serviceable way of adjudicating disputes but is *the required form* of such adjudication; a position as presidency of a university is not merely a given administrative arrangement but is *the officially endorsed* arrangement; and a general scheme of a social order, such as a democratic society, is not merely one of several alternative forms of organizing a society but is *the particular form* that has to be followed and respected.

As these scattered illustrations show, legitimacy confers an additional quality on the content of the given social object. This additional quality, in the form of an authoritative sanction, undergirds social arrangements and indeed holds a social order together. It prevents people from moving off freely in different directions in fashioning modes of behavior or developing principles of conduct. Legitimacy limits conduct and belief, directs conduct and belief along fixed channels, prescribes and maintains regularized lines of action and thus serves as a supreme control over the web of social relations. Legitimacy can be seen as a shield of social protection to whatever it covers. The content of a social feature may be disliked, evaluated adversely, seen to be deficient, and indeed experienced as very unsatisfactory, without the social feature's losing its legitimacy. Legitimacy lies not in the content of the social feature or in the experiences of people with that content but, instead, in the transcending group stamp of approval of the social feature. An object having legitimacy is seen as natural, as an appropriate part of what is established, as part of things as they are and as they have a right to continue to be. Thus, the legitimate object is grounded in the thinking and feeling of people in the given social setting and is supported by the official custodians of the related institutions. A legitimate object exercises a claim on people for its observance and its retention.

The renouncing of the legitimacy or authoritative status of a given social arrangement thus exposes that arrangement to criticism, to denunciation, to a denial of its claim to acceptance, and thus puts people in a position of readiness to change the social arrangement. As long as a social arrangement is accepted as authoritative and legitimate, as being in the order of things, it is secure and protected, however much it may be disliked and however harsh may be its effects. In not questioning its legitimacy people are not oriented to doing anything about it; they continue to endure inconvenience, discomfort, deprivation and hardship under it without collective remonstrance or protest, accepting the social arrangement as a natural part of the order of life. The groundwork for social unrest is laid when people begin to challenge and disown the authoritative status of a given social arrangement and thus feel free to take action against the social arrangement. This rejection of the legitimacy of the social arrangement is a crucial matter, since it implies not merely the possibility of changing the social arrangement but also a more serious matter of impugning and attacking the principle of authority and legitimacy itself. This is why the manifestation of social unrest, particularly in the form of protest, is likely to evoke grave and spirited reaction from authorities and from the public that is attached to the existing order; the manifestation is seen as not merely a plea for the change of a given social arrangement but as a flouting of authority and legitimacy. In this sense, however restricted may be its initial area of concern, social unrest always conveys a taint or implication of revolutionary change—an attack on the principle of legitimacy that undergirds the existing social order. To understand the nature of social unrest and to grasp its implications it is necessary to recognize the central position of this ingredient of rejecting the authoritative status of an established social arrangement.

The more profound causes of social unrest must be sought in the conditions which bring about this changed posture toward authoritative status instead of being sought in mere dislocation in ways of living or in intensified dissatisfaction. The failure to recognize that the causes lie in these conditions is the most serious deficiency in the analysis by scholars who seek to explain the causes of one or another instance or type of social unrest. For example, current social unrest among blacks in the United States is due far more to a disowning by them of the legitimacy of the racial arrangement than it is to changes in their modes of living or to an increase of harsh treatment of them. An event such as the desegregation decision of the United States Supreme Court in 1954 had its primary significance in undermining the legitimacy of a long-established relationship between the races and thus helping to open the doors to the expression of dissatisfactions which had been long endured but not protested against. My remarks are perhaps sufficient to show that the major necessary condition to social unrest is a disowning and rejection of the legitimacy of given existing social arrangements.

2. Discontent.

The second major ingredient of social unrest consists of feelings of dissatisfaction with a given area of social arrangements. It is important to recognize that there are two kinds of such feelings in the case of social unrest. In part, the dissatisfaction consists of dislike of specific features of existing social arrangements which are the object of grievance and complaint, such as not being allowed to vote in the case of blacks in certain southern areas of the United States. These features consist of particular practices or requirements that have been found galling or unsatisfactory. Such specific sources of dissatisfaction are opened to expression as authoritative status is stripped away from the given area of social arrangements. This is why the loss of legitimacy usually releases large numbers of complaints that have been previously restrained and covered over. However, the dissatisfaction which enters into social unrest is composed, in addition, of vague and general feelings that transcend specific complaints and pertain to the structure of social arrangements. This additional type of dissatisfaction arises not from one or another specific disliked condition within a given area of social arrangements but, instead, from a general unsatisfactory character of the social arrangements. This general unsatisfactory condition is traceable to the way in which the people come to conceive their general lot—their social position in relation to other groups under the social arrangements. In the case of social unrest, people have come to form a new collective conception of themselves that carries the implication of new rights, new privileges and opportunities. With this revised conception of themselves people find that their general lot is no longer agreeable or tenable and hence they become dissatisfied with their position as such. The question that arises is not so much the correction of this or that recognizable grievance as it is the kind of new social arrangement that is needed to measure up to the new collective self-conception. This general or nonspecific form of dissatisfaction is fundamental in social unrest. It consists of vague and diffuse feelings—a sense that one's position or lot is wrong and unfair, without any clear comprehension of precisely what needs to be corrected or introduced to provide a remedy. This general dissatisfaction gives social unrest an amorphous character, leading to groping efforts in place of clearly seen action toward definite and fixed objectives. This explains why the satisfaction of specific grievances fails so frequently to dissipate social unrest.

Let me add one other observation to this discussion of dissatisfaction. It is important to note that an expansion of dissatisfaction usually follows in the wake of an expanded rejection of the authoritative status of existing social arrangements. As participants in a given instance of social unrest extend their disowning of legitimacy from a given social practice to the rules that uphold it, thence to the authorities enforcing the rules, thence to the functioning apparatus of the institution embodying the institution and rules, thence to the supposed purposes and objectives of the institution, and perhaps even to the fundamental values of the society, the range of dissatisfaction increases. In social unrest, dissatisfaction is intimately linked to the areas of authoritative legitimacy that are being denied.

3. Chafing Against Restraint.

The third major ingredient of social unrest is the frustration or balked feeling of having to live in and abide by a social arrangement whose legitimacy has been disallowed and whose practices and form are a source of dissatisfaction. The condition of being required to live under a galling social arrangement which has lost its claim to social acceptance provides the impetus to work out a suitable adjustment. As we shall see later, it is this condition which sets the stage for the formation of social unrest along several significantly different directions. Here I merely wish to point out that the chafing experience of having to abide by what is unsatisfactory and unacceptable provides fuel to the development of social unrest. It impels people who are so affected to discuss their situation, to define its nature, to try to work out some kind of adjustment, and to engage in various forays of collective action. It is necessary to add that the condition of feeling balked and frustrated at the hands of the existing social order is, itself, interpreted and reinterpreted during the formation of social unrest; the feeling may be intensified, dampened, and construed in different ways during the course of developing such unrest, especially in the light of the experiences which participants have with authorities and the general public.

It is important to note that in the formation of social unrest the three specified ingredients usually incite and abet one another. Thus, as already mentioned, a growth in delegitimation tends to spur and release dissatisfaction. Correspondingly, where delegitimation is already in process increased dissatisfaction usually adds fuel to further delegitimation. A similar cumulative interaction takes place between chafing and dissatisfaction, also between chafing and delegitimation. In general, as one would expect, the three basic components of social unrest are incitants to one another when the process of forming social unrest is under way. However, one should keep in mind the key role of delegitimation; without a rejection of the authoritative status of objects dissatisfaction remains dormant and chafing against restraint does not arise.

The three basic ingredients of social unrest, operating inside the interaction of participants who are faced with an arena of action, account for typical symptoms of social unrest: heated and unrestrained denunciation of given social arrangements and of authorities; agitational efforts to arouse people against the social arrangements; subterranean or closed meetings among participants, appearing frequently to have the character of plotting; the voicing or making of seemingly extreme demands and threats; engaging in new and odd forms of expressive behavior, such as singing, dancing, cultist activity, or unusual modes of dressing; outbreaks of attack, either peaceful or violent, against authorities; and the spread of all these from place to place. These symptoms are essentially scattered and unfocused attempts to express feelings in overt action. The overt actions are usually improvised to meet the immediate situation; they seem to be erratic and confused; they frequently take bizarre and queer forms; and they are particularly likely to appear as indecent and shocking to those attached to prevailing social arrangements. The symptoms of social unrest signify that participants are disturbed with sets of social arrangements without being clear as to exactly what in the social arrangements disturbs them, poised against these arrangements yet uncertain where to go, chafing under restraint but confused as how to escape, and prone to engage impulsively in immediate action instead of designing their acts to meet more ultimate ends. The development of social unrest should not be seen as merely an unfolding expression of these features but instead as a groping effort to clarify dissatisfaction, to identify what is wrong in the social arrangements and, above all, to move toward a more ordered line of action with regard to the social arrangement.

The people who are caught up in social unrest are typically not a compact congregation, nor a well-defined territorial group, nor an established social group, nor an organized party. Instead, they are a new and unorganized collection of people, drawn usually from a variety of established groups and from various backgrounds. Particularly they are a *selection* of people from such groups and backgrounds in that many of their fellow members in such groups and backgrounds do not share their unrest. Those who are so selected constitute a collectivity in that they enter and participate in an arena of interaction in which they discuss their complaints and dissatisfactions, assess critically the area of social arrangements with which they are concerned, infect one another with their unrest, and grope toward lines of action with regard to the social arrangements. The arena of interaction is diffuse and varied in makeup, consisting of such forms as discussion within small groups of friends and acquaintances, public meetings, rallies and demonstrations, correspondence between participants, and dissemination of leaflets, newspapers and publications among those who are literate. People become involved in such interaction in diverse degrees, with new entrants into the interaction from time to time and others dropping out along the line. It can be seen from these few remarks that those who share the social unrest constitute an amorphous group, with no well-defined boundaries, with little or no established organization, with no traditional set of relations between the participants, and with no lines of action that have been mapped out for themselves or for the society in which they live. They represent a collectivity that is in a process of formation instead of being a group that is already established and structured—an amorphous collectivity that is seeking to get its bearings and to develop lines of action toward a given social arrangement rather than an already constituted group with established structure, leaders, doctrines and goals.

I wish to close this brief characterization of the nature of social unrest with a few remarks about the social arrangements which may become the object of social unrest. Obviously, there is great variety in the sectors and aspects of social life around which social unrest may develop. The social arrangement under challenge may be as various as working conditions in an industrial community; an unpopular national government engaging in respressive acts; the practices and mode of operation of an institution, such as a university or a church; the position of a given class of people in a society, such as a subordinate racial group or an aspiring social class, or a social class that finds its privileged position being undermined; a given style of life in a society, such as a puritanical ethic or a profit-seeking career; or basic tenets of a social order itself. Thus, social unrest may be confined to a small local population or extended to a vast populace, it may be focused on a restricted area of social arrangements or turned toward a wide area of social life, and it may be relatively specific or highly diffuse in its object of reference.

To understand the role and importance of social unrest it is necessary to recognize (a) that it is a process with a varying and uncertain career of formation, (b) that its fundamental function is to develop new perspectives among participants and thus to prepare them for new lines of action with regard to social arrangements, and (c) that there is profound difference between the alternative lines of action along which social unrest may move. These are the primary matters which I wish to discuss now.

THE FORMATION OF SOCIAL UNREST

Social unrest does not suddenly bloom into existence as a complete product. Instead, it undergoes a process of growth, usually in a slow and protracted manner, and develops into a particular form. This process of growth usually starts from obscure conditions, requires a number of suitable facilities, is subject to the play of dramatic events, and takes direction from the interaction between its participants in the light of the opposition they encounter from authorities. It has, accordingly, a variable and uncertain career in the course of which it, so to speak, hews out its lines of movement. As indicated in the opening paragraphs of this essay, it is not only erroneous but foolhardy to think that the growth of social unrest is preset or pushed along in a determinate direction by antecedent factors or conditions. Instead, the formation of social unrest and the hewing out of its pathways are dependent on the contemporary happenings that occur during the course of its formation. These happenings influence and shape the three major ingredients of social unrest, affecting the intensity of social unrest, accelerating or halting its growth, and above all shaping the alternative forms into which social unrest may become resolved. It is thus necessary to see social unrest as an active process—one which undergoes variable formation. Our task is to identify the more vital factors which affect its career. These vital factors are the following: (1) predisposition to social unrest, (2) role of dramatic events, (3) interaction among the participants, (4) effect of the overt expressions of social unrest, and (5) interplay between the restless groups and outside groups. The career or fate of social unrest is dependent on these factors, not on the alleged causes of social unrest. It is the interlinked operation of these five factors which determines whether a given instance of social unrest dwindles or dies or becomes a powerful pressure to transform social arrangements. Thus, we need to consider their character and their operation.

Predisposition to Social Unrest.

Most scholars view social unrest as little more than a release of predispositions which are seen as lodged either in individual makeup or in the social setting. Thus, they assert that social unrest is but a reflection of personal instability or an expression of acute structural strains in the existing social order. While the gross deficiency of these views of causation has already been pointed out in the introductory section of this essay, the topic of predisposition to social unrest deserves some additional consideration.

Undeniably a marked selective process takes place in instances of social unrest, in the sense that out of a given population in the same social situation some people enter easily and quickly into the condition of social unrest, some are indifferent to its presence and play, and others are vigorously opposed to the social unrest developing in their midst. For example, in the case of current student unrest, there are thousands of students who are not touched by it. This is true, similarly, of all other types and instances of social unrest, whether it be women's unrest, peasant unrest, labor unrest, nationalistic unrest or revolutionary unrest. Yet, while there is unquestionably a selective process at work in terms of those who are drawn into social unrest, there is no solid evidence that such people are of a particular psychological or social type. We have to look askance at certain popular views, to the effect that social unrest springs from unstable personalities, from indigenous troublemakers, from people who hate society, or from individuals with deep-seated emotional conflicts set by early childhood experiences. Two relevant observations need to be made. Such disturbed or destruction-prone individuals are to be found in liberal numbers among those in the same population who are indifferent to the instance of social unrest or who vigorously oppose it; in the case of current student unrest, there are many instable and emotionally disturbed students who are untouched by the unrest. More important, if we group together a large number of different historical instances of social unrest, we readily see that people who come to be caught up in social unrest are a very heterogeneous array of individuals. In the several scores of instances of social unrest which I have studied, the evidence is clear that the participants vary along all significant psychological and social dimensions. They may be intelligent or stupid, sophisticated or naive, educated or illiterate, idealistic or materialistic, unstable or well balanced, impulsive or deliberate, misfits or respected citizens, wealthy or poor, introverts or extroverts, spiteful or well intentioned, belligerent or benign, deeply troubled with personal problems or light-hearted and gay, and so on with regard to other lines of comparison. Under given circumstances all kinds of people, irrespective of psychological or social type, can come to question the legitimacy of given social arrangements, experience dissatisfaction with such arrangements, and chafe under having to abide by such arrangements. In my judgment the evidence gives no support to contentions that social unrest springs from individuals who are psychologically unstable, or emotionally pathological, or inveterate troublemakers, or habitual rebels against social restraints. People with such kinds of makeup are to be found among those caught up in any given instance of social unrest; they are also to be found among those indifferent or opposed to the given instance.

The parallel view that the predispositions to social unrest lie in the structural imbalance or strains in a society has a measure of truth, but only if properly interpreted. The following observations are definitely in order. Structural strains in the sense of gross inequalities in social position, or in sharing the goods and rewards of life, or in the competitive striving of groups or organizations may exist in a profound way over long periods of time without any social unrest. Even when such social disparity is marked by social discontent there need be no social unrest. As has been pointed out earlier, what is crucial is not social discontent but the disowning of the legitimated character of the social arrangement. This shifts the focal point of importance from the so-called structural strain to the way in which the structural strain is *interpreted*. The mere presence or existence of structural strains does not at all signify that the given social arrangements will be interpreted in such a way as to cause people to renounce their authoritative status. Societal predispositions to social unrest lie not in the structure of the society but in the interpretative process in play in the society. To get at these predispositions it is necessary to see how people are defining their mode of life, their institutions, the important groups in their world, their authority figures, and the stream of events taking place in their experience. Further, to grasp this interpretative process it is obviously necessary to note the new definitions that are being introduced into their operating world from the outside. New definitions such as the principles of democracy, a concept of liberty or "Uhuru," a vista of a more enjoyable material life, a new doctrine of individual rights and privileges, a depiction of authority figures as corrupt or irresponsible—these are the kind of outside definitions which lead people to reassess their positions, themselves, and the authoritative character of their institutional arrangements. It is in this on-going process of definition and interpretation that one must seek the so called societal predispositions to social unrest.

Finally and of major importance, individual or societal predispositions to social unrest cannot even at their best account for the formation or the career of social unrest. The career depends, instead, on incidents, the interaction between participants, the situations that have to be faced, the resistance and opposition that are encountered, and the success in coping with such resistance and opposition.

Dramatic Events

The nucleating point in the formation of social unrest is constituted by a dramatic event or a closely allied series of dramatic events. It is the dramatic event which incites and focalizes predispositions, and brings them to bear on a concrete situation; which shocks, arouses, enlivens, and shakes people loose from their routines of thought and action; which catches collective attention and stirs imagination; which attracts and engages people who have been indifferent to a given sector of life; which suddenly poses issues which are unknown or which lurked dimly in the background; which incites heated discussions and initiates intense interaction; and which stimulates the novel proposals and the impulsive tendencies that are so characteristic of social unrest. Without dramatic events, potential social unrest never comes into being, never acquires any liveliness, and never, so to speak, gets off the ground. Further, even after being brought into being, the subsequent career of social unrest is affected enormously by the occurrence of new or other dramatic events.

A few examples of dramatic events chosen from diverse instances of social unrest are: an unwarranted attack on a leadership group, the mass arrest of people, the assassination of a leader, a sudden and seemingly high-handed cutting of wages, a brutal police action in breaking up a peaceful procession, a radical decision of a high tribunal such as the 1954 desegregation decision of the United States Supreme Court, an arrogant administrative act, a spectacular defiance of established authority such as the Boston Tea Party or the Storming of the Bastille, a sudden and novel defiance of a deeply established custom such as the restaurant sit-ins by black students in the South, disclosure of offensive corruption and chicanery in high government circles, and a sudden appropriation of the homes and property of people. The dramatic events inducing and starting off social unrest vary enormously. They are predominantly adventitious and undesigned even though they may on occasion be fabricated and staged. They invariably bring into sharp focus a contest between established authoritative social arrangements and challenging forces—a contest which takes place along either of two lines. The first is the arousing of passions of moral indignation against a social arrangement and its symbols. Given people view the dramatic event, such as a brutal police attack or a callous administrative action, as an intolerably inhuman act that violates fundamental virtues of justice, decency, and fairness. Their indignation constitutes or leads to a sudden questioning of the legitimated character of the social arrangement on behalf of which the act was taken, as well as a recasting of attitudes toward the administrative heads, government officials, and functionaries regarded as responsible for the act. Dramatic events arousing bitter condemnation of authority are the primary crucible in which the authoritative status of given social arrangements is dissolved. The second line along which dramatic events set the contest between authoritative social arrangements and challenging forces is quite different in nature; here the dramatic act is in the form of a bold and encouraging attack on the social arrangement—such as the Supreme Court decision on desegregation, or sit-ins, or the Boston Tea Party. Dramatic events of this sort are significant, not along the line of arousing moral indignation against the authoritative status of the social arrangement, but along the line of suggesting the fragility of the authoritative status and of indicating that this status is open to direct attack. This type of dramatic event opens vistas of action and also inspires further action.

The great importance of dramatic events in the initiation and formation of social unrest should not lead us to overlook two other significant matters relating to their influence. One is that the dramatic event evokes a response not only from those who are brought by it into the fold of social unrest but also from authorities and an outside public. The interpretation of the dramatic event by these latter groups may lead to action which affects profoundly the course of formation of social unrest. We will consider this matter later. The second matter pertains to the role of general public moods in affecting how people interpret and respond to the dramatic event. There can be no question that public mood is a decisive factor, very likely the most decisive factor, in determining how people see and respond to dramatic events. A given kind of dramatic event which at one time may evoke profound indignation and arouse spirited discussion may at another time be viewed and treated with conspicuous indifference. Regrettably, our scholarly knowledge of public moods is practically nothing; the recognition and study of public moods is one of the most neglected matters of scholarly concern. I merely note that the state of public mood affects significantly the interpretation of dramatic events in the formation of social unrest.

The Process of Circular Interaction

Interaction among people who feel aggrieved or dissatisfied with a social arrangement, who are disowning the authoritative status of that arrangement and who are agitated by dramatic events, is the primary process by which social unrest is nursed and cultivated and through which social unrest is directed and takes form. People who are initially disaffected have to meet, voice their feelings, express their views, and propose

actions in order for social unrest to be formed and sustained. Such interaction should not be treated as a casual or incidental matter or regarded
as a mere medium through which antecedent conditions or underlying
factors result in subsequent behavior. The interaction is a formative process in its own right, forging feelings, forming interpretations, shaping
perspectives and working out lines of action. Only a little reflection is
needed to recognize that this interaction serves not only to spread but to
intensify feelings as people express to one another their complaints, indignation and condemnation of persons, practices, acts and positions associated with a social arrangement about which they feel aggrieved. Not
all participants contribute equally—prestigeful persons, aggressive individuals and those expressing strong self-assurance exercise greater influence. It is this process in which participants stimulate and reinforce and
sanction each other's feelings and convictions that justifies us in identifying the interaction as being circular. In addition, the interaction serves to
define matters of concern to the participants—to develop characterizations of such objects as opponents, persons in authority, institutional
practices, and individual rights. The objects which are so formed represent the way in which the participants come to see their world. Finally,
the interaction is taken up in large measure with discussion of immediate
acts to be performed—what they should be and how they should be
carried out. It should be evident that in serving such purposes, the process of interaction among participants is of central importance in the
formation of social unrest.

The interaction among the participants in social unrest is spread over
time, occurs in many different settings (e.g., small congenial groups, rallies, large meetings, mass assemblies, or conventions), takes many different forms (e.g., expressions of indignation, public haranguing, debates,
argumentative discussion, and strategy planning), and typically shifts in
content almost day by day. It is a fluid and changing kind of interaction,
marked by uncertainty and excitement. To settle down in form, to take on
a routine character, or to be a mere repetitive discussion of the same
things is a sure sign that the interaction has lost its character as social
unrest. The interaction in social unrest is not an expression of fixed intentions, nor a realization of established values, nor a pursuit of established
norms. Instead, it has the character of an excitable and mercurial groping
for a social arrangement whose character is as yet shadowy and uncertain.
This groping character is manifest in the well-known fact that while the
proponents of social unrest are usually clear and definite in saying what
they are against (i.e., the given social arrangement or features of it) they
are markedly uncertain and shifting with regard to what they wish to set
up as a substitute. Objectives are improvised, set up impulsively to meet
the immediate situation without much foresight to their consequences,

and readily shifted in the light of new events. This is but a reflection of the fluid and uncharted nature of the interaction that takes place in social unrest.

Overt Expressions of Social Unrest

The overt expression of social unrest should be seen as an important factor in itself in affecting and shaping the formation of social unrest. The expressions set the stage for subsequent steps in the course of formation and thus help to guide the direction of that formation. The expressions have a double line of effect—an effect on fellow participants in social unrest and an effect on outsiders, particularly authorities, who respond to the expressions. The response of fellow participants and of outsiders reacts back on the formation of social unrest. While this should be immediately obvious, insufficient attention is given to its importance. Clearly, overt expression of social unrest—through such forms as the voicing of criticisms, denunciations, public meetings, demonstrations, acts of defiance and direct attacks—shape participants and prepare them for subsequent participative action. The overt expressions function to solidify shared feelings and convictions, to establish a sense of camaraderie, to buoy up the participants in a feeling of successful mission. The effect of overt expressions of unrest is particularly pronounced in the case of the dramatic and spectacular instances of such expression; these are likely to have an electrifying effect on the participants in arousing feelings, imparting enthusiasm, establishing conviction and generating greater energy. Spectacular expressions of social unrest which appear to be successful—such as a strike, sit-in, seizure of property, a huge rally, or defiance of authority—are especially likely to become immediate models in spreading and sustaining social unrest. It is scarcely necessary to add that overt expressions of unrest which fail, which lack imaginative spark, which are devoid of excitatory feeling, and which take on the form of mere ritual have a dampening effect and ultimately a paralyzing effect on the formation of social unrest. This observation suggests at once the importance of the responses of outsiders to the overt expressions of social unrest. Clearly, the actions or lack of actions by outsiders are of the greatest significance in affecting the course of social unrest. In the immediately following portion of this essay I shall identify the outsiders and indicate the parts they play. Here I merely wish to say that the responses of local and remote authorities and of segments of the general public to the overt manifestations of social unrest enter into the arena of social unrest, set conditions that have to be faced and met, and operate as either facilitating or repressive factors in the growth of social unrest.

Interplay Between the Restless Group and Outside Groups

Social unrest must be seen as emerging and operating in an arena, with the career of social unrest dependent on the succession of situations which are encountered therein. The arena is not constituted merely by those who are imbued with the social unrest and by a surrounding ring of potential participants. Instead, the arena embraces other significant groups whose actions have telling significance on the formation and the fate of social unrest. These other groups are primarily authorities and their agents, interest groups with a special concern that is affected by the social unrest, and a general public that pays attention to the expressions of social unrest. The formation and career of social unrest is profoundly affected by the interaction between the four groups mentioned: those caught up in the social unrest and the potential recruits to social unrest, local and remote authorities, special-interest groups, and a general attentive public.

The initial alignments of these groups is almost self-evident. Since social unrest represents a renunciation of the legitimacy of a given social arrangement, it carries the threat of an attack on the social arrangement. By definition, authorities are committed to the retention of the social arrangement and accordingly to its defense. Thus, opposition of authorities to those animated by social unrest is natural and inevitable. Similarly, groups that have vested interests in the given social arrangements view the social unrest with apprehension and so fall into an opposition group; contrariwise, there may also be groups that have vested intersts in some anticipated changes. Finally, the initial position of the general public is unfavorable to the social unrest. This is true because, as earlier discussion has indicated, the general population usually accepts the legitimacy of the social arrangement. Thus, it views the manifestations of social unrest as out of order. In the light of these observations it is clear that, logically, the growth and formation of social unrest takes place in the face of opposition from authorities, from most special-interest groups and from the general attentive public. The manner in which, and the intensity with which, such opposition is expressed influence greatly the growth and fate of social unrest.

The interplay among the groups mentioned—restless people, authorities, interest groups, and attentive public—can and does vary a great deal, with corresponding different effects on the fate of social unrest. While the varying intricacy of the interplay bars the formulation of a neat theoretical scheme capable of embracing all instances of social unrest, some general principles may be advanced. I shall identify these principles by participating group and enumerate them for purposes of convenience.

The Social Unrest Group

1. The initial expressions of social unrest are usually made through the accepted channels present in the society for hearing and acting on complaints, grievances, protests, and demands for change.* However, such efforts to work through the established machinery characteristically encounter frustration and blockage. The forms of such frustration and blockage are typical: refusal of authorities to listen to the protestors, or to listen but take no action; the requirement that protests and demands be presented first to lower-echelon authorities and then be passed upward in a lengthy protracted manner before reaching the higher authorities who alone are authorized to make decisions; declarations by authorities that they are not empowered to consider, much less to grant, given kinds of demands; lengthy delays and periods of inaction by authorities; unfavorable characterizations of the protesters and ridiculing of the protest by authorities in place of viewing the protesters and their cause impartially; the offering by authorities of trifling concessions and their refusal to consider what the protesters feel to be momentous. Such experiences lead the protesting group to believe that it is futile to rely on established machinery for registering protests and seeking redress. They come to feel that the machinery is inept or inadequate or in the hands of unsympathetic persons—indeed, in the hands of enemies; that they cannot get a fair hearing; that their efforts become bogged down in a quagmire of bureaucratic complexity; and that their efforts are met by callous disregard and deceptions. Faced with such obstacles and frustrations by authorities, protesters turn typically to direct tactics—tactics that circumvent established procedures and that bring unconventional pressures to bear on authorities.

2. The resort by the protesting group to unsanctioned procedures and direct attacks introduces a new operating situation in the formation or career of social unrest. It almost always moves authorities to the use of repressive and punitive measures. These, in turn, reset the position of those caught up in social unrest and require a redefinition by them of their operating world and of their tactics of procedure. Interaction between protesters and authorities shifts from dependence on discussion to reliance on power play.

3. The sense of being blocked by authorities and of being subjected to repressive treatment by them intensifies social unrest and widens its coverage. It contributes to a further stripping away of the legitimate

---

*The unusual cases of an immediate initial use of direct action tactics occur when the social unrest group (a) is the heir to a revolutionary or direct action tradition, (b) has before it a model of other groups which are engaging successfully in direct action, or (c) is thrown into the condition of an aggressive crowd.

character of the social arrangement in question; this is an interesting case where the exercise of authority undermines its acceptance. Further, and more important, the disowning of legitimacy is extended to embrace the established machinery which exists to handle grievances and also the functionaries who operate the machinery. Finally, the blocking and repressive actions of authorities sharpens the sense of grievance; the seeming unwillingness or fear of authorities to face the complaints or protests confers on complaints an extra validity in the eyes of the protesters.

4. Social unrest capitalizes, so to speak, on stupid or inhuman acts committed by authorities in the use of repressive action. Repressive and primitive actions which appear brutal, excessive or inhuman arouse indignation and intensify resentment among those caught up in social unrest. Such actions evoke sympathy for the protesters among people who feel some kind of identification with those manifesting the unrest and so bring new recruits inside of the fold.

The Authorities

1. In its early stages, social unrest is likely to be treated lightly by authorities. Unless authorities are already in a state of alarm the early expressions of unrest are given only slight attention and are not viewed seriously. The expressions seem strange and abnormal. Because of their aberrant character and their usually scattered appearance they are viewed as not worthy of credit. Those who voice or express the unrest are regarded as crackpots, troublemakers and unbalanced individuals who are unlikely to attract any sizable or serious following.

2. When authorities are forced to take account of social unrest and to deal with the actions of the protesters their approach is typically to preserve and protect the existing social arrangement and, above all, to insist on the sanctity of the established institutional machinery for hearing and taking action on complaints. This is to be expected. By definition they are entrusted with the operation of institutions in accordance with the established goals and rules of the institutions. And they are committed to the smooth and orderly functioning of the machinery that has grown up to accomplish these purposes. Consequently, they look askance at demands, claims and pressures that threaten either established institutional objectives or functioning machinery—especially, of course, when such demands come from groups who have no acknowledged right or claim to decide the course of the institutional arrangement. Accordingly, their typical position is one of opposition to protest. This initial posture of opposition is hardened and solidified when protest turns to direct attack and unconventional procedures. Such direct attack is seen as a defiance of authority itself—a challenge to the inherent validity of authority and to the status of those who have the acknowledged right to exercise that

authority. With their direct commitment to the preservation of their institution in its established form, their interest in its smooth and orderly functioning, and their acknowledged right to exercise their authority, they see themselves as forced into the position of being the opponents of protest. The actions which they take from this position are bound to influence the fate of social unrest.

3. Authorities, especially the local sort, are captive to their institutional position in seeking to handle the protest that stems from social unrest. Even when tolerant of the protest and sympathetic to some of its demands (this happens here and there among authorities, especially in the early stages of unrest), authorities are limited in what they can do and, furthermore, they are subject to pressures which seriously reduce their autonomy. Institutional rules and established procedures restrict the free exercise of their authority; it is not unusual, accordingly, that even though they may see justice and merit in certain demands, they are unable to grant them. In addition, the actions of lower authorities and administrative heads, who by necessity are the ones who have to deal with the protesters, take place in an open fishbowl of public observation. They are particularly subject, accordingly, to scrutiny and pressure from higher authorities, interest groups, and the general public. Pressures which emanate from these groups are of telling importance in influencing local authorities in the way they deal with social unrest.

4. *Generally,* the line of development in the handling of social unrest by authorities is a movement from initial indifference, through vacillating tolerance, to increasing firmness and ultimately to reliance on the police power of the state. It is important to note that authorities are themselves subject to the actions of others in the arena of social unrest, particularly the actions of special-interest groups and the general public. Accordingly, the line of their efforts is influenced significantly by the posture of these latter groups.

Special-Interest Groups

1. The formation and career of social unrest are usually influenced to a formidable extent by the activities of particular groups having special interests that are either threatened by the unrest or that may be furthered by exploiting the unrest. Groups of people who feel that they stand to lose advantages from changes in the social arrangement that is under attack are certain to take action against the social unrest and oppose its efforts. Groups which feel that the social unrest and the accompanying protest constitute a challenge to law and order usually voice their positions vigorously; such groups in our society are likely to include business organizations, law enforcement agencies, certain civic organizations, and given political organizations. Further, groups and individuals, such as politi-

cians, who perceive prospects of advantage in parading themselves as opponents of the protesters are likely to become active participants in the arena of social unrest.

2. The actions of such special-interest groups are brought to bear especially on authorities and on the general public. The action on authorities range from a mere expression of views to a direct intercession in the making of decisions by the authorities. The action on the general public is in the form of denouncing the protesters, ridiculing their claims, denying that there are valid grounds for the social unrest, and depicting the protesters in reprehensible terms. Their rallying call is usually that of maintaining "law and order." Since special-interest groups are particularly favored in access to the media of communication, their influence on the general public is pronounced.

The General Public

1. The position of the general public is dependent on how the social unrest and its manifestations are defined to the public and by the public. Generally, the public is uninformed about the given case of social unrest, is unfamiliar with the experiences of those at the center of the unrest and consequently is not able to put itself in the position of those voicing protest. These limitations have a double effect on the general public. First, they shield the public from seeing the protested social arrangement as improper or illegitimate. It should be borne in mind, as earlier discussion has indicated, that in an established social order most people accept the legitimacy or authoritative status of the prevailing arrangements. Lacking familiarity with the events and experiences that bring into being the particular instance of social unrest, they are unable or unprepared to accept the view that the social arrangement is illegitimate. Hence, their position tends to be one of inability to understand the unrest and of disapproval of the protest activity that stems from it. The criticisms, intellectual attacks and demands advanced by the exponents of social unrest appear outlandish, and the overt actions—particularly direct actions outside of conventional channels—taken by them appear strange and out of order. Given its natural position, the public tends to recoil from social unrest and its manifestations. This tendency is tempered, of course, by the extent of identification on other grounds with those in the restless group.

Second, ignorance of the conditions provoking the unrest and unfamiliarity with the experiences of those caught in it make the general public easy prey to the way in which it is characterized to them. The depiction of the unrest and of the protesters through the various media of communication is very influential in shaping the public outlook. Since the media of communication are particularly open to use by authorities and to the representatives of special-interest groups unsympathetic to the social unrest, the definitions that are presented usually lead the general public to an unfavorable characterization of the unrest and its exponents.

2. The general public acts back on the career of social unrest in two important ways; first, as a pressure on authorities to steer a given course in meeting the social unrest and in handling the protesters. We see here the interesting case of authorities and special-interest groups, who are largely responsible for shaping the images of the public, asserting that they are responding to the interests and the demands of the public. Second, by its posture the general public creates a social atmosphere which affects the individuals caught up in social unrest or potentially sympathetic to it. Expressions of public attitudes as conveyed in family conversations, talk on the street, in meetings, in other public utterances, and in the media of communication play upon those identified with the social unrest and those sympathetic to it. One should not undervalue the influence of such expressions in contributing to an atmosphere of deterrence and intimidation around the participants in social unrest.

3. Generally, however, the public is moved to sympathy for those expressing social unrest, by what appear to be cruel, inhuman and unconscionable actions against them. Thus, repressive or punitive actions by authorities occurring in a dramatic and spectacular manner which are seen as grossly violating sentiments of justice, decency, and fair treatment can swing support to the cause of the protesters. In the face of the generally intolerant attitude of the public at large toward the protesters, dramatic acts of brutality and indecent treatment of them by authorities or other opponents are the chief means of gaining public support for the protesters.

The foregoing discussion should be sufficient to make clear that social unrest does not come into being, in full form and character, as a result of so-called underlying or preceding causes. Instead, it acquires its substance, its form, its growth, and its direction from the interplay of factors in a contemporary process. The most important of these factors, as we have noted, are predispositions to unrest, the play of dramatic events, the interaction that takes place among those who are infected by the unrest, the character of the expressions and outbursts of the unrest, and, importantly, the resistance and opposition that are encountered by those espousing the unrest. Whether social unrest grows, declines or is arrested. whether it takes root or is evanescent, whether it assumes violent or peaceful forms of expression, and whether it becomes directed to one or another set of objectives—all of these vital parts of its being are an outcome of what happens in the arena of its operation and formation. We have noted earlier that the basic ingedients of social unrest are a collective disowning of the legitimated character of a social arrangement, a development of shared dissatisfaction with the social arrangement, and a preparation to take collective action against the social arrangement. These three ingredients are aroused, cultivated, directed and forged by what takes place in the very process of formation through which social unrest passes. It should be evident, thus, that in its formation social unrest does not follow any preordained path. Instead, its career line is uncertain and precarious.

SOCIAL UNREST AS A DEFINING PROCESS

The primary significance of social unrest is that it is a process by which people redefine or recast the images of their world and so prepare themselves to act toward the world. This is the function of social unrest. In the intricate interplay of factors in the formation of social unrest people come to revise the way in which they see given social objects and values, social practices, institutional arrangements, systems of authority, authoritative figures, and the social order itself. Parallel to such redefinitions, people form new conceptions of themselves. The new definitions of their world and of themselves in relation to it set the way in which people become prepared or sensitized to act. This preparation or sensitization to act constitutes the outcome or resolution of social unrest. As we shall see in the next section of this essay, the ways in which social unrest may be resolved differ profoundly. The advance recognition of this difference calls attention to the importance of the defining process that takes place in the formation of social unrest. Also, it points to the need of seeing that social unrest is a fluid process—one which may take different directions, depending on the nature of the redefinitions that are made during the course of its formation.

At the inception of social unrest people who are caught up in it are vague, uncertain, and differ from one another in their ideas of their disturbed situation. They are far from clear about what is disturbing them, about what it is that they are seeking, about the aspects of the social arrangement that disquiet them, about what they are condeming, about whom to blame for the conditions they feel to be wrong, about the extent and pinpointed character of the legitimated authority that they are disowning, and about the lines of action they should take. The formation of social unrest is a process through which clarity on these matters is sought and worked out within the context of happenings in the arena of social unrest. The reader should bear in mind that people in the state of social unrest engage in lengthy discussions among themselves, in which they voice their divergent criticisms of social arrangements, express their complaints and grievances, talk about what they think is wrong, express their feelings about different social values, present their versions of existing authoritative arrangements, discuss their present situation, venture judgments as to what they should do, and propose tactics that should be employed. Such discussions are recurrent, sometimes virtually continuous affairs, necessarily shifting in content and focus as the people find themselves confronted with new situations with the movement of events. The success or failure which they experience at one or another point in their actions, the picture of what is being done by fellow participants elsewhere, the opposition and frustration which is experienced at the hands of authorities, the resistance met from the general public, and their own inner differences and disputes—all these enter into the defining process, that takes place among them.* As a result of their discussions and reflections in the wake of the events and situations they encounter, people evolve their views of the world that concern them and of themselves in relation to it. They form a more definite idea of what they are dissatisfied with, a revised picture of the authoritative arrangements and figures which they reject, and a new stance or position as a result of their interpretation of the opposition and resistance which they encounter.

One can appreciate the nature of this defining process by focusing attention on the most important strand in the formation of social unrest. This strand is the disowning of legitimacy in social arrangements and the working out of a generalized position as a result of resistance and opposition. Typically in the formation of social unrest the area of rejected legitimacy widens and the objects that are rejected become more fixed. Whereas in the beginning of social unrest the rejection of authoritative status may be confined to a particular practice or to a given adminstrative act, it may readily expand serially to include the administrators themselves, the whole apparatus of authority in the given social or institutional arrangement, the basic purposes and objectives of the institution and ultimately the sanctioned style of life of the social order itself. Such an expansion of what is rejected as no longer authoritative occurs, of course, primarily because of the resistance and repression that is experienced in trying to achieve the immediate short-term objectives that crop up here and there in the formation of social unrest. The opposition encountered in the pursuit of what are felt as worthy objectives—particularly what is seen as procrastinating, unfair and unyielding opposition from authorities and the general public—easily leads to disenchantment with wider circles of established authority and with larger portions of the conventional social

---

*All of this is to be seen, for example, in current social unrest among blacks in the United States, among college and university students in the case of student unrest, and in the case of women's unrest that is looming or the horizon. It is to be noted, also, in the many instances of nationalist unrest, industrial unrest, revolutionary unrest, and colonial unrest in the past.

order. One illustration of this expanding rejection of authoritative status is the familiar "radicalization" of people as a result of what they see as inconsiderate or indifferent treatment by authorities or as unfair denunciation by an intolerant public. If we recognize that from its beginning social unrest represents some form and degree of opposition to established arrangements and that, in turn, it is met by opposition from authorities and different segments of the public we can understand that the initial idea of what is wrong may expand to include more crucial features of the established order. Administrators, institutional heads and governmental executives who are regarded as instigating the counteropposition come to be regarded as enemies and the authoritative character of their posts comes to be challenged. Functionaries and agents of such heads and leaders come to be seen as lackeys, and the validity of their roles is thrown into question. The integrity of the institutions which are the seats of the counteropposition comes to be doubted; these institutions come to be seen as betraying their proper objectives. Established social values and styles of life which are seen as undergirding the counteropposition begin to lose their authoritative character. The extent to which such increasing rejection of the established order occurs depends, of course, on the events and experiences that take place and on the way they are defined by those who are caught up in the developing unrest. We need to keep in mind that the increasing disowning of established social arrangements that takes place in the formation of social unrest is an outcome of the *defining* process that is in play and not the result of factors that antedate that process.

Not only does this interpretative process establish and set the lines of opposition against the social order, but it shapes the nature of that opposition. As the following section will explain, social unrest may develop into significantly different forms of opposition to the established social order. It may take the form of a suppressed and immobile disgruntlement with the established order but without any action being taken; it may take the form of aggressive efforts to change social arrangements; it may take the form of fleeing from the established order of life and finding refuge in a radically different mode of life; it may take the form of a radical self-transformation leading to the creation of a transcendental world which supersedes the established order; or it may take the form of a life of hedonistic satisfaction inside of, but in a sense detached from, the established social order. Such radically different resolutions of social unrest constitute an additional reason for recognizing the importance of the defining process that takes place in the formation of social unrest. As participants interact with one another, discussing their experiences, evaluating their world, meeting the opposition of authorities, encountering condemnation of and disdain for the expressions of their unrest, setting models for one another, weighing the success or failure of their initial efforts, and judging their future prospects, they move toward the development of given stances or positions toward the established social order.

LINES OF RESOLUTION OF SOCIAL UNREST

I use the term, "resolution," to refer to the outcome of the formation of social unrest, to the form that is developed through the process of rejecting legitimacy and dealing with a refractory established order. Resolution represents a conversion of vague and uncertain dissatisfaction with established social arrangements into a definite feeling of the unsuitability of such arrangements, a shift from a mixed and unsettled view of the social order to a singular and fixed conception of it, and the development of a new stance or posture toward the social order. This stance becomes the anchor point for collective action and sets the direction of such action.

I wish to identify and discuss the major forms into which social unrest may be resolved in the course of its formation. As suggested in a few remarks above, they may be identified as (1) an accommodated acceptance of established social arrangements, (2) collective and aggressive protest against the arrangements, (3) a flight from established social arrangements, (4) the creation of a transcendental world of belief that overshadows the existing order, and (5) a resort to a life of hedonistic satisfaction within the existing social order. As can be noted, the last four of these forms of resolution of social unrest represent incubating grounds for the emergence of social movements, but movements that differ profoundly from one another. I wish to discuss each of the five lines along which social unrest may be resolved.

Accommodation to Existing Social Arrangements

The run of experience of those caught up in a given instance of social unrest may have no other outcome than to lead them to a grudging acceptance of existing social arrangements because of an inability to accomplish any change. This is indeed the fate of the great majority of instances of social unrest. Participants find that despite their agitation, their excited discussions, their public meetings and demonstrations, their pressing of demands on authorities, their planning and their strategy, and their momentary successes at one or another point they are not able in the last analysis to achieve anything that corresponds to their wishes and hopes. The opposition of authorities may prove to be unyielding and the condemnatory attitude of the general public may not give way. Participants find themselves in a position where their activities become fruitless, where they seemingly have no way to turn, and where prospects for effective action in the foreseeable future are vague. Leaders lose hope and flounder, members lose enthusiasm and determination, morale and spirit decline, and the drive behind the unrest dries up. If the run of experiences is interpreted and met in this way by the participants, their collective unrest may disappear, becoming reduced to mere dissembled attitudes as people accommodate themselves to what they cannot change. Their accommodation to the existing arrangements is typically a grudging one. The people still cling to their beliefs that given social arrangements are wrong and unjust, that the arrangements and indeed wider areas of authority are unacceptable, and that the arrangements deserve to be changed. But the individuals reconcile themselves to acting conventionally within the social arrangements, awaiting at the best some future turn of events that might bring about the change they had sought.

Collective Protest

I use the term, "collective protest," to refer to social unrest that becomes centered in persistent aggressive efforts to change social arrangements irrespective of the opposition that is encountered. It differs from the accommodative type of resolution that I have just discussed in that the resistance and opposition it encounters do not deter or dissolve the intention to achieve a change in the social order. Encountered resistance and opposition become the occasion for new effort, for attempts in new directions, for devising new objectives or new strategies. Collective protest differs from the three remaining forms into which social unrest may become resolved (to be discussed below) in that it remains a direct attack on the social order and thus has to be met by the authorities and defenders of the established order. It thus sets up a clear and central arena of battle in a way that does not arise in these three other resolutions of unrest. It is this combative character, this entrance into the arena of power play, that is the distinguishing mark of collective protest—a combative motif that sets its course and determines its modes of procedure. Collective protest is less a symbolic expression of dissatisfaction, as in the earlier stages of unrest, and more a direct maneuvering to achieve specific objectives. The crystallization of social unrest into collective protest becomes a bridge to the formation of social movements having an avowed and specific commitment to change existing social arrangements. I shall discuss collective protest at some length in the final section of this essay.

Flight from the Social Order

Social unrest may become resolved along directions that are markedly different from collective protest. One of these directions is to flee from the established social order and to find refuge in a new scheme of life that seems to offer prospects of satisfying new interests, hopes and tastes. For purposes of convenience, I use the label, "flight unrest," to refer to this line of development of social unrest. Flight unrest has three cardinal features: a rejection of the legitimacy of established social arrangements, an abandonment of efforts to change these arrangements, and a formation of a new scheme of life that immures participants so far as possible from the value demands of the existing social order. Flight unrest may take one of two alternative forms. One form is for the participants to separate themselves physically from the existing social arrangements, such as by setting up a communal colony in a secluded geographical location. Such physical withdrawal, particularly in the form of so-called utopian societies, has been very common over time in the case of major instances of social unrest. Such physical separation allows participants to form and engage in a scheme of collective life at variance with the established social order with a minimum of abrasive contact with that order. The second type of flight unrest is in the form of psychological detachment, such as establishing a cult or embracing a new unconventional philosophy. In this case the participants remain within the physical confines of the existing social arrangements but immerse themselves within a separate scheme of group life built around an unconventional set of beliefs and rituals. This separate scheme of life is elevated to a position of top priority so that it exercises a major claim on the participants' interests and commitments. Thus, while the participants continue to live and act within the established social arrangements, they lose concern with these social arrangements and, metaphorically, turn their backs on these social arrangements. Psychologically, they barricade themselves against the value demands of the existing social order, without seeking to protest against such demands or to change them.

The abandonment of efforts to change existing social arrangements provides the clue for understanding how flight unrest takes form. One obvious source of its formation is the emergence of a conviction among the participants that it is fruitless to try to change or bend the existing social order so that it conforms to the new wishes, interests and tastes. The opposition either encountered or anticipated from authorities, and particularly the resistance coming from the general public and its exponents, come to be seen as shutting the doors to desired changes. Expressions of condemnation and scorn directed against participants by parents, relatives, institutional heads and spokesmen of the established order are interpreted to mean that the established order is irrevocably set against the desired types of change. Harassment and lack of sympathy by authorities help to cement the conviction that it is fruitless to try to achieve a change in the social order.

The abandonment of hope of changing existing social arrangements does not mean, however, settling into the accommodative type of resolution of social unrest discussed above. Instead, the renunciation of the established order is so great and the wish for a different scheme of life so strong that refuge is sought in the form of flight. A second and somewhat similar source of flight unrest is an inability on the part of the participants to see or to develop a substitute for the established social arrangements that they disown. In not having a relatively clear or stable conception of the type of life they would like or are seeking, they are particularly prone to an aimless and exploratory quest. They seek a place of refuge and refrain from trying to change the social order, not because of the opposition or resistance of the social order but because they lack even a vague understanding of a substitute arrangement. Hence, they are led to strike out in divergent directions in their effort to find something that answers to and satisfies their restlessness, usually along the line of resurrecting obscure cults of the past, borrowing bizarre cults from other lands, experimenting in developing new cults of their own, or exploring and embracing varieties of unconventional philosophy. Periods of profound social unrest are almost always marked by the emergence of a plethora of such divergent cults and philosophies. They represent a rejection of the social order without a correlative effort to change it.

Creation of a Transcendental World of Belief

One of the very important lines along which social unrest may become resolved is to develop a transcendental world of belief and a correlative collective life of ritual that overbridges and overshadows the existing social order. This is, of course, the type of resolution that we note in the emergence of genuine religious sects. Indeed, it may be spoken of as the religious resolution of social unrest. This type of resolution shares with the other types a rejection of the authoritatative status of existing social arrangements; indeed, it usually signifies a rejection of the entire social order, not merely some part of it, and a denigration of basic values of the social order. Yet the social order is left intact and no steps are taken to change it. The basic forms of the social order are followed and its basic values are observed. The adherence to the basic forms and values of the established order is not a grudging acceptance of them as in the case of the accommodative type of resolution of social unrest discussed earlier. Instead, as we shall see, it is a case of stripping vital meaning from such forms and values so that to obey or follow them is regarded as inconsequential. Finally, the direction taken by this type of unrest is not a matter of seeking a secluded haven of refuge inside of the social order as in the case of flight unrest. It is a matter of constructing a transcendental scheme of life which relegates the existing social order to a place of inferior

significance. The existing order, while stripped of its legitimacy, is toler-
ated as having no value in the real order of existence, since the real order
of existence is redefined in the new transcendental terms.

What causes the formation of social unrest to move along this line of
fashioning a transcendental world of belief and value in place of taking
other directions, such as becoming set in the direction of changing existing social arrangements, or of becoming accommodated to an indefinite
postponment of efforts to achieve such changes, or of seeking a position
of refuge within the social order? As we have seen, resistance by the
general public and opposition from authorities are major factors, usually
the major factors, in bringing about these latter forms of resolution of
social unrest. However, public resistance and official opposition play only
a minor role in leading social unrest to move toward the construction of a
transcendental world. In the case of this type of social unrest public
condemnation and official repression are minimal since the thrust of the
unrest is not to seek changes in the existing order. In offering little direct
challenge to prevailing social arrangements there is, correspondingly,
little occasion for confrontation.* Further, since there is a disposition to
relegate existing institutions, their directors and their upholders to a lower
position in what is conceived as the real world of importance, opposition
stemming from these sources is not seen as important in shaping the
direction of what is being sought. The opposition that is encountered
serves to cement solidarity among participants in this type of social unrest
without having much influence in setting the line along which the social
unrest takes form.

Instead, the line of formation of this type of social unrest is laid out by
the way in which dissatisfaction and discontent with life in the social order
are defined. Such dissatisfaction or discontent—which is usually
profound—is seen primarily not as stemming from difficulties between
people and the existing social order but as rooted in difficulties between
people and a transcending universe. What is held to be wrong is not this or
that deficient institution or social arrangement but, instead, being out of
touch or step with a superior power of the universe. What is called for is
not a reorganization of the existing order but, instead, the establishment
of a proper and harmonious relation with a transcending power and being.
It is not the existing social order that is at fault; it is the people who have
gone astray. The course to be followed is the transformation of people and
not the transformation of prevailing social arrangements. The pursuit of

---

*This does not mean that a group seeking to form a transcendental world necessarily
escapes repressive acts by authorities; the persecution of the group may be indeed very
severe. Such persecution is due to what the religious group symbolizes and not because of
any frontal attacks.

this course involves the construction of a transcendental world of belief and value and a moral transformation of individuals to embrace and fit into the transcendental world.

This is not the place to trace the way in which such a transcendental world of belief and value takes form. The process is familiar to those who have studied carefully the emergence of primitive religious sects. I merely wish to note that the formation of a transcendental world is one of the important directions along which social unrest may become resolved. This form of social unrest arises clearly out of dissatisfaction with life in a given social order, it signifies acute disharmony between people and that social order, it involves a career of intense interaction among participants in which they are defining their situation to one another, it implies clearly a rejection of the compelling authoritative status of the existing social order, yet it represents a line of adjustment in which the social order is not challenged but is left intact. It is not a matter of fleeing from the social order; it is a matter of relegating the social order to a plane of inferior significance.

Resort to a Life of Hedonistic Satisfaction

The remaining significant direction along which social unrest may move in its formation is toward a life of immediate sensual gratification. Such hedonistic satisfaction may be sought in such forms as dancing, music, expressive conversation, exotic behavior, sex activity or the use of drugs. These forms of behavior are lifted out of their normal restricted and subordinate position in the social order and elevated to the status of both immediate and final ends. They become the center of schemes of collective life, with accompanying codes, set of rituals, and a justifying philosophy. The emergence of such kinds of collective behavior is not infrequent in periods of social unrest, particularly if the social unrest is intense and if disillusionment with the social order is profound.

What conditions lead the formation of social unrest toward seeking a life of hedonistic satisfaction? The crucial matter seems to be a disillusionment with the existing order of life with no hope of changing it or finding a substitute for it. Conventional goals, career lines, and styles of life lose their value and appeal, and avenues to new career lines and to the building up of a new order of collective life appear to be completely closed. Under these conditions of disillusionment with the existing order of life and in the absence of any substitute scheme toward which participants might strive, the resort to a life of immediate sensual gratification can readily occur.

This brief characterization of the conditions which favor this outcome of social unrest invites consideration of the path that is followed in its formation. One finds present, of course, the same fundamental ingredients that belong to social unrest in general: dissatisfaction and discontent with existing social arrangements; a loss of credibility in the authoritative status of conventional values, demands, and styles of living; vexation and distress in having to abide by these values, demands and styles; incipient efforts to protest and to alter these conventional forms; and the awareness of condemnation and resistance by authorities and the public to such efforts. The distinguishing features of this type of unrest are the greater disillusionment with the existing order and the greater sense of hopelessness of devising or finding any scheme of life to take its place. The disillusionment gets expression in the loss of a sense of career; the future of life in the existing order seems bleak and uninspiring. The absence of prospects of finding or devising a new promising order of life cements the sense of hopelessness of the future. The result is to seek self-realization in the immediate present in the form of heightened feelings of sensual indulgence. This outcome, as one can readily perceive, is profoundly abetted by the resistance of the public and authorities—a resistance that is interpreted as not merely reflecting profound indifference to the plight and complaints of the participants but as being so deeply implanted that there is no hope of changing it. It is not surprising, accordingly, that the resort to hedonistic satisfaction carries a strain of bitterness against the established order—a dash of vengeance. The hedonistic behavior is likely to be excessive and extravagant and to take expressions that shock and insult authorities and the public.

SUMMARY REFLECTIONS ON SOCIAL UNREST

The identification of five alternative lines along which social unrest may move in its formation should reinforce the recognition that social unrest represents, metaphorically, a fluid state and that its direction is set by the interpretation of events and happenings that occur during the course of its formation. The course of formation cannot be accounted for by the conditions that precede the formation. While such antecedent conditions undeniably fashion predispositions they do not determine the career of social unrest. Instead, the kinds of events that occur, the nature of circular reaction among participants, the kind of official opposition and public resistance that are encountered, and the kinds of interpretations that are made in this interplay are the decisive factors which shape the formation of social unrest. It is necessary to understand this process of formation of social unrest in order to grasp the character of social unrest and to comprehend its outcome.

It should be understood that the resolution of social unrest into the five indicated forms does not take place instantaneously or abruptly, except in rare cases. Usually, the development takes place over relatively long periods of time, involving definition and redefinition of situations and goals. Predispositions and early events may give an initial slant to the direction along which social unrest may form; however, the direction is set chiefly by what is experienced in the middle and later stages of formation. It may be said that tendencies toward all five directions are present in the early stage of unrest. Certainly, aroused dissatisfaction with social arrangements, rejection of their authoritative status, and vexation over having to continue to endure them provoke a disposition to protest them. Almost simultaneously there is a readiness in the face of opposition and resistance to buckle into an accommodative acceptance of the disliked social arrangements. Also, there is a tendency to seek refuge, whether in a secluded location or a detached cultist world. Similarly, there are people who are ready to turn toward a life of hedonistic satisfaction. And, finally, because of acutely experienced personal disturbance, there are people poised, so to speak, to move toward a transcendental world scheme as a means of salvation. These tendencies exist side by side, with the result that in periods of particularly profound social unrest, all five types are to be found. Yet, it is not these initial tendencies that set the course that is taken by social unrest in its formation. Instead, it is the interplay of the major factors previously considered that set the course. Under their impact an initial orientation of social unrest may shift to a different direction. Such reorientation is especially pronounced in the shift away from a protest posture to other lines of resolution—a shift which, as we have said, occurs from the way in which resistance and opposition are defined. But, under the play of the defining of experience, shifts can take place in other directions in the formation of social unrest.

Social unrest, when resolved or achieving form, is essentially a preparation for collective action. This is not true, of course, of social unrest which has taken the direction of reluctant accommodation to the existing social order. The other four types of resolution, however, prepare and poise participants for immediate collective action along their respective lines—protest, flight, moral regeneration, and hedonistic experience. All four are at odds with the established social order. Their mere existence constitutes a challenge to the social order. Their overt expression in collective action represents in varying degree either a direct or indirect attack on that social order. This presence and this attack invite and provoke counteraction from the guardians and supporters of the established institutions. Thus, even though the direction of each of the four types of social unrest has become set, the participants are still caught in continuing efforts to achieve an order of life that corresponds to their respective line of interest. It is this continuing effort that sets the stage for the emergence of social movements. Social unrest which has become set in its direction is in this sense a bridge to the egression of social movements. Since collective protest is the form of social unrest that is central in a direct attack on the social order, I wish to single it out for discussion.

COLLECTIVE PROTEST

My concern is with collective protest that emanates from social unrest. Such collective protest needs to be distinguished from other kinds of related collective action and from other forms of social protest with which it is frequently confused. To begin with, it needs to be set apart from the other terminal types of social unrest that have been discussed above. One can say that the flight to a secluded unconventional world inside of the established social order, or the effort to establish a transcendental world of moral regeneration, or the resort to a life of hedonistic gratification signifies protest against the estabished order. Yet, as our earlier discussion has sought to make clear, these forms of unrest are not direct attacks on the social order—they do not seek to correct, change or reorganize social arrangements. I use the term, "collective protest," to refer to this latter direction of social unrest.

Next, collective protest that has its roots in social unrest needs to be distinguished from forms of protest which do not stem from social unrest. There are multitudes of such latter instances, such as by groups of people who are incensed by an authoritative act or prospective authoritative act or by an outrageous breach of proper conduct. An administrative decree, a law, or a prospective institutional policy which endangers the interests of a particular set of people is likely to provoke social protest from that group. Also, a seemingly outrageous act such as a dastardly crime or a gross impropriety on the part of a public official can evoke strong expressions of public protest. Such forms of protest activity, which are very common in modern societies, do not spring from social unrest; they do not arise from general dissatisfaction nor do they presuppose a denial of the legitimacy of given social arrangements. Next, we need to set apart those kinds of immediate direct attacks which are outbursts of transitory or episodic crowd excitement. Lynchings, riots and vandalistic attacks, although involving momentary defiance of authorities, are not instances of collective protest stemming from social unrest unless they are grounded in a disowning of the legitimacy of established arrangements. Finally, we must distinguish collective protest that arises out of social unrest from mere expressions of disapproval of some given area of social arrangements. In this regard, collective protest, indeed like social unrest itself, is frequently confused with a mere state of dissent, as in speaking of current student dissent. Mere dissent is not social unrest, and the verbal expression of dissent need not be a protest expression of social unrest. Collective protest emanating from social unrest signifies not merely a criticism or disapproval of an existing social arrangement but, instead, a rejection of the right of that arrangement to continue; it signifies also not merely a denunciation of that arrangement but a readiness to take direct action in defiance of its authoritative status. In summarizing these various lines of distinction we can say that collective protest which grows out of social unrest has the following marks: (a) its source of dissatisfaction and intention is deep-seated and enduring, (b) it signifies a persisting denial of the legitimacy or authoritative claims of the institutional area under protest, and (c) it represents a readiness to engage in direct attack, circumventing established channels of protest, and defying authorities. This brief identification of collective protest that is rooted in social unrest provides the clues to an understanding of its characteristic features. I wish now to spell out these features, enumerating them for convenience. Henceforth, in using the term, "collective protest," I shall be referring to collective protest that arises from social unrest.

1. Collective protest in any of its instances is a continuing affair, extending over time, taking usually a variety of expressions, and moving from one object or target to another. It is not a momentary occurrence that comes into being over a single incident, only to disappear as soon as the incident has passed. Since it springs from a complex of persisting dissatisfaction, abiding rejection of authoritative status, and continuing vexation with what is felt to be an abrasive social arrangement, it is, itself, a continuing matter. The recognition of this has two noteworthy consequences. First, collective protest should be seen as following a career or course—a course which, as we shall see, is very precarious and uncertain since it is dependent on differing factors at work in the arena in which collective protest occurs. Second, it is erroneous to believe that an effective handling of any single manifestation of collective protest, whether, let us say, by granting a set of demands of the protesters or by ruthlessly suppressing the protest expression, will dissipate it. This is a view commonly taken by authorities—a view that fails to note the continuing base of collective protest. As long as dissatisfaction, rejection of authoritative status, and chafing under a given social arrangement continue to exist, the mere handling of one of the thrusts of protest is not likely to end it.

2. By its very nature collective protest has no clear, specific and fixed goals as to what should be sought; instead, its course is a series of concern with immediate happenings that arise from point to point. This feature is so fundamental that it needs to be spelled out. Earlier discussion has emphasized that the dissatisfaction component of social unrest is made up of complaints over specific features of a given social arrangement and a vague general dissatisfaction with one's lot under the arrangement. The

specific complaints represent the concrete experiences that have been found to be onerous and distasteful in living under the arrangement; the general dissatisfaction arises from new self-conceptions implying a claim to a different social position, to new rights, privileges and opportunities and to a new order of life. Both the specific complaints and the general dissatisfaction hamper the formulation of distant goals which might guide the protest activity. Specific complaints almost always differ greatly among the participants, setting a difficulty in trying to establish an order of priority among them. Further, there is pronounced difficulty in trying to incorporate specific complaints into workable sets of objectives. Sets of demands composed solely of such specific complaints proliferate into seemingly minor and trivial matters that do not meet the sense of general dissatisfaction that is felt. Thus, the array of specific complaints found among the participants do not yield a set of objectives suitable to guide collective protest during the course of its movement. The sense of general dissatisfaction is even less qualified to supply such guiding objectives. The feeling of general dissatisfaction, which is by far the more important part of the dissatisfaction component of social unrest, is not accompanied by any clear goals of what should be sought, any specific and fixed idea of the new social order or new set of social arrangements that should be set up. The feeling of general dissatisfaction sensitizes people to detect social ills in conditions that have been accepted previously as natural, and it feeds upon discussion of such ills. But while it serves thereby to delineate things to which people are opposed, it does little to identify practical arrangements that should be sought. This character is aptly summed up in the frequent charge hurled against people in a condition of social unrest to the effect that they know fairly well what they don't want but do not know what they do want.

The absence of clearly defined distant objectives that offer prospects of meeting the conditions of dissatisfaction turns collective protest in the direction of dealing with immediate situations on a largely improvised and *ad hoc* manner. Without the guidance of clearly conceived remote objectives, such as exist in the case of an organized social movement, protest activity comes to be centered on immediate events. A dramatic happening, a seemingly stupid administrative act, an outburst of indignation over some repressive act, an opportunity to confront suddenly a detested authority figure, a sudden turning of public attention to an acute grievance—these are particularly the kind of happenings on which collective protest seizes and on which it thrives. Because of this dependency of collective protest on immediate events and immediate situations the course of collective protest tends to be erratic, shifting from one object to another, taking unexpected turns, and marked by uncertainty as to what may be the next target—a condition which occasions despair among sensitive authorities who must deal with collective protest. Collective protest appears as consisting of tactics without strategy; whatever strategy may occur is short-termed and not in the service of distant objectives.

Even though collective protest becomes centered on immediate issues that are brought up by the run of events, considerable discussion goes on in the restless group with regard to long-range objectives. This is inevitable in the continuing course of protest. For one thing, participants find it necessary to reconcile their divergent and vague notions as to what kind of social arrangement they are seeking. More importantly, they are forced to assess the results of their protest efforts, as they encounter opposition or find that immediate "victories" turn out to be empty. Such conditions lead them to try to formulate more general objectives that seem to explain and justify their general protest.

An apt example in the case of current student unrest is the formulation of a goal of "student power" in place of an earlier concern with one or another instance of administrative abuse. Such formulations of general objectives, one may say parenthetically, should not be regarded as explaining or being the cause of the given type of social unrest and collective protest. This is a grievous error that scholars make all too frequently. Such formulations are the products and not the causes of social unrest and collective protest. Finally, it should be noted that, even after such formulations are reached, they have minor influence in directing the expressions of collective protest. Protest continues to follow a course that is dominated by response to the demands and opportunities of immediate situations in place of being guided by long-range policies. This character of collective protest changes, of course, when social unrest solidifies into a social movement. When and as a social movement takes form, collective protest shifts from spontaneous expressions of "populist" feelings to calculated use on behalf of long-range policy.

3. The preoccupation of collective protest with immediate events allows us to recognize the purposes or interests that are served by collective protest. Collective protest has four lines or dimensions of purpose. These can be labeled as *expressive, unifying, symbolic,* and *coercive.* Instances of collective protest can be helpfully analyzed and understood in terms of these four dimensions.

The *expressive* dimension of collective protest refers to the use of collective protest merely to express feelings that have been touched off by immediate incidents or issues. In this form, protest is no more than a means or opportunity to voice or release feelings that have been stirred up by the incident or issue. The feelings may be indignation, anger, vengeance, enthusiasm, glee and the like, as these may be aroused by such incidents as a shocking administrative action, a provocative or insulting declaration by an authority, an unusual opportunity to challenge a distasteful public policy, a brutal police action, or a display of authoritative vulnerability that invites exploitation. In this case collective protest serves primarily to express feeling rather than to effect change, being largely a matter of crowd excitement. To a very large extent collective protest emanating from social unrest has this expressive character of merely releasing and satisfying feelings that have been collectively aroused by given incidents rather than of trying to achieve calculated ends. This is especially true in the early stages of collective protest, taking precedence over the other purposes or functions of collective protest. This expressive dimension of collective protest continues in varying degree throughout the course of collective protest.

The *unifying* dimension or purpose of collective protest refers to the influence of protest in introducing a sense of camaraderie and solidarity among the protesters. One does not have to point out the crucial importance of such camaraderie and solidarity among the participants. Since they have no organization, or at best only a loose, indefinite and changing organization, participants are very dependent on a sense that they are being directly supported by one another. Without being sustained by such a realization that there are many others who share their feelings and approve their purposes and practices, participants lose fervor and readiness to act. This explains why outward collective expressions of protest are significant in themselves as important sources of stimulation and support. A big turnout for a rally or demonstration, vigorous expression of shared feelings gaining hearty applause at a public meeting, a large following behind a delegation presenting demands, a sizable number of simultaneous disruptive actions, and similar displays of protest unite and buoy up participants in collective protest. In this sense, collective protest feeds on its own expressions. Conversely, if numbers are small or drastically below expectations in given expressions of protest, the sense of solidarity is weakened and protest effort loses vigor. In seeking to analyze and understand collective protest one should not minimize the role of its various expressions in imparting a sense of unity to its participants and in sustaining their collective purpose. Frequently, this is a major consequence of collective protest, a consequence that may be of great importance in laying a basis for subsequent formation of an organized movement.

I use the term, "*symbolic* dimension," to refer to the use of collective protest to make an impression on the outside public—to make the community and its influential members recognize the importance and worthiness of the protest. A strong strain to achieve such an effect runs through collective protest. The protesters see their protest activity as being on display and thus as exerting influence on those who pay attention to it. Nevertheless, protesters are usually naive and unanalytical as to the impression that their protest will make and similarly so with regârd to how their protest should be expressed in order to achieve a certain impact. Commonly, especially during the early stages of protest, protesters assume that the mere voicing or expression of their protest is sufficient to make the general public recognize its merit and the deficiency of what is being protested. Such a result is almost taken for granted. It is assumed or implied that in witnessing the display of the protest the outside public or at least its intelligent members will see matters as the protesters see them and thus respond sympathetically. It is unusual, especially in the early stages of protest, for the protesters to consider seriously and to think through the question of how a given expression of their protest is likely to be judged and responded to by the general community. The usual absence of such a consideration of possible responses by the general public helps to explain why a breach may begin between the protesters and the public, with the former being astounded that the merit of their protest is not automatically recognized, and with the public repelled by what appears to be the oddness and unwarranted character of the protest. We can conclude by saying that in relation to the outside audience the protesters are far more interested in making an impression than they are in thinking through what that impression will be.

The *coercive* dimension of collective protest refers to the deliberate effort of the protesters to force authorities, usually local authorities, to meet requests and demands—to take a given line of action or to desist from a line of action. This is the major objective of protest. Since what is sought can be achieved only through actions taken by authorities, protest activity is directed primarily and ultimately toward authorities. Authorities become the targets. The thrust of protest is to force the relevant authorities to accede to a given request or demand. Initial efforts to gain such assent through the mere presentation of the request are typically fruitless; indeed this is why protest comes into being. Hence protest efforts readily and quickly take the direction of coercion. Whether by a show of strength, a display of resolute intention, a persistent refusal to desist, a threat of disruption or an actual act of disruption, collective protest becomes a pressure on authorities to take a desired form of action.

It should be evident that collective protest may shift from one to another of the four lines of purpose that have been indicated—sometimes serving merely to express feelings, sometimes merely to invigorate and unify participants, sometimes primarily to get the general public to pay attention and listen, and sometimes to force authorities to take action. Misunderstanding of given instances of protest may easily occur as a result of faulty interpretation of the purpose underlying the protest. The two most conspicuous forms of such misinterpretation should be noted. One is the failure of observers to perceive the general dissatisfaction that lies behind the expressive dimension of protest. The expression of feelings by protesters as a result of particular immediate events that evoke their protest may easily conceal their general dissatisfaction with their lot and with the state of the world. Authorities and the general public are especially prone to preoccupation with the immediate instances of protest and with the behavior displayed in them with the consequence that they fail to detect the underlying general dissatisfaction that is the major source of the protest. This failure is an important reason for the polarization of authorities and protesters that we shall soon discuss. A second noticeable type of misinterpretation is to treat the expressive and the symbolic aspects of protest as if they were coercive acts. If authorities and the general public construe expression of feelings and appeals for attention as coercive acts they are led to adopt a defensive stance and thus are easily inclined to a repressive line of response.

4. As it pursues its course, collective protest tends to develop a polarized relation between the protesting group with their sympathizers on one side and authorities with their supporters on the other side. Under the play of given events this tendency toward polarization may become extreme, leading the two parties to enter into a warlike relation and to form a typical psychology of warfare. The conditions that promote such polarization are easy to identify.

First, merely the way in which protest happenings are typically reported, whether in informal word-of-mouth transmission or in the formal channels of news dissemination, overemphasizes the theme of conflict relations. The relating of protest happenings, especially through modern mass media of communication, picks out and stresses opposition, confrontation, and combative crisis. These are the features that are dramatic, that catch the public eye and that tap latent dispositions. Journalists, news analysts, commentators, politicians and kindred figures thrive on depicting such antagonistic opposition. Their efforts serve not merely to reveal in strong relief the opposition inherent in the protest but to elevate this opposition to a dominating position at the expense of the many other matters that are involved in the protest situation. The result of this overemphasis on the combative motif is to establish and shape in a profound way a general framework of perception through which the public and the participants are led to view and judge the protest situation and the happenings in it. Such a general framework of perception or scheme of interpretation conduces enormously to the formation of polarized relations in the case of collective protest.

Next, collective protest must be seen in itself as fostering increased opposition in the course of its development. In challenging sectors and principles of the prevailing social arrangements, and in seeking to bring about changes in them, collective protest initially pits the protesters against authorities and against people who uphold the legitimacy of the given order. This initial opposition is intensified when and if the protesting group pursues action outside of the sanctioned channels for the expression of protest. As our earlier discussion has indicated, it is very common for collective protest emanating from social unrest to turn toward forms of direct action that bypass lines of expression allowed by law or by administrative regulations. The cumbersome, slow-moving and frequently ineffectual operation of the established apparatus for handling protest, plus a belief that the apparatus is in the hands of unsympathetic opponents, readily lead the protesters to resort to direct and unsanctioned forms of action. A refusal to follow prescribed procedures of dealing with lower-echelon officials, the holding of assemblies and marches in defiance of their prohibition, the massing of participants in a picket line preventing access to given buildings or areas, the blocking of traffic, and the staging of sit-ins represent the kinds of unsanctioned actions to which protesters may resort. In turn, such forms or direct action evoke punitive reactions from authorities and usually outcries of indignation from segments of the general public. The result is to intensify the sense of opposition between protesters and their sympathizers on one hand and authorities and their supporters on the other. The authorities are led to reinterpret the protest as not merely an expression of dissatisfaction but as a defiance of their invested power and sanctioned responsibility; the protesters view the punitive and repressive reactions of the authorities as definite proof of an inability to get any sympathetic consideration of their claims. This polarized position of the parties is intensified and cemented further with the introduction of violence into their respective lines of action. In their use of unsanctioned means of protest, the protesters may be led to engage in violence in the form of attacks on property and on persons; on the other side, law enforcement agencies called in by authorities may be violent in their handling of protesters and others caught in the sweep of police action. I shall deal later with the place of violence in protest. Here, I merely wish to note that the introduction of violence into the arena of collective protest is a factor of major weight in polarizing the positions of protesters and authorities. Finally, polarization is pushed to an ultimate position by repressive legislation or governmental decree which so compresses protest as to make it ineffectual, and by judicial procedures and court trials which appear to the protesters as not prosecution but persecution. Such seemingly repressive legislation and unjust judicial procedure may be regarded by the protesters as a total collapse of the legitimacy of the established social order. Such a belief gives great impetus to converting collective protest into an organized social movement.

The polarization introduced and developed through collective protest has two very significant consequences. One is to place protesters and authorities into a warlike relation with a resulting inability of either to understand the other. The other consequence is for the combative relation to engulf and conceal the conditions of social unrest which gave rise to the collective protest. Each of these two consequences needs to be spelled out.

An increasing sense of opposition between protesters and authorities produces the ingroup-outgroup relationship that is so familiar to sociologists. Each of the two parties is inclined to identify the other as an enemy and thus to form an unfavorable image of it as deceitful, untrustworthy, and evilly intentioned. This imagery gains expression in degrading characterizations of the other party and the application to it of contemptuous labels. Each party views its own position as virtuous and its own actions as fully condonable; at the same time each party regards the actions and intentions of the other party as venal and unpardonable. Each party develops a world of its own, a framework of perception and evaluation that is in contrast to that of the other party. It is not surprising, consequently, that understanding and meaningful communication between the two break down. As polarization increases, the two parties move farther apart and lose, correspondingly, the ability of each to place itself in the position of the other. Their relation moves from a struggle between adversaries to a contest of power between enemies. Logically, an adversary relation between opponents implies a neutral and impartial third party which, acting under codes and principles, can render a decision between the competing claims of the opponents. This relation disappears to the extent that authorities (legislatures, governmental agencies, and courts) become part of an in-group aligned against the protesters as an out-group, thus abandoning the transcending role of an authority, as an impartial referee. Under these circumstances, the relation between protesters and authorities becomes essentially an exercise of power. Since, except under conditions of a collapse of acceptance of authority, authorities have command over far greater power than that available to the protesting group, the position of the authorities prevails over that of the protesters. The realization by the protesting group of its relative impotence, plus a belief that the agencies of authority are solidly committed to suppressing and extirpating all protest efforts, induce feelings of desperation and generate angry and rash action. In turn, such action is likely to evoke harsh retaliatory action by the authorities. As antagonism and hostility between protesters and authorities mount, the gulf between them widens, with increasing inability of each to understand the other, indeed a failure of interest and effort to understand each other. The relation shifts to that of two warring parties, each bent on vanquishing the other.

This warlike relation between the parties calls attention to a second noteworthy effect of polarization, namely, that each party loses sight of the issues out of which the protest arose. The protesters, in seeing the authorities as a hostile group bent on smashing the protest, reply with hostile feelings of their own. The expression of these feelings may become the primary concern of the protesting group, taking such forms as defiance for the mere sake of defiance, a flouting of symbols of authority, and on occasion vengeful and violent attack on the agents and the physical symbols of the authoritative arrangement. To the extent that protest activity comes under the sway of hostile feelings toward the authoritative establishment, the original meaning of protest as an expression of dissatisfaction and complaint recedes to secondary importance. A corresponding development takes place on the side of the authorities and their supporters. They are led to form a stereotyped image of the protesters as flouting established values, as disrespectful of law and authority, and as committed to the destruction of vital institutions of society. Their posture becomes one of hostility toward the protesting group and their aim becomes that of blocking the protest activity and, if need be, of destroying the protesters as persons or as a viable group. With such a posture and aim, authorities and their supporters lose sight and understanding of the dissatisfaction underlying the protest and bypass consideration of the conditions of the social order that may have given rise to the dissatisfaction. In the light of the observations made in this paragraph the reader should see that increasing polarization adds a new central element to the protest situation, shifting the focus away from the causative background of the protest to a warlike contest between the parties. Condemnation of each other and struggle against each other become primary considerations, with fading attention to the conditions of the social order out of which the protest arose.

5. The place of violence in collective protest merits special consideration. We begin with the commonplace observation that violence is not present in most expressions of protest. Predominantly, collective protest is expressed in an array of forms that do not involve any physical attack on property or person, as in the case of meetings, rallies, parades, marches, distribution of pronouncements and manifestos, picketing, and presentation of petitions. In addition, unsanctioned forms of protest such as sit-ins, mass picketing, forbidden parades, and occupation of buildings may be conducted in a nonviolent manner despite their unauthorized or illegal character. The occurrence or use of violence in collective protest must be recognized, accordingly, as an unusual and special condition. Let us inquire into the circumstances that bring it into being.

It is erroneous and unworthy of scholarly credence to ascribe violence in collective protest to a pre-established violent makeup of protesters, such as is done in the naive view that protesters are inveterate troublemakers inflicting their ill feelings on society. Instead, the sources of violence lie in developments in the arena of collective protest—in the particular direction of interaction between protesters and authorities. Violence is a product of a combination of mounting hostility and of frustration in action that are experienced by each party in dealing with the other. The use of violence may be from either side. Indeed, its appearance and growth are typically a result of reciprocating violent actions between the two parties. It is this process that needs to be traced.

The major steps in this process have already been mentioned from time to time in earlier remarks. The starting point is the opposition that is set logically between protesters and authorities as protesters indicate a rejection of the legitimacy of given social arrangements that authorities are required, by definition, to honor and preserve. Denunciation of such arrangements and of the authorities who have to maintain them is an early step in the generation of hostility. The response by authorities and by spokesmen of the established order along the line of belittling the protest and demeaning the protesters contributes to hostility among the latter. Such initial ill-feeling between the parties is increased as the protesters experience and voice their frustration in trying to work through the sanctioned institutional apparatus. Impatience and disappointment in trying to get a hearing and to gain action on demands by going through a cumbersome and seemingly unyielding apparatus increases hostility toward authorities. If, in turn, authorities drag their heels and deliberately slow down or block the functioning of the apparatus (this is not unusual) protesters have extra grounds for becoming hostile. The role of bad manners on the part of both parties in these early stages of the protest process is of great weight in adding to mounting hostility. The use of rude language and grating demeanor by protesters is a source of great irritation to authorities, particularly since such conduct implies a disrespect or contempt for their authority. In turn, curt behavior by authorities and an officious display of their authority produce ire among the protesters. A firm foundation for a hostile relation is laid when each party feels that it is being insulted and demeaned by the other party. Hostility is accelerated when protesters resort to the use of unsanctioned, forbidden, or illegal forms of protest. Such action is typically regarded by authorities and their supporters as in defiance of their constituted prerogatives and thus as calling for the use of police power, not merely to uphold the legitimacy of orders, regulations and laws but to inaugurate a punitive process against the violators. Under the circumstances, the protesters are easily led to see the police action as designed to destroy the protest movement rather than to uphold law and order. Such an interpretation is abetted by police action that takes unprincipled forms, such as harassment, brutal use of force, and the framing of innocent victims. The hostility that is thereby engendered among protesters is only a razor's edge away from expression in violence. In turn, police agents who are caught in the ingroup-outgroup polarization discussed above may be easily governed by a mood of hostility in approaching and handling protesters. Particularly, if they are subjected to disrespectful and vicious taunts, police agents readily view protesters not as law violators but as enemies. The factor of frustration must be introduced alongside generated hostility to understand fully the appearance of violence. When hostile feelings are strong but are subject to seemingly intolerable restraints, dispositions to violence become acute. Protesters who feel angered by what they regard as mistreatment by authorities and their agents but who feel impotent before the power of authority are especially prone to violence. Correspondingly, the agents of authority who feel themselves reviled or treated with disrespect but who feel restrained by operating procedures from expressing their hostility are particularly keyed to violence. Each party, metaphorically speaking, would like to get at the throat of the other party but is restrained by impotency or by rules. It is, accordingly, not surprising that violence breaks forth in crisis situations where restraints weaken or collapse.

Not all violence that occurs in the arena of collective protest comes into being as a result of the escalation of hostility and frustration that has been sketched. Some violence may take place as mere crowd excitement, usually in the form of revelry of outsiders attracted to the scene of protest. Youngsters, gangs, "underworld" groups, bystanders, and others not identified with the protesting group may take advantage of a condition of disturbance to engage in violence, with the opprobrium for its occurrence being placed on the protesters. Other violence may be no more than an expression of a customary mode of police procedure. Authorities may have an operating policy built up from previous experience or from their philosophy that leads them automatically to apply violence in their approach to any appearance of collective protest by a disliked group, even to the extent of using provocateurs to incite violence. However, these two forms of violence—that of outsiders and that coming from a confirmed policy of authorities—are limiting forms and do not represent the typical nature or source of violence in collective protest. Violence in collective protest is characteristically built up over time instead of being preformed or adventitious. It is an outcome of interaction between protesters and authorities in which each incites the other to mounting hostility within a framework of galling restraint. It is fundamentally a product of an intense ingroup-outgroup relation of polarization in which each party believes its position to be justifiably correct and that of the opposite party to be morally indefensible.

6. Our treatment of collective protest, as explained previously, is restricted to protest that emerges from a background of social unrest and that develops prior to becoming converted into an organized movement. A few remarks are in order with regard to the conversion of collective protest into

an organized movement. The conditions which promote or lead to such a conversion should be clear. The absolute or relative failure of collective protest because of the strength of opposition and resistance constitutes the basic reason for the emergence of an organized movement. Opposition and resistance from authorities and their supporting institutions are usually, almost typically, effective in hedging and blocking the course and development of collective protest. But such opposition and resistance may be very ineffective in allaying the social unrest that underlies the collective protest; indeed, such opposition and resistance may reinforce the sense of general dissatisfaction and the conviction that prevailing social arrangements have sacrificed their claim to legitimacy. Thus, impetus to change existing social arrangements continues. This impetus is abetted by the additional feelings of hostility that are generated by the polarization of protesters and authorities into an ingroup-outgroup relation. Given these conditions, unless the collective protest is completely smashed and the protesters fully immobilized, the groundwork is laid for the formation of an organized movement.

The emergence of an organized movement signifies a radical transformation of collective protest. Collective protest now falls inside of the framework of a working organization. A stable leadership is established (a leadership that is legitimate within the movement), a secretariat is set up, membership replaces mere participation, members are organized and given positions, rules are established to guide their actions, an ideology is developed and formulated, long-range objectives are established, and strategies are worked out to effect the achievement of objectives. Under these conditions protest loses spontaneity and preoccupation with immediate events and, instead, comes under the direction of established lines of strategy and established social policies. To understand collective protest it is highly important to distinguish between protest that is a natural expression of feelings of social unrest and protest that is a calculated step in long-range plans of an organized movement. Authorities and the uninformed general public are particularly prone to miss this distinction, being all too ready to see conspiracy and organized direction in the collective protest that is a mere expression of fluid social unrest.

A few final observations should be made with regard to the conversion of collective protest into organized social movements. One should note, first, that it is a common occurrence for collective protest to wither away in the face of strong opposition and not to pass over into an organized movement. In this event, the participants in the protest accommodate themselves to the existing social order in the manner explained earlier in discussing the accommodative resolution of social unrest. Also, as many historical instances show, collective protest that has been blocked and paralyzed may lead to the alternatives of flight, moral regeneration, and hedonistic gratification that have been previously considered. However, collective protest which is balked or blocked may take the direction of forming an organized movement dedicated to changing established social arrangements. The analysis of this formation falls appropriately in a discussion of social movements, a topic of the greatest importance in its own right but one which falls outside of the present essay. However, it should be noted that organized movements emerging from collective protest follow either the line of reform or the line of revolution, very frequently with both types of movement arising from the same setting of collective protest. The distinctive mark of a reform movement is that it seeks to achieve its objectives by using the established and sanctioned institutional apparatus of the given society, seeking to gain public support and to use political influence. In contrast, the distinctive mark of a revolutionary movement is to seek its objectives through a paralysis and the eventual overthrow of constituted authority. These respective orientations place a very different stamp on each type of movement, establishing objectives, ideologies, strategies and tactics of a profoundly different sort. Our interest here is merely to note that the way in which collective protest has been met by authorities and their supporters is of exceedingly great importance in determining whether an organized movement emerging from collective protest will take the direction of reform or revolution. The typical picture is that the revolutionary direction is taken if authorities are seen as merely committed to the suppression of the protest and if the influential segments of the public are seen as merely abetting the position of the authorities. A conviction that the established institutional arrangement of decision making and of power is solidly aligned against consideration of the claims and dissatisfaction underlying the protest turns continuing protest effort into a revolutionary channel.

CONCLUDING REFLECTIONS ON COLLECTIVE PROTEST

Collective protest should be viewed not as linear behavior of a protesting group but as a disturbed state of society in which various groups are thrown into contention with one another. Thus, the proper object of scholarly concern is not the protesting group but the *arena* of collective protest. One does not understand collective protest by merely studying the protesting group, by trying to find out what kinds of people compose it and their views, their motives and their actions. One must identify the other groups acting in the arena (echelons of authority, agents of authority, interest groups, and the general public) and observe what they do. Above all, it is necessary to see how the actions of these participating groups set the stage for one another and influence each other. Collective protest is a *joint* development, involving the interplay of different groups and moving in diverse directions as a result of the interplay.

We should recognize that collective protest is a natural means by which people thrown into a state of social unrest endeavor to bring about changes that will meet their dissatisfaction with given social arrangements. Springing from social unrest, their dissatisfaction is both deep and diffuse, imparting persistency to their protest inclinations and irregularity to their protest efforts. That protest is met with resistance by authorities and by an uninformed public is to be expected, since collective protest implies by definition a challenge to the legitimacy of given social arrangements. That protesters, in the face of such resistance, are likely to resort to the use of unsanctioned forms of expression is also to be expected. This resort to unallowable lines of action sets the critical points in the course of collective protest, the points at which the greatest administrative skill and sagacity are required. It is at these points that authorities may take action, under the principle of law and order, that irrevocably propels the protest situation into a polarized relation of two warring groups.

Such polarization is the perverting and imperiling factor in the development of collective protest. As our earlier remarks have indicated, polarization casts protesters and authorities into a warlike relation in which the underlying causative conditions of the protest disappear from sight and each party becomes preoccupied with triumphing in combat. Intense polarization is the breeding ground for the use of violence by both parties. Polarization becomes particularly perilous when authorities are swept into the position of being merely a combatant aligned against the protesters and their sympathizers. When authorities abandon the role of neutral arbiters standing above the combat and become themselves solely a combatant, the doors are closed to the resolution of collective protest through consideration and accommodation of claims.

It is precisely the ambiguity between the role of authorities as enforcers of regulations and laws and their role as arbiters transcending the conflict that is the source of fundamental difficulty in dealing with collective protest. Faced with collective protest, authorities are necessarily led into an adversary position. As the guardians of established arrangements and as the upholders of the regulations and laws that sustain the arrangements authorities automatically stand over against the protesters and their demands. This role as adversary is inescapable. To forfeit this role by automatically acceding to demands solves nothing and merely postpones the day of reckoning. The uncertainty of the protesters as to what they are seeking in the way of new social arrangements forces authorities to take a stand of opposition at some point, precisely because of earlier concessions given without hard discussion and bargaining. Yet, if authorities abandon, either by choice or pressure, the role of an adversary capable of making accommodations and move into the role of a committed combatant, the effective resolution of protest is blocked. We have seen the conditions of polarization which foster such a switch in the role of authorities. Ordinarily, higher authorities—top administrators, top governmental officials, legislators and the judiciary—are in the position of viewing and approaching collective protest from a transcending position of greater impartiality. If such authorities, however, are swept into the position of resolute opposition to the protest (as frequently happens under conditions of general unrest and disturbance) the political process is closed to an effective resolution of collective protest. An effective resolution of collective protest is not made if the protest is merely curbed and suppressed without taking action with regard to the social unrest out of which the protest arises. For authorities to resort to, or be maneuvered into, the position of resolute opposition to collective protest is the most serious consequence of polarization.

Modern complex societies have so far failed to devise political instruments or a political apparatus suited to an effective handling of the more tenacious and escalating forms of collective protest. There is absent a politically approved code that would allow officials to tolerate unsanctioned forms of protest so as to maintain the adversary process and to ward off intensified polarization. Above all, there is lacking political machinery that would enable authorities and protesters jointly to probe into conditions of social unrest and into the state of social arrangements under protest, while at the same time allowing authorities to execute their functions of operating institutions and of upholding the regulations and laws incidental to such operation.

To pose the problem in this fashion may seem to be proposing a combination of irreconcilable opposites. Yet this is the need in political machinery. Collective protest emanating from social unrest is an indication of a serious impairment in the social order brought into being by changing conditions. It is a call for the recognition and analysis of the impairment. The recognition is a legitimate demand on authorities who should be sensitive to adminstering a social order that is responsive to social change, despite the fact that the sway of established belief, the pressure of vested interests, and the opposition of an uninformed public militate against such recognition. But the mere recognition of the impairment is not sufficient. An analysis of the impairment is necessary. This analysis cannot be made by the authorities alone, however much they entertain testimony and seek counsel, since the protesters themselves are not clear about their unrest or what they are groping for. The need is for authorities and the protesters jointly to probe into the impairment, to develop a joint understanding of it, and to seek jointly to devise policy and a line of action with regard to it. The protesters have to guide authorities to see what the authorities are insensitive or blind to; the authorities have to help the protesters to work out and understand what the protesters are gropingly seeking. In the absence of machinery that allows for such a joint undertaking, the course of collective protest is thrown back into an arena of power contest.

ORGANIZATIONAL CRIME: A THEORETICAL PERSPECTIVE

Edward Gross UNIVERSITY OF WASHINGTON

More than some areas of sociology, studies of crime and delinquency usually have a strong theoretical base. Further, they are often comparative, as when the relative strength of structural-functional, labeling, subcultural, or learning theories are being applied to a body of data. Yet all of the leading theories seem to share a disturbing bias—they focus attention on the behavior of individuals, or groups of them. This tendency may be a consequence of the nature of Western law which usually seeks to assign responsibility for behavior to individuals. After all, only concrete living persons commit crimes and it seems only logical that they should be locked up or otherwise punished.

Whatever the explanation may be, it is our claim that we must begin to pay attention to the fact that all societies are increasingly dominated by large-scale organizations. Although there remain strong interests in com-

Studies in Symbolic Interaction—Volume 1, 1978, pages 55–85.

munes and other forms of nonbureaucratic organizations, there does not appear much threat to the dominant position of large-scale organizations in the foreseeable future.

We recognize that students of crime and delinquency have not ignored organization itself, as illustrated in studies of openly criminal organizations (39a), of crime within organizations, such as shoplifting or embezzling (24, 39, 64), of crimes against organizations (145), or of criminal "behavior systems" (33, 154). But we are here calling attention to hospitals, government bureaus, factories, businesses, public schools, prisons, universities, social work agencies, old-age homes, army bases, political parties, voluntary associations—the whole class of social arrangements that are familiar and constitutive of everyday life in modern society.

It is with regard to such organizations that we make the following claim: *all organizations are inherently criminogenic*. By this claim we do not refer merely to pilferage or crimes against bureaucracy (145). We mean that there is built into the very structure of organizations an inherent inducement for the *organization* itself to engage in crime.

The theory that accounts best for such a result is, it seems to us, a variation of the classic Mertonian theory of the divergence between means and ends.[1] Of course, that theory has been subject to much criticism as an approach to understanding juvenile and other crime. It ignores or deals poorly with crime for "kicks," it assumes everyone accepts the success goals of American society, it ignores agencies of social control, and it assumes a functionality which is not supportable (cf. 32, 120). But the theory works very well in organizations, and that follows from the very nature of organizations.

PERFORMANCE EMPHASIS

Organizations are typically defined as social arrangements which coordinate effort toward the attainment of collective goals. The focus on goals is seen by most students of organizations as its central characteristic. Parsons (123) claims that ". . . primacy of orientation to the attainment of a specific goal is used as the defining characteristic of an organization which distinguishes it from other types of social systems." Blau and Scott (18) state that an organization is ". . . established for the explicit purpose of achieving certain goals," and Etzioni (53) echoes this idea when he states that organizations are ". . . deliberately constructed and reconstructed to seek specific goals." Although this focus has been criticized (4) because of its overly narrow concern, still there is no denying that organizations are justified and evaluated in terms of their success or failure in goal attainment. The goals are multiple and conflicting and there goes on a continual battle to define them. But still, if organizations are distinct at all, it is in the fact that it is felt to be legitimate to evaluate them in terms of how effectively and efficiently they are pursuing their goals. We can speak of this feature as performance emphasis.[2] Of course, persons engage in much behavior in organizations for "kicks," but they do not hold their jobs for long. Further it seems that most persons in organizations either accept their goals or at least are indifferent to them. Opposition is furtive, and indeed, usually involves trying to change the goals to suit particular groups or craft interests.[3]

Now, as arrangements which are committed to goal attainment or performance, organizations will often find themselves in difficulties. They live in competitive environments, even in socialist society, in which there are always insecurities and uncertainties in supplies, money, sales, and securing support. They try to routinize everything (127) but they never succeed. The pictures offered by journalists of organizations as smoothly running, irresistible juggernauts are little more than monster stories intended to frighten the uninformed. Even the famous assembly line actually involves worried foremen who spend their time repairing breaks in the line and trying to make sure workers are kept satisfied (15, 144, 166).

Given a situation of uncertainty in attaining goals, and one in which the organization is judged (directly, or indirectly by sales or other indicators) by its success in goal attainment or performance, one can predict that the organization will, if it must, engage in criminal behavior to attain those goals. Thus, Staw and Szwajkowski (149), examining data on violations by private firms of antitrust laws and the Federal Trade Commission Act between 1968 and 1972, find an inverse relationship between the "munificence" of the organization's environment and the likelihood of its being cited for unfair market practices and restraint of trade activities. In short, when private organizations have trouble reaching their profit goals, they engage in illegal acts to try to do so. So too Bensman and Gerver (10) found that an illegal device, a metal tap, was *routinely* employed in an airplane factory since, under pressure, it was the *only* way the organization could meet its goal of high-quantity production.

In one sense, we are examining a special case of the effects of emphasis on performance as an end in itself. The generalization takes the following form: whenever individuals are placed in a position where performance is emphasized, there will be pressure to violate norms, if necessary.[4] For example, cheating on examinations is related to emphasis on doing well and to the rewards of high marks in securing entry to professional schools or securing occupational licenses. Similarly, Leonard and Weber (92) and Farberman (56) report that auto dealers are pressured into kickbacks and nonpayment of taxes by tight profit margins imposed by the manufacturer, a situation they call a "criminogenic market."[5]

But organizations, while subject to the same kinds of pressure, are not mere analogues of individuals. Individuals, after all, while exposed to the temptation to commit crime, do have contrary pressures operating on them. There is guilt or shame and any other residua of their early socialization, there is fear of getting caught, and other kinds of deterrents. As Matza (106) reminds us, there is no determinism here—one can only speak of persons being exposed to pressures or temptations, not as having their behavior caused by those pressures or temptations.[6] And surely the experience of criminologists and students of delinquency in the area of corrections provides sufficient evidence that it is doubtful that we can cause law-abiding behavior by applying pressures either. For this reason proposals to reduce or deter organizational crime by greater legal attacks on corporate officers (e.g., 62) are not likely to have much more effects than they have had on other criminals, even though some insist that corporate-class officers are more sensitive to public opprobrium than working-class offenders.[7] But there is a much more important set of reasons than the limited effectiveness of measures against individuals. Organizations are not individuals but instead exhibit certain features which make their criminogenic tendencies much more difficult to overcome.

ORGANIZATION-INDIVIDUAL CONTRASTS

First, while individuals have goals and are frequently judged by their success in attaining them, they are not mere goal-pursuing entities. They are also concerned with consummatory activities and are, in a basic sense, appreciated as whole persons. We may even come to love our friends for their very defects. By contrast, goals are, as we have said, central to and essential for organizations and it is impossible to think of them without calling goals to mind. A manufacturing company produces tractors and a profit, a public school is supposed to be preparing students for participation in society, the Internal Revenue Service, as we are annually reminded in April, collects taxes. Such statements verge on the obvious but their implications are frightening, for organizations are held accountable for their goals and have built-in mechanisms to increase the probability of their attaining them in an efficient manner. All organizations have special departments which monitor performance and provide continuous feedback on the returns from any practice. Such units—accounting departments, personnel departments, time-and-study departments, research divisions—generate frequent reports which are employed to try to keep the organization on target, should it be found to stray (30). Indeed, the importance of such monitoring activities led Weber to single out the keeping of records as a central characteristic of bureaucracies. But even he hardly anticipated the accountability movement[8] which has risen to mountainous proportions in recent times, being applied to government offices, mental hospitals, prisons, and public schools (171). Even the Catholic Church has been subjected to a management study (Management Audit, 1956). What we are saying, then, is that organizations, far more than persons, are subject to continual scrutiny of their performance and put under pressure to perform well. While organizations seek to escape such scrutiny by creating backstages (Camp David for the U.S. government, the Bohemian Grove for business and other elites (44), they do not have the benefit of the protective etiquette which we accord to persons in their backstages.[9] Instead organizations must be protected by barbed wire and armed guards. Their very existence is taken to imply that organizations are up to some dirty business which will not stand exposure. Nor, of course, are such suspicions without foundation, as the newspapers reveal daily.

More important (and a second organization-individual contrast), organizations engage in what Thompson (157) spoke of as strategies for "reducing uncertainty," that is, for increasing the likelihood of goal attainment by eliminating anything that might get in the way. Thompson described means by which organizations seal off their technical cores from environmental change, such as buffering through building up inventory or stores of supplies, smoothing peak loads through special inducements, anticipation of future demands, and rationing of services according to preplanned priorities.[10] If the environment becomes too threatening, a parent organization may shift a subsidiary to a less threatening environment, including moving to another country, as multinationals do routinely. Then, behavior that is regarded as criminal in one setting may be freely engaged in where it is not so regarded. Where such escape is not possible or too costly, organizations write off punitive fines as "nonrecurring losses"—although their record suggests that this is not entirely accurate. The $7 million fine which was levied against the Ford Motor Company for environmental violations (151:40) was certainly more than a slap on the wrist, but it rather pales beside the estimated $250 million loss which the company sustained on the Edsel. Both represent environmental contingencies which managers are paid high salaries to handle. We know they handled the latter—the first seven years of the Mustang more than offset the Edsel losses. One can infer that they worked out ways to handle the fine too.

A third difference between organizations and individuals lies in the structure of control. Wide personality splits in individuals are assumed by many psychiatrists to be symptomatic of some disorder. In organizations, the division of labor and departmental specialization are not indicative of some process of schizophrenia but rather are the very stuff of organizational structure and its special virtue. Such departmentalization means that organizational goals get translated into subgoals, and then those subgoals become *the* goals as far as the members of the department are concerned (42). Further, the reward structure is such as to encourage attainment of those subgoals (77a). When Ralph Cordiner became the chairman of General Electric, one of the things he did was to divide up the company into "profit centers," whereby each unit became a more or less autonomous company, with each president assigned the responsibility for a high level of profit. They were told the goal and then dismissed, with a warning from the company lawyers of what the antitrust laws said (146). The participation of the executives in the price-fixing with competitors which followed was not so difficult to understand. There is, further, a break between the sense of liability that a subunit feels and overall corporate responsibility. Producing plants hardly take into account the sort of problem that corporate headquarters may face in an antitrust action. It is simply not a part of the variables under their control, and is not supposed to be. As Stone (151) puts it:

> The potential for future lawsuits—that is, the possibility that the comptroller of the corporation will someday have to write some plaintiff a check from corporate headquarters (perhaps five or six years thereafter, given the delays of litigation) is not merely a distant event to the life of the producing plant: *It is not even a part of its reality.* (Italics in original)

Of particular importance is the isolation of the legal department. Just as accountants are people who make their living by checking up on others, and hence are disliked, so too lawyers are persons whose main power lies in their ability to say "no," and hence to put up obstacles. So, except for advice on income tax matters, investments, and major organizational changes, production and sales people try to have as little to do with lawyers as possible. Further, if there is trouble at lower levels, the tendency is for such "bad news" to be screened from those at the top, especially if such bad news may involve possible trouble with the law. A job of the lawyers is often to prevent such information from reaching the top officers so as to protect them from the taint of knowledge, should the company later end up in court. One of the reasons former President Nixon got into such trouble was that those near him did not feel such solicitude but, from self-protective motives, presumably, made sure he did know every detail of the illegal activities that were going on. In sum, the complexity of the organization creates situations in which one part of an organization may achieve its ends at the cost of another part of an organization for which it is not responsible and which it may not even know about. Of course, all this information might, ideally, be stored in a central computer, but if anything, the current popularity of decentralization makes it less and less likely that anyone will coordinate all information, especially if it offers "bad news."

All put together, organizations find themselves under heavy pressure to meet their goals, with a structure which means that responsibility for tasks is delegated, enabling some units to pass off onto other units the risky consequences of questionable behavior, but in which trouble with the law is one of many environmental contingencies which must be handled. Sometimes individuals can engage in comparable strategies—they can seek to escape accountability by "techniques of neutralization" (155), by "copping pleas," by claims of "temporary insanity" or by clogging the judicial process with repeated challenges, objections, and appeals. These same strategies are, of course, open to the executives or administrators of organizations—with all the resources of their organizations available to counsel and aid them. But when organizations themselves are accused of crime, such resources may attain huge impacts. And, as we shall see, when all the defenses that individuals are able to offer collapse, organizations have one device left to save them—they can sacrifice those individuals so that the organizations to which they belong may, as Coleman (37) suggests, perhaps live forever.

EVIDENCE FOR ORGANIZATIONAL CRIME

The evidence for organizational crime is extensive, though unfortunately not collected in as systematic a manner as are the Uniform Crime Reports. We are too often forced to depend on revelations of Congressional investigations or the muckraking of Nader and his associates (52, 57, 77, 119, 161). Still, the evidence supports a claim that organizational crime is widespread.

The recent revelations about corporate and governmental crime have led many to look for causes in recent events. Much blame is placed on the Vietnam War as a cause of erosion in faith in government and as legitimation for subsequent governmental malfeasance. Loss of U.S. leadership in international economic affairs is claimed to be responsible for the bribes that officials of oil and airplane manufacturers are reported as having given to agents in other countries. Yet Sutherland's (153) classic study of white-collar crime was originally published in 1949. Unfortunately, many persons are familiar with the concept largely from Sutherland's presidential address and see it as little more than a label. Sutherland's book is actually a research report on the criminal behavior of seventy top representative corporations, a report of their behavior since their founding—many going back into late nineteenth century or earlier. He focused on convictions or decisions against them for restraint of trade, misrepresentation in advertisements, patent infringements, unfair labor practices, giving of illegal rebates, financial fraud, and violation of trust, as well as other crimes. He reports an average of fourteen decisions against each corporation. If one restricts his attention solely to the decision made by criminal courts. Sutherland (153) writes:

> . . . 60 percent of the seventy larger corporations have been convicted in criminal courts and have an average of four convictions each. In many states persons with four convictions are defined as "habitual criminals."

A similar case could be made for governmental organizations. We have seen Watergate, but earlier generations were equally shocked by the Teapot Dome scandal.[11] And Sutherland includes data on fifteen power and light companies which, though "vested with the public interest," do not appear to present a very different picture. As for other organizations—hospitals, prisons, social work agencies, universities, opera companies—the data are even more difficult to come by. We do not refer here to crime data but data of any sort. We can only offer the hypothesis that they will be under pressure to engage in criminal action if they get into trouble. And here we need some specification of the general claim. If the goal orientation of organizations is seen as a crime-generating feature, then we should expect less crime from organizations which can, somehow, reduce emphasis on goals. Although it may seem like a contradiction in terms, some organizations do indeed manage to do as little as they can get away with, perhaps because they are not currently held accountable for much. Some prisons escape pressure because, though they make claims that they are rehabilitating their inmates, in fact these prisons are not expected to do any more than keep them from escaping or from rioting. On the other hand, when universities try to get into the big time by going after large amounts of federal research funds, they find themselves branded as violators of affirmative action and other federal laws or regulations (70). In sum, when they begin acting like other aspiring organizations, crime rears its head soon after.[12] A study of nonprofit organizations assigns blame for their current troubles to government rather than to their own management. The author explains (164):

> The non-profits by themselves are hardly responsible for getting themselves into the mess they currently occupy; indeed, most of them are so ineptly managed that they can hardly get themselves into trouble, let alone out.

Some organizations get into no trouble with the law because their managers do not know how! These examples suggest that organizations will vary in their criminogenic tendencies but such variation is not random. In the following section we suggest some of the dimensions that help specify such variation.

SPECIFICATION

Limitations of space prevent us from detailed specification of the claim that organizations are criminogenic, but we may advance some suggestions drawn from the growing literature on the structure of organizations. Organizations exhibit structural variations, and such variations may be related to their vulnerability to crime. First, a plausible hypothesis is that the more the organization is subject to accountability, the greater the likelihood that it will engage in crime. Accountability is simply the obverse of goal-emphasis: to hold an organization accountable is to set up norms or criteria by which its success in goal-attainment is judged. Some organizations have built-in accountability mechanisms, such as those we discussed earlier (accounting departments, etc.). But some of these originate from outsiders—and those are more directly related to crime for they cannot be so easily "handled" by internal controls. The more frequent the accounting, the greater the likelihood of crime. Berliner's (13) accounts of the uses of "blat" and *tolkachi* ("influence agents") describe the problem of Soviet managers faced with intense pressures to meet targets but deprived of ability to control supplies (see also 21). In capitalistic societies, one of the functions of profit, as a goal, is to provide a continuous accounting of how the organization's managers are spending the stockholders' money. As Galbraith (60) suggests, private corporations are not dedicated to profit as such, only to enough profit". . . to make accustomed payments to stockholders and provide a supply of savings for reinvestments." Such efforts help insure the autonomy of the techno-structure, whose members may go on then to pursue other more personal goals, such as those that can be realized by organizational growth.

Second, organizations vary in the degree to which their outputs are measurable or the extent of agreement on the value of outputs. For example, manufacturing organizations can be judged in terms of volume of output, costs per unit (marginal costs), profitability and other relatively objective measures. By contrast, Perrow (126) reports that hospitals find it difficult to utilize "objective" measures. Since those contributing sophisticated equipment or other devices (which might be used as "intrinsic" measures) object to publicity, hospitals are driven to publicity about extrinsic measures, such as unlimited visiting hours, telephones in the rooms, attractively prepared food, and other cosmetic features. Although the medical staff may feel that this is a diversion from presumably more relevant criteria, nevertheless, organizations that can make use of such devices to control the organization's image clearly can escape the goal pressure to which manufacturing organizations are subject. We would speculate that human-service organizations generally (hospitals, prisons, social work agencies, schools, universities) would be generally less subject to pressure to engage in deviant practices because of the fact that their goals are more diffuse and more subject to "image management" than are manufacturing, retailing[13] and banking organizations.[14]

Third, pressure to engage in crime is likely to be inversely related to goal displacement. This phenomenon, as discussed by Michels (109), Lipset (95), Messinger (108), Scott (140), and others, refers to the tendency of organizations to make their "means" into ends in themselves. Hence, organizations such as Mobilization for Youth (20), faced with threats to their egalitarian goals, shifted to more conservative goals in the interest of survival. In sum, a device that reduces the need for an organization to adopt deviant means to achieve its goals is the renunciation of those goals in favor of the minimal efforts needed to keep the organization alive. Another device is that of concentrating on activities that lend themselves to counting (telephone inquiries, number of publications) and which presumably reflect more intangible goals (167).

Fourth, we may advance a hypothesis that breaks up the monolithic conception (cf. 83) of organizations; namely, in general, those parts of the organization most exposed to its environment (113) will be those parts most subject to pressure to deviate. What has come to be called "contingency theory" (8, 9, 23, 90, 128, 136, 142) concerns itself with interactions between organizations and their environments. Although the area is still being subjected to extensive research (cf. 148), we think a plausible conclusion from that research is that organizations faced with uncertain, complex, rapidly changing environments differentiate their structure, so as to cope with that environment (but see 117, 118, 125). As such, we expect that those departments or units most exposed to that environment will be those most likely to exhibit deviant behavior, departments such as sales and other marketing units, purchasing, for example, in contrast to accounting (47) and production (131). In universities, we would predict that the evening college and other units subject closely to "consumer demand" (cf. 31) as well as those units of a more applied nature (professional schools) would be under pressure to deviate.[15]

THE AGENTS OF ORGANIZATIONAL CRIME

Although organizations are here held to be criminogenic and although courts no longer exhibit much hesitation in charging the organization itself with crime, organizations of course cannot themselves act—they must have agents who act for them. Who will the persons be who will act for organizations in their criminal behavior? While the Mertonian theory appeared to be useful for dealing with organizational crime, the identification of the agents seems to follow more directly from symbolic interaction theory, in conjunction with a set of reasonable assumptions about upward mobility in organizations. Since we maintain that organizations are criminogenic, we are led to examine the question of whether there exists in organizations a set of selective processes which propel certain kinds of person to positions of influence, or which require of those in positions of influence kinds of behavior which, under conditions of difficulty in goal attainment, may result in crime. Our approach will be to ask whether there are certain distinctive kinds of conduct associated with achieving top organizational positions.

As Chinoy (28) noted long ago, studies of mobility tend to focus on intergenerational analysis (16, 104)[16] or on the social origins of elites (2, 19, 58, 89, 122, 168). This neglect[17] of career mobility has been especially evident in the study of organizations, though such mobility has not been ignored entirely (69, 74, 93). Hence, we must proceed by making reasonable inferences, using such data as are available.

At the outset it is worth noting that those that strive for high positions in organizations seem to make up a small minority of those in organizations. Moore (118a, Chapter XII) draws a distinction between "strainers" (who do wish to move to the top) and others whom he calls "secure mobiles."[18] Whereas the former might be fairly described as climbing a ladder, the latter, he feels, may be more appropriately pictured as on an escalator. "Once they successfully mount the bottom step," he writes, "it would take positive effort to avoid going to the next level" [Moore (118a, p. 171)]. Many others do not even get onto the bottom step.

The evidence, while not systematic, does seem to support such a picture. Tausky and Dubin (156) draw a distinction between two types of career "anchorage"—one in which persons judge their progress by the distance yet remaining between where they are now and the top to which they are aiming ("upward" anchorages), as opposed to those who judge their progress by how far they have come from where they started ("downward" anchorages). The "upward" group may constitute an approximation to Moore's "strainers." Tausky and Dubin (156) report that only 11 percent of their sample of northwest coast managers (and 8 percent of the "specialists") had an "upward" anchorage, compared to 45 percent of the managers (and 58 percent of the "specialists") who exhibited a "downward anchorage. These "downward" persons probably include high proportions of persons who are "satisfied" with their present middleman position, many of whom got there through seniority and do not expect to move any higher. Even the remainder (whom Tausky and Dubin call "ambivalents") were "dissatisfied" but were also unwilling actively to pursue success and resembled the "downwards" more than the "upwards" in their behavior (readership of magazines or *The Wall Street Journal,* expenditures for business suit or dwelling, and whether they played golf or not). Ghiselli (68) gives us a somewhat similar picture. In a careful study of managerial talent, he seeks to offer validation for his measures of talent by applying them to a "large financial organization." Though there is only one organization involved, the data are worth reporting since it is one of the very few longitudinal studies available. Ghiselli followed a group of eighty-one men from the time of their being hired to a point ten to eighteen years later. He reports that 12 percent of the original cohort were eventually advanced to "high positions" in the company. A study by Goldthorpe, *et al.* (75) of two-hundred English blue-collar workers reports that only 7 percent inquired about or applied for foreman jobs, whereas only 3 percent had gone as far as taking some action such as attending a training course. Some 74 percent responded that they "have never thought seriously of becoming a foreman." Such a finding suggests the generality of Chinoy's classic study of autoworkers in which he tells us that "success" in the form of promotion is heavily discounted. In the words of a thirty-nine-year-old oiler, "If you're secure, then you're getting ahead" (28, 29). The studies by Coates and Pellegrin (34, 35), though not offering comparable statistics, provide us with a contrast between the expressed attitudes of fifty "top-level executives and fifty first-line supervisors employed in bureaucratic industrial, business, and administrative organizations in "Bigtown," a southern metropolitan area" (35). The former provide an approximation to Moore's strainers, while the latter seem to be closer to the "secure mobiles." The authors quote a supervisor as saying that in contrast to top exeutives who are "totally different," "most supervisors want to get so high and no higher because they don't want big responsibilities" (35). Of top executives, Coates and Pellegrin (34) write that "The job itself is at the very core of the executive's life. . . ." Sketchy as they are, these studies do support the claim that only a small proportion strive for (or eventually get to) high organizational positions, and that such persons seem to be rather different from those who fail to make it or try to. How, then, do they differ?

DISTINCTIVE FEATURES OF THOSE WHO ATTAIN TOP POSITIONS

Since we are seeking general features (ignoring interorganizational differences as well as structural and situational influences), correlations with success in attainment of such positions are bound to be low (cf. the difference of views between Mahoney *et al.* (101) and Nash (115).[19] Further much of the literature employs some measure of "effectiveness" as a test of validity and it is not clear that there is a strong relationship between such effectiveness and making it to the top.[20] Still we think that the available literature supports a claim that those who make it to the top of large-scale organizations exhibit the following personal characteristics to a major degree.[21]

1. *ambitiousness*

As we have suggested, only a small proportion of lower-level persons aspire to top positions, but as one moves up, the proportion of those who do increases until, near the top, the amount of competitiveness becomes fierce. In their classic study of successful mobile big-business leaders, Warner and Abegglen (168, 169) wrote:

> They share a high level of energy, an ability to expend enormous effort on achieving a desired end. This factor is closely related to the capacity for complete concentration. To them the career and its immediate environs are all that matter. They can focus their entire selves on their job, to the exclusion of all other matters, daydreams, family, social life, or any extra interests that might intrude.

In an intensive study of 468 managers in a variety of organizations in Minnesota, Mahoney *et al.* (102) characterize the more effective managers as "more aggressive, persuasive and self-reliant." Coates and Pellegrin (35) found that lower-level supervisors, in contrast to high executives, ". . . simply lack the determination to climb further up the executive ladder." Such supervisors define success as liking one's job, being well treated, having security, and leading a satisfying and happy life off the job. In contrast, high executives define success in terms of a sense of accomplishment, pride is helping others, and living up to the expectations of superiors and others (34, 35). In one of the technically most sound of all studies of managerial success, Ghiselli's (68) study of 306 managers in ninety different U.S. business and industrial organizations finds more successful managers to exhibit a measurably stronger need for occupational achievement, or more generally, a desire for achievement. At the opposite end (on a scale of methodological rigor) is the study by Dill, *et al.*

(43) of thirty graduates of a masters' training program who were inter-viewed at various stages of their career when they were showing clear signs of success (or failure). Dill, *et al.* (43) focus on what they call the "heuristics" utilized by these men to advance their careers. They tell us that men who are advancing rapidly exhibit behavior" . . . governed by the desire to do managerial work or to achieve managerial income and status." In contrast, men who progressed slowly showed more limited aspirations—less desire for power, income or status, less tolerance to-ward the perceived costs of becoming a manager, and more commitment to present jobs and working conditions. Miner (114, 115, 116) makes of the desire for top managerial positions a whole theory of managerial effec-tiveness, claiming that only those motivated to do an effective job will do such a job. In studies of managers in a variety of hierarchical organiza-tions by use of a specially constructed scale, Miner finds successful man-agers to have (in contrast to less successful managers) a stronger desire to compete, greater assertive motivation, a desire to exercise power, a desire for a distinctive position and a willingness to carry out routine administra-tive functions.[22] Lastly, we may mention the several studies carried out by Porter and his associates (134, 131) of 635 managers in a variety of organizations to test the claims that industry is recruiting more "other-directed" than "inner-directed" managers. They conclude that the more successful managers tend to be more inner-directed. But such a finding lends support for our general claim, since inner-directed is operationalized as "forceful," "imaginative," "independent," and "de-cisive." In sum,[23] the men (and they tend overwhelmingly to be men in this perhaps most sexist of all occupations) who are found in top positions in organizations are men who have fought their way to the top by winning out in a strong competition.[24] There is no escalator here, nor many oppor-tunities for the shy. As Lewis and Stewart (94) put it: "The meek shall not inherit top management."[25]

2. shrewdness

Practically all studies report that successful managers of all organiza-tions are men of high intelligence. They tend overwhelmingly to be college graduates (22, 104) as well as to show up relatively well on standard intelligence tests (11, 68, 168, 169). But mere intelligence (in the everyday sense of ability to solve problems) is not enough and in any case does not distinguish managers as such from scientists and persons in professions which call for brilliance of thinking or of depth of reasoning power. What is needed is the ability to apply one's intelligence to spot the main chance, to figure out what is coming next, to size up potential enemies—in short, one must be shrewd. Mills, in describing the shift from entrepreneurial to bureaucratic mobility among white-collar workers, called this ". . . the stress on agility rather than ability" (112). Ghiselli (68), summing up his carefully analyzed data, writes of the need not simply of intelligence but of a "creative and effective intelligence." Martin and Strauss (105) use the term "discernment" and call attention to the fact that the "perceptive" individual is one who can pick up cues, such as the pattern of advancement in the organization,[26] or the ability to recognize whether a proposed shift is a promotion or a demotion.[27] In a study of 149 managers in a large industrial firm, Goldner (73) ascertained the "perspectives" of managers five years previous to their attainment of their present positions. He reports that those who had been promoted "most clearly saw and understood the complex nature of the organization" in contrast to demoted persons who ". . . were naive about the nature of organization." In the study referred to earlier, Dill, *et al.* (43) call attention to what they name "sensitivity," one aspect of which is ". . . a man's ability to see himself, his surroundings, and his job the way that his superiors do—even though he need not always act as they would." This problem is compounded by the fact that persons typically got little objective feedback from superiors about their performance or chances for advancement. The same authors (43a) also call attention to the discovered fact that it was not enough for an aspiring manager to be competent: others must become aware of that competence. Hence assignments which allow for such visibility must be sought out. In sum, those who would reach the top of organizations are not simply effective managers of their departments or effective managers of men: they are also clear-minded and determined managers of their own careers. They do not sit idly by waiting for the great chance: they watch for it and actively seek it out.

3. *moral flexibility*

It is pleasant if one's own morals happen to coincide with the values of the organization. Then one has no conflicts to wrestle with in the darkness of one's soul. But if they conflict, one has a dilemma: one can rethink one's moral beliefs and perhaps amend them, or go on suffering. The latter alternative interferes with efficiency of effort and hence makes promotion less likely. The person who would seem to have a clear advantage is the one who can change his moral beliefs with little distress so that they match whatever is called for by the organization. This is not to say that such a person is necessarily immoral. Rather, he has developed the ability to change his morals, or his morals are relatively vaguely defined so that they do not contradict any other set of morals. There is considerable evidence that such a characterization fits those who make it to the top of large-scale organizations. In a study of U.S. federal executives,

Warner, *et al.* (170) write of those executives: "They can be part of the larger whole and can subordinate themselves to the welfare and purposes of the organizations. It requires above all the capacity, and these men have this capacity, to internalize the needs of the organization so that its needs become the needs of the self." A down-to-earth interpretation is given of the concept of "anticipatory socialization" by some writers in the business area. Strauss and Sayles (152) in a widely used personnel administration text summarize what they refer to as "recent research dealing with successful, rapidly promoted managers." Among the findings is: "[The successful manager] engages in 'anticipatory socialization': at each step he copies the values of those a step above him (152)."[28] Miner (114) reports that successful managers in the Research and Development Department of a large corporation were persons who felt it important to "behave in ways which do not provoke negative reactions from their superiors; ideally they will elicit positive responses." Similar findings are reported for studies of executives in businesses, in school districts of various sizes and in a state employment service (116).[29] Coates and Pellegrin (35) in their study of higher executives in contrast to lower supervisors refer to the importance of the acquisition of ". . . the attitudes, values and behavior patterns of successful superiors." Persons are cautioned (by other managers) not to be a "copy cat" but to exercise this practice shrewdly.

On the question of the relationship between personal and organizational values, Dill, *et al.* (43a) report that those who find what the organization requests distasteful to their own values tend to leave the company. Miner (116) quotes a personnel recruiter who sought management trainees but discovered that their values had changed (around 1970). These new recruits ". . . show a great deal of social concern. . . . We have had individuals quit or transfer to another division where they would not face any ethical conflict. These people were exit interviewed." For many, the problem does not seem to arise. For example, Bass and Eldridge (6) report findings on the willingness of managers to spend money on decisions which forced a choice between a moralistic alternative and one which would involve saving the company money, e.g., whether to spend money to eliminate a safety hazard, to risk a strike, improve a low-quality product as opposed to increasing advertising on that product, or whether to reduce pollution in a stream or accept the legal costs of refusing to do so. Managers were divided into those who were above their rank for people of their age or below the average age for people for their rank. Such persons are named "accelerates" and compared to others who have made less progress. The authors report that U.S. accelerates favored the cost-saving alternatives in all of the alternatives offered, especially in eliminating stream pollution. Such a finding is confirmed for United Kingdom managers, and (with some modification of definition) for German managers as well.[30]

In sum, then, the men at the top of organizations will tend to be ambitious, shrewd and possessed of a nondemanding moral code. Their ambition will not be merely personal, for they will have discovered that their own goals are best pursued through assisting the organization to attain its goals. While this is less true, or even untrue at the bottom of the organization, those at the top share directly in the benefits of organizational goal achievement, such as seeing their stock values go up, deferred compensation, and fringe benefits.[31]

Further, being at or near the top, these persons are those most strongly identified with the goals of the organization. While a case can be made that those further down will be less identified with those goals and some (in prisons, for example) are even opposed to them and fight them, such a claim cannot be made for those at the top. They believe in the organization, they want it to attain its goals, they profit personally from such goal attainment.[32] So they will try hard to help the organization attain those goals.

Finally, if the organization must engage in illegal activities to attain its goals, men with a nondemanding moral code will have the least compunctions about engaging in such behavior. Not only that, as men of power, pillars of the community, they are most likely to believe that they can get away with it without getting caught. Besides, they are shrewd.

Still another element is pointed to by Geis (63) who reports that those he calls "avocational criminals" do not conceive of themselves as criminals at all. They seek to redefine their activities as noncriminal, as simply part of their jobs. Many go further and drape themselves in self-sacrificing motives.[33] Just as Al Capone is reported to have conceived of himself as a "public servant," so too corporation executives and government cabinet ministers insist that they themselves profited little if at all from their activities. They were doing it as a sacrifice, for the organization. And, indeed, some of them were sacrificed and spent (short) periods in jail. Others may even be indemnified for their financial losses. The new Delaware Corporation Code, already perhaps the loosest in the nation, empowers corporations to purchase insurance against such liability for their executives "whether or not the corporation would have the power to indemnify [them] against such liability under the provisions" of the rest of the Delaware law (151).

Putting these elements together, we would predict that persons who will engage in crime on behalf of the organization will most likely be the officers of the organization, its top people. The experience of the conspiracy among the electrical-equipment manufacturers, the subsequent scandal among the plumbing-supply manufacturers, the later exposures of

folding-box manufacturers, payment of bribes and illegal campaign contributions and similar adventures all featured crime by the top officers.
This made these cases newsworthy, but really the results were quite
predictable.

CONCLUSION

Our argument has taken two forms. On the one hand, we have sought to
show that the internal structure and setting of organizations is of such a
nature as to raise the probability that the attainment of the goals of the
organization will subject the organization to the risk of violating societal
laws of organizational behavior. These will be genuine crimes—the organization being charged in court as a corporate person and made to pay
organizational damages in the form of fines or being subject to injunctions
requiring that certain corporate behavior shall cease. On the other hand,
we have suggested that the persons who actually act for the organization
in the commission of such crimes will, by selective processes associated
with upward mobility in organizations, be persons likely to be highly
committed to the organization and be, for various reasons, willing and
able to carry out crime, should it seem to be required in order to enable
the organization to attain its goals, to prosper, or, minimally, to survive.

Let us make two final points. First, nothing we have said gives any
special comfort to those who identify crime with the pursuit of profit and
who might see in our remarks an argument against capitalistic forms of
organization. The problem with organizations is goals—whatever the
goals happen to be. Some organizations seek profits, others seek survival,
still others seek to fulfill government-imposed quotas, others seek to
serve a body of professionals who run them, some seek to win wars, and
some seek to serve a clientele. Whatever the goals might be, it is the
emphasis on them that creates the trouble. We would argue that socialist
societies probably have *more* crime than do capitalist societies on the
grounds that the former are more demanding and exercise greater
monitoring of private activities than do the latter. Hence, they probably
are more goal-oriented.[34] Indeed, many successful communes, the
apotheosis of socialist dreams, exhibited an undeviating concentration on
a set of unquestioned goals. Deviants were rife and had to be continually
punished through exposure or expulsion. Capitalistic societies are a good
deal sloppier, some of that sloppiness, of course, being related to the
greater richness of capitalistic societies. Only rich societies can afford
sloppiness. The stage of development is also important. Most modern
socialistic societies are newer than the capitalistic societies and some of
their monitoring of private activities reflects their desire to modernize in a

hurry. How efficient that approach is, is another matter: police forces are not cheap.

Our second point has to do with the vaunted efficiency of large-scale organizations. Weber (66) wrote: "The decisive reason for the advance of bureaucratic organization has always been its purely technical superiority over any other form of organization." Although Weber is careful to state his generalization in comparative form, others are not so cautious. Two authors have recently written of an "organizational imperative," which they state as follows:"*Whatever is good for man can only be achieved through modern organization.* The question of what is 'good' for man is left open; what must be beyond question is the conviction that the only way to achieve that good is through modern organization" (84). (Italics in original.) Others while not going quite so far still identify organizations with "efficiency" (17). But the fact of organizational crime must be set down beside those claims. If a man wins a footrace by bribing the officials, surely we must raise a question about his running ability. If organizations can only attain their goals by bribing government officials, we must raise a similar question about their ability as organizations. If a corporation cannot outsell a competitor in a fair fight but instead finds it must collude with it to control the market, or simply destroy its competitor, surely its effectiveness and efficiency are questionable. Organizations may turn out to be the only way to achieve what is "good" for man, but if that should turn out to be the case, it may not be because organizations are more efficient or effective, but simply that organizations have gained such a commanding position that they allow for no alternatives.

FOOTNOTES

1. May we avoid the compulsory footnote to Merton's famous paper on social structure and anomie? According to Miles (110), it has been reprinted twenty-nine times. Cole (36) uses it as a case example in a study of citations—providing a nice picture of how frequently it has been cited or criticized. Perhaps by now we can assume that it is not necessary to refer to it as such—a type of flattery that Cole refers to—any more than we need any longer cite Karl Pearson or R. A. Fisher when we use basic statistical concepts.

2. The concept of "performance" may help answer some of the criticisms of the goal concept. For example, Yuchtman and Seashore (174) prefer to evaluate organizations in terms of their ability to exploit their environments in "the acquisition of scarce and valued resources." Whether this formulation avoids the need to speak of goals is a question we cannot deal with (for example, the word "valued" suggests that the resources must be valued *for* some end). But the acquisition of resources is clearly a major performance. Similary, Georgiou's (65) searing criticism of what he calls the "goal paradigm" ends with a proposal for a "counterparadigm" in which attention focuses on the manner in which persons "exchange activities for incentives"—a way of saying, presumably, that persons will do whatever the organization wishes if they think it worth their while. (cf. 1) But what is the

organization asking them to do? And we presume that the "incentives" offered will have to bear some calculated relationship to the activities performed. So again, performances are evaluated.

3. A related perspective is that of the ethnomethodologists who see rules and goals as statements which members must take account of in order to routinely organize their work. Such "taking account of" may include direct obedience to rules, subversion, explanations, making exceptions and other devices, depending on the context. See (14, 175).

4. Haas and Drabek (81) advance a theory of organizational stress which rests on the "degree of discrepancy between organizational demands and organizational capacity." Although the authors advance a number of possible hypotheses which employ terms such as "normative inconsistency" and "normative dissensus," these are not spelled out. Some of them might include crime. Drabek and Haas (45) in a laboratory simulation of organizational stress refer in passing to a study of the 1964 Alaska earthquake in which it is reported that ". . . many items were purchased without official authorization." But they see this as a way of "cutting the red tape." It may be that Haas and Drabek's use of disasters as a model tends to shift one's attention from seeing what goes on as criminal. As they point out, in emergencies, the rules and even the laws may be temporarily suspended or violations allowed without culpability.

5. In a survey of studies of task-goal attributes in employee performance, Steers and Porter (150) note that there is fairly strong evidence that the institution of clear and specific goals increases production. However, goal difficulty appears to have less predictable effects. In laboratory studies such difficulty seems to stimulate performance (up to a point), but in field studies it is found to lead to "creative behavior" on the part of foremen to discover the causes of poor performance. The latter is the conclusion from a study by A. C. Stedry and E. Kay in 1964, cited in Steers and Porter (150).

6. A similar point is made by Dunham (48) where he calls this procedure a "logical error" involving jumping from social system to individual levels.

7. The disenchantment with the social programs of the 1960s and the emergence of evaluation research (cf. 12) has led to renewed interest in deterrence theories. See Silberman (143).

8. A colleague raised the question of whether Protestantism might not be conceived of as a kind of accountability ethic—a most intriguing idea. Yet, if anything, one would think that the Catholic conception of being rewarded in the afterlife for good works on this earth is an even more obvious way of holding persons accountable for their conduct. At least in the early period, the Calvinists rejected any notion of grace as a reward for good works. Still, perhaps later notions of success in this world as a sign of grace might be said to produce a powerful incentive to hold oneself accountable for all of one's behavior.

9. I am indebted to Gregory P. Stone for this observation.

10. A study of departments in a state employment security agency offers suggestive findings on the possible relationship between task uncertainty and crime. Van de Ven, et al. (163) report that as tasks increase in uncertainty, forms of coordination change. In particular, coordination through hierarchy and impersonal programming yield to coordination by "mutual work adjustments" (horizontal communication channels and group meetings). Although these authors say nothing about the implications of this finding for crime, one may speculate that the emergence of meetings provides the opportunity for various "innovative" solutions which may include, of course, criminal actions. The manner in which organizational crime involves frequent meetings of top executives is noted by practically all writers (e.g., Geis, 61).

11. A journalistic treatment of U.S. history (111) seeks to show that corruption in government is "as American as apple pie." However, the clearly tendentious orientation of the

author leaves one with an uneasy feeling of selectivity of data. Further, most of the illustrations deal with venial crime—persons in positions of trust taking advantage of their position to steal whatever they could lay their hands on. Such behavior is not what we here understand by organizational crime.

12. Gollin (76), describing the battle of some Catholic religious orders to avoid bankruptcy, points out how some have come perilously close to criminal liability. In 1973, the Attleboro, Massachusetts, province of the La Salette Fathers was warned by the Securities and Exchange Commission that the bond-lending practices of its St. Joseph Trust were almost certainly in violation of the SEC laws. Because of absence of criminal intent, the SEC decided not to prosecute, provided the bonds were backed financially. To this end, the La Salettes had to sell their property (including land at Cape Cod) and ask for help from other orders. According to Gollin, "Pope Paul himself sent two checks, one for $46,000, the other for $10,000" (76).

13. A study of department stores by Ouchi and Maguire (121) contrasts the use by managers of behavioral control versus dependence on measures of output. They conclude: "The use of output measures is largely a result of the demand for quantifiable, simple measures. Paradoxically, output measures are used most when they are least appropriate: in the face of complexity, interdependence and lack of expertise. Under such conditions . . . the manager is suspected of poor performance and, as a result, he goes to great lengths to provide evidence of his contributions to the organization."

14 A good example is provided in a study of the crisis intervention unit of a community mental health clinic in Southern California. Faced with what Emerson and Pollner (50) call "imperfect patients" (those for whom little can be done because they are "hopeless," have already used up community resources, or who resist, yet to whom the crisis team felt that something *had* to be done), the team managed to preserve its image of itself as a psychiatric team by claiming that such work was "shitwork," that is, dirty work. The authors claim that such designations" . . . serve to reaffirm performance criteria, to express moral distance from a particular performance and to tutor an observer into the preferred interpretation of a particular encounter . . ." (50). When such redefinitions of activities are possible (and can be made to stick), there is no need for illegal or any other activities to demonstrate fidelity to organizational goals.

15. We cannot enter into the question of differential distribution of crime among the various types of organizations identified by different writers, e.g., Blau and Scott (18); Haas, *et al.* (81), and others.

For example, Etzioni's (55) well-known types (coercive, utilitarian and normative) are *all* subject to pressure to engage in criminal behavior, but probably the kinds of pressures are different. The sorts of crime found in prisons and mental hospitals have been well documented and are related to the problems of pursuing "order goals." Utilitarian organizations are subject to the kinds of pressures we have been considering since their goals involve measurable kinds of production and distribution. Normative organizations, which persons join because they accept their goals as their own values or because they, "like" the people already at work, are subject to a special kind of crime which has been relatively ignored in the deviance literature; namely, crime in the service of "higher laws." Being *"wertrational,"* persons will engage in "whatever it takes" to attain the organization's "sacred" goals. (cf. 139) If such behavior turns out to be unlawful, persons are undeterred. This is not the same as "nonconforming" (108) behavior, since such persons are not seeking to change the rules—they simply are indifferent to them.

One might also speculate about the relationships of market structure (oligopolistic vs. atomistic) to conduct (collusion, interdependence, independence), The cases that reach the newspapers seem to involve oligopolies, yet, as Bain (5) points out, excessive competition in atomistic industries (bituminous coal, groceries) has historically also led to vicious and violent "predatory and exclusionary" tactics. But the data for such a study have hardly even been assembled, let alone analyzed.

16. Blau and Duncan also consider career mobility in their analysis of how first job predicts later job.

17. There are important exceptions; e.g., Lipset and Bendix (96), Wilensky and Edwards (173).

18. Cf., the distinctions made by Presthus (135) between upwardmobiles, indifferents, and ambivalents.

19. Summaries of the literature on the relationship between various personality traits and job effectiveness for executives differ in their conclusions. Ghiselli (67) reviews a large number of studies in which correlations with such abilities as intelligence, perceptual accuracy, interests and other personality measures yield average correlations around .25. Guion and Gottier (79) conclude that personality and interest measures are of dubious value, but feel more hopeful about "homemade" measures, specially adapted to particular settings or problems. Johnson and Dunnette (88) seem impressed with measures of interest, partly because they seem to yield scores that remain stable over time. Campbell, et al. (25) finally conclude that any attempt to predict success from individual characteristics alone is doomed to come out with low (at best) correlations, with possible exceptions; cf., Finkle (59). They propose that "opportunity," environment, and feedback need also to be taken into account (Chapters 2 and 16).

20. Measures include estimates by superiors or others who are in a position to make evaluations; e.g., Dunnette and Kirchner (49); Mahoney, et al. (100) or, less commonly, performance or outcome measures, such as volume of grievances or turnover, output rates, and the like; e.g., Turner (162) [See England et al. (51)]. But such measures are applicable to any level of management and do not bear directly on the question of "who makes it to the top," except that there is probably a relationship between such effectiveness and who is chosen.

21. These features are alluded to by Tullock (160). However, he advances them as speculations without supporting evidence, It is important also to point out that, although many of the researchers to be cited refer to these features as "personality" characteristics, that is not our claim, or belief. We find ourselves agreeing with Becker's (7) conception of changes in adult life as associated with "situational adjustments." That is, the kinds of behavior to be described are very much called for by the situations in which the mobile executive finds himself. Hence, we find no inconsistency in the oft-noted fact that corporate criminals are also pillars of the community, churchgoers, etc.

22. The relationship between these motivations and success is less evident in nonhierarchical organizations such as schools, as well as in government offices.

23. Other studies confirming this conclusion may be briefly cited. Smigel (145) calls attention to the severity of competition among associates in large law firms, as well as the importance of "hard, hard work." Triandis (159) reports that more effective managers have a more strongly "instrumental and task-oriented" approach than do the less effective managers. Bentz (11), summarizing many studies of Sears executives, emphasizes the presence of a "powerful competitive drive for position of eminence and authority." Finally, a study of business managers by Cummin (40) reports that the more successful exhibit higher n achievement and n power scores (Murray's categories) than do the less successful. Although some authors place considerable faith in such studies of the achievement motive, it is probably more relevant for explaining the behavior of independent businessmen than those in large organizations. Cf. McClelland and Winter (100); Hornaday and Aboud (87); and Wainer and Rubin (165).

24. There are other roads to the top than climbing the ladder in a complex organization, of course. Lewis and Stewart (94) call attention to the possibility of inheriting top positions in

family-owned businesses, or of starting one's own business. Such possibilities may be somewhat more in evidence in France and Italy, for example. But they remain a minority of opportunities and are probably decreasing in importance. Even where one may inherit one's father's position, it is likely that the son will have to learn the ropes and demonstrate ability before he is allowed to take over.

25. Such a conclusion is all the more interesting in that it runs contrary to the professed values of managers in positions of power in American organizations. Such persons typically devalue "power," saying they are not interested in it or have little of it (60, 86). Such a claim reaches an apex in American universities. Lunsford (98) argues that such declarations constitute myths which have not only institutional but self-justifying functions. He reports (from an empirical study of 526 university administrators), that administrators are ambivalent on the subject of power, and employ various kinds of rhetoric in articulating their own positions vis-à-vis "politics" and "pressures." Reisman (138) similarly calls attention to the "cult of amateurism" in American culture: ". . . what is wanted (for a university administrator) is a Ph.D. who temporarily gives up his profession to become a part-time amateur manager, and either actually hates such work or appears to despise it."

26. A good example is provided by Sofer (147) in a study of upward mobile managers in England. Among the most commonly used strategies he reports that of choosing "jobs that are stepping stones." A similar reference to steppingstone jobs is reported by Glickman, *et al.* (71).

27. Since moves in organizations are often unclear and since firms are reluctant to add insult to injury by making demotions clear, many moves deliberately put persons into holding patterns or give them compensatory titles. See Goldner (72).

28. Dalton's (41) classic study of informal factors in career achievement reported that some of his subjects ". . . dropped Catholicism as they groped to find the avenues to advancement."

29. Related to the finding that successful managers have favorable relations with superiors is the frequently reported finding that owners of small businesses report having had trouble with authority, and, hence, as seeing owning one's own business as an escape from such relationships. See Collins *et al.* (38); Hornaday and Aboud (87); and Litzinger (97).

30. Nonsignificant findings in the same direction are reported for several other countries, but the reverse seems to be true for Denmark and possibly for Italy and Japan (the Japanese sample is, however, very small). Studies by England and associates also show successful managers to be more pragmatic and less moralistic than less successful managers in the United States, Korea, and Japan, but find the reverse to be true for Indian and Australian managers. See England *et al.* (51). Since youth are often reported as being moralistic and, hence, often unwilling to accept jobs in large corporations, the finding of Rettig and Pasamanick (137) is relevant. They report greater leniency in moral values in various spheres as college graduates experienced later adult socialization. In the economic area, such leniency was evident in response to opinions about the following kinds of situations: "An industry maintaining working conditions for its workers known to be detrimental to their health"; "A prosperous industry paying workers less than a living wage."

31. Akers (3), in support of a "social learning" theory of deviance, emphasizes such economic rewards as well as the extent to which organizational crime is learned. We do not doubt the presence of these elements, but feel that exposure to temptation and opportunity to learn are not sufficient for, as many have noted, most persons so exposed do not commit crime. We think, therefore, that the process of selectivity that we have described in which those who make it to the top are likely to be ambitious, shrewd and morally flexible, creates a set of persons who would be especially likely to respond to such opportunities, whether they personally profit from them or not. [Cf., Lemert (91).] In Becker's terms, their commitments have become very large, precluding any serious alternative career or behavior (7).

32. In a careful study of a large sample of managers, Porter (129) reports that need fulfillment went up with job level—higher managers experiencing more such need fulfillment than did lower managers. This finding held for the needs of esteem, autonomy and self-actualization, but not for security and social needs. The finding was, however, reversed in small companies (130). See the literature evaluation in Porter and Lawler (133).

33. Although the language is often puffed, such claims do not differ in any substantial way from the standard defenses offered by the second-story man or embezzler. The revelations of illegal corporate contributions that dominated the news in 1975 and 1976 provide many examples from corporate defenders. John J. McCloy (formerly president of the World Bank, chairman of the Ford Foundation, and chairman of the board of the Council on Foreign Relations, Inc. and of the Chase Manhattan Bank), head of a Special Review Committee to study the use of corporate funds by Gulf Oil Corporation, offers the claim that members of corporation boards of directors ". . . are incapable of consciously conniving or conspiring to contravene the law" (99). But faced with his own concession that corporate political contributions were against the law, he laments the fact that only corporations got blamed, whereas the politicians who received such funds often escaped culpability. Then he goes on to claim that we are in a moral "gray area," wherein illegality or impropriety are not clear. He opposes bribes (what he prefers to call "outright" bribes) but is less sure of what to do about "gratuity payments" to foreign agents to "expedite" paper work. Yet he does not think a code of ethics which might clarify such vague matters would help much. See also Guzzardi (80).

34. In a description of bureaucratic organizations in present-day China, Whyte (172) comments: "No aspect of the life of an individual is regarded as completely irrelevant to his organizational performance. Informal contacts within the organization, outside recreation with friends, marital relationships, and many other factors are seen as affecting the performance of individuals. The leaders of a Maoist organization are to try to make sure that all these influences support, rather than undermine, organizational goals" (172, p. 155).

In advancing a claim that, in spite of their low reputation among sociologists, basic human needs probably do exist, Etzioni (54) offers the hypothesis that one such need is recognition. As test, he offers the following hypothesis: ". . . where collectivism is predominant, the rate of individualist deviance will be much higher than collectivist deviance in industrialist systems." In our terms, the claim would be that there is more individual crime in (say) Russia than corporate crime in the United States.

REFERENCES

1. Peter Abell, *Organizations as Bargaining and Influence Systems*. Halstead Press, New York, 1975.
2. S. Adams, "Trends in the occupational origins of business leaders." *American Sociological Review* 16:541–548 (1954).
3. Ronald L. Akers, *Deviant Behavior: A Social Learning Approach*. Wadsworth, Belmont, California, 1973.
4. Martin Albrow, "The study of organizations—objectivity or bias?" in Graeme Salaman and Kenneth Thompson (eds.), *People and Organizations*. Longmans, London, 1973.
5. Joe S. Bain, *Industrial Organization*. Wiley, New York, 1968, ch. 12.
6. Bernard M. Bass and Larry D. Eldridge, "Accelerated Managers' Objectives in Twelve Countries." *Industrial Relations* 12:158–171 (1973).
7. Howard S. Becker, "Personal change in adult life." *Sociometry* 27:4–53 (1964).
8. S. W. Becker and G. Gordon, "An Entrepreneurial Theory of Formal Organizations, Part 1." *Administrative Science Quarterly* 11:315–344 (1966).
9. ———, and D. Neuhauser, *The Efficient Organization*. Elsevier, New York, 1975.

10. Joseph Bensman and Israel Gerver, "Crime and Punishment in the Factory: The Function of Deviancy in Maintaining the Social System." *American Sociological Review* 28:588–598 (1963).
11. V. J. Bentz, "The Sears Experience in the Investigation, Description and Prediction of Executive Behavior," in F. F. Wickert and D. E. McFarland (eds.), *Measuring Executive Effectiveness*. Appleton-Century-Crofts, New York, 1967.
12. Richard A. Berk and Peter H. Rossi, "Doing Good or Worse: Evaluation Research Politically Re-examined." *Social Problems* 23:337–349 (1976)
13. Joseph S. Berliner, *Factory and Manager in the USSR*. Harvard University Press, Cambridge, Mass., 1957.
14. Egon Bittner, "The Concept of Organization." *Social Research* 31:239–255 (1964)
15. Peter Blau, "Formal organization: Dimensions of Analysis." *American Journal of Sociology* 63:58–69 (1957).
16. ――― and Otis Dudley Duncan, *The American Occupational Structure*. Wiley, New York, 1967.
17. ――― and Marshall W. Meyer, *Bureaucracy in Modern Society*. Random House, New York, 1971, ch. 8.
18. ――― and W. Richard Scott, *Formal Organizations*. Chandler, San Francisco, 1962.
19. T. B. Bottomore, *Elites and Society*, Basic Books, New York, 1964.
20. George Brager, "Commitment and Conflict in a Normative Organization." *American Sociological Review* 34:482–491 (1969).
21. Arvid Brodersen, *The Soviet Worker*. Random House, New York, 1966, ch. VI.
22. Charles G. Burck, "A Group Profile of the Fortune 500 Chief Executive." *Fortune* (May 1976); 173 ff.
23. Tom Burns and G. M. Stalker, *The Management of Innovation*. Tavistock, London, 1961.
24. Mary O. Cameron, *The Booster and the Snitch: Department Store Shoplifting*. The Free Press, Glenco, Ill., 1964.
25. J. P. Campbell, Marvin D. Dunnette, E. E. Lawler, and K. E. Weick, *Managerial Behavior, Performance and Effectiveness*. McGraw-Hill, New York, 1970.
26. Richard O. Carlson, *Executive Succession and Organizational Change*. Midwest Adminstration Center, University of Chicago, 1962.
27. Eli Chinoy, "The Tradition of Opportunity and the Aspiration of Automobile Workers." *American Journal of Sociology* 57:453–459 (1952).
28. ――― *Automobile Workers and the American Dream*. Garden City: Doubleday, Garden City, N.Y., 1955a.
29. ――― "Social Mobility Trends in the United States." *American Sociological Review* 20:180–186 (1955 b).
30. Neil C. Churchill and William W. Cooper, "Effects of Auditing Records: Individual Task Accomplishment and Organizational Objectives," in W. W. Cooper, H. J. Leavitt, and M. W. Shelly II (eds.), *New Perspectives in Organization Research*. Wiley, New York, 1964.
31. Burton R. Clark, *Adult Education in Transition*. University of California Press, Berkeley, 1956.
32. Marshall B. Clinard, (ed.), *Anomie and Deviant Behavior*. The Free Press, New York, 1964.
33. ――― and Richard Quinney, *Criminal Behavior Systems: A Typology*. Holt, Rinehart, and Winston, New York, 1967.
34. Charles H. Coates and Roland J. Pellegrin, "Executives and Supervisors: Contrasting Self-Conceptions and Conceptions of Each Other." *American Sociological Review* 22:217–220 (1957 a).
35. ――― and ―――, "Executives and Supervisors: Informal Factors in Differential Bureaucratic Promotion." *Administrative Science Quarterly* 2:200–215 (1957 b).

36. Stephen Cole, "The Growth of Scientific Knowledge: Theories of Deviance as a Case Study," in Lewis A. Coser (ed.), *The Idea of Social Structure: Papers in Honor of Robert K. Merton*. Harcourt Brace Jovanovich, New York, 1975, pp. 175–220.

37. James S. Coleman, *Power and the Structure of Society*. W. W. Norton and Company, New York, 1974.

38. Orvis F. Collins, D. G. Moore, and D. B. Unwalla, *The Enterprising Man*. Bureau of Business and Economic Research, Michigan State University, East Lansing, Mich., 1964.

39. Donald R. Cressy, *Other People's Money*. Free Press, Glencoe, Ill., 1953.

39a. ———, *Criminal Organization*. Harper Torchbooks, New York, 1972.

40. Pearson C. Cummin, "TAT Correlates of Executive Performance." *Journal of Applied Psychology* (1967).

41. Mellville Dalton, "Informal Factors in Career Achievement." *American Journal of Sociology* 56:407–415 (1951).

42. DeWitt C. Dearborn, and Herbert A. Simon, "Selective Perception: A Note on the Departmental Identifications of Executives." *Sociometry* 21:140–144.

43. William R. Dill, Thomas L. Hilton, and Walter R. Reitman, "How Aspiring Managers Promote Their Own Careers." *California Management Review* 2:9–15 (1960)

43a. ———, ———, and ———, *The New Managers*. Prentice-Hall, Englewood Cliffs, N.J., 1962.

44. G. William Domhoff, *The Bohemian Grove and Other Retreats*. Harper Colophon, New York, 1974.

45. Thomas E. Drabek, and J. Eugene Haas "Laboratory Simulation of Organizational Stress." *American Sociological Review* 34:224–238 (1969).

46. Robert Dubin, "Deviant Behavior and Social Structure: Continuities in Social Theory." *American Sociological Review* 24:147–164.

47. ——— and S. Lee Spray, "Executive Behavior and Interaction." *Industrial Relations* 3:99–108 (1964).

48. H. Warren Dunham, "Anomie and Mental Disorder," in Marshall B. Clinard (ed.), *Anomie and Deviant Behavior*. Free Press, New York, 1964.

49. Marvin D. Dunnette, and W. K. Kirchner, "Validation of Psychological Tests in Industry." *Personnel Administration* 21:20–27 (1958).

50. Robert M. Emerson and Melvin Pollner, "Dirty Work Designations: Their Features and Consequences in a Psychiatric Setting." *Social Problems* 23:243–254 (1976).

51. George W. England, O. P. Dhingra, and Naresh C. Agarwal, *The Manager and the Man: A Cross Cultural Study of Personal Values*. Kent State University Press, Kent, Ohio, 1974.

52. John C. Espositio, *Vanishing Air*. Grossman, New York, 1970.

53. Amitai Etzioni, *Modern Organizations*. Prentice-Hall, Englewood Cliffs, N.J., 1964.

54. ———, "Basic Human Needs, Alienation and Inauthenticity." *American Sociological Review* 33:870–885 (1968).

55. ———, *A Comparative Analysis of Complex Organizations*. Free Press, New York, 1975.

56. Harvey A. Farberman, "A Criminogenic Market Structure: The Automobile Industry." *Sociological Quarterly* 16:438–457 (1975).

57. Robert Fellmeth, The Interstate Commerce Omission. Grossman, New York, 1970.

58. Michael R. Ferrari, *Profiles of American College Presidents*. Graduate School of Business Administration, Michigan State University, East Lansing, 1970.

59. Robert B. Finkle, "Managerial Assessment Centers," in Marvin D. Dunnette (ed.), *Handbook of Industrial and Organizational Psychology*. Rand McNally, Chicago, 1976, ch. 20.

60. John K. Galbraith, *American Capitalism*. Houghton Mifflin, New York, 1952. ch. 15.

61. Gilbert Geis, "The Heavy Electrical Equipment Antitrust Cases of 1961," in Marshall B. Clinard and Richard Quinney (eds.), *Criminal Behavior Systems: A Typology*. Holt, Rinehart and Winston, New York, 1967, pp. 139–151.

62. ———. "Deterring Corporate Crime," in Ralph Nader and Mark J. Green (eds.), *Corporate Power in America*. Grossman, New York, 1973, ch. XI.

63. ———, "Avocational Crime," in Daniel Glaser (ed.), *Handbook of Criminology*. Rand-McNally, Chicago, 1974, ch. 8.

64. D. M., Gelfand, *et al.* "Who Reports Shoplifters?" *Journal of Personality and Social Psychology* 25:267–283 (1973).

65. Petro Georgiou, "The Goal Paradigm and Notes Towards a Counter-Paradigm." *Administrative Science Quarterly* 18:291–310 (1973).

66. Hans H. Gerth and C. Wright Mills, from Max Weber, *Essays in Sociology*. Oxford University Press, New York, 1958.

67. E. E. Ghiselli, *The Validity of Occupational Aptitude Tests*. Wiley, New York, 1966.

68. ———, *Explorations in Managerial Talent*. Goodyear Publishing Company, Pacific Palisades, California, 1971.

69. Barney G. Glaser (ed.), *Organizational Careers*. Aldine, Chicago, 1968.

70. Nathan Glazer, *Affirmative Discrimination: Ethnic Inequality and Public Policy*. Basic Books, New York, 1975.

71. A. S. Glickman, C. P. Hahn, E. A. Fleishman, and B. Baxter, *Top Management Development and Succession*. Macmillan, New York, 1968.

72. Fred H. Goldner, "Demotion in Industrial Management." *American Sociological Review* 30:712–724 (1965).

73. ———. "Success vs. Failure: Prior Managerial Perspectives." *Industrial Relations* 9:453–474 (1970).

74. ——— and R. R. Ritti, "Professionalization as Career Immobility," *American Journal of Sociology* 72:488–502 (1967).

75. J. H. Goldthorpe, D. Lockwood, F. Bechhofer, and J. Platt, *The Affluent Worker: Industrial Attitudes and Behavior*. Cambridge University Press, Cambridge, Mass., 1968.

76. James Gollin, "There's an Unholy Mess in the Churchly Economy." *Fortune* 93:223–248 (1976).

77. Mark Green, *et al. The Closed Enterprise System*. Grossman, New York, 1972.

77a. Edward Gross, "The Definition of Organizational Goals," *British Journal of Sociology* 20:277–294 (1969).

78. R. H. Guest, "Work Careers and Aspirations of Automobile Workers." *American Sociological Review* 19:155–163 (1954).

79. R. M., Guion, and R. F. Gottier, "Validity of Personality Measures in Personnel Selection." *Personnel Psychology* 18:135–164 (1965).

80. Walter Guzzardi, Jr., "An Unscandalized View of Those 'Bribes' Abroad." *Fortune* (July 1976): 118ff.

81. J. Eugene Haas and Thomas E. Drabek, *Complex Organizations: A Sociological Perspective*. Macmillan, New York, 1973.

82. ———, Richard H. Hall, and Norman J. Johnson, "Toward an Empirically Derived Taxonomy of Organizations," in Raymond V. Bowers (ed.), *Studies on Behavior in Organizations*. University of Georgia Press, Athens, Georgia: 1966, pp. 157–180.

83. Richard H. Hall, "Intraorganizational Structural Variation: Application of the Bureaucratic Model." *Administrative Science Quarterly* 7:295–308 (1962).

84. David K. Hart and William G. Scott, "The Organizational Imperative." *Administration and Society* 7:259–285 (1975).

85. William E. Henry, "The Business Executive: the Psychodynamics of a Social Role." *American Journal of Sociology* 54:286–291 (1949).

86. C. Addison Hickman and Manford H. Kuhn, *Individuals, Groups, and Economic Behavior*. Dryden, New York, 1956.
87. J. A. Hornaday, and J. Aboud, "Characteristics of Successful Entrepreneurs." *Personnel Psychology* 24:141–153 (1971).
88. J. C. Johnson and Marvin D. Dunnette, "Validity and Test Retest Stability of the Nash Managerial Effectiveness Scale on the Revised Form of the Strong Vocational Interest Blank." *Personnel Psychology* 21:283–293 (1968).
89. Suzanne Keller, *Beyond the Ruling Class*. Random House, New York, 1963.
90. Paul R. Lawrence and J. W. Lorsch, *Organization and Environment*. Harvard University Press, Cambridge, Mass., 1967.
91. Edwin M. Lemert, "Social Structure, Social Control, and Deviation," in Marshall B. Clinard (ed.), *Anomie and Deviant Behavior*. Free Press, New York, 1964, pp. 57–97.
92. William N. Leonard and Marvin Glenn Weber, "Automakers and Dealers: A Study of Criminogenic Market Forces." *Law and Society Review* 4:407–424 (1970).
93. Bernard Levenson, "Bureaucratic Succession," in Amitai Etzioni, *Complex Organizations: A Sociological Reader*. Holt, Rinehart, and Winston, New York, 1961, pp. 362–375.
94. Roy Lewis and Rosemary Stewart, *The Managers: A New Examination of the English, German, and American Executive*. The New American Library, New York, 1961.
95. Seymour Martin Lipset, *Agrarian Socialism*. University of California Press, Berkeley and Los Angeles, 1950.
96. ⸺ and Reinhard Bendix, *Social Mobility in Industrial Society*. University of California Press, Berkeley, 1960.
97. W. D. Litzinger, "The Motel Entrepreneur and the Motel Manager." *Academy of Management Journal* 8:268–281 (1965).
98. Terry Lunsford, "Authority and Ideology in the Administered University," in Carlos E. Kruytbosch and Sheldon L. Messinger (eds.), *The State of the University*. Sage Publications, Beverly Hills, Calif., 1970.
99. Myles L. Mace, "John J. McCloy on Corporate Payoffs." *Harvard Business Review* 54:14ff (1976).
100. D. C. McClelland and D. G. Winter, *Motivating Economic Achievement*. The Free Press, New York, 1969.
101. T. A. Mahoney, T. H. Jerdee, and A. N. Nash, "Predicting Managerial Effectiveness." *Personnel Psychology* 13:147–163 (1960).
102. ⸺, ⸺, and ⸺, *The Identification of Management Potential*. Brown Management Audit, Dubuque, Iowa, 1961.
103. ⸺, ⸺, and ⸺, The Roman Catholic Church. Special Audit No. 137, Vol. V., no. 15, 1956.
104. Hiroshi Mannari, *The Japanese Business Leaders*. University of Tokyo Press, 1974.
105. Norman H. Martin, and Anselm L. Strauss, "Patterns of Mobility Within Industrial Organizations." *Journal of Business* 29:101–110 (1956).
106. David Matza, *Becoming Deviant*. Prentice-Hall, Englewood Cliffs, N.J., 1969, ch. 1.
107. Robert K. Merton, "Social Problems and Sociological Theory," in Robert K. Merton and Robert A. Nisbet (eds.), *Contemporary Social Problems*. Harcourt, Brace and World, New York, 1961, pp. 723–728.
108. S. L. Messinger, "Organizational Transformation: A Case Study of a Declining Social Movement." *American Sociological Review* 20:3–10.
109. Robert Michels, Political Parties. The Free Press, Glencoe, Ill. 1949.
110. Mary Wilson Miles, "The Writings of Robert K. Merton: A Bibliography," in Lewis A. Coser (ed.), *The Idea of Social Structure: Papers in Honor of Robert K. Merton*. Harcourt Brace Jovanovich, New York, 1975, pp. 497–522.

111. Nathan Miller, *The Founding Finaglers*. David McKay, New York, 1976.
112. C. Wright Mills, *White Collar*. Oxford University Press, New York, 1951.
113. Sergio E. Mindlin, and H. Aldrich, "Interorganizational Dependence: A Review of the Concept and a Reexamination of the Findings of the Aston Group." *Administrative Science Quarterly* 20:382–392 (1975).
114. John B. Miner, *Studies in Management Education*. Springer Publishing Company, New York, 1965.
115. ———, *The Management Process: Theory Research and Practice*. Macmillan, New York, 1973.
116. ———, "The Real Crunch in Managerial Manpower," in John B. Miner, *The Challenge of Managing*. Saunders, Philadelphia, 1975.
117. D. L. Moberg and J. L. Koch, "A Critical Appraisal of Integrated Treatments of Contingency Theory." *Academy of Management Journal* 18:109–124 (1975).
118. L. B. Mohr, "Organizational Technology and Organizational Structure." *Administrative Science Quarterly* 16:444–459 (1971).
118a. Wilbert E. Moore, *The Conduct of the Corporation*. Random House, New York, 1962.
119. Ralph Nader and Mark Green, *Corporate Power in America*. Grossman, New York, 1973.
120. Gwynn Nettler, *Explaining Crime*. McGraw-Hill, New York, 1974, ch. 7.
121. William G. Ouchi, and Mary Ann Maguire, "Organizational Control: Two Functions." *Administrative Science Quarterly* 20:559–569 (1975).
122. Geraint Parry, *Political Elites*. Frederick A. Praeger, New York, 1969.
123. Talcott Parsons, "A Sociological Approach to the Theory of Organizations," in *Structure and Process in Modern Societies*. The Free Press, New York, 1963.
124. Roland J. Pellegrin and Charles H. Coates, "Executives and Supervisors: Contrasting Definitions of Career Success." *Administrative Science Quarterly* 1:506–517 (1957).
125. J. Pennings, "The Relevance of the Structural-Contingency Model for Organizational Effectiveness." *Administrative Science Quarterly* 20:393–410 (1975).
126. Charles Perrow, "Organizational Prestige: Some Functions and Dysfunctions." *American Journal of Sociology* 66:335–341 (1961).
127. ———, *Complex Organizations*. Scott, Foresman, Glenview, Ill., 1972, pp. 166–167.
128. Jeffrey Pfeffer and H. Leblebici, "The Effect of Competition on Some Dimensions of Organization Structure." *Social Forces* 52:268–279 (1973).
129. Lyman W. Porter, "Job Attitudes in Management: I. Perceived Deficiencies in Need Fulfillment as a Function of Job Level." *Journal of Applied Psychology* 46:375–384 (1962).
130. ———, "Job Attitudes in Management: IV. Perceived Differences in Need Fulfillment as a Function of Size of Company." *Journal of Applied Psychology* 47:386–397 (1963).
131. ——— and Mildred M. Henry, "Job Attitudes in Management: VI. Perceptions of the Importance of Certain Personality Traits as a Function of Line Versus Staff Type of Job." *Journal of Applied Psychology* 48:305–309 (1964a).
132. ——— and ———, "Job Attitudes in Management: V. Perceptions of the Importance of Certain Personality Traits as a Function of Job Level." *Journal of Applied Psychology* 48:31–36 (1964 b).
133. ———, and Edward E. Lawler III, "Properties of Organization Structure in Relation to Job Attitudes and Job Behavior." *Psychological Bulletin* 64:23–51 (1965).
134. ——— and ———, *Managerial Attitudes and Performance*. Irwin, Homewood, Ill., 1968.
135. Robert Presthus, *The Organizational Society*. Knopf, New York, 1962.

136. D. S. Pugh, J. D. Hickson, and C. R. Hinings, "Dimensions of Organization Structure." *Administrative Science Quarterly* 13:65–105 (1968).
137. Solomon Rettig and Benjamin Pasamanick, "Changes in Moral Values as a Function of Adult Socialization." *Social Problems* 7:117–125 (1959).
138. David Riesman, "Predicaments in the Career of the College President," in Carlos E. Kruytbosch and Sheldon L. Messinger (eds.), *The State of the University.* Sage Publications, Beverly Hills, Calif., 1970.
139. Roberta Lynn Satow, "Value-Rational Authority and Professional Organizations: Weber's Missing Type." *Administrative Science Quarterly* 20:526–532 (1975).
140. Robert A. Scott, "The Factory as a Social Service Organization." *Social Problems* 15:160–175.
141. Stanley E. Seashore, and Ephraim Yuchtman, "Factorial analysis of organizational performance." *Administrative Science Quarterly* 12:377–395.
142. Stephen M. Shortell, "Contingency Theories of Organizations: Where Do We Go from Here?" Paper presented to meetings of American Sociological Association, New York City, August 1976.
143. Matthews Silberman, "Toward a Theory of Criminal Deterrence." *American Sociological Review* 41:442–461 (1976).
144. Richard L. Simpson, "Vertical and Horizontal Communication in Formal Organizations." *Administrative Science Quarterly* 4:188–196 (1959).
145. Erwin O. Smigel and H. Laurence Ross, *Crimes against Bureaucracy.* Van Nostrand Reinhold, New York, 1970.
146. Richard Austin Smith, "The Incredible Electrical Conspiracy." *Fortune* 63(April 1961):132–137 and (May 1961):161–164 (1961).
147. C. Sofer, *Men in Mid-Career.* Cambridge University Press, Cambridge, Mass., 1970.
148. William H. Starbuck, "Organizations and Their Environments," in Marvin D. Dunnette (ed.), *Handbook of Industrial and Organizational Psychology.* Rand McNally, Chicago, 1976, ch. 25.
149. Barry M. Staw and Eugene Szwajkowski, "The Scarcity-Munificence Component of Organizational Environments and the Commission of Illegal Acts." *Administrative Science Quarterly* 29:345–354 (1975).
150. Richard Steers and Lyman Porter, "The Role of Task-Goal Attributes in Employee Performance." *Psychological Bulletin* 81:434–452 (1974).
151. Christopher D. Stone, *Where the Law Ends.* Harper and Row, New York, 1975.
152. George Strauss, and Leonard R. Sayles, *Personnel: The Human Problems of Management.* Prentice-Hall, Englewood Cliffs, N.J., 1972.
153. Edwin H. Sutherland, *White Collar Crime.* Holt, Rinehart and Winston, New York, 1961.
154. ———, and Donald R. Cressey, *Criminology.* Lippincott, Philadelphia, 1974, ch. 13.
155. Gresham M. Sykes and David Matza, "Techniques of Neutralization." *American Sociological Review* 22:664–670 (1957).
156. Curt Tausky and Robert Dubin, "Career Anchorage: Managerial Mobility Motivations." *American Sociological Review* 30:725–735 (1965).
157. James D. Thompson, *Organizations in Action.* McGraw-Hill, New York, 1967, pp. 19ff.
158. James D. Thompson, Robert W. Avery, and Richard O. Carlson, "Occupations, Personnel, and Careers." *Educational Administration Quarterly* 4:6–31 (1968).
159. Harry C. Triandis, "Differential Perceptions of Certain Jobs and People by Managers, Clerks and Workers in Industry." *Journal of Applied Psychology* 43:221–225 (1959).
160. Gordon Tullock, *The Politics of Bureaucracy.* Public Affairs Press, Washington, D.C., 1965.

161. James S. Turner, *Chemical Feast*. Grossman, New York, 1970.
162. W. W. Turner, "Dimensions of Foreman Performance: A Factory Analysis of Criterion Measures." *Journal of Applied Psychology* 44:216–223 (1960).
163. Andrew Van de Ven, André L. Delbecq, and Richard Koenig, Jr., "Determinations of Coordination Modes Within Organizations." *American Sociological Review* 41:322–338 (1976).
164. Bruce C. Vladeck, "Why Non-Profits Go Broke." *The Public Interest* 42:86–101 (1976).
165. H. A. Wainer and I. M. Rubin, "Motivation of Research and Development Entrepreneurs: Determinants of Company Success." *Journal of Applied Psychology* 53:178–184 (1969).
166. Charles R. Walker, Robert A. Guest, and Arthur N. Turner, *The Foreman on the Assembly Line*. Harvard University Press, Cambridge, Mass., 1956.
167. W. Keith Warner and A. Eugene Havens, "Goal Displacement and the Intangibility of Organizational Goals." *Administrative Science Quarterly* 12:539–555 (1968).
168. W. Lloyd Warner and James C. Abegglen, *Big Business Leaders in America*. Harper, New York, 1955a.
169. ———, *Occupational Mobility in American Business and Industry*. University of Minnesota Press, Minneapolis, 1955b.
170. ———, Paul P. Van Riper, Norman H. Martin, and Orvis F. Collins, *The American Federal Executive*. Yale University Press, New Haven, 1963.
171. Stanton Wheeler, *On Record: Files and Dossiers in American Life*. Russell Sage Foundation, New York, 1969.
172. Martin King Whyte, "Bureaucracy and Modernization in China: The Maoist Critique." *American Sociological Review* 38:149–163 (1973).
173. Harold Wilensky and Hugh Edwards, "The Skidder: Ideological Adjustment of Downward Mobile Workers." *American Sociological Review* 24:215–231 (1959).
174. Ephraim Yuchtman and Stanley E. Seashore, "A System Resource Approach to Organizational Effectiveness." *American Sociological Review* 32:891–903 (1967).
175. Don H. Zimmerman, "The Practicalities of Rule Use," in Jack D. Douglas (ed.), *Understanding Everyday Life*. Aldine, Chicago, 1970.

CRIME AND THE AMERICAN LIQUOR INDUSTRY*

Norman K. Denzin**UNIVERSITY OF ILLINOIS—URBANA

INTERACTION, SOCIAL ORDERS AND PROBLEMATICS IN THE AMERICAN LIQUOR INDUSTRY: A CASE STUDY

The field of organizational studies is ripe for reconceptualization and re-examination. There is an increasing recognition that the interactions of individuals within the arenas of bureaucracies and organizations must be fitted into any theory of complex organizations. (See Blau [12]; Scott [70]; Collins [21]). The perspective of symbolic interactionism which stresses the negotiated, constructed and defined features of organizational structures seems well-suited for an emergent theory of persons and their organizations. (See Glaser and Strauss [37]; Strauss, *et. al.* [83, 84]; Blumer

Studies in Symbolic Interaction—Volume 1, 1978, pages 87–118.

87

[14]). This article applies the interactionist point of view to the study of complex organizations.

More specifically, the present discussion derives from Bell (7) and Gross (42, 43) who have proposed that all complex organizations are "inherently criminogenic." Built into the very structures of complex organization are personal motives which "induce members to engage in criminal activities." This theme will be examined through a case study analysis of the growth and expansion of the American Liquor Industry since Repeal in 1934.

Focus and Data Base

Practical constraints limit discussion of the operation of this industry to one community, Champaign-Urbana in the state of Illinois, and to the state of Illinois more generally. Historical, journalistic, ethnographic and interview data will be brought to bear upon this industry as it operates at the international, national, regional, state, and local levels. See Abrahamson (1); Baldwin (3), Bretzfield (18); Cavan (19); Clough (20) in process; Distilled Spirits Institute (28); Dobyns (29); Durrell (30); East (31); *Fortune Magazine* (35, 35a, 35b); Fosdick and Scott (36); Gusfield (44); Henderson (47); Horowitz and Horowitz (48); Jennings (50); Kane (51); LeMasters (53); *Liquor Handbook* (54); Martin (58); Merz (63); Pitman and Snyder (65); Roebuck and Frese (66); Rosenbloom (67); Simon (72, 73, 74); Sinclair (75); Spradely and Mann (78); Switzer (86); Warburton (90).[1]

Over a three-year period (1974–1976) data of the above order have been gathered from national publications of the industry, national distillers, manufacturers, regional managers of large distilling corporations, metro-managers in large urban areas, wholesalers, or distributors, retailers, former liquor commissioners in "Twin Cities", as well as from the Illinois State Liquor Control Commission. Persons active as bootleggers during prohibition were interviewed, as were state managers for distillers, street salesmen for wholesalers and distillers, tavern owners, tavern managers and restaurant owners. Interviews at the distiller, distributor, and retail level were, whenever possible, made with the highest-ranking officials. The data base includes statements from corporate vice-presidents, corporate presidents, and presidents or co-owners of distributorships. The interviews were of an open-ended nature, each building upon the preceding, with efforts to validate hypotheses as the research progressed (26). In each case, the focus was on the informants' relationship to competitors, their stances toward the liquor laws, their view(s) of drinkers, their shifting conceptions of the entire liquor enterprise and of their place within that enterprise—whether at the local, state, regional or national level.

Research Question

The criminogenic hypothesis will be examined as follows: The growth and expansion of the industry since prohibition is, in part, a function of the situation it confronted in 1934 when the federal government returned control of the alcoholic beverage industry back to the states and encouraged direct, local control at the community level. (See Fosdick and Scott [36]). This relinquishment of national control produces forty-eight separate situations (state units) that the industry had to confront, manage, define, interpret, accommodate and fit themselves to. This situational ambiguity produced a structure of social relationships, accommodative agreements, and negotiated understandings that permitted the industry to grow, expand and develop in the face of highly specific legal statutes governing the production, distribution and sale of alcoholic products. Ambiguity and specificity went hand in hand, and the industry exploited this situation to its own advantage. With expansion appeared semi-illegal and semi-corrupt behavior, as well as outright illegal and corrupt behavior. Pay-offs, deceptions, deceit, bribes, and conflicts of interest quickly became survival as well as expansion tactics. The exploitation of this situational ambiguity accounts, in large measure, for the industry's recovery from the restraints of prohibition.

OVERVIEW

The discussion is organized as follows. First, the interactionist approach to the study of industrial and organizational behavior is briefly reviewed. Second, the American liquor industry is placed within a specific historical context. It is argued that this context set the stage for the emergence of a unique industry within the American marketplace. Third, the relational structure of the liquor industry is explored, and five distinct levels, or interconnecting social worlds, are examined. Fourth, the acts and objects that make up these worlds are discussed, with special attention given to the place of the object called alcoholic beverage. Fifth, the negotiations and agreements that occur between the multiple levels of the liquor world are presented. Sixth, the shifting realities, some more obdurate than others, that the industry must take a stance toward are presented. State laws, the antitrust laws in particular, are examined. Seventh, manipulative strategies within the industry, including attempts to negotiate the legal order, are reviewed. Survival and expansion tactics are examined. Eighth, the conditions that permit such behaviors are explored. Finally, the relevance or utility of the symbolic interactionist approach for the study of social structure, economic relations and the liquor industry in particular is addressed.

THE SYMBOLIC INTERACTIONIST APPROACH TO THE STUDY OF ORGANIZATIONAL AND INDUSTRIAL RELATIONS

The interactionist views any organization in terms of the arenas that organization affords its members. (See Blumer [14], Strauss, et al. [83], Becker, et al. [4], Goffman [38], Dalton [25], Gusfield [44]). Selznick's (71) proposals for the foundations of a theory of organizations suggest that the interactionist examines and stresses the informal, as opposed to the formal, attributes of any organizational complex. Organizations are viewed as negotiated productions that differentially constrain their members. As Thompson and McEwen (87) stress, organizations exist within other interactional contexts that differentially impinge upon and shape the behaviors of their members (10, 23, 76). Organizations outlive the lives of their respective members; they take on histories that transcend individuals, conditions and specific situations. Organizations like the Licensed Alcoholic Beverage Industry are best approached as complex, shifting networks of social relationships. The sum total of these intertwined relationships—whether real or only symbolized, assumed and taken for granted, or problematic and troublesome—constitute the organization as it is sensed, experienced, organized and acted on by the individual or the relational member. Power, control, coercion and deception are central commodities that are negotiated over in those arenas that make up the organization (39, 40, 41). Persons stand in varying degrees of control over one another and may or may not have the ability to expand their spheres of influence beyond the specific confines of their particular subworlds of specialization.

The organization can be likened to what Norton Long (57) has called an ecology of games. This network of games, or interrelated affairs, cuts across territorial, personal, social, economic, political, and at times religious, ethnic and racial boundaries. Matters of personal and professional skill, expertise, experience, reputation, sponsorship and colleagueship are basic to the underlying gamelike structure of the organization. Members are ranked in terms of their standings in the respective games that make up this matrix of social relationships. As Long (57) notes, the most relevant activity in this ecological structure may be the social game.

THE AMERICAN LIQUOR INDUSTRY: HISTORICAL CONTEXTS

Whiskey has been produced in the United States since 1640 and has been intermittently taxed by the federal and state governments since 1791. Since November 1, 1951, the federal tax per gallon of distilled alcohol has been $10.50 per proof gallon. The distilling industry made its first great expansions during the 1870s and 1880s at which time nearly sixty distillers, under the Whiskey Trust, controlled more than 50 percent of the total distilling capacity in the United States (64). The Eighteenth Amendment in 1920 and the Volstead Act of 1919 stopped the growth of the industry and made the production of alcoholic beverages illegal except for purposes of medicinal, sacrimental and scientific research. While a few distillers remained in production under strict governmental control, the majority of distillers were driven out of legitimate business to become or to be replaced by bootleggers.

Prohibition set the basic situational context for the subsequent growth and development of the large distillers, and while the Eighteenth Amendment was basically unenforceable (29), its enactment set six conditions that make the liquor industry a unique enterprise within the American economic marketplace (see Oxenfeldt [64]). First, it basically destroyed an industry that was over two hundred years old, and for thirteen years exposed the producers of alcoholic products to a systematically organized governmental, public, community, moral, political, legal and financial attack. Following repeal, the industry emerged in 1934 with the four largest whiskey distillers prior to prohibition in the same position of control. These four distillers were: (1) Distillers Corp.—Seagrams Ltd., (2) Schenley Distillers Corp., (3) National Distillers Products Corp., and (4) Walker (Hiram)—Gooderham and Worts, Ltd. During prohibition in the United States all four had production bases in Canada. (Oxenfeldt, [64]). In conjunction with Distillers Corporation Ltd. (DCL), a Scottish-based conglomerate was formed in 1876 that today controls 75 percent of the world's scotch supply.

As a consequence, we are dealing with an industry that has a long history and has become concentrated in the hands of a relatively small number of individuals. First, it is a shrinking industry. In 1972 there were 140 breweries; in 1973, 125. In 1973 there were 318 distilleries; in 1974, 308. Three states dominate in the location of distilleries: California, Kentucky, and Illinois. It is estimated that by 1980 this will be a $10.7 billion industry. (*United States Industrial Outlook* [89].) Second, relatively few people are engaged in the production of whiskey. This is a high-capital-, low-labor-intensive industry. The maintenance of one's position rests on the ability to make the large expenditures that go to the federal government in the form of taxes. Competition has been kept to a minimum, which is not unique to the liquor industry. Third, the leaders of the distilling and brewing corporations found themselves attacked daily in the nation's newspapers. (See Dobyns [29].) Abrahamson [1] suggests that whiskey provoked high public controversy, as revealed in the attacks of the Anti-Saloon League. There emerged a general conviction that uncontrolled liquor traffic was dangerous. High governmental regulation was regarded as right and proper.

This third point is illustrated in the following account of the industry just before and immediately after repeal. On November 27, 1933, nine days before repeal, President Roosevelt created a Code of Fair Competition for DCL. One day later Owsley Brown (president of Brown-Foreman Distillers) sent telegrams to thirty companies calling for a meeting on December 2, 1933. A code authority consisting of Brown, L. S. Rosensteil (Schenley's) and Frank Thompson (Seagrams) was elected. They took the name of the Distilled Spirits Institute. On December 4, 1933, President Roosevelt established the Federal Alcohol Control Administration. On December 5, 1933, the Twenty-First Amendment was ratified. On December 14, 1933, DSI was incorporated in the State of New York. General Frank Schwengel, a retired brigadier general, was retained in this same month as a marketing adviser by the Bronfmans for the American-based Seagram operation. The code authority was directed by Roosevelt to draw up a set of guidelines for the federal regulation of their industry. In the immediate post-repeal days the industry worked closely with the federal government, a government-industry relationship which may be without precedent in American history.

General Schwengel (*Beverage Executive* [30] made the following observations:

> In order to forestall attacks from various dry organizations, which the WCTU spearheaded, we emphasized one of the basic principles of Distilled Spirits Institute: moderation, moderate drinking. This was the universal theme. Don't oversell, don't overdrink.

The power of Schwengel's theme and the influence of the original group assembled by Owsley Brown is evidenced in the fact that they or their relatives still control DSI.

DSI encouraged high government regulation and taxation. While they appeared to meekly accept a weak position, they learned from their industrial counterparts in oil, railroads, and automobiles how to cover their ever-expanding behaviors through the newly emerging and complex anti-trust laws. They quickly moved in the directions of vertical and horizontal integration, but acted as if they were not. They kept a low profile, dramaturgically managed themselves, and some forty years later emerged as new participants in the competitions of the multinationals. (See the discussion of Heublein's, Inc., below.)

Fourth, like the drug industry, the whiskey industry has an illegal counterpart—the bootleg trade, which consists of the production of moonshine or "white lightning,"—and for the modern bootlegger, the hijacking of legal merchandise, or along the nation's southern border, smuggling. (See Klokars, *The Professional Fence* for other illegal market transactions.) In 1932 the federal government spent in excess of $40 million enforcing prohibition. In the early 1970s the government was losing an excess of $20 million in taxes on illegally produced alcohol. (See Warburton [90]; *The Liquor Handbook* [54].)

The fifth situational and historical factor set by prohibition that put the liquor industry in a special category in the American economy is that it is one of the most widely regulated and taxed industries in our society; others include the tobacco industry and the utility companies. In 1973 the tax on alcohol accounted for $16.6 million (*Statistical Abstracts of the United States,* [79]). In addition to the federal government's $10.50 excise tax on every gallon of distilled alcohol, state excise taxes may be as high as $2.50, and some communities further impose a local option excise tax. Federal and state excise taxes *must be* paid by the distiller when the product leaves the warehouse. The distiller passes on to his distributor a markup of between 15 and 20 percent, the distributor duplicates this markup, and the retailer averages a 10 to 15 percent markup. Distillers say that the cheapest product in their industry is the alcoholic beverage. Containers, barrels, grain, labor, taxes, transportation and advertising raise the cost of the beverage to the present high levels. This situation also produces deals made to those distributors and retailers who can buy in large quantities.

The sixth consequence of prohibition was to introduce what came to be termed the *three-tier system* of distribution in the wine and spirits industry. Under this system (86),

> the three levels of supplier, wholesaler and retailer must be maintained separate and independent of each other, and the supplier must sell only to the wholesaler, and the latter only to the retailers. The retailer, in turn, may buy only from the wholesaler. The manufacturer or supplier, who is normally the brand owner, may not deal directly with the retailer. The wholesaler, therefore, stands between the retailer and the manufacturer.

Hidden in the above language is one basic point which had been the touchstone of the Anti-Saloon League—namely, the saloon or tavern as a source of evil and immorality (75). It was argued that distillers and brewers owned or staked tavernkeepers, imposed quotas upon them, and forced them to take needed money out of the pockets of the thirsty drinkers, who were also family men. "Tied taverns," or the "tied" houses as they were called, permitted outside interests to control the politics, moralities and drinking patterns of local communities. By placing the wholesaler between the manufacturer and the retailer, the states and federal government attempted to break the tied-tavern relationship—on the surface at least.

Prohibition and repeal did not represent legal, moral, political or economic acts that would unilaterally take the liquor industry in one direction or another. Rather, as in other situations of rapid or proposed social change, the effects of the change could not be fully predicted beforehand. Each distiller, wholesaler, retailer and tavern owner had to adapt his own attitude toward these laws and respond accordingly. Some acted together, others separately; some disappeared, some reappeared in new forms.

LEVELS, RELATIONSHIPS AND PERSONS WITHIN THE AMERICAN LIQUOR INDUSTRY

As Hamilton (45) has observed, there is no such thing as a single industry. At least five different tiers resolve into distinct social worlds which constitute those collective realities that make up this particular industry. The Twenty-first Amendment recognized the three tiers of distiller, wholesaler and retailer. Closer inspection reveals the presence of two additional tiers—first, the drinkers themselves; and second, those individuals and agencies committed to the enforcement of the liquor laws: local liquor commissions, the police, the FBI, and the Treasury Department's Bureau of Alcohol, Tobacco and Firearms (BATF). The industry is best viewed as a loosely structured network of social relationships which cut across political, associational, organizational, territorial, ethnic, racial, family and personal boundaries. Some of the parties to this complex ecology of relationships and games are close friends, others are hostile enemies. For instance, one of the principal liquor retailers in Champaign-Urbana, when asked to comment on his chief competitor, stated. "It is my goal to drive that s.o.b. out of the business. Even if I have to lose money on a particular deal I will make a fool out of him" (field interview, May 1975).

Other participants are family intimates. In 1944 thirty-four families controlled sixty of the eighty local taverns in Champaign-Urbana. Since 1944 the number of taverns has more than doubled and the same families control a large proportion of these enterprises. One family controlled all but one of the local retail outlets, of which there were five. That family now has a virtual monopoly on retail sales. Family control typically extends through three generations. Eight of the ten wholesalers in the seventeen-county area under consideration are related either through marriage or direct kin. Of the four major whiskey producers, all but National Distillers are family controlled, with control extending into pre-prohibition days. (For an illustration of one such family, see *Newsweek* August 25, 1975: 16–17). The same pattern appears to hold for breweries and wineries, at least until quite recently (48).

At the executive level of top rival distilling firms, hostile, not cordial or congenial relationships, appear to be the pattern, although these participants will seldom permit personal animosities to enter into profit-making decisions. Oxenfeldt (64) notes that the executive offices of the large distillers are all located in New York City, within a short radius of one another. (There has been a recent regional shift to Chicago.) The executives meet often and know one another very well. With few exceptions they all belong to the same organizations and clubs, including Distilled Spirits Institute and the Licensed Beverage Industries Institute. They also contribute to the same charities, all in the collective name of the industry.

Wholesalers often find themselves in a situation where a particular distiller has "dualed" a product in their territory. Territories are typically marked by county boundaries, although these boundaries are not always clear. Wholesalers cannot sell outside of their own territories. This means two wholesale houses have the right—often verbally granted—to sell the same product to the same audience, e.g., retail outlets. "Dualing" leads to deals and special favors that are often illegal. The participation in these deals appears to give one wholesaler prime rights over the product in question. Other participants are go-betweens or representatives between warring bodies. They include bureaucrats, chemists, agro-economists, market analysts, truck drivers, secretaries and loading bosses. On one occasion we interviewed a wholesaler who was proudly wearing the latest "western belt buckle" from his brewery, as he was giving away free frisbees with the name of his brewery on the side. One street salesman, about to retire after thirty years with the same wholesaler, was wearing the latest tie with a new insignia designating a new product about to be marketed by his principal distiller. Others wear special tie clasps, display corporate calendars, show off the latest Eskimo ice chest they have won, or the ballpoint pen set they were just given. Distillers also engage in product promotion. One distiller gives his corporate executives a "Friday package" each week consisting of a bottle of gin, vodka and blended whiskey. This is expected to last them a week, and they are expected to display these products on social occasions. Each Friday afternoon at four o'clock these executives leave their offices with their gifts wrapped in brown paper bags. Their corporate identity is maintained, although the price of their gift is hidden.

Other member participants are college students who work as bartenders, barmaids, and assistant bar managers. Some are professional athletes who have chosen to invest in the industry, often at the local level; others are local amateur athletes who serve as bouncers. Certain bars within the city routinely hire university football players on a part-time basis for the above function. In at least one case the bar owner knew high-ranking members of the athletic department on a first-name basis.

Some members of this world take part in the advertising of the industry and collectively bid against one another at the agency level to capture ever bigger drinking audiences for the producer, the distiller and the retailer. Although the industry does not utilize the most expensive media, T.V., brewers and certain vintners do. Major advertising outlets are outdoor displays, magazines, newspapers and "point of sales" displays. Total magazine expenditures in 1973 for distilled products amounted to $84,310,843; a 20 percent increase over the previous year (54). This figure is probably deflated. Interviews with two major distillers revealed that they never gave an accurate accounting of their advertising expenses. The above figure, if these interviews are correct, should be at least one-third higher. The advertising arm of the industry points to perhaps the largest, if not the most heterogeneous sector of the liquor world: the drinker who is the ultimate point of contact for all the interactions that make up this world. The drinker can make or break new programs. (See Stone (81) on drinking clubs.) Their purchasing patterns determining package programs, advertising campaign, and their shifting moods regarding taste, product, and brand enter into the long-range planning programs of the distiller, wholesaler and retailer. The decision not to advertise on television extends back to fears generated during prohibition, as well as a general reluctance on the part of the Federal Communications Commission, until 1960, to permit such advertising. A bloc of Southern senators succeeded in representing the sentiments of their "dry" constituents.

The most important advertising commodity, or medium, is the street salesman, who links the distributor to the retailer and thereby connects the customer to the distiller, brewer, or vintner.

Two examples will serve to document the centrality of the drinker-consumer in this process. First, after eight years of planning, testing and field experimentation in the fall of 1975, Heublein, Inc., introduced on the market a new product named "Hereford Cow," which comes in chocolate, mocha and strawberry flavors. Aimed for youth, it was simultaneously introduced in two test cities: Champaign-Urbana and the South Side of Chicago. Since its introduction, another distiller has come out with a new product, "Angus Cow." The Hereford Cow was *forced* onto the shelves of all the bars served by the local distributor and within four weeks was rejected by all bars. While its initial sales in South Chicago of 150,00 cases in two weeks far surpassed expectations, it has since dropped

off in sales and Heublein is searching for a new product for this particular audience.

The second example comes from a street salesman who has to serve
small racial and ethnic retail liquor outlets in South Chicago. The drinkers
in this area prefer to make their purchases in pint-sized quantities, and
they prefer to purchase only the most prestigious scotches, bourbons,
gins and vodkas; but they change their taste patterns almost weekly,
leaving the salesman either understocked or overstocked for his
wholesale outlets. These drinkers, who make up over 50 percent of the
drinking population in Washington D.C., Chicago and New York City, are
particularly problematic for the distilling industry (54).

Some individuals trace their membership in this large social world to
preprohibition days, and they may cut across the specific worlds of the
distiller, the wholesaler, or the retailers. These individuals stand in sharp
contrast to people like recent law school graduates who view the liquor
industry as a promising field for legal careers. These new entrants (and
they may be distillers, wholesalers, or retailers as well as lawyers) have
little if any collective understanding of the historical roots and foundations of the industry. Nor do they express any sympathy for those whose
historical past extends into the early 1920s when prohibition, the Anti-
Saloon League and World War I questioned not only the legality but the
morality and financial future and security of the industry. In general,
pre-prohibition individuals, or those who entered the business in the early
1930s, feel that the industry has slipped through their fingers, and while
they can talk about the past with fond remembrances, they look with
distaste upon the present. A retail store owner recalled:

"I started in 1934 with a corner shop and couldn't even get a sign in the door. I paid
$200 a month rent. I paid off the bootleggers, the police, I kept up my bills. I didn't let
the outsiders drive me out. What do these people in the chain stores, the grocery stores
and drug stores think they can do? They don't know the business. They'll never drive
me out." (field interview, June 1975).

The modern retailer, on the other hand, reads the *Liquor Store
Magazine*. He permits the distiller to rent shelf space in his store, to
display his company's products prominently, and thinks in terms of more
efficient ways to increase profits on point-of-sales transactions.

These two groups stand in deep contrast to one another; the one keeps a
past alive, the other discards that past and adapts to a future that equates
the sale of whiskey, beer and wine with the marketing of standard
grocery-store items. The vice-president of sales of a large corporation

which holds sole United States rights to the marketing of one of the top four scotches in the world remarked: "Scotch is no harder to sell than shoestrings or overalls. It's a matter of marketing, promotion and packaging" (field interview, July 1975).

A RECOGNIZABLE NEGOTIATED ORDER: ACTS AND OBJECTS

Five tiers within the liquor industry have been established. Each of these levels is interconnected, often in ways that are hidden or taken for granted by their participants. Numerous examples can be given to document this conclusion. A major distillery has an exclusive club that only presidents of distributorships can belong to. Membership in the club is passed on from father to son. Should a father fail to produce a son, he must marry his daughter off to a man who is willing to enter the business. Once the male heir assumes control, the father relinquishes his membership in the club. A salesman of thirty years with this distributorship had never learned of this club. His skills and successes as a salesman did not depend upon his knowledge of this exclusive club. Few if any drinkers of this distiller's products are aware of the club's existence.

A common practice of this company is to schedule a two-week family vacation in some exotic resort area for its distributors and their wives. A portion of the vacation time is spent in "consciousness expanding" sessions where notables such as Gloria Steinham, Tom Hayden, Hewey Newton, Merle Miller, Walter Hinkle, Bill Cosby and Don Rickles have lectured and entertained.

Further amplification of this hidden, taken-for-granted character of the industry emerged from an interview with the previous president of the Illinois Liquor Control Commission. When asked about Regulation 6, Article 4, which requires all distillers to file with the state liquor commission the territories where they have granted distributors' exclusive sales rights, he remarked, "I have never heard of this rule; if it was important I would know about it" (field interview, June 1975). This rule, in part unique to Illinois, sets firm guidelines for maintaining a separation between distillers, distributors and retailers. It is intended to reduce monopolistic control over local liquor sales. Furthermore, few drinkers are aware of the laws that limit the number of retail outlets in any city, nor are the prices of licenses commonly known. Additional complexity is introduced when multinational corporations buy up specific breweries, distilleries, and purchase exclusive sales rights to specific brands. One retailer remarked: "You never know from day to day who owns these damned corporations, or what their policies are."

This negotiated order operates on shifting levels of knowledge and information. In a certain sense gossip and rumor bind all participants into an illusory world of common understanding.

A negotiated order, consisting of all the diverse social relationships outlined above, draw these diverse persons into a semi-common, semi-consensual world of understandings, meanings, experiences and discourse whose central focus is the alcoholic beverage. The fact that this social object arouses noncensensual, contradictory and competing definitions (e.g., how should it be bottled; how should it be priced, sold, branded; who should drink it; when should it be consumed; how should it be consumed, etc.) is itself nonproblematic. These contradictions and failures in consensus set the stage for new rounds of interaction between the central players in the negotiated worlds of the liquor enterprise—from the drinker to the corporate president of Heublein's. From level to level, tier to tier, wholesaler to wholesaler, retailer to retailer, drinker to drinker, the word goes out concerning new brands, new mixes, and good buys on fine wines.

The substance called alcohol and those acts referred to as distilling, producing, rectifying, wholesaling, retailing, and drinking make up the negotiated order of the liquor industry. Each tier is bound to every other tier, and each tier assumes certain recurrent behaviors on the part of the other. This negotiated order produces for its co-participants realities and objects that are assumed, taken for granted, at times problematic, on other occasions impossible to obtain.

This negotiated order is made up of easily recognizable names, and to these names are attached persons who have careers, the central focus being an act or set of activities directed toward the alcoholic beverage—whether this be grapevines, vats of sour mash, grain elevators, semi-trucks with built-in coolers, warehouses, bottles and kegs, federal stamps, tax receipts, or letters exchanged between a brewer and the director of a state liquor commission. Persons have careers through, and careers with, the products and activities of their respective organizations, be it Schenley Industries or the Do-Drop Inn. These enterprises belong to a recognizable, if not taken for granted and assumed, negotiated order.

NEGOTIATIONS AND AGREEMENTS

The five tiers that make up the liquor industry intersect and interrelate along moving and shifting lines of accommodation, acceptance, cooperation, co-optation, tolerance, competition and, at times, rejection and open hostility. Various tiers or combinations of tiers may band together, as when the brewers cooperated with temperance forces during prohibition

(75). Subgroupings of the public may be co-opted into propaganda campaigns to further the sales of a new product just released by a distiller. Outright competition can occur when distributors vie with distillers for new products. Informants report that these competitions are best seen at the annual conventions of the liquor industry when various distillers court distributors, and when distributors court distillers. Corruption, payoffs, and deals can arise when new liquor licenses are under consideration. Loopholes in local statutes can permit preferred individuals to obtain licenses whereas others are denied such privileges. Blocks of votes can be purchased when local, state and national politicians take a stand on temperance, prohibition, expanded liquor licensing, or increases in the federal or state tax on alcoholic products (47).

Distributors can make agreements with specific retailers or tavern owners to supply them with specific goods or services, any or all of which may be illegal or semi-illegal. In 1944 the Illinois Liquor Control Commission Code made it illegal for any distributor to provide a tavern owner with walk-in coolers, free glasses, free calendars, clocks, bar equipment, mirrors, or outside display signs. The economic slump of 1971–1974 led brewers to begin enforcing this law informally, telling their favorite tavern owners that "the feds had come down on them and they could no longer provide those services" (field interview with bar manager of fourteen years, August 1975).

Distillers must negotiate with one another over the relative prices they will set for their respective products. Federal law requires that no distiller market a product at a price lower than the one he lists in what is termed an *affirmation state* [86]. New York, Florida, and Michigan are affirmation states. Twice a year, all distillers must file in those states at a designated time the lowest price for each of their marketable items. Deceit, deception, misrepresentation, and "unintended leaks" of information abound at these times, and at least one large scotch manufacturer is now facing suit because of its latest filing procedures. The manufacturer filed four hours early, and then one minute before midnight on the designated date entered a lower price for its scotch. This was managed by lowering the FOB price per barrel as the product left the docks in Glasgow, Scotland.

Distributors must negotiate the payments they receive for delivered goods to retailers. The State of Illinois demands that all beer be paid for upon delivery and allows thirty days for all other alcoholic products. If a retailer or tavern owner fails to meet a payment deadline, he (or she) goes on a delinquent payment list filed in the state capital every Wednesday. No distributor can deliver goods to a retailer whose name is on the delinquent list. However, bargains, side deals and arrangements can be made, as when a distributor agrees to *take back* portions of an order that a customer cannot pay for. In a similar fashion, tavern owners and retailers can bargain with patrons on the payment of received goods, and while local statutes prohibit charge accounts at retail liquor stores, "preferred" customers are allowed to receive such privileges.

Distributors can negotiate with one another. The Illinois Liquor Control Act prohibits distributors from selling in territories where they have no right. Such violations are not uncommon. Distributors found guilty can have their licenses suspended from two to twenty days. In Champaign-Urbana, in response to a recent labor strike at the Anhueuser-Busch factory in St. Louis, the local distributor holding the sole rights to Busch products found himself out of stock. He began selling what he termed "brand X," which upon inspection was found to be Old Style Beer. The local distributor who holds the rights to that beer denied selling it to the distributor in question. The matter is now under investigation by the executive director of the State Liquor Commission. Some distributors agree to ignore infractions and permit each other to serve old customers, usually family friends, who in fact reside in another distributor's territory (field interview, September 1975). Such agreements engender goodwill and lead distributors to help one another out when they find themselves short of some needed product.

Retailers can manipulate distilling corporations into making special deals with them, simply because they can move large volumes of a particular product. In some situations a retailer can make arrangements to be served by a distributor who actually resides in another territory. In these instances the size and power of the retailer lead him to take control over the local market distribution of a particular product.

Retailers can negotiate with one another. They can agree to set a bottom price on a certain product, or a retailer bent on running a competitor out of business can buy a product in a sufficiently large quantity (e.g., 2,000 cases) and systematically undersell his competitor, who can only buy in ten–twenty–or fifty–quantities.

At the tavern tier it is common for groups of tavern owners to agree to take a hard or soft line on enforcing the drinking-age law, and they may or may not cooperate in the organization of a communication network that warns fellow competitors of an impending police raid. Retailers can agree to cater only to certain drinking audiences, and in a campus town such agreements often flow along the organizational lines of housing units, sororities and fraternities. On the other hand, outright battles may occur when a new bar owner enters the public drinking arena and attempts to take stable patrons from other bars. Bar managers hire "spies" to check on new competitors.

Drinkers, too, enter into this negotiated arena, and this is best seen when they agree to boycott a particular bar because of a change in ownership, decor, menu, or entertainment. Drinkers are often regarded by bar owners as fickle. One local bar which had been in existence for twenty-five years changed hands in the summer of 1975. The new owner completely changed the decor and pinball arrangements in the "new bar," and immediately lost a regular crowd that had historical roots going back twenty-five years. He is still in the process of regaining that lost clientele.

RECAPITULATION: NEGOTIATED COMMODITIES AND OBDURATE REALITIES

Liquor licenses, bar locations, delinquent payment lists, product prices, territorial boundaries, gifts, agreements, alignments, commitments, patrons, fines, laws, fees, filing dates and relationships with public officials constitute a significant proportion of the negotiated commodities that make up the world of the liquor industry. These commodities are varyingly negotiable, and some are more obdurate and real than others.

At the national level the industry must deal with a complex set of laws and procedures that are unique to every state in the United States. (See *Summary of the State Laws and Regulations Relating to Distilled Spirits,* [27].) These procedures include rulings ranging from tax collection procedures, size of retail containers, local option rulings on retail sales, to license permits for distillers' representatives and revocation procedures.

States and Their Relative Obdurate Realities

There are basically two state models the industry must deal with. Monopoly states permit the sale of bottled distilled spirits only in state-owned stores. The state buys directly from the distiller and sells through its state-controlled stores.

License states are states where distilled spirits are sold under a licensed private enterprise system. There are three types of license states. The first have the standard three-tier system between distiller, distributor and retailer. Distillers and distributors can have no involvement in the direct sale of alcoholic beverages. The second type of license state requires that wholesalers be residents of the state. These states permit licensed resident manufacturers to sell beverages manufactured in the state to retailers. The third type permits suppliers or manufacturers to hold wholesale licenses whereby they can bypass the wholesaler and thus produce a two-, not a three-tier system. This permits out-of-state suppliers to secure wholesale licenses.

Every major distiller, brewer and vintner employs a legal staff whose chief function is to monitor the changing laws within each state, to keep in touch with relevant legal representatives of the industry, to represent the best interests of the industry to local, state and national political entities.

Above all, they insure that their corporations do not grossly violate any statute or ruling that would inhibit the sale of their products.

The industries' stance toward the legal system is reflected in the following statement from a high-ranking official in an internationally known distilling firm: "We break the laws every day. If you think I go to bed at night worrying about it, you're crazy. Everybody breaks the law. The liquor laws are insane anyway. We worry more about the antitrust laws" (field interview, August 1975).

Antitrust laws were of special relevance for this individual. The corporation he represents recently acquired the United States rights to a major scotch line as a result of an antitrust suit brought to bear against one of the top four world distillers.

ANTITRUST LAWS AS NEGOTIATED PROBLEMATICS

Antitrust suits take on major significance for the distiller. Large corporations can hide behind complicated corporate structures which allow them to gain major holdings in competing lines, or to diversify within the same product line.

A case in point is offered by the history of Heublein, Inc., which incorporated in 1915. In 1964 they acquired Arrow Liqueurs Corp. In 1965 they acquired Theo. Hamm Brewing Co. It was sold in 1973 for $6 million. In June of 1966 they acquired Coastal Valley Canning Co. in California for 247,000 common shares. In 1968 they acquired Don Q. Imports, Inc., of Florida. In 1969 they acquired an 82 percent interest in Allied Grape Growers, Inc., a subsidiary, by issuance of 1,734,621 shares of stock. In 1969 they acquired Beaulieu Vineyard of California for $7,480,000. In 1970 they acquired Grape Factors, Inc., for 149,005 common shares. In 1971 they acquired Regina Grape Products Co., in exchange for 60,000 common shares. .In June 1971 they acquired Kentucky Fried Chicken Corp., through an exchange of 5,489,477 common shares. During 1972 they acquired Hart's Inc. of Tennessee for 200,000 common shares. In 1972 they acquired Gillam's Take-Out, Inc., and Midwest Franchise Corp. for 16,667 common shares; and Cameri Pty, Ltd., Australia, for 64,000 common shares, and also merged with Spring Valley Foods, Inc., through an exchange of stock.

In 1970, Heublein, Inc., and J. M. da Fonseca of Lisbon, Portugal, built a $1,600,000 winery south of Lisbon to produce 750,000 cases of wine a year with provision to expand to 2,000,000 cases a year. In 1969, Indian Head, Inc. entered into a joint venture to build and operate a $16 million glass container plant in Madera, California. In 1972, the company signed an agreement to acquire Drury's S.A.–Fabrizio–Fasano group, a whiskey maker in Brazil. Subsidiaries of Heublein, Inc., include Allied Grape Groups (82 percent controlled), United Vintners, Inc., Kentucky Fried Chicken Corp., Heublein (Canada, Inc.). Heublein International Ltd., Smirnoff Beverage & Import Co. This company produces vodka, mixed cocktails, dry gin, cordials, beer, rum, table wines, sherries, all wines sold under the names of Italian Swiss Colony, Inglenook, Lejon Petri, and Gambarelli & Davito. They also produce A1 Sauce, Escoffier sauces, Snap-E-Tom tomato cocktail, Grey-Poupon Mustard, and Regina wine vinegars and cooking sauces.

They have achieved at least partial *vertical* and *horizontal* integration. They have purchased their own vineyards for growing their own wines, and they have set up their own bottling firms *(vertical integration)*. They have bought out competitors—*(horizontal integration)*.

This situation led the Federal Trade Commission to issue a complaint in 1972 challenging the 1968 acquisition of the controlling interest in United Vintners, Inc. The FTC charged that this acquisition eliminated competition in the wine industry and could prevent new wineries from entering business and inhibit existing wineries from expanding. The FTC alleged that this acquisition violated the Clayton Anti-trust Act. Heublein's denied the charges and asserted that "its 82 percent interest in United Vintners gave California grape growers a marketing arm to meet industry competition" (*Moody Industrial Manual*, 1975:236). Heublein's still controls 82 percent of the United Vintners, Inc.

Under a complex corporate umbrella, Heublein's Inc. has followed the pattern of many of the major distillers, brewers and vintners. While they flirt with antitrust laws, they are seldom brought to court, and when this happens, they usually win, or a handful of individuals receive a handsome price for relinquishing their shares in a competing corporation. Antitrust laws are more troublesome than problematic. The following interview, with a former president of a major United States distiller, reflects this fact. In 1934 his brother joined forces with a Canadian distiller, and they profited hugely in post-prohibition days. During the 1950s this individual joined another firm. That firm acquired the rights to a particular brand of scotch. At that time they held controlling shares in the three best-selling scotches in the world. In 1968 the FTC brought an antitrust suit against his firm. The antitrust suit was tied up in the courts for six years. The FTC won and forced him to sell his shares in the company. He sold his shares for a 50 percent profit to a newly emerged multinational corporation that was interested in moving into the liquor industry. The vice-president of that corporation had been the previous manager of the parent scotch company in Scotland. The FTC's suit made profits for everyone and elevated at least one person to the position of multinational vice-president (see Abrahamson [1] for similar examples immediately after repeal.)

NEGOTIATING CONSTRAINTS, MANIPULATING THE LEGAL ORDER AND NORMALIZING THE TAKEN-FOR-GRANTED WORLD

Repeal opened the way for a small group of distillers at the national level to capitalize on a relatively new and ambiguous situation. Not only did they have to redefine themselves for the federal government, but they also had to formulate a collective self-image that could be sold to the public. The foregoing illustrations of negotiations, negotiated commodities, and the manipulation of obdurate realities suggest that the industry accomplished its ill-defined goal of becoming a legitimate American economic enterprise. Taverns were cleaned up. Tied houses disappeared. Gross instances of corruption and illegal behavior became clouded behind complicated corporate laws and local statutes. In the end, drinkers, tavern owners, retailers, wholesalers, and manufacturers all profited. Deception and illusion became marketable commodities. Bootleg liquor gradually disappeared. Upgraded alcoholic products appeared on the market. Sophisticated advertising campaigns were organized to appeal to the diverse tastes of a multiplicity of drinkers. A normalized system that assumed a taken-for-granted nature emerged, solidified, and gradually became institutionalized into local, state and national laws.

This normalized, taken-for-granted system contains within itself a variety of behaviors, actions, and ideologies that justify self-serving manipulations of the legal order by its participants. The liquor industry in the middle 1970s appears to be a highly legal, stable, and normalized enterprise. Yet hidden behind its corporate structures, state statutes, and local codes are a variety of illegal behaviors that mirror those that produced the Eighteenth Amendment and prohibition.

EXPLOITATION, MANIPULATION AND DECEPTION IN THE LIQUOR INDUSTRY: THE RELEVANCE OF POWER AND CONTROL

An analysis and presentation of exploiting, manipulating and deceiving behaviors within the liquor industry must be organized in terms of the five separate worlds that make up this enterprise. However, it must be recognized that the most powerful force within these interconnected social worlds is the distiller, or manufacturer. The alcoholic product originates with the manufacturer who has the greatest amount of revenue involved in the industry.

Distillers: Not only do manufacturers violate antitrust laws, but they also exert tremendous pressure upon distributors, who in turn pass this pressure along to the retailer. In response to such pressure, retailers often deceive the customer into believing that they are getting a good buy on a particular product.

Consider the following situation, reported in *Liquor Store Magazine* (55). William S. Lynch, the chief of the Justice Department's Organized Crime and Racketeering Section, recently called for greater liquor law coordination between federal and state governments. A specific problem that ties the distiller to the wholesaler and the retailer is the "off-invoice" strategy which arises from the competition among wholesalers. It often takes the form of free liquor to retailers. Distillers put pressure on wholesalers to move a particular product by threatening to withhold supplies of a top-selling item. They demand that he buy more of this item than he can move in a month's time. To get his money out of his unnecessary inventory, the wholesaler will give retailers extra liquor, off the liquor invoice as long as the retailer buys a portion of the premium liquor. This violates several laws. The retailer may make the sale but not ring it up on his cash register and thereby avoid federal and state taxes. The wholesaler, who has paid the proper taxes on the products he has received, violates federal and state laws by keeping a second set of books which falsify his invoice orders to the retailer. (See Farberman, [32] for a similar instance in the auto industry.)

A second form of distiller-manufacturer behavior, which does not violate any specific laws but which openly deceives the customer, is the practice of multiple branding. In 1951 it was estimated that there were over 30,000 rival brands of whiskey on the national liquor market which were controlled by less than forty separate distillers. Single companies may have as many as fifty to one hundred brands. National Distillers markets ten brands of bourbon whiskey. Each of these brands appeals to a different clientele, yet is marketed by the same distiller. Abrahamson (1) reports that distillers believe that consumers have only the haziest notions of the differences among whiskeys. Accordingly, the more brands a distiller can offer, the greater the likelihood that he can capture a broader sector of the market. Immediately after prohibition, when the stock of aged whiskey was at an all-time low, blended whiskeys came on the market. In order to encourage the purchase of their products, distillers prefaced all their labels with the word "old"—thus Old Taylor, Old Rip Van Winkle, Old Charter, etc. (1).

Distillers create competing corporations within their own corporate structures, and while not informing the public of the variety of brands they market, they pit each corporation against the others. One international distiller has created seven such distinct marketing competitors. Although the executives within this corporation share the same office building, the same cocktail lounge, and the same sauna bath, they never meet directly and do not know one another socially.

Branding produces product identification, which is intended to produce self-identification on the part of the drinker. The distiller endeavors to cultivate drinkers who will purchase only prestige items, and through advertising campaigns they communicate the image that sophisticated individuals drink only the best gins, the oldest scotches, and the finest blended whiskeys. The distiller manipulates the drinker and attempts to maintain the illusion that certain brands continue to be distilled by the same families who originated the product in 1716 in Glasgow, Scotland. Most, if not all, original scotches and bourbons initially tied to specific families have long since been purchased by large-scale corporations who simply maintain the original brand name and label. In this way the distiller attempts to manipulate the self-images and social relationships of the drinker. His success is monitored each month; and at the end of each year, planning sessions are organized to further buttress these drinking identities of the consumer.

Quasi-tied houses represent a third form of distiller-brewer manipulation of the legal codes. While the three-tier model prohibits the intervention of the distiller-brewer in the actual sale of his product, informal agreements arise which tie taverns to brewers. This tie is made through the wholesaler, who does favors for tavern owners. They make special runs. They stop by up to three times a week to chat with tavern owners and managers. They fill special orders and also fix up special deals for favorite customers. The *norm of reciprocity* (40) is expected to operate. In return for special services, the tavern owner is expected not to solicit, or indulge in, the services of another distributor, even if his "tied" distributor cannot deliver the products he needs. This norm locks the tavern owner into a compromising and at times uneasy relationship with the wholesaler. The tavern owner must sell products to make a profit. Furthermore, brewers produce free frisbees, revolving clocks, wall calendars, monogrammed glasses, walk-in coolers and bar stools. The three-tier system does not operate as intended by the Twenty-first Amendment.

Distributors: These represent the weakest link in the three-tier model. They can be rejected by retailers, dualed, totally ignored, or find themselves without a contract from the distiller. They are in a poor bargaining position and are under constant pressure from the distiller. This leads them to deal directly with the retailer and the tavern owner. The greatest corruption appears at the wholesale-retail level, for retailers can turn elsewhere. Without distiller contracts, franchises and retail accounts, the wholesaler is out of business.

The Wall Street Journal (52) featured an article noting that kickbacks to retail stores seem common in New York City. They go on to note that at the wholesale level (a) salesmen carry cash from store to store to offer kickbacks to retailers; (b) wholesalers ship free loads of whiskey to retailers and account for the missing whiskey by reporting a warehouse theft; (c) wholesale firms list sales persons who receive high commissions, and these commissions go to retailers who patronize certain wholesale houses; (d) some wholesale houses print lists indicating the amount of kickback money that is available when a retailer purchases certain products; (e) street salesmen, under union contracts, receive a 3.4 percent of the gross sales to retail stores, bars and restaurants.

Participants in the wholesale industry denied the above charges, but a member of the New york state liquor authority remarked: "All of those guys [who founded the distribution firms] were in bootlegging—that's how they got into the wholesale liquor business." The article confirms observations made in the State of Illinois, namely,

> When prohibition was repealed in 1933, state governments considered applications for liquor-distribution licenses. And the people best prepared to enter the business were the ones already in it illegally.

Territorial violations represent a second form of illegal behavior on the part of the distributor. As noted above, they often cross one another's territory and make illegal sales. *Delinquent list manipulations* constitute a third semi-illegal act on the distributor's part. He can withhold a name from his delinquent list, re-buy overstocked products with his kickback fund, or extend illegal credit to a retailer or tavern owner by doctoring his invoice books.

Retailers who achieve sufficient size are in an enviable position, for they can control wholesalers and exert pressures through wholesalers back to the manufacturer. Some retailers bypass wholesalers and deal directly with the distiller—a direct violation of the Twenty-first Amendment. In one instance, a retailer virtually controls both a wholesale house and a distilling house. He buys outside his territory and refuses to permit his major distillers to deal with his chief local competitor. Should they deal with that individual, he threatens to cancel all contracts with the house in question. Retailers can be manipulated by wholesalers, as when a wholesaler unloads an undesirable product. Powerful retailers refuse wholesaler control and quite literally control the wholesaler. Retailers are in a direct position to violate the under-age drinking law; and they can also receive kickbacks from distillers and wholesalers. The retailer is the most entrepreneur-like and independent operator in the entire system, and is thereby most free to manipulate, deal and negotiate agreements that are in his own best interests. He is least likely to violate any clear-cut liquor laws.

Tavern owners violate the laws every day. They serve under-age drinkers and they fail to meet local building sanitation and wiring codes. They may make deals with wholesalers. Their violations come under the direct scrutiny of the local liquor commissions, and they are frequently monitored by police departments through raids and periodic checks.

The legal order: The federal and state monitoring of liquor laws and liquor violations is weak. In Illinois a six-person Liquor Control Commission consisting of a president, secretary and director, plus three adjunct members, oversees the operation of the state's liquor code. This commission is reappointed after each gubernatorial election and has a nine-member investigative team that covers the entire state. The federal government, except through the operations of the BAFT and FTC, which are understaffed, is also in a weak position to monitor violations of the liquor codes. The failure of the state and federal governments to cooperate has led to a situation that is currently being exploited by organized crime (55, 68).

At the *local level* corruption, payoffs, and conflicts of interest can be observed in any of the following areas: (1) license renewals; (2) license applications; (3) protection of licenses; (4) protection against raids; (5) alterations of zoning laws so "dry" areas can be converted into "wet" areas where new licenses can be awarded. When licenses are renewed, the applicant, by optional state law, is fingerprinted and asked if he (or she) or any member of his corporation has ever been convicted of a state or federal crime. The applicant must pay his license fee at the time he is fingerprinted. Local liquor commissioners often use this opportunity to remind the applicant that it is a special privilege to hold such a license.

Licenses can be suspended for up to thirty days by Illinois state law. At least one mayor over the past thirty years drove two tavern owners out of business because they refused to "protect" their licenses and because they "habitually" served under-age drinkers. In one instance a dry township was converted into a wet township (as negotiations were under way to establish a large out-of-town shopping center) when a construction worker moved into the dry township for one month. A construction firm set up a house trailer for him and paid all his expenses. He was the only resident of the township. At the end of the month he called for a referendum to vote the township wet. Since he was the only resident in the township, the vote carried. The owner of the construction firm was a local politician (field interviews, 1975).

Recapitulation

This discussion has attempted to apply an interactionist conception of organizational and relational behaviors to the multilayered worlds that make up the American liquor industry. The interrelationships among these orders, as set partly by historical contexts and partly as consequences of negotiations and access to negotiable commodities, have been identified. It has been suggested that this industry engages in corrupt, semi-legal and illegal behaviors and that these behaviors have roots that predate prohibition and the Eighteenth Amendment. This analysis has rediscovered what E. Sutherland (85) termed "white collar crime." We have identified—on the part of all or some participants in the liquor world—misrepresentations of financial statements, manipulations of stock holdings, commercial and personal bribery of public officials, misrepresentation of funds and products, and at times clear-cut instances of conflict of interest. The liquor industry, as Al Capone suggested, is a "legitimate racket."

The fact that we have identified such behaviors in an American industry should not be surprising; that it occurs in such a seemingly supervised and regulated industry is more difficult to explain.

CORRUPTION IN THE LIQUOR INDUSTRY: A COMPARISON OF MODELS

Corruption, or corruptive behavior, serves multiple functions, as Merton (62) and Smelser (77) have noted. Such activities meet needs that other institutions do not—like the bootlegger during prohibition. Corruption expresses certain attitudes, beliefs and values on the part of the public—e.g., to drink at social occasions or to expand a community's center of commercial activity.

The functional model assumes that there are deficiencies in a system which are known and consensually defined. Such a model has difficulty dealing with the situations confronted by the liquor industry immediately after repeal. A normalized system for legally producing alcoholic beverages was not legitimated. There was no apparent need for corruption to occur. Yet it did occur. Perhaps the functionalist emphasis on the systems level of analysis, with a relative neglect of the interactional and relational side of organizational, industrial and societal relations, accounts for its inability to fully explain the central role corruption and illegality played in the expansion of the liquor industry since 1934 (42, 43). Corruption and organizational crime, as witnessed in the liquor industry, serve to define the minimum and maximum boundaries of illegal behavior any society will tolerate. Corruptive acts, embedded in complex organizational procedures, serve no vital purposes for society at large. Such acts are entirely self-serving in nature. This assertion, which reverses the commonly held view of Durkheim (Matza [60]) suggests that organizations need societies if their corruption is to operate successfully. Societies, as complex arrangements between interacting individuals, become willing, but more often unwitting, participants in the illegal acts and activities of organizations.

The Twenty-first Amendment clarified the ambiguity for the liquor industry. It also presented the industry with a bewilderingly complex array of states and situations to contend with. However, this amendment provided the industry with the necessary legal information they could then use to manipulate the very system that had now made them legitimate. And, as noted earlier, they assisted in the writing of the laws that would regulate them. Corruption best operates in those situations where rules and guidelines are clear-cut, for the commodities in such situations are more easily assembled, bartered over and exchanged.

Facilitating Factors

The factors that facilitated the rapid growth of the industry after Repeal are as follows:

First, Repeal ushered in an attitude toward the temperate use of alcohol on the part of the liquor industry. This defused the forces of the Anti-Saloon League and produced a disinterested public who felt that the liquor industry was now under proper control. Second, relatively weak functionaries at the local, state and national levels were placed in control of the industry. Third, the laws that were brought into play were viewed as fair. The industry went along with this myth of fairness and permitted local tavern owners to take care of themselves. Fourth, when the industry was sanctioned, the sanctions failed to have any lasting effects at the local, state or national level. Fifth, when the industry did engage in behaviors of an illegal or semi-illegal nature they kept these behaviors to themselves. Sixth, the industry provided a product the public wanted and they did so with precision, speed and efficiency. Seventh, the tangible benefits of this new system were quickly realized and the industry endeavored to increase the numbers of the drinking population through the introduction of new brands, products, mixes and types of drinks. It produced the illusion that no member of the public was being ignored; they had something for everyone. Consequently, a relatively contented public and a legal bureaucracy permitted the industry to grow in any direction it chose to take.

Had the above conditions not been met, the days of prohibition would have reappeared and the industry would once again have been driven underground. Three conditions could have produced this destruction.

First, a fully informed and enraged public could have stopped repeal, or made repeal a slight variation of prohibition. Such a public did not come into being. Second, a public that remained outraged over the morality concerning alcohol, would, if present, have produced a rigidly controlled legal system (44). Third, the industry's abilities to corrupt and expand could have been controlled if a monopoly method of distribution had been universally adopted. This would have broken the link between the manufacturer, the wholesaler and the retailer and would have fit the highly workable system utilized in England (36). Instead, a set of officials, some subject to periodic election, took control of the system, and others were absorbed within complex governmental bureaucracies where their mandates were less than clear-cut.

These three conditions were not created and this in large part is a credit to the industry.

As a consequence of repeal, the industry skillfully found itself in the position of being the main monitor of its own behavior. It, not the government, filed taxes; it, not the government, filled out tax accounts; and it, not the government, filed delinquency lists. It vertically and horizontally integrated with great speed. The government made it accountable for the management, control and supervision of the very system the government had previously so carefully controlled and manipulated. This situation served to place in positions of control not only those who could be corrupted more easily (wholesalers), but it also placed those same individuals in a situation where they could corrupt those who were intended to control them—local, state, and national officials. As a result, the interactional consequences of the Twenty-first Amendment were to collapse or combine into one unit—the liquor industry—the essential ingredients of power, control and corruption. The industry took control over itself. While the public and government created the periodic illusion that the industry was under governmental control, this was illusion.

This situation placed a wedge between the members of the liquor industry, the public and the polity. As one moves from the local level to the state, regional, and national levels, the immediate problematics of the actual drinking transaction and the drinking act become less and less problematic. What emerges as problematic is the production, distribution, and sale of a single product—the alcoholic beverage. This, however bottled, branded, endorsed, packaged, priced or displayed, must somehow reenter the system where its last contender exited, be this the storeroom of the wholesaler, the shelves of the retailer, or the consumer's refrigerator. These two entities—one an actor, the other a product—constitute the essence of the American liquor industry. They must be brought together, over and over again, and American society has given the liquor industry the license and mandate to join those two commodities in a variety of ways. The industry controls itself, monitors itself, all the while giving the illusion that it is here to serve the public, at the behest of the federal government and in terms of the highest moral and legal standards. Such realization and success has seldom been achieved in other industries, for few have had to confront the range of problems faced by the liquor industry in 1934. Further case studies of an interactionist and comparative nature should serve to illuminate the processes by which an industrial complex manages to work itself into such a position of self-control.

CONCLUSION

The realities, illusions and productions of the complex organization constitute a fact of life for the member-participants of all contemporary industrialized societies. If the American liquor industry is representative of these organizational structures, then it can be argued that criminogenic behaviors are basic to the day-to-day behaviors of those individuals who constitute the essense and fabric of these organizational-economic sectors. Symbolic interactionism offers one framework to study and analyze this seldom examined element of everyday life.

FOOTNOTE

*An earlier version of this manuscript was presented to the third Annual Meeting of the Society for the Study of Symbolic Interaction, University of Missouri, Columbia, Missouri, April 5-7, 1976. This must be regarded as a preliminary analysis. Many of the theoretical, historical and economic formulations are grounded in less than satisfactory data.

**I am indebted to Patricia T. Clough for her assistance in collecting the historical documents and interviews which constitute the body of this analysis. Her assistance in conceptualization and problem formation is gratefully acknowledged, as are the comments and editorial suggestions of Evelyn K. Denzin, Sidney J. Kronus, William Cockerham, Stanley Cross, and Julian Simon. Portions of this research were supported by the Graduate College Research Board and the Department of Sociology of the University of Illinois, Urbana. Ethnographic data drawn from certain drinking establishments were gathered by graduate students in Sociology 415-416, a departmental research practicum. Their assistance is also acknowledged. Without the assistance and cooperation of the informants, whose names and organizational affiliations remain anonymous, this research could not have been conducted.

[1] Since the repeal of the Eighteenth Amendment the Distilled Spirits Council of the United States (DISCUS) has issued annual in-house statistical reports on the progress of the industry for DISCUS members. Statistical data may also be derived from annual reports of the U.S. Internal Revenue Service; the United States Brewers Association; the U.S. Treasury Department; the Licensed Beverage Industry; the Federal Alcohol Administration, Bureau of Alcohol, Tobacco and Firearms. (The BATF is primarily responsible for reporting the

illicit production, transportation and sale of "boot-leg" whiskey and is most active in those Southern states that are primarily "dry.")

In addition to the above data sources, each major distiller, brewer and wine producer generates his "in-house" monthly records on the sales of competitors, including shifting popularities in brands and sizes, as well as prices. These data are supplied from state sources, based on distiller-wholesaler reports, and are assembled by DISCUS. Marked confidential, they are for the use of DISCUS members only. These reports come out monthly. Since the repeal of prohibition and the Eighteenth Amendment in 1934, the Distilled Spirits Council of the United States has issued annual in-house reports on the progress of the industry for its members. By and large, the above cited studies draw their data from DISCUS-supplied documents.

Whether or not these data supplied by the distiller-wholesaler are accurate, inaccurate, or deliberately distorted is irrelevant. DISCUS members treat them as "real" social facts. Data supplied by the federal government are somewhat more accurate, for every bottled key of whiskey, scotch, or case of gin (for tax purposes) must be federally stamped by gallonage and date of storage. The above remarks are intended to establish one basic point. The data most central to any analysis of the past, present or future of the American liquor industry must confront the fact that most of the data will come from the industry.

REFERENCES

1. Albert Abrahamson, "Whiskey—Incidence of Public Tolerance in Price Policy," pp. 395–429 in Walton Hamilton and Associates, eds., *Price and Price Policies.* McGraw-Hill, New York, 1938.
2. E. B. Alderfer and H. E. Michl, *Economics of American Industry.* McGraw-Hill, New York, 1957.
3. Leland D. Baldwin, *Whiskey Rebels: The Study of a Frontier Uprising.* University of Pittsburgh Press, 1939.
4. Howard S. Becker, Blanche Geer, Everett C. Hughes, and Anselm L. Strauss. *Boys in White.* University of Chicago Press, 1961.
5. Daniel Bell, *The End of Ideology: On the Exhaustion of Political Ideas in the Fifties.* The Free Press, New York, 1960a.
6. ———, "The Breakup of Family Capitalism: On Changes in Class in America," pp. 37–42 in Daniel Bell, *The End of Ideology,* The Free Press, New York, 1960b.
7. ———, "Crime as an American Way of Life," pp. 115–136 in Daniel Bell, *The End of Ideology.* The Free Press, New York, 1960c.
8. ———, "The Racket-Ridden Longshoremen: The Web of Economics and Politics," pp. 159–190 in Daniel Bell, *The End of Ideology.* The Free Press, New York, 1960d.
9. J. Kenneth Benson, "The Interorganizational Network as a Political Economy," *Administrative Science Quarterly,* Vol. 20 (June 1975): 229–249.
10. Ralph L. Blankenship, *The Emerging Organization of a Community Mental Health Center,* unpublished doctoral dissertation, Department of Sociology, University of Illinois, Urbana.
11. Ralph L. Blankenship, "Organizational Careers: An Interactionist Approach." *Sociological Quarterly,* Vol. 14 (Winter 1973): 88–98.
12. Peter M. Blau, ed., *Approaches to the Study of Social Structure.* The Free Press, New York, 1975a.
13. ———, "Introduction: Parallels and Contrasts in Structural Inquiries," pp. 1–20 in Peter M. Blau, ed., *Approaches to the Study of Social Structure.* The Free Press, New York, 1975b.

14. Herbert Blumer, "Sociological Theory in Industrial Relations," *American Sociological Review*, Vol. 12, No. 3 (June 1947): 271–278.
15. ———, "Industrial Relations and the Laboring Class," *Sociological Quarterly*, Vol. 1, No. 1 (January 1960): 4–14.
16. ———, *Symbolic Interactionism*. Prentice-Hall, Englewood Cliffs, N.J., 1969.
17. Herbert Blumer, Talcott Parsons, and Jonathan H. Turner, "Exchange on Turner: 'Parsons as a symbolic interactionist,'" *Sociological Inquiry* Vol. 45, No. 1 (1975): 59–68.
18. Henry Bretzfield, *Liquor Marketing and Liquor Advertising: A Guide for Executives and Their Staffs in Management, Sales and Advertising*. Ablelard-Schuman, New York, 1955.
19. Sheri Cavan, *Liquor License*. Aldine, Chicago, 1966.
20. Patricia Clough, in process, *The Lantern: A Study of Middle Class Drinking Behaviors In a Public Place*. Doctoral dissertation, Department of Sociology, University of Illinois, Urbana.
21. Randall Collins, *Conflict Sociology*. Academic Press, New York, 1975.
22. Lewis A. Coser, ed., *The Idea of Social Structure: Papers in Honor of Robert K. Merton*. Harcourt Brace Jovanovich, New York, 1975.
23. Steven Cox, *Ideology, Negotiation and Emergent Organization: A Comparative Analysis*. Unpublished doctoral dissertation, Department of Sociology, University of Illinois, Urbana (1971).
24. *Daily Illini*, Vol. 105, No. 129 (March 31, 1976), Bob Weiss, "State Probes Beer Delivery," p. 1.
25. Melville Dalton, *Men Who Manage*. John Wiley, New York, 1959.
26. Norman K. Denzin, "The Methodological Implications of Symbolic Interactionism for the Study of Deviance," *British Journal of Sociology*, Vol. 25, No. 3 (September 1974): 269–282.
27. Distilled Spirits Council of the United States, Inc., *Summary of State Laws and Regulations Relating to Distilled Spirits*, 21st Edition. 1300 Pennsylvania Building, Washington, D.C.
28. Distilled Spirits Institute, Inc., Annual Report (1942–1949). National Press Building, Washington, D.C. (presented by year).
29. Fletcher Dobyns, *The Amazing Story of Repeal: An Exposé of the Power of Propaganda*. Willett, Clark & Company, Chicago–New York, 1950.
30. Raymond Durrell, "The Story of the DSI: Part 1: Repeal and the Blue Eagle Hatch the DSI," *Beverage Executive* (April 1, 1967): 1–4.
31. Ernest E. East, "The Distillers' and Cattle Feeders' Trust, 1887–1895, *Illinois State Historical Society Journal*, Vol. 45, No. 2 (Summer 1952): 101–123.
32. Harvey A. Farberman, "A Criminogenic Market Structure: The Automobile Industry," *Sociological Quarterly*, Vol. 16, No. 4 (Autumn 1975): 438–457.
33. R. E. L. Faris, ed., *Handbook of Modern Sociology*. Rand McNally, Chicago, 1964.
34. Dennis D. Fisher, "Coles Found Guilty of Tavern Owner Shakedowns," *Chicago Sun Times*, (March 1976): 8.
35. *Fortune Magazine* "Whiskey," Vol. 8, No. 5 (November 1933): 28–47; 112–131.
35a. ———, "Name, Schenley; Age, Three," Vol. 13, No. 5 (June 1936): 100–166.
35b. ———, "The Fortune Directory of the 300 Largest Industrial Corporations Outside the U.S. (August 1975): 155–162.
36. Raymond B. Fosdick and Albert L. Scott, with a Foreword by John D. Rockerfeller, Jr., *Toward Liquor Control*. Harper & Brothers, New York, 1933.
37. Barney G. Glaser and Anselm L. Strauss, *Awareness of Dying*. Aldine Publishing Company, Chicago, 1965.

37a. ———, *A Time for Dying*. Aldine Publishing Company, Chicago, 1968.
38. Erving Goffman, *Asylums*. Doubleday, Garden City, N.Y., 1961.
39. Alvin Gouldner, "Metaphysical Pathos and the Theory of Bureaucracy," *American Political Science Review,* Vol. 49 (1955); 496–507.
40. ———, "The Norm of Reciprocity: A Preliminary Statement," *American Sociological Review,* Vol. 25 (1960): 161–178.
41. ———, "Reciprocity and Autonomy in Functional Theory," pp. 241–270 in L. Gross, ed. *Symposium in Social Theory*. Harper & Row, New York, 1959.
42. Edward Gross, "Organizational Sources of Crime: A Theoretical Perspective, *"Social Problems Theory Division Newsletter,* The Society for the Study of Social Problems, No. 5 (Winter 1976a): 15–17.
43. ———, "Organizational Crime: A Theoretical Perspective," in manuscript (1976b.).
44. Joseph R. Gusfield, *Symbolic Crusade: Status Politics and the American Temperance Movement*. The University of Illinois Press, Urbana, 1963.
45. Walton Hamilton and Associates, *Price and Price Policies*. McGraw-Hill, New York, 1938.
46. ———, "The Affairs Called Industry," pp. 1–26 in Walton Hamilton and Associates, *Price and Price Policies*. McGraw-Hill, New York, 1938.
47. Yandell Henderson, *A New Deal for Liquor: A Plea for Dilution*. Doubleday, Doran, Garden City, N.Y., 1934.
48. Ira Horowitz and Ann R. Horowitz, "Firms in a Declining Market: The Brewing Case," *Journal of Industrial Economics,* Vol. 14, No. 2 (March 1965): 129–153.
49. ———, "Entropy, Markov Processes and Competition in the Brewing Industry," *Journal of Industrial Economics,* Vol. 16, No. 3 (July 1968): 196–211.
50. Walter W. Jennings, *A History of Economic Progress in the United States*. Thomas Y. Crowell Co., New York, 1926.
51. Frank Kane, *Anatomy of the Whiskey Business*. Lake House Press, Manhasset, N.Y., 1965.
52. Jonathon Kwitny, "Booze Business: Liquor and Corruption Are Drinking Buddies," *Wall Street Journal,* Vol. 55, no. 103 (March 11, 1975): 1–18.
53. E. E. LeMasters, *Blue-collar Aristocrats: Life-Styles at a Working Class Tavern*. University of Wisconsin Press, Madison, 1975.
54. *Liquor Handbook,* Gavin-Jobson Associates, Inc., New York: 1975.
55. *Liquor Store Magazine,* Vol. 81, no. 1 (July 1974).
56. ———, Vol. 81, no. 4 (October 1974).
57. Norton E. Long, "The Local Community as an Ecology of Games," *American Journal of Sociology* Vol. 44 (1958): 251–261.
58. A. N. Martin, Jr., and E. E. McCleish, *State Liquor Legislation,* Vol. 4. Prepared by the Marketing Laws Survey. U. S. Government Printing Office, Washington, 1941.
59. Wilfred B. W. Martin, *The Negotiated Order of the School*. Macmillian of Canada, Montreal, 1976.
60. David Matza, *Becoming Deviant,* Prentice-Hall, Englewood Cliffs, N.J., 1969.
61. Robert K. Merton, "Structural Analysis in Sociology," pp. 21–52 in Peter M. Blau, ed., *Approaches to the Study of Social Structure,"* The Free Press, New York, 1975.
62. ———, *Social Theory and Social Structure,* rev. and enlarged ed., The Free Press, New York, 1957.
63. Charles Merz, *The Dry Decade*. Doubleday, Garden City, N.Y., 1930.
64. Alfred R. Oxenfeldt, *Industrial Pricing and Market Practices*. Prentice-Hall, Inc., Englewood Cliffs, N.J., 1951. (Chap. 9, "Case Studies as Summary and Synthesis: Whiskey Prices: 447–488).

65. David J. Pittman and Charles Synder, eds., *Society, Culture, and Drinking Patterns.* John Wiley, New York: 1962.
66. Julian B. Roebuck and Wolfgang Frese, *The Rendevezous: A Case Study of an After-Hours Club.* The Free Press, New York, 1975.
67. Morris Victor Rosenbloom, *The Liquor Industry: A Survey of its History, Manufacture, Problems of Control and Importance.* Ruffsdale Distilling Company, Braddock, Pa.: 1935.
68. Jonathan Rubenstein, *City Police.* Farrar, Straus and Giroux, New York, 1973.
69. Paul A. Samuelson, *Economics.* 7th ed. McGraw-Hill, New York, 1967.
70. W. Richard Scott, "Organizational Structure," pp. 1–20 in Alex Inkeles, James Coleman and Neil Smelser, eds., *Annual Review of Sociology,* Vol. 1. Annual Reviews, Inc., Palo Alto, Calif., 1975.
71. Phillip Selznick, "Foundations of the Theory of Organizations," *American Sociological Review,* Vol. 13 (1948): 25–35.
72. Julian L. Simon, "The Price Elasticity of Liquor in the U.S.: And a Simple Method of Determination," *Econometrics,* Vol. 34, No. 1 (January 1966a): 193–205.
73. ———, "The Economic Effects of State Monopoly of Packaged-Liquor Retailing," *The Journal of Political Economy,* Vol. 74, No. 2 (April 1966b): 188–194.
74. ———, "The Effect of Advertising on Liquor Brand Sales," *Journal of Marketing Research* Vol. 6 (August 1969b): 301–313.
75. Andrew Sinclair, *Era of Excess: A Social History of the Prohibition Movement.* Harper & Row, New York, 1964. First Harper Colophon edition, first published in 1962 by Little, Brown under the title *Prohibition: The Era of Excess.*
76. Mark Singer, *Careers, Negotiations and Ideology in Two Treatment Settings,* unpublished doctoral dissertation, Department of Sociology, University of Illinois, Urbana.
77. Neil J. Smelser, "Stability, Instability, and the Analysis of Political Corruption," pp. 7–29 in Bernard Barber and Alex Inkeles, eds., *Stability and Change: A Volume in Honor of Talcott Parsons.* Little, Brown, Boston, 1971.
78. James P. Spradely and Brenda J. Mann, *The Cocktail Waitress: Woman's Work in a Man's World.* John Wiley, New York, 1975.
79. *Statistical Abstracts of the United States,* 95th annual edition, Washington, D.C. 1974, p. 226.
80. Barry M. Staw and Eugene Szawjkowski, "The Scarcity-Munificence Component of Organizational Environments and the Commission of Illegal Acts," *Administrative Science Quarterly,* Vol. 20 (September 1975): 345–354.
81. Gregory P. Stone, "Drinking Styles and Status Arrangements," pp. 121–140 in David J. Pittman and Charles Synder, eds., *Society, Culture and Drinking Patterns.* John Wiley, New York, 1962.
82. Anselm Strauss, *Negotiations and Negotiated Orders* (in process).
83. ———, *Psychiatric Ideologies and Institutions.* The Free Press, New York, 1964.
84. Anselm Strauss, Leonard Schatzman, Danuta Ehrlich, Rue Bucher, and Melvin Sabshin, "The Hospital and Its Negotiated Order," pp. 147–169 in Eliot Freidson, ed., *The Hospital in Modern Society.* The Free Press, New York, 1963.
85. Edwin H. Sutherland, "White-Collar Criminality," *American Sociological Review,* Vol. 5, No. 1. (February 1940): 1–12.
86. Frederick M. Switzer, *The Three-Tier System of Distribution in the Wine and Spirits Industry.* Wine and Spirits Wholesalers of America, Inc., St. Louis, 1975.
87. J. D. Thompson and William J. McEwen. "Organizational goals and environment: goal-setting as an interaction process." *American Sociological Review.* Vol. 23: 23–31.

88. Jonathan H. Turner, *The Structure of Sociological Theory*. Homewood, Ill.: Dorsey, 1974.
89. *United States Industrial Outlook: 1975–1980*. U.S. Printing Office, Washington, D.C. 1975.
90. Clark Warburton, *The Economic Results of Prohibition*. Columbia University Press, New York, 1932.

A SOCIAL WORLD
PERSPECTIVE*

Anselm Strauss, UNIVERSITY OF CALIFORNIA

Since the early days of Chicago-style interactionism, the term "social worlds" has been used sporadically, sometimes descriptively (1, 3, 7), rarely conceptually (4, 5). The best known, though brief, discussion of social worlds as such is by Tomatsu Shibutani who, in arguing the collective and communicative aspects of reference groups, suggested four aspects of social worlds (4). Each social world is a "universe of regularized *mutual response.*" "Each is an *arena* in which there is a kind of organization." Also each is a *"cultural area,"* its boundaries being "set neither by territory nor formal membership but by the limits of effective *communication.*" (my emphasis.)

Before following through on Shibutani's provocative and rather overlooked discussion, I want to underline what this paper is designed to do. Primarily its purpose is to argue that a focus on, and study of, social

Studies in Symbolic Interaction—Volume 1, 1978, pages 119–128.

worlds might provide a means for better understanding the processes of social change. Beginning with some assertions about what I believe are some strengths and weaknesses of the interactionist tradition, I shall then outline several features of social worlds, including some of their implications. In the final pages, the main argument will be taken up again. Of course, many issues attending the idea of social worlds will be ignored or skipped over lightly, although I plan to address them in future publications.

Among the greatest strengths of the Chicago tradition, especially as developed by Thomas and Park, is its central focus on the problems of social change, with concomitant emphasis on large-scale interaction—the history of group conflict and encounter—as setting the most significant limits for social action (2). The earliest generation of interactionists tended to think that the most significant group encounters involved ethnic, racial and nationalistic groups. Their style of conceptualization was national or international in scope, although studies were also made on smaller terrain. Later generations have tended to focus on smaller territories and looked especially at professional, occupational and deviant groups while retaining the conflict-encounter aspect so characteristic of interactionism. Given the range of potentially significant group encounters in the contemporary world, the interactionist choice of encounters seems unnecessarily restrictive.

This tradition is also strongly antideterministic, emphasizing the creative potential of individuals and groups acting in the face of social limitations. Creativity is not seen as untrammeled; nevertheless, social limitations are viewed in terms of potential for human action. I concur with that tradition wholeheartedly and with the implication that sociologists need to study processes. Again, though, the range of processes thought to be significant in how people are shaped by (and *shape*) their societies seems to have been unduly narrowed.

A third theme in interactionism is found in Mead, whose views of social change and communication signify an enormous, unlimited and ceaseless proliferation of functioning groups which are not necessarily clearly boundaried or tightly organized. Mead's views of society seem analytically underdeveloped (in contrast, certainly, to his social psychology) and tied to his commitment to civilizational evolution. There is no reason why we cannot view some groups as contributing to what he termed the widening scope of consciousness, while seeing that some groups do not do so. Likewise, while some proliferate and expand, other groups contract and die—even the ones we ourselves might name as progressive. The Meadian emphasis on the endless formation of universes of discourse—with which groups are coterminous—is extremely valuable, yielding a metaphor of groups emerging, evolving, developing, splintering, disintegrating or pulling themselves together, or parts of them falling away and perhaps coalescing with segments of other groups to form new groups, in opposition, often, to the old.

In short, I am suggesting that this Meadian "fluidity" and the interactionists' general emphases on antideterminism and group encounter at any scale or scope be worked through for its implications, rather than restricted to certain kinds of groups of processes, and certainly not restricted to "micro" or "macro" studies of these matters. I believe that one means for doing that job is to study worlds and to take "a social world perspective."

Many worlds produce literatures or generate commentary by social scientists and, of course, aspects of many are studied by social scientists (the gay world, the world of the taxi dancer). But we have not developed a general view of social worlds as a widespread, significant phenomenon, nor have we developed a program for studying them systematically. Nor do we have an adequate appreciation of what a social world perspective might signify for classical sociological issues. There is also too little awareness of the significance for interactionism itself of social world analysis.

Now, before following through on Shibutani's implicit directives for studying social worlds, let us look at them ostensively, so that they do not fade into a misty nothingness, in contrast to seemingly hard realities like formal organizations with clear boundaries and known memberships. Though the idea of social worlds may refer centrally to universes of discourse, we should be careful not to confine ourselves to looking merely at forms of communication, symbolization, universes of discourses, but also examine palpable matters like activities, memberships, sites, technologies, and organizations typical of particular social worlds.

Ostensively, there are countless discernible worlds: those of opera, baseball, surfing, stamp collecting, country music, homosexuality, politics, medicine, law, mathematics, science, Catholicism. . . . Some worlds are small, others huge; some are international, others local. Some are inseparable from given spaces; others are linked with sites but are much less spatially identifiable. Some are highly public and publicized; others are barely visible. Some are so emergent as to be barely graspable; others are well established, even well organized. Some have relatively tight boundaries; others possess permeable boundaries. Some are very hierarchial; some are less so or scarcely at all. Some are clearly class-linked, some (like baseball) run across class. But note that the activities and communications within these worlds focus differentially around matters intellectual, occupational, political, religious, artistic, sexual, recreational, scientific; that is, social worlds are characteristic of any substantive area.

One can pick up any newspaper or magazine and read of the social worlds about us. Recently an avant-guard composer and promoter, Pierre Boulez, was visiting at Stanford where a group of musicians and engineers are working on methods of great importance for his French-based group. Soon, other musicians and engineers, from everywhere, will doubtless be visiting him at his new center in Paris (also a central site in the world of contemporary music). *Science* reported that 5,000 scientists and technicians, representing a host of disciplines "from 72 countries, aided by 1000 land stations, 40 ships, 12 aircraft, and 6 satellites [recently] were engaged in a coordinated research effort, spread over 20 million square miles" in an enterprise attempting "to understand the workings of the tropical atmosphere." In all of that, of course, organizations were involved, but so, in vital ways, were representatives of social worlds and subworlds. To quote *Science,* "overall [this] has been an impressive sample of cooperative big science at its best, an auspicious first step for the Global Atmospheric Research Program." Similar phenomena occur in areas far distant from science or music and are present in virtually every substantive area. The customary social science perspectives and concepts of formal organizations hardly do justice to those enterprises and evolving structures.

In each social world, at least one primary *activity* (along with related clusters of activity) is strikingly evident; i.e., climbing mountains, researching, collecting. There are *sites* where activities occur: hence space and a shaped landscape are relevant. *Technology* (inherited or innovative modes of carrying out the social world's activities) is always involved. Most worlds evolve quite complex technologies. In social worlds at their outset, there may be only temporary divisions of labor, but once under way, *organizations* inevitably evolve to further one aspect or another of the world's activiities.

These features of social worlds can be converted analytically into subprocesses; for instance, site finding, funding, protecting, competing for sites. Technological innovation, manufacturing, marketing, and the teaching of technical skills are also evident. Organizational building, extending, defending, invading, taking over, and converting also occur. The discovery and study of such subprocesses and of their relationships, including conflictful and "power" relationships, are essential parts of research into social worlds.

Two other major processual features seem inevitable and immensely consequential. First, social worlds *intersect,* and do so under a variety of conditions. Where services are needed, technology is borrowed and technical skills are taught and learned. Where other worlds impinge (as when worldly action is questioned as harmful or illegitimate or inappropriate), alliances are deemed useful. Thus, a major analytic task is to discover such intersecting and to trace the associated processes, strategies and consequences. As examples, I mention only the discovering of seemingly relevant other worlds; of intersectional advocacy by bridging agents; and of the penetrating of subworlds by servicing agents, cover agents, and even in a certain sense by clients.

Analysis can become very complicated because of a second important process, the *segmenting* of social worlds. Most seem to dissolve, when scrutinized, into congeries of subworlds. Indeed a processual view leads quickly to the understanding that these activities result in a never-ending segmenting. Some of the contributing conditions pertain to the evolution of technology, to differential experiences within the world, to the evolution of new generations of members, to the recruitment of new kinds of members, and to the impinging of other worlds. This segmenting leads to the intersecting of *specifiable subworlds*. Intersecting, in other words, occurs usually not between global worlds but between segments. Such subworld formation signifies not only new activities, sites, technologies, and organizations, but also signifies new universes of discourse.

Intersection and segmentation imply that we are confronting a universe marked by tremendous fluidity; it won't and can't stand still. It is a universe where fragmentation, splintering, and disappearance are the mirror images of appearance, emergence, and coalescence. This is a universe where nothing is strictly determined. Its phenomena should be partly determinable via naturalistic analysis, including the phenomenon of men participating in the construction of the structures which shape their lives.

The social world perspective yields the usual interactionist vision of a universe often bafflingly amorphous. But this perspective has analytic thrust and implicit directives. Here are additional concepts and some related research questions.

At first blush, anyone who is *in* a world (or subworld) is associated with its activities. But some are thought to be (or think of themselves as being) more authentically of that world, more representative of it. *Authenticity* seems to pertain to the quality of action, as well as to judgments of which acts are more essential (6). So there are analytic questions about who decides (or which organizations decide) which members are more authentic and via what social mechanisms? Who has the "power" to authenticate? and how? and why? Do the subprocesses include sponsoring, launching, assigning, placing, licensing? Is not coaching an important subprocess pertaining to the giving of competence and sponsorship? Power features need to be spelled out but presumably include the allocating, assigning, and depriving of resources. Basic processes like segmenting cut across authenticating; thus, people will form a new subworld because newcomers are flooding into the old one (or aren't allowed in or all the way in, like the impressionist painters). The development of new styles and canons of authenticity can be noted. Also, within the larger world, organizations or subworlds, not just persons, may compete for claimed and awarded authenticity (Harvard? The Wisconsin Department of X?). Nonauthenticating processes (like excommunication) and strategies evolve ("it's not research; it has no statistics"). Some activities and products of activities can be discounted as nonauthentic. This raises questions about near fakes, downright fakes, and production only of the "real stuff" as well as the manipulation or perspective of differential audiences and markets. Out on the symbolic margins are the arts and products which raise debates about the authentic boundaries of the social world. Is conceptual art really art? Is the trimarin really a sailboat? Some people are defenders of a world's "shape"; others wish to change the shape.

Socialization is associated not only with degrees and kinds of authenticity but also with how people enter and leave social worlds and subworlds. Rather than looking simply at organizational mechanisms such as recruitment, we should also be looking at how people get contacted by, encounter, rub up against, introduced to, drawn into, and hooked on social worlds. What is the role of "accident," of networks of acquaintances and friends in the hooking, explaining, wising up, plugging in, and coaching for this process? What is the part played by formal and informal coaches, scouts, and sponsors? Most socialization theory assumes *de novo* entry, but probably most social world and subworld entries involve *orbiting* processes; i.e., moving from one to another, retaining both or dropping the original, plus simultaneous memberships. Hence, there is a calculus of compatibility, neutrality, and incompatibility. This stands in relation of ease of movement, to probability of remaining, to marginality and to experienced nonauthenticity.

Within each social world, various issues are debated, negotiated, fought out, forced and manipulated by representatives of implicated subworlds. These *arenas* involve political activity but not necessarily legislative bodies and courts of law. Issues are also fought out within subworlds by their members. Representatives of other subworlds (same and other worlds) may also enter into the fray. Some of these social world issues may make front-page news, but others are known only to members or to other interested parties. Social world media are full of such partially invisible arenas. Wherever there is intersecting of worlds and subworlds, we can expect arenas to form along with their associated political processes. And can we view organizational evolution and change in terms of such processes?

As for the larger public issues (what to do about pollution or alcoholism), there the sociologist needs to ask not only which social worlds are represented in the larger arena but also which segments of which social world. Furthermore, to *what other* (internal world) arenas is representation in this (multiple world) arena interrelated? The multiple-world issues do not get settled independently of the larger context of internal-world political activities. This phenomenon is not adequately taken into account in current theories of public opinion formation nor in political sociology.

Organizations are commonly viewed as relatively closed in their boundaries, and there are few good analyses of interorganizational relations. The social world perspective tells us that some organizations are relatively embedded within a social world, while others stand at intersections, indeed may have been intentionally constructed that way. The understanding of organizational evolution, change, and functioning requires an examination of relations embedded in the same or intersecting worlds. Some and possibly most organizations can be viewed as arenas wherein members of various subworlds or social worlds stake differential claims, seek differential ends, engage in contests, and make or break alliances in order to do the things they wish to do. Organizational theory which ignores these considerations is likely to sell us very short.

Social movements are not features merely of explicitly political or religious realms—what our sociological literature on movements is mostly about—but are features of all social worlds. There are movements, as we all recognize, in architecture, in painting, in poetry, certainly in the academic disciplines, and probably in ship building and in banking, too. Many movements, of course, spill over to engage or affect other worlds and generally result in new organizations or affect old ones. Historians and the acting natives give us ample data, but we need analyses.

Other phenomena probably can be usefully reconceptualized in terms of social worlds. Thus *fashions* flourish in every world, so their appearance and disappearance should surely be studied in relation to social world processes. The concept of *careers* needs to be expanded also. Careers are not simply organizational or occupational in character; many if not most are pursued and promoted within the context of specifiable social worlds. The cosmopolitan/local dichotomy reflects such considerations but is overly simple.

Mass-circulation magazines may either appeal to very large social worlds or to the members of multiple worlds. In contrast, the magazines of most social worlds or subworlds never reach the newsstands—or the desks of scholarly experts on the mass media. The total American readership of these world-specific magazines must be enormous, even without mentioning the readerships in other industrialized nations. Even casual scrutiny of an in-world medium suggests its many functions: giving technical tips and instructions; teaching how to minimize danger while pursuing worldly activities; promoting or giving information about sites, upcoming events, advertising various items; reporting on past events; and disseminating information and opinions about topical world issues. The readership for any social world is neither a discrete aggregate of people who never talk together about what they have read, nor is it a group of people who are passive to what they read. Indeed, the very smorgasbord coverage of subworlds suggests that readers will be highly selective and actively responsive in their reading. The social world perspective reminds us that their participants may bring active perception and judgment as well as a great deal of knowledge and even study to the events of their social worlds. Furthermore, the spectators of many events, including sports events, themselves are or have been active in such activities. They are not all strangers to it or lending a casual eye to it. They may even be "scouting the act" for cues as to how to improve their own performances.

What does this social world perspective signify not only for interactionism but also for any style of sociology that rests on some of the same assumptions and has some of the same aims? The following points pertain fairly directly to the discussion of interactionists' strengths/weaknesses touched on earlier.

1. Social worlds can be studied at any scale, from the smallest (say a local world, on local space) to the very largest (in size or geographic spread). The commitment is to study social worlds across many scales with emphasis upon worlds which are substantively different yet intersect on a broad scale with other social worlds.

2. The interactionists insist on the importance of process as central to the study of social worlds. The above pages should make it evident that it is difficult to think about worlds without considering processual issues. In fact, examination of specific worlds or subworlds tends to force one's focus on the characteristically salient processes. Thus, for exploding worlds like tennis, these include the processes attending the increased numbers of participants, the growth of spectator crowds (including those watching TV matches), the increased visibility of the world, and the management of celebrity careers. For the subworld of recombinant genetics, salient processes include both external threats as well as internal responses to that threat. The process of a recent increase in public visibility has produced a fear that external agencies will gain control over the subject matter of this subworld. The process of internal response will likely take the form of attempts to ward off or minimize external regulation. While I am not overlooking the possibility that processes can be discovered independent of a focus on social worlds, the social world perspective makes processual study virtually mandatory. As the previous

examples illustrate, it also puts processes in alignment with the structural features of the particular social worlds under scrutiny.

3. The interactionist tradition, in common with other sociology, has tended to focus on contemporary life while either avoiding history or using it as a backdrop for the analysis of ongoing organizations and processes. Indeed, the split between historical and contemporary (mainly fieldwork) research is particularly glaring in the instance of interactionism, which inherits a distinction between (and continues to keep separate) the areas of collective behavior/social movements and areas like professions/occupations and work (2). Studies of social worlds train our attention on the history of that social world; that is, what are its origins, where is it now, what changes has it undergone, and where does it seem to be moving? Is it evolving, disintegrating, splintering, collaborating, coalescing?

4. The antideterministic stance of interactionism, though not insured, is not at all threatened by a social world focus. However, we need not make hidden assumptions about whether the social worlds under study are contributing to "progress" or not. If we do wish to assume that, then we must spell out their nature and the associated criteria by which "progress" or lack of it can be judged. (I say that because much of the interactionism, and indeed sociology in general, does proceed on such hidden assumptions. When interactionists do that, they break the interactional frame—and they do this with some frequency [2].)

A consistent interactionism, with its dual emphasis upon group constraints as well as group/individual creativity, will ask appropriate questions about social worlds. These will surely include the more obvious one concerning how segments are formed and enter into collaborative new enterprise with other segments. Less obvious questions include how members of some worlds or subworlds struggle against severe social constraints. These constraints include the employment of insidious institutionalized canons of legitimacy and authority as well as the continual threat and occasional use of force, excommunication, and other coercive means.

5. I have little to suggest about the methodological thrust of social world research. However, there should be much supplementation to the interactionist reliance on fieldwork and interviewing with the focused use of historical and contemporary documentation. An understanding of the arenas within which large-scale public opinion is fought must embrace a comprehension of the elements of opinion formation within the smaller interactional worlds which form that larger arena. Our research methods must capture both levels of interaction as well as reflect its full historical development, diversity, and sweep. The social world perspective, because it asks new questions, literally demands new methods (the evolu-

tion of public opinion that led to an environmental regulatory agency illustrates this range of issues). (Cf [8])

6. This perspective also urges us to build general theory about social worlds rather than merely to aim at substantive research on particular ones. Some research, at least, should be done on the basis of emerging theory; that is, with cognizance of theoretical sampling and of the universe of others similarly working on social world phenomena. At the very least, sampling of worlds and subworlds in accordance with the Weberian idea of the historical movement should be considered. Which social worlds are likely to be viewed by later generations as the levers of history? In the 1970s, will it be genetics, high-energy physics, underwater geography-geology, computerization, or international banking? Or, should the question more properly be formulated as which levers of which histories—and whose histories—are we considering?

*The heart of this paper was given as a keynote address to the Society for the Study of Symbolic Interaction, August 1976. The beginning and ending pages are new.

REFERENCES

1. Paul G. Cressey, *The Taxi-Dance Hall,* University of Chicago Press, 1932.
2. Berenice Fisher and Anselm Strauss, "Thomas, Park and Their Successors." *Symbolic Interaction.* In press.
3. Robert Park, *Human Communities,* Free Press, Glencoe, Ill., 1952.
4. Tomatsu Shibutani, "Reference Groups as Perspectives," *American Journal of Sociology* 60 (1955): 522–529.
5. Anselm Strauss, *Mirrors and Masks,* Free Press, New York: 1958, reprinted San Francisco, Sociology Press, 1969.
6. Barbara Suczek, *The World of Greek Dancing,* doctor's thesis, Department of Social and Behavioral Sciences, University of California, San Francisco, 1977.
7. Carol A. Warren, *Identity and Community in the Gay World,* Wiley, New York, 1974.
8. Carolyn Wiener, *Drunken Power: The Politics of Alcoholism,* doctor's thesis, Department of Social and Behavioral Sciences, University of California, San Francisco, 1973.

TOWARD A SYMBOLIC INTERACTIONIST THEORY OF LEARNING: A RAPPROCHEMENT WITH BEHAVIORISM*

Edward Gross, UNIVERSITY OF WASHINGTON

Abstract. The author outlines the shape of a symbolic interactionist theory of learning, giving special attention to the role of motives and sequences. He argues further that most of the claims for behaviorism, of the Skinnerian variety, turn out to be assimilable to a symbolic theory. In particular the role of reinforcement and reward may be seen as reducible to incentives and cognitive elements in a symbolic theory. The explanatory value of the theory is hence considerably enhanced.

For the most part symbolic interactionists have given little attention to the phenomenon of learning. This is in striking contrast to the enormous amount of attention that the subject receives on the part of psychologists (12). The word "learning" turns up in the symbolic interactionist literature, of course, but for the most part its use tends to be vague, or else it is employed in an everyday manner. Actual discussions of learning usually

Studies in Symbolic Interaction—Volume 1, 1978, pages 129–145.

occur in connection with the broader topic of socialization, but here again the attention is much less extensive than is found by the psychologist (33). For example, Becker's (4) classic discussion of becoming a marijuana user is often cited as an illustration of the symbolic interactionist approach to learning, and indeed Becker uses the term. He says:

> The first step in the sequence of events that must occur if the person is to become a user is that he must learn to use the proper smoking technique in order that the use of the drug will produce some effects in terms of which his conception of it can change (p. 414).

After describing the process Becker concludes,

> A person, then, cannot begin to use marijuana for pleasure, or continue its use for pleasure, unless he learns to describe its effects as enjoyable, unless it becomes and remains an object which he conceived of as capable of producing pleasure (p. 421).

However, Becker does not tell us *how* persons learn other than merely to assert that it takes place. The best that he offers is the claim that there is some process of imitation or modeling that is involved. He refers to the words of another smoker who instructs the first one, telling him that he should hold the smoke in the lungs for a period of time. The matter is not described any further. Presumably if the person follows instructions and experiences some pleasure, then that is the end of the matter. There is no implication here that practice is necessary nor any notion of how much practice, or whether one form of practice may be better than another. Although there are hints, the matter is certainly not discussed systematically.

Rose (21) is one of the few symbolic interactionists that give particular attention to it, but even he passes over the subject by simply claiming that symbolic learning is relatively easy, and therefore presumably requires little explanation. He writes:

> Through tests with readings or lectures using new material, it has been found that a normal, alert person can learn over a hundred new meanings in the space of an hour, that most of this new learning can be retained for weeks without reinforcement. In most human learning involving trial and error (except for learning manual skills), it has been found that only one failure is enough to inhibit the false response, and usually one success is enough to affix the correct response—unlike trial and error learning among other animals, where many failures and successes are necessary to fix the new correct response (p. 9).

Rose's claim can certainly be disputed by persons who have attempted to learn foreign languages, and in any case, he makes an unfair comparison between trial-and-error learning among animals, which after all typically involves some type of muscular activity, and symbolic learning in humans. Humans seem to experience just as much difficulty in learning muscular skills as do other animals. Nor does Rose explain why it is that symbolic learning apparently is so quick. For that matter, errorless learning has also been demonstrated among pigeons, the favorite experimental animal of the behaviorists (31). Shibutani (25) takes a similarly casual view of learning, equating it to a functional matter of solving problems in a "gratifying" manner, a theory which seems little different from that of the behaviorists.

I should note in passing that these rather casual views of learning have something quite contrary to the spirit of symbolic interactionism about them, for they seem to imply that the person is himself a relatively passive part of the whole process, that he just sits there, as it were, and things are done to him or things happen to him relatively easily. There is no picture suggested here of a struggling, puzzling, uncertain self at work (33).

The writer feels further that it is particularly important for the symbolic interactionists to advance their own theory of learning since the behaviorists appear to have taken the area over and to have made quite exaggerated claims for their version of the stimulus-response approach. Particularly disturbing is the conversion of a number of sociologists to this approach and their attempts to apply it quite broadly (1, 6, 24). It is ironic that the sociologists appear to be excited by this scheme at the very time when psychologists are beginning to question it, although, of course, a number of enthusiasts remain committed to it. A number of phenomena appear to present insoluble problems to the behaviorists, particularly the concept of reinforcement (5). More to the point, the Skinnerians, particularly the more enthusiastic among them, can be shown to be backing, unknowingly, into symbolic interactionist theory (16), as I shall suggest later in the paper, for I believe that a symbolic interactionist theory will explain much, though not all of their work, better than they do and a lot besides.

THE SHAPE OF A SYMBOLIC INTERACTIONIST THEORY OF LEARNING

What then would a symbolic interactionist theory of learning look like? We may begin with Dewey and Bentley's famous aphorism: "To name is to know" (29). The claim here is that learning requires the identification of something as a social object and that this is often facilitated if the object is given a name. Thus Becker, in the article referred to earlier, tells us that the budding marijuana smoker must learn to recognize what a "high" is, that is, he is unable really to attain one until he is able to give this name to sensations which he is experiencing. So, too, the classic discussion of Helen Keller, it will be recalled. deals with her first realization that objects have names. Strauss (29) in discussing the conversion of persons to communism in China mentions the importance of a new vocabulary which is taught to the candidates that enables them to reevaluate objects and events and to reinterpret their familiar world. So, too, the practice of teaching a mathematical proof by breaking it down into a number of recognizable, and even named, steps is familiar to all of us.

Without denying the importance of naming and giving names in learning, we see immediately that this approach leaves important gaps. First, it is immediately evident that there are other kinds of symbols than names, and these too are quite as important as names in learning. An obvious example is music, which has its own complex symbol system which is not translatable into words and where the names, such as the names of the notes, contribute very little to one's ability to handle that symbol system. It is also a remarkable fact to which relatively little attention has been paid, in my judgment, that music itself is often learned much more rapidly than other symbol systems. Indeed, as all teachers know, one of the fastest ways by which a child may learn a poem is to set the poem to music. We may expand the Dewey and Bentley notion, then, to say not simply that "to name is to know," but rather "to symbolize is to know."

But even this extension is not completely satisfactory, for there appear to be no consensually validated ways to symbolize a great many events and situations that are learned, nevertheless. Thus, in the learning of mathematical proofs, many algorithms are involved that contain steps to which no name can be given other than simply to call them Step 1 or Step 2. Although one can often claim that calling something Step 1 or Step 2 is giving it a name and that the person eventually learns a collection of items that seem to go together, there is something missing in this explanation which all of us can remember from our difficulties in learning mathematics in school. There is something that goes on which enables us to think of something as a step, and the naming of it does not really seem to help. Sometimes what is going on, in my judgment, is that calling something a step refers really to a sequence of some sort which one is told one must follow, and therefore the step procedure refers, rather, to the way the material has been organized. There is something here that is closely related to the learning of muscular skills in which a sequence is essential, but the naming of the sequence is not the critical matter except as it aids one to perform the activity in the needed order. Once the activity has been learned, the steps vanish, and a smooth performance is expected and essential. Indeed, it can be claimed that if a person must proceed by steps, he has not learned it, and the activity may not take place at all. Further, there is no question that a good many activities are learned without any awareness of names or indeed symbols, as in Piaget's (19) concept of the "operation." In one of his famous tests showing that a child has moved from the sensorimotor stage to the pre-operational stage, a glass of liquid is poured from a short, fat glass into a tall, thin glass. The child is then asked whether there is more or less liquid in the taller glass. Piaget believes that an essential stage in the child's cognitive development occurs when the child recognizes that the amount of liquid is the same in both glasses. He sees this as what he calls an "operation," a term he uses to refer to reversible processes. In this case the child could regenerate the amount in the original glass by simply pouring from the tall glass back into the short, fat glass and discovering that the amounts are the same. Yet all of this takes place, Piaget maintains, at a very young age (one and a half to two years) at which the child's ability to symbolize, let alone name, is still at a very primitive stage.

Finally, identifying learning with naming and symbolizing does not seem to be enough. There are no motives involved. The approach seems, then, to be overly cognitive, as if there is some inevitable imprinting on the brain or the self that results directly from merely naming or pointing to something. One can certainly learn names and symbols by pointing, but such an operation, while it surely takes place, does not explain *why* one learns names or symbols. Hence it is surely insufficient, although it is a necessary element in a learning theory. It should be recognized, too, that merely learning names does not deal with what is perhaps the central feature of learning, and that is that elements are related to one another. Learning *begins* by giving names to objects. It is essential for many kinds of learning, although not all. But of course, what is learned are relationships among the symbols, and the mere calling of attention to the fact that symbols are involved does not explain this relationship or how different kinds of symbols come to be connected to one another.

We therefore point out at the outset that a symbolic interactionist theory will have to show somehow or other how symbols come to be related to one another, and the entire process will have to be shown to involve appropriate motives for making such relationships. For example, Rose (21) points out that symbols get connected to each other in the form of clusters, and one important such cluster is made up of a role or other kinds of social structures. In a new situation, one may manufacture a cluster, as for example in the device used by music teachers to teach pupils the names of the lines, E, G, B, D, F. Some such sentence or mnemonic, as "every good boy deserves fudge," or something like that is used. The suggestion here is that symbol systems become elaborated and that symbols are connected to each other by other symbols. This is a useful clue that does not deal with the question of the sequence in which the symbols are connected to each other to form the new symbol, nor again does it deal with the question of why any music pupil should want to memorize such a meaningless sentence.

We will deal with the two problems, then, of motives and of symbol connections in that order.

MOTIVES

A key element in learning consists of the discovery of a motive which will relate a symbol or object to an identity. To put it in everyday language, the subject or activity to be learned must make a difference to the person. The person must, after the learning is completed, be a different person. In a broad sense, then, this general approach follows the classic emphasis that Dewey placed on "doing" and is related to the importance which Stone (28) placed on the attitude in its relationship to the identity. To put it in Stone's terms, learning requires that the attitudes to be assumed must affect the identity in a valued way. As we shall see presently, it is also essential that there should be an appropriate mood. In a report on toilet-training children, Azrin and Foxx (3) claimed startling results such as being able to toilet-train children in less than a day. These results they tend to attribute largely to behaviorism of the Skinnerian variety. In fact, they make use of a heavily symbolic interactionist approach, as illustrated in what they refer to as Friends-Who-Care Procedure. Thus, when the child succeeds in any portion of the toilet-training, a list of persons whom the child admires is used, including fictional persons. For example, the trainer or parent is advised to proceed as follows:

> When you give approval for an action, continually give the approval in the name of one of those persons—such as "Tommy is sitting on the potty; Grandmother will be so happy," or "Eddy (his brother) will say, 'Tommy is a big boy.'" Also describe the similarity between your child's approved actions and those of the close friends—for example, "Good boy, Tommy, you flushed the toilet. Just like Daddy." Or "Your pants are dry. Just like Captain Kangaroo's." Rotate the use of names in such a way that you name all persons on the Friends-Who-Care list several times. Whenever possible, describe the anticipated approval of a friend in a manner that actually can be carried out soon. For example, "When Daddy comes home today, he'll say, "Tommy is a big boy. Tommy has dry pants." Or, "When Eddy sees you go potty, he'll be so happy"; or "Grandma will be so happy when we call her." Then as soon as training is completed that day, have Grandma tell him of her pleasure over the phone, and have his father and brother do likewise when they arrive home (p. 75).

In the above we have a striking illustration of the sort of team which Foote (10) described in his classic paper on identification, except that in this case the team, rather than merely existing, is created to suit the particular child.

When learning is related to identity, we see an important link between studies of learning and the many studies of socialization which have involved descriptions of transformations of identity as well as the studies which make use of the word "becoming" (25). Here we may sum up the basic point insofar as it concerns learning as follows, namely, the assumption of a new identity or any substantial change in an old identity means that one behaves differently. For example, Dornbusch's (9) famous description of changes in the self-image of the Coast Guard Academy recruit calls this to our attention. He writes: "If a cadet falters on the parade ground, he is told, 'You're marching like a reserve.' Swabs are told to square their shoulders while on liberty, 'or else how will people know you are not a reserve?'"

Later, describing developing self-confidence on the part of the cadet and the way in which the cadet changes his view of himself, Dornbusch quotes one cadet as saying, "I used to be shy. Now I'm reserved." A key element in identity shift is the occurrence, as Caplow (8) has pointed out, of new involvements. The university freshman finds himself surrounded by persons who are just as capable as he, and since many such persons were among the top performers in their high schools, that experience is likely to be upsetting to many students. Further, the university may become increasingly competitive as one moves through the system. Caplow points out that socialization involves not simply the development of new relationships but the abandonment of old. He writes:

> For the recruit, the convert, the newly elected, adopted, or graduated, there is always the awareness that becoming what one is now means forgetting what one was before. The bride is no longer a maiden; a new chief is expelled from the peer group. The extent and importance of the old relationships that are abandoned usually determine what kind of socialization process is necessary. In those cases in which socialization takes a drastic form, the severity of the new experience is explained not so much by the difficulty of learning a new part as by the difficulty of forgetting the old (p. 171).

An outstanding description of the process of forgetting or of eliminating prior statuses is provided by Goffman (11) in his description of the process of mortification in mental hospitals. In occupations and organizations this is often accomplished by sequestration. Such sequestration may be ecological, in which persons are sent off to retreats, or may be temporal, in which the whole of the day and the night or longer periods may be given over to training. In such cases one lives in separate communities, as Lipset *et al.* (14) have described for the case of the printers.

Shifts in identities typically involve changes of value as well, as have been illustrated, for example, by Merriam and Mack (15) for members of the jazz community or the way in which nurse trainees change their view of their work from a lay conception to a more technical one (20, 26). Westley (32) has called attention to the fact that the police operate in a world which is often hostile to the police function itself. As a result, the police have been pushed into isolation and secrecy in their work. This leads, he finds, to a pervasive secretiveness and to a willingness to condone violence. One result is that the police often see themselves as being concerned with defending the police from society as much as defending society from criminals. The point of such studies in the present context is that such teaching or learning of values would seem to be possible only in realistic situations, either on the job or in learning situations themselves. Further, it would seem to be necessary that such values be communicated subtly. For example, Olesen and Whittaker (18) show how laughter and silences are utilized by nursing instructors as teaching devices.

It is essential, however, that learning not be equated only to such remarkable identity transformations in which change is vivid and obvious. My way of putting it above, namely, that learning requires that the subject or matter to be learned must make a difference to one, is sufficiently broad to include much less momentous changes. Thus, the behaviorists' use of reward may be interpreted in the present context as an indication of whether a given behavior change makes a difference to one or whether it is worth it. Thus, in Roy's (23) famous studies of gold-bricking among industrial workers, he calls our attention to the fact that the worker, offered the opportunity of earning money through a new piece work system or a change in a piece rate, does not reject the opportunity out of hand. Rather, he tries it and attempts to discover whether or not he can make money on the new scheme. He discovers how much he can make and then evaluates the money that can be made in the light of the amount of effort required. He then makes an assessment as to whether or not the extra effort is worth the money. If it is not, he simply does not respond to the incentive system and goes about his work being satisfied to accept simply his daily guarantee.

The reference to reward brings us now directly to what is the central concept in the behaviorist theory of learning, namely reinforcement. Presumably the purpose of all payment, food, and other kinds of devices used to provide reinforcement in the psychologists' experiments is to encourage production of products or, in the case of scientists, of ideas, talent, inventions, and so forth. But a special study of scientists' productivity by Zuckerman (34) suggests a rather different interpretation of reward. She reports a decline in productivity by Nobel scientist laureates *after* they were honored, a decline which is considerably greater than can be attributed to age. Seeking an explanation for this paradox, Zuckerman takes the view that the Nobel prize is not just any honor but "almost in a social category by itself. . . . The prize . . . assigns a new status to the laureates. The newly crowned laureate is socially defined not only as a great man of science but also as a celebrity and a sage" (pp. 398–399). As support she presents a Durkheimian analysis which suggests that the impact of the prize differs according to the size of the status increment represented by the prize. The decline in productivity is greater for those catapulted to sudden eminence than for those for whom the prize came after many earlier prizes and other indications of status. In sum, the prize disorganizes the previously obscure, creating anomie.

But something other than the special character of the Nobel prize is involved here. In explaining the special character, Zuckerman has shifted from a reinforcement theory of rewards to what might be called a symbolic interactionist theory of rewards. Lesser rewards may reinforce desired behavior, but greater ones apparently serve to mark you off as a special sort of person—and it is that identity transformation that may be disorganizing if it occurs too suddenly. In sum, rewards may do more than merely affirm and reinforce existing roles—rewards may actually create new roles. It is my belief that such a view of rewards is not necessarily limited to the great rewards only. Giving an employee a salary increase or making him teacher of the year might also affect his self-conception with significant consequences for his career.

In a case known to the author, a member of a Sociology department was up for promotion. He had published very few articles over the years, but had recently begun to work on possible articles. However, most of the department had apparently given up any hope that the person would ever be a prolific producer of research papers. In the discussion of whether the individual should be promoted or not, the question of the articles he was reputed to be working on was raised. At that point, a member of the department proposed that the individual should be told that he would be promoted if one of the articles was accepted for publication before next year. In other words, the proposal was that a behaviorist theory of rewards should be employed. Another member of the department, however, suggested the symbolic interactionist approach. In effect he said, "Let us promote him now. Then what we do is change his identity. We change him from an assistant professor to an associate professor. The point is that associate professors are people who publish, not merely people who promise that they may publish." With considerable misgivings, the latter course was followed. And in fact, the person did present a paper at meetings the following year which was well received. As of this moment, we do not know if the paper was published, but the results are indeed consistent with the position being presented here. In the Azrin and Foxx (3) study of toilet-training, the authors illustrate the teaching procedure in a composite picture of a woman's attempt to toilet-train her son Mickey. Mickey has a brother named Ronnie and a sister named Renée who are older and already toilet-trained. Azrin and Foxx write as follows:

> Approximately ten minutes had elapsed since the training had begun. She began asking him a series of questions, all of which were designed to inform him of how happy all his family, friends, and heroes would be when he was a big boy who could potty by himself. She also wanted to point out to him that all of these people used the toilet by themselves and thereby kept their pants dry. She wanted him to identify with and emulate these people. She began by asking, "Mickey, does Daddy wet his pants?" She had waited until he was looking at her before she asked the question; that way she could be sure that he was listening to her. Mickey shook his head and said, "No." She repeated his answer: "No, Daddy doesn't wet his pants. Daddy is a big boy. He keeps his pants dry. He pees in the potty. Does Daddy wear diapers?" "No," Mickey said. "Are you a big boy?" "Yes," Mickey answered. "Will you keep your pants dry?" "Yes," he said. "Does Ronnie wet his pants?" "No." "Does Renée wet her pants?" "No." "Does Mommy wet her pants?" "No." "Only babies wet their pants. Are you a baby?" "No." "That's right. You don't wet your pants. You're not a baby. You're a big boy!" (pp. 109–110).

In the above quotation we see one further element of reward that enables us to assimilate the concept to symbolic interactionist theory, namely, that rewards are a way of calling attention to the assumption of an identity, that is, persons who have a particular identity are entitled to certain kinds of rewards. They go with the identity. They do not cause the learning; rather, they are coming to the person and are appropriate. Space forbids us to elaborate this point, but it is of obvious importance in handling the whole phenomenon of what have been called status symbols, such as trappings of office and other aspects of appearance that go with a given identity.

RELATING SYMBOLS TO ONE ANOTHER

Our discussion so far, however, deals only with roughly half of the problems of learning. We have provided basically a picture of the manner in which motives may be related to learning, with giving reasons why persons should learn or why they should be interested in learning. We have said in effect that one learns when what there is to be learned makes a difference to one's identity in some way. Otherwise, one is bored, and while some kind of learning can take place under such conditions, it appears to be slow and laborious. But none of the above actually deals with the question of content of learning, with the material itself that is to be learned. A person may have every reason to learn to ride a bicycle because big boys or girls ride bicycles, for example, but that alone will not teach him how to ride a bicycle. The same is true of other technical skills. We deal here with the recognized problem in all learning, of how difficult it is to acquire any new skill and where we can no longer get away from the recognition by psychologists of the importance of repetition and others of what seem to be purely psychological elements. A symbolic interactionist theory must come to grips with this problem.

It is our belief that the key element here is one of sequencing. The learning of any body of content, a set of symbols or a set of manual skills involves, we believe, coming to an appreciation and being able to indicate to oneself that a particular sequence is required. The problem is one that all parents who have sought to teach their child to ride a tricycle have experienced. The child puts his two feet on the pedals and proceeds to press both pedals simultaneously, often leading to frustration and crying. It takes some time before the child appreciates that he must first move one pedal while relaxing the pressure from his foot on the other and to do so in a regularized sequence. At a more advanced level, timing is recognized as of major importance in manual skills. It is our belief that a similar argument can be made for learning symbol systems. These, too, occur in a particular sequence, except that the sequence here may not simply be one in time but may involve quite elaborate patterns.

A widely used procedure for the teaching of sequences and patterns is through modeling, which can include taking the role of the other. Here the role of the coach, as described insightfully by Strauss (29), is relevant. As Strauss defines it,

> A coaching relationship exists if someone seeks to move someone along a series of steps, when those steps are not entirely institutionalized and invariant, and when the learner is not entirely clear about their sequence (although the coach is). The football coach attempting to turn out a good halfback, Iago seeking to induce Othello along the path of jealousy, the piano teacher trying to make a concert pianist out of a young man, the revivalist trying to work his audience into a frenzy of conversion, the psychiatrist carefully maneuvering his patient back to better psychological integration, and the confidence man manipulating his victim through sequential steps of involvement in an illicit deal: all are instances of coaching relationships, albeit each has different aspects. In each instance there is a man who has yielded himself (whether he knows it or not) to a teacher who guides him along at least partly obscure channels (p. 110).

Strauss's discussion is particularly insightful since in the case of the coach we have a melding of the importance of the change of identity and the learning of sequences. Persons may often identify with their coaches, which leads to problems of disidentification later on when a person must move beyond his coach as well as the dangers of betrayal when the coach has failed him or when the coach feels that his pupil has failed him.

An important method for teaching sequences involves the use of rewards in still another sense than the uses described up to this point. Rewards may be not only consummatory in significance, but may also be cognitive. Psychologists, for example, have become impressed with latent learning, a phenomenon which was given a great deal of attention by the psychologist Tolman. In a classic experiment, Buxton (7) ran rats through a complex maze without any food reward. After a considerable time lapse, the unrewarded rats were suddenly presented with a reward at the end of the maze. It was found one half of them moved from the beginning of the maze directly to the reward without error on the first trial. Tolman's conclusion was that rats develop what he called a cognitive map and that this map was invoked when necessary. In sum, the rats learned the maze, but did not display the behavior because they had no incentive for doing so. Only when a reward was offered did they then show that they knew all along, as it were, how to get to that end if ever it was worthwhile for them to do so.

Such a conception would seem to be applicable to humans without question. Indeed, the puzzle here is that rats are able to demonstrate what we might at first have thought was an exclusively human quality, namely, the ability to anticipate or imagine a reward being present when one was not present. Guthrie was critical of Tolman's approach, complaining that he left the rats "buried in thought," a criticism which Tolman accepted when he suggested that it was not enough that there be an incentive, but in addition the rat must want the food, that is, that he must be hungry. In the case of humans, the incentive concept would seem to be highly useful. In another study for which behaviorists take credit, Ayllon and Azrin (2) describe what they call a token economy. The authors made use of tokens in a state mental hospital in order to control and modify a good deal of patient behavior. Typically, the study, which was carefully done, points out a variety of situations in behavior which in the opinion of guards and others was not modifiable—in fact, could be modified. They did this through making use of payments to the patients of tokens for doing various things, which tokens could in turn be exchanged for food or other kinds of privileges the patients valued.

In one of their studies, for example, they were able to show that they could get patients to participate in the exercise program by giving them tokens for doing so. Furthermore, the number of patients who would participate was directly related to the number of tokens given for attendance at the exercise session. I report on this small study here, because in this case the authors refer to spontaneous verbal comments made by the patients during the study. They tell us that, at first, when participation in the activity did not produce tokens, the patients rarely took part and verbally stated that they disliked exercise. Later, when substantial numbers of tokens were being earned, patients commented that the activity was fun and that they enjoyed participating in it and felt they were getting a lot out of it. When the number of tokens was reduced to zero, patients stated again that they didn't like it and for that reason would not participate in it. The authors claim that this "verbal behavior" is a *consequence* of the reinforcement or lack of it. Basically, their model suggests that exercise is followed by reinforcement, mainly the giving of tokens, which in turn is then followed by more exercise accompanied by verbal comments that they liked the exercise. However, a symbolic interactionist approach would suggest a modification of this model. Exercise might be given followed by reinforcement or tokens. Then an attempt would be made to assess the effect of the reinforcement on the self-image that the person has, or on his conception of whether the number of tokens was worthwhile. Based on his view on the token situation, he might decide that the tokens given implied a certain view of himself, and therefore whether he wished to respond to the tokens or not. We then would predict that how he assesses the tokens and what they mean for his own self-perception would predict whether the patient would participate in the exercise program or not.

In the test, we would vary the self-image. For example, after tokens are offered, an experimenter might say to patients, "You see, this means they think you're worth being taken into account. They don't treat you like dirt." Another set of patients might be told, "This is just a gimmick to get you tired out so that you'll be less trouble." The assumption would be that even though the number of tokens in both cases would be the same, that they would participate in exercise in the first case to a greater extent (17). Another approach would be to take advantage of the variation that exists in the population already in the interpretation of self-image among patients. It would be predicted, for example, that patients with a low self-image would respond because it is assumed that the offered tokens would elevate their self-image. On the other hand, those with a high self-image would not respond since they would not require tokens in order to assure themselves that they enjoy the favorable evaluation of others, that is, that others are interested enough in them to be willing to pay them for an activity.

What we are saying in effect, then, is that rewards may have cognitive significance; that is, they may be assessed for their relationship to one's self-image. But they may also be assessed as indicators of the sequence of symbols in a learning situation (27). Rewards may simply *call attention* to given directions in which learning should proceed, and the same may be true of punishments in reverse. In learning how to ride a bicycle, if given behavior moves one in a fruitful direction so that the bicycle moves forward, one will continue to do that, not because moving in a desired direction is rewarding, but rather because that is an indication of a goal which in this case one is seeking. So, too, doing something else which produces pain tells one that that is not the way to go. Rewards in this sense are signals which map out a route which one may take, provided he is interested in the reward in much the same manner as Tolman's rats. So, too, persons may frequently explore an area of a city which they have never seen before, discover an attractive view or restaurant they did not know about, but move on because at the moment they haven't the time nor are they hungry or interested. At some future time, however, if a person is interested, he can return to the same spot.

In the Ayllon-Azrin (2) study much of what occurred can be interpreted in cognitive terms. The attempt was made in this study to relate as much behavior as possible to tokens. The researchers were also extremely careful in trying to prevent patients from beating the system. For example, they were very careful to control theft or other forms of deviance, and they supervised the behavior of the patients very closely in the manner which is familiar to all of us in total institutions. It is my judgment, however, that the close control of behavior and the giving of tokens for practically anything the patient might want to do says two things to the patient in symbolic interactionist terms. They say, first, "We are interested in you, you are important to us; every item of your behavior is important to us; we are interested in everything you do." This interpretation is supported by the authors' attempt to discover appropriate reinforcers by the simple device of using "probability of occurrence" of the behavior as a basis for choice. That is, the kind of behavior that the patients engaged in when the opportunity exists was assumed to be reinforcing. Their tokens enabled them, in effect, to purchase that kind of behavior. For example, it was noted that certain patients often hoarded various items under their mattresses to make them inaccessible to other patients and to staff. So this was considered to be a reinforcer. The keys to a locked cabinet in which they could conceal their private possessions were made available to patients in exchange for tokens which they earned by engaging in other kinds of behavior.

Another example was that patients were often observed to conceal themselves in several locations in the ward in an effort to enjoy some degree of privacy. The researchers therefore decided an appropriate reinforcer would be a portable screen which a patient could put in front of her bed. Basically, reinforcing behavior, then, is natural behavior. In providing patients with the opportunity to earn tokens by which they could purchase behaviors that they desired, experimenters were saying to their patients, "You are important. We respect you as you are. We will provide you with the opportunity to engage in behavior you prefer to engage in."

A second consequence is more relevant to the general subject of learning. It would seem that by providing tokens and by carefully controlling behavior, the experimenters were demonstrating to their subjects that they could realize or attain their goals in this environment. They were transmitting to their patients an important message, namely, that at least here the world is a meaningful place, that here there is a connection between what you do and what you get, and that this is basically, therefore, not the kind of anomic place in which the patients had lived before coming to the mental hospital and which indeed may have been responsible for some of their disturbances. The authors are careful that given forms of behavior will always enable them to obtain tokens as promised. This is not, of course, the situation in the world outside in which what happens may include many kinds of chance events, as well as situations in which the reward is rigged against one.

What we are claiming, then, is that in the behaviorist literature the significance of reward may be interpreted in symbolic interactionist terms. Offering a student or learner a potential reward may be seen not as reinforcing the particular behavior, but rather as calling attention to the possible consequences of a given form of behavior. The learner can take this into account, and it will be of importance in leading to learning depending on how important the reward is felt to be. This will obviously be related to the identity of the person, how greatly he values the reward, what it might mean to him. It calls attention to a particular direction which is necessary, since the reward always exists in some place or some time, so that the sequence which precedes it is indicated in some way by the location in time and space of the reward itself.

In conclusion, it is worth noting that a symbolic interactionist theory, powerful as it is and even though it may be able to include the emphasis on reward reinforcement, still leaves certain psychological elements which in my judgment remain to be explained. For example, a behaviorist theory might help explain nonsymbolic behavior, the learning that occurs on the part of persons before they have a self, as in the case, say, of newborn infants or in the case of persons who have suffered brain damage or have other kinds of disturbances or who may be suffering from various kinds of cognitive lacks, such as what Rose (21) spoke of as incomplete socialization. It is not clear how important such nonsymbolic situations are, and indeed Harry Stack Sullivan (30) doubted that they were of any great interest since even the most obvious sorts of nonsymbolic behavior very quickly become surrounded by or suffused with symbolic elements. There are other kinds of situations, though, which would not seem to be easily explainable in symbolic terms. It has been claimed [and doubted (27)] that it is possible to learn some types of sequences without awareness or without making self-indications.

The figure-ground principle seems also to be important: in order for a person to learn something, he must be able to see or appreciate the particular sequence that must be learned. Thus Azrin and Foxx (3) emphasize that in toilet-training a child, one must first get the child's attention before one gives it an instruction. This may seem like an obvious point, but it is not. The child must be directly faced, and the person must be sure the child is looking at him before he gives it an instruction. In other words, an access phenomenon is absolutely essential for learning, and it has undoubtedly features of its own, not only psychological but probably physical as well. But the net result is still to reduce such elementary psychological elements to relatively minor status and to elevate symbolic interactionist theory as a truly powerful approach to the study of learning.

*A revised version of a paper delivered at the meetings of the American Sociological Association, New York City, August 1976.

REFERENCES

1. Ronald L. Akers, *Deviant Behavior*. Wadsworth, Belmont, California, 1973.
2. Teodoro Ayllon and Nathan Azrin, *The Token Economy*. Prentice-Hall, Englewood Cliffs, N.J., 1968.
3. Nathan H. Azrin and Richard M. Foxx, *Toilet Training in Less Than a Day*. Simon and Schuster, New York, 1974.
4. Howard S. Becker, "Becoming a Marijuana User," in Jerome M. Manis and Bernard N. Meltzer (eds.), *Symbolic Interaction: A Reader in Social Psychology*. Allyn and Bacon, Boston, 1967 (originally published in 1953).
5. Robert C. Bolles, "Reinforcement, Expectancy, and Learning," *Psychological Review* 79, No. 5 (September 1972): 394–409.
6. Robert L. Burgess and Don Bushell, *Behavioral Sociology*. Columbia University Press, New York, 1969.
7. Buxton, C. E. "Latent Learning and the Goal Gradient Hypothesis," in Winfred F. Hill, *Learning*. Chandler, San Francisco, 1963, pp. 118–119.
8. Theodore Caplow, Chapter 5 in *Principles of Organization*. Harcourt Brace and World, New York, 1964.
9. Sanford M. Dornbusch, "The Military Academy as an Assimilating Institution," *Social Forces* 33 (May 1955): 316–321.
10. Nelson M. Foote, "Identification as a Basis for a Theory of Motivation," *American Sociological Review* 16 (February 1951): 14–21.
11. Erving Goffman, *Asylums*. Doubleday, Garden City, N.Y., 1961.
12. Ernest R. Hilgard and Gordon H. Bower (eds.), *Theories of Learning*. Appleton-Century-Crofts, New York, 1966.

13. Philip J. Hilts, *Behavior Mod.* Harper, New York, 1974.
14. S. M. Lipset, M. Trow, and J. S. Coleman, *Union Democracy.* Doubleday, Garden City, N.Y., 1962.
15. Alan P. Merriam and Raymond W. Mack, "The Jazz Community," *Social Forces* 38 (March 1960): 211–221.
16. Walter Mischel, "Toward a Cognitive Social Learning Reconceptualization of Personality," *Psychological Review* 80 (1973): 252–283.
17. W. Mischel and N. Baker, "Cognitive Appraisals and Transformations in Delay Behavior," unpublished manuscript, Sanford University. Cited in Mischel, *ibid.*
18. Virginia L. Olesen and Elvi W. Whittaker, "Adjudication of Student Awareness in Professional Socialization: the Language of Laughter and Silences," *Sociological Quarterly* 7 (Summer 1966): 381–396.
19. Jean Piaget, *The Origins of Intelligence in Children.* International Universities Press, New York, 1952.
20. George Psathas, "The Fate of Idealism in Nursing School," *Journal of Health and Social Behavior* 9 (March 1968): 52–64.
21. Arnold M. Rose, "Incomplete Socialization," *Sociology and Social Research* 44, No. 4 (March–April 1960): 244–249.
22. ———, "A Systematic Summary of Symbolic Interaction Theory," in Arnold M. Rose (ed.), *Human Behavior and Social Process.* Houghton Mifflin, Boston, 1962.
23. Donald Roy, "Quota Restriction and Goldbricking in a Machine Shop," *American Journal of Sociology* 57 (1952): 427–442.
24. John Finley Scott, *Internalization of Norms: A Sociological Theory of Moral Commitment.* Prentice-Hall, Englewood Cliffs, N.J., 1971.
25. Tamotsu Shibutani, *Society and Personality.* Prentice-Hall, Englewood Cliffs, N.J., 1961.
26. Ida Harper Simpson, "Patterns of Socialization into Professions: the Case of Student Nurses," *Sociological Inquiry* 37 (Winter 1967): 47–53.
27. Charles D. Spielberger and L. Douglas DeNike, "Descriptive Behaviorism versus Cognitive Theory in Verbal Operant Conditioning," *Psychological Review* 73 (1966): 306–326.
28. Gregory P. Stone, "Appearance and the Self," in Arnold M. Rose (ed.), *Human Behavior and Social Processes.* Houghton Mifflin, Boston, 1962.
29. Anselm L. Strauss, *Mirrors and Masks.* Free Press, New York, 1959.
30. Harry Stack Sullivan, *The Interpersonal Theory of Psychiatry.* Norton, New York, 1953.
31. H. S. Terrace, "Discrimination Learning with and without Errors," *Journal of Experimental Analysis of Behavior* 6 (1963): 1–27.
32. William A. Westley, *Violence and the Police.* M.I.T. Press, Cambridge, Mass., 1970.
33. E. F. Zigler and I. L. Child (eds.), *Socialization and Personality Development.* Addison-Wesley, Reading, Mass., 1973.
34. Harriet Zuckerman, "Nobel Laureates in Science: Patterns of Productivity, Collaboration and Authorship," *American Sociological Review* 32, No. 3 (June 1967): 381–402.

THE SOCIAL PSYCHOLOGY
OF SEXUAL AROUSAL: A
SYMBOLIC INTERACTIONIST
INTERPRETATION*

Jeffrey S. Victor, STATE UNIVERSITY OF NEW YORK

THE SOCIAL PSYCHOLOGY OF SEXUAL AROUSAL: A SYMBOLIC INTERACTIONIST INTERPRETATION

Until quite recently, the study of human sexuality has been dominated by specialists in biology and medicine. Sociologists are now making important contributions to the investigation of premarital and extramarital relations and certain forms of deviant sexual behavior, such as mate-swapping, homosexual behavior and prostitution. Social psychologists are making similarly important contributions in research focused upon sex-role socialization and responses to pornography. The 1970s have witnessed a rapid growth of college courses concerned with sex roles and sexual behavior, in both psychology and sociology departments. Recent social psychology textbooks are finally beginning to offer chapters cover-

Studies in Symbolic Interaction—Volume 1, 1978, pages 147–180.

ing a social psychological approach to sexual behavior (39). Gagnon and Simon (19) have written a major theoretical work, in which they have attempted to integrate behavioral sex research within a framework of symbolic interactionist theory. Another important symbolic interactionist theoretical analysis of sexual behavior has been written by Plummer (69). Articles are finally beginning to appear in interdisciplinary professional journals concerned wtih human sexuality, which introduce scholars of varied disciplines to this hitherto unfamiliar perspective on sexual behavior. Gecas and Libby (21) have presented a short survey of key issues in the study of human sexuality, as seen from the symbolic interactionist viewpoint. Much of the future of symbolic interactionist theory lies in its potential for illuminating scholarly problems which concern researchers outside the confines of traditional sociology.

In relation to interdisciplinary concerns, it is heartening that recent developments in psychological learning theory have moved it closer to a symbolic interactionist position. Social learning theory is increasingly being combined with insights from cognitive psychology, so that more attention can be focused upon the brain's symbolic information processing. The synthesis of these efforts is already being called "cognitive social learning theory (56)." Although its terminology and micro-level analysis differs from that of symbolic interactionism, its theoretical orientation is essentially similar. Already practical applications to human problems are taking shape. There has been a modification of behavior modification therapies in the direction of greater attention to cognitive learning and symbolic processes (2).

This chapter focuses attention upon a key issue in understanding human sexuality: the nature of sexual arousal. (In the popular language of today, the question concerns "what turns people on" sexually.) Sexual arousal refers to the activation of sexual desire and behavior directed toward the attainment of erotic, sensual pleasure. Research on the physiology of sexual response, such as that of Masters and Johnson (54), has focused attention almost exclusively upon biological dimensions of sexual arousal. A symbolic interactionist approach to sexual arousal, instead, focuses attention upon human meanings attributed to interpersonal interaction. More specifically, the concern centers upon the effects of cognitive-affective information processing in response to sexual experience.

BIOLOGICAL FACTORS IN SEXUAL AROUSAL

A basic question about human sexuality concerns the relationship between bodily functioning and social learning in erotic behavior. Traditional beliefs hold that bodily factors initiate and direct sexual responsiveness and behavior. The exact links between body and behavior are vaguely believed to be "instincts" or "hormone regulation," or some sort of inborn "biological forces." These vague notions are inadequate and basically incorrect. Instead, there exists a complex interrelationship between biological and learned factors.

Before it is possible to explore the social psychological aspects of sexual arousal, it is necessary to review some recent research concerning the biological elements in sexual arousal. Bodily factors provide the potential of sexual arousal, but it is ultimately learned and interpersonal factors which activate that possibility.

The Effects of Androgenic Hormones

In both males and females, the same androgenic hormones, particularly testosterone, create the bodily conditions which enable sensual, erotic pleasure to be experienced. These bodily conditions include: 1) an intensified sensitivity of the genitals (penis or clitoris and labia) to stimulation, and 2) a build up of sexual response to such stimulation until orgasm (74). Without the presence of the necessary hormones and bodily conditions, a person cannot experience erotic pleasure. Certainly a person may experience other forms of pleasure in bodily contact with others, such as affection, joy, warmth and relatedness. These can multiply the pleasures of sexual activity. Yet, they exist as distinct and different from erotic pleasure. It is necessary to recognize this distinction, in order to avoid confusion about the meaning of eroticism.

Various sources of evidence point to the conclusion that androgen is essential to sexual arousal in both sexes (51, 59). In women, removal of the ovaries as a source of estrogen does not necessarily bring about an elimination of sexual desire, but the removal of the adrenal glands as a source of androgen does so, almost always (89). The absence of estrogen in women, (resulting from ovariectomy or menopause) however, does cause sexual intercourse to become difficult, due to insufficient vaginal lubrication (60). In many cases, an administration of androgen to women increases their sexual desire, probably by increasing clitoral sensitivity (51). (It also has the unfortunate side-effect of increasing bodily and facial hair.) In adult men, removal of the testes (castration) does not always eliminate sexual desire and the capability of erection, probably because the adrenal glands continue to supply a small amount of androgen (62). In most cases, however, castration does diminish or terminate genital sensitivity and the possibility of sexual arousal. The administration of androgen to castrated men usually reestablishes their sexual sensitivity and capability of erection (51). A drug has recently been developed which counteracts the bodily effects of androgen. When this anti-androgen drug was administered to male sex offenders who volunteered for a study in

Germany, their sexual desire was greatly diminished or eliminated (45). There is no complete agreement among physiologists that androgen is the only hormone affecting sexual arousal, but no other bodily agent has yet been identified.

Androgen is essential for sexual arousal, but it does not produce sexual desire. Psychological factors are necessary to account for sexual desire. This is shown in cases in which men and women who are sexually unresponsive and inorgasmic ("impotence" and "frigidity") are treated with testosterone hormone therapy. The results usually do not establish sexual desire in such patients (59). Hormone therapy for these problems is now generally considered useless, if not potentially harmful. Instead, one form or another of psychological or behavior therapy is most effective.

Since a bodily chemical must be present in order for a person to experience sexual arousal, it is necessary to ask about the effects of differing amounts. Do high and low levels of circulating androgenic hormones affect sexual desire and sexual behavior in any way? Only recently has there been adequate research into this question, primarily due to improved methods of determining hormone levels directly from blood samples. Basically, the research to date indicates that the relative levels of androgenic hormones circulating in the blood have no effect upon either sexual desire or sexual behavior. One study, for example, compared men having extremely low testosterone levels ("eunuchoid") with normal men, in terms of their frequency of sexual intercourse (71). No significant differences were found between these groups of men in their frequency of intercourse. The researchers concluded that normal men produce a "superabundance" of testosterone and that only extremely low amounts are needed for erotic activity. This research is also important to an understanding of male-female differences. Recent investigations indicate that adult men may have five to ten times more testosterone circulating in their blood than do adult women (62). The implication is that this difference in hormone levels has no effect upon frequency of sexual behavior, if only micro-amounts are sufficient for sexual activity to occur.

Frequency of sexual activity and levels of testosterone have been found to be related, however, in an unexpected way. One study of twenty men, over a two-month period, found that sexual activity resulted in an immediate increase in their testosterone levels. After several days of sexual inactivity their testosterone levels decreased from that peak (44). Yet, when comparisons were made between different men, it was found that more sexually active men had lower average testosterone levels than those men who were less sexually active. Sexually inactive men had higher average testosterone levels over the two month period, even though sexual activity resulted in an immediate increase in each individual's level of testosterone. This research shows that we must be very cautious about drawing any conclusions about the relationship between the amount of testosterone and the frequency of erotic activity.

Some physiologists have speculated that different people have different "response thresholds" to individually different levels of androgen (44). Therefore, individually different levels of androgen may be irrelevant to genital sensitivity. These "response thresholds" may be a function of the ability of the cells of genital tissue to respond biochemically to androgen. Further speculation suggests that the cellular biochemical reaction is determined genetically or during fetal development.

Biological Maturation

Research on the effects of androgenic hormones is also important to an understanding of erotic development during childhood and adolescence. There has not yet been much adequate research which has measured evolving levels of androgen during childhood. The available research, however, does indicate that androgen is present in boys and girls from infancy (28, 66). Androgen production begins to increase markedly at about the age of eight or nine in both sexes. Then, during early adolescence, androgen production levels off in girls, but continues to increase in boys. Ultimately, adult men produce substantially more androgen than adult women. (The excess androgen in males may be more closely associated with the development of male body characteristics, than any difference in erotic response.) Indeed, the existence of androgen in children is probably sufficient to account for childhood erotic activities, such as masturbation. Erotic sexual activities between children is commonplace in some societies (17). In conclusion, it appears that the biological basis for erotic behavior exists from early childhood, and that the social environment inhibits or permits its expression below a certain age level.

It is unlikely that increased androgen production during puberty results in a sudden interest in dating and heterosexual activity. Instead, when adolescents begin to develop the outward appearances of an adult male or female body, they begin to be "seen" as sexual (erotic) persons. In American society, it is then that a person begins to be exposed to a new eroticized social environment composed of dating, petting, sex jokes, sex information and misinformation. Once a person is socially "seen" as a sexual being, the erotic responsiveness becomes channeled, by parents and peers, in the direction of socially approved goals of sexual expression.

Evidence that social learning is necessary to the activation of heterosexual erotic interests and behavior comes from studies of children who experience precocious puberty. Unlike early maturation, precocious puberty is a very rare condition in which the bodily sexual changes of puberty may begin as early as four to six years of age. By the time such children are preadolescent, they have an adult physical appearance and body functioning, except for a lasting shortness of height. Research on precocious puberty has found that such children usually do not develop erotic interests and behavior parallel to their hormonal and bodily changes (57, 61). Instead, their erotic development is consistent with that of other children their own chronological age. The erotic development of children follows from interpersonal experience and the cognitive social learning of erotic meanings, rather than from any direct hormonal influences.

At the other end of the life cycle, popular belief holds that a decline in hormone production destines the elderly to erotic inactivity. This belief is simply not true. When this false assumption is held by an elderly couple, it may actually bring about a self-fulfilling prophecy, by inhibiting sexual desire. As far as it is known today, the decline in sexual activity with advanced age is primarily a result of interpersonal and psychological factors. Many people in their sixties, seventies, and even eighties can and do enjoy sexual activity (49). Certain physiological conditions of bodily aging may diminish sexual responsiveness, but the termination of sexual desire is essentially a psychological matter. Men may experience a decreased skin sensitivity in the penis, less rapid erection, and less copious seminal fluid during ejaculation. Women may experience less vaginal lubrication and a relaxation of the vaginal muscles. Yet, the ultimate inhibitions to erotic pleasure derive primarily from the attitudes generated by an elderly couple's past sexual relationship with each other (68).

The Psychological Effects of Genital Anatomy and Physiology

Certain other biological factors have consequences for the psychology of erotic response; particularly in understanding male-female differences. These include penile erection and the accumulation of seminal fluid in males.

Some psychologists have suggested that the difference between male and female genital anatomy has important implications in the development of erotic responsiveness in both sexes (6). The erection of the penis is an obvious indicator of sexual arousal in males. In that sense, it offers dramatic feedback information to a boy of his body's response to certain forms of stimulation. In contrast, the clitoris, which is the center of female genital sensitivity, is small and recessed into the body. Its erection in young girls easily goes unnoticed. It is not easily stimulated by incidental external friction, such as that from movement against clothing or bedding. The larger size and external anatomy of the penis means that male children are more easily and consistently exposed to bodily excitation from genital stimulation. The erection of the penis offers feedback information, which localizes the source of that excitation in the genitals. Therefore, the suggestion is that women, particularly when young, are less easily aware of their genital excitation. They have less bodily feedback information than do men (except when vaginal lubrication is copious). Some women even have difficulty identifying whether or not they have experienced an orgasm. Men do not have any such difficulty, due to the feedback information from erection and ejaculation.

Few researchers have given any attention to the effects of the accumulation of semen in male sexual arousal. However, at least one theorist has suggested that males behave as if they are under constant physiological tension to accumulated seminal fluids (81). It is a widespread belief among men that genital tensions derives from internal "pressures" of accumulated semen. At least as far as is known, the accumulation of semen does not generate any direct genital tension (40). Instead, men may learn an attitude of pleasurable anticipation ("tension"), in response to subtle bodily sensations associated with the build-up of seminal fluids (in the seminal vesicles or prostate gland). It is known, however, that the amount of semen ejaculated is related to the intensity of orgasmic pleasure in men (54).

At an early age, men and women begin to develop differing attitudes toward their genitals (not due to any invidious comparison). While menstruation may be considered to be the central concern of female body consciousness during adolescence, ejaculation is the central focus of male body consciousness at that age. Differences in the nature of menstruation and ejaculation point to a basic distinction between female and male body consciousness (19). Menstruation is directly associated with reproduction. It usually has no erotic significance. Ejaculation is more directly associated with erotic pleasure. Consequently, men experience their bodies as a source of erotic pleasure more immediately and easily than do women. In contrast, women's body consciousness points them in the direction of a parental role more immediately and easily than men. This difference between male and female body consciousness is also revealed in the type of sex information sought by teenagers. Girls tend to be much more concerned about reproductive processes (menstruation, pregnancy, childbirth), while boys focus their curiosity upon techniques of erotic stimulation. On another level, this distinction is related to differences in attitudes toward the genital area of the body. Among adolescent boys, the penis is primarily a source of pleasure; but among adolescent girls, their genitals are primarily a source of anxiety and displeasurable emissions. As young men and women become involved in genital petting and initial sexual intercourse, their differing body consciousness predisposes them to attribute different kinds of meanings to that experience.

THE SOCIAL PSYCHOLOGY OF SEXUAL AROUSAL

The term "sexual pleasure" usually connotes exclusively physical, bodily experience. Sexual desire is usually portrayed as some sort of strong biological "urge" for relief from physiological tensions. Sexual arousal is often regarded as springing almost automatically from a biological potential for physical pleasure, imagined to begin some time during puberty. Sexual stimuli are regarded as physical "triggers," which turn on sexual arousal. The underlying assumptions in this chapter are entirely different. It is assumed that the biological potential for sexual arousal does not have any consequence unless it is activated by psychological forces. It is assumed that the biological roots of sexual pleasure must be nurtured by psychological and social forces, in order to become more than a mere potential. It is also assumed that sexuality, as erotic responsiveness, is learned and does not spring into existence automatically. Perhaps most fundamentally, the assumption is made that sexual desire is not particularly forceful or dangerous in human life, but instead it is easily molded to nonsexual purposes (19).

Cognitive Brain Functioning

In humans, sexual arousal is not a simple result of genital friction. Instead, the cerebral cortex of the brain and its cognitive functions play the central role in erotic sexuality among human beings (8). Cognitive functioning gives erotic meaning to external stimuli, to daydream fantasies, and even to the very bodily sensations which a person may (or may not) regard as being pleasurable. The cerebral cortex in human beings also accounts for the crucial influence of learning in human sexual behavior.

Some recent research provides evidence of the importance of cognitive processes in sexual arousal. Several experiments have investigated the effects of cognitive processes in the inhibition of sexual arousal. One such study found that men who were shown a sexually explicit movie could voluntarily control the possibility of erection by thinking about nonsexual matters (35). Another experiment confirmed the hypothesis that cognitive distraction interferes with erection in men (22). Sex therapists have long noted that "mental" (e.g., cognitive) distraction interferes with sexual stimulation and reduces sexual arousal (54).

In contrast, a concentration of attention upon thoughts of erotic pleasure appears to intensify sexual arousal. Interview research has found that women who concentrate upon erotic fantasies during sexual intercourse report that such imagery intensifies their sexual responses (31). Some sex therapists now advise patients who have problems in achieving orgasm to concentrate on erotic mental imagery in order to avoid distracting thoughts which induce anxiety, guilt, or fear of failure (4). Men and women both experience sexual arousal in response to erotic fantasies alone, without body contact (34). Some people, though very few, are even capable of fantasizing to orgasm (41). In addition, sexual arousal in response to sexually explicit photographs, movies and literature is ultimately a response to the stimulation of cognitive imagery. (Lower animals do not exhibit sexual arousal to such indirect stimulation.) Much more research into the sexual effects of cognitive processes is needed. However, the available research indicates the central importance of cognitive processes in the inhibition and intensification of sexual arousal. It appears that cognitive interference inhibits sexual arousal, while a concentration of attention upon erotic imagery intensifies sexual arousal.

It is not at all unusual that brain functioning should affect other physiological processes in the human body. The effects of brain functioning on the body may include such distresses as ulcers, hypertension, gastric disorders, and even skin rashes. In certain neurotic disorders, brain functioning in response to life experiences may simulate the bodily symptoms of blindness, deafness, or even paralysis. Therefore, it should not be surprising to find that brain functioning can intensify or inhibit genital sensitivity. The exact physiological mechanisms involved are not yet understood. However, it is known that feelings of affection can intensify sexual arousal, while feelings of anxiety, guilt and depression can inhibit sexual arousal. It is believed that the connection between emotional responses and physiological responses operates through the limbic system of the brain.

Social Learning

Behavioral scientists have developed a reasonably adequate understanding of the general principles of human learning in everyday social interaction. Three basic mechanisms of social learning can be recognized, including: 1) conditioning, 2) modeling, and 3) cognitive learning. These three mechanisms of learning usually occur simultaneosuly, so that it is a bit artificial to focus upon one or another in an actual situation.

Conditioning involves learning which is the result of the effects of rewards and punishments. People are constantly being exposed to an environment which rewards and punishes their behavior. Generally, actions which are constantly rewarded tend to be continued, while ones that are constantly punished tend to be discontinued. These experiences of pleasure and pain may be direct, or indirect and symbolic. (For example, giving candy to a child as a reward is a direct gratification, while praise is symbolic and indirectly satisfying. When a child receives a spanking, it is a directly painful experience; while receiving ridicule is symbolic and indirectly painful.)

It is not only actions which can be shaped by conditioning, but also bodily responses. Sexual arousal can be effected by rewards and punishments. When sexual arousal is frequently rewarded, sexual desire is intensified (29). However, when punishments are applied to sexual arousal, the effect can be the inhibition or depression of sexual desire. Sexual desire, then, becomes associated with an unpleasant bodily state. For example, a child may find that stimulating its genitals provides it with pleasure. The reward of pleasure will enhance sexual desire, as well as encourage the behavior which results in pleasure. If a parent often punishes a child for such behavior, it will occur less frequently. In addition, punishment will become associated with its sexual desire. When both rewards and punishments become associated with sexual arousal, a person experiences sex anxiety (3).

The second mechanism of learning is modeling. Modeling involves observation and imitation, usually of intimate associates. Children, especially, learn a great deal by imitating the behavior which they observe in their parents and close friends. They use the behavior of another person in certain situations as a model for their own behavior, when they encounter similar situations. Rarely, however, is observational-imitation a matter of conscious and deliberate planning. Usually, the model is cognitively programmed and remains latent in subconscious memory, until a relevant situation activates it.

In our society, there is scarce possibility for children to observe adult sexual activity. However, modeling does play a very important role in sexual learning among children, as they observe interpersonal behavior indirectly associated with sexual activity. A child may observe its parents embrace, caress each other and express words of affection. Later on in life in male-female relations, that model will be repeated more easily than if it had never been experienced. (How much later in life may become a parental worry.) A child who sees its parents worried about nudity in the home will likely become anxious about nudity, even though it may not know why (80). In general, role models can provide positive or negative associations with sexual desire and arousal.

Cognitive learning involves learning which depends upon language. Language consists of a code of spoken and written symbols which have no meaning in themselves. Instead, linguistic symbols represent human meanings which have become culturally associated with sounds and writing. Linguistic symbols are able to convey complex chains of associations which are only indirectly linked to concrete experiences. Cognitive learning about sexual matters derives from stories, jokes, direct explanation and sometimes even from books. Such learning involves structuring the brain's pathways. It can be compared with learning the details of a very complicated map.

Certain kinds of abstract symbols are particularly important in sexual learning. These include beliefs, values and rules for behavior. Many beliefs about the nature of sexual stimuli affect sexual arousal. Human values are constantly applied to evaluate sexual stimuli, and also sexual desire itself. These may be evaluated as a benefit or burden of being alive. In addition, sexual arousal is influenced by personal standards of conduct, which can be the basis for feelings of self-esteem or guilt.

Some examples illustrate the influence of cognitive learning upon sexual arousal. In American society today, most women and many men learn the value that sexual pleasure should be associated with love. Love is not directly experienced, but symbolized in expressions of affection. When this value is strongly internalized, it may be difficult for a person to respond sexually, without anxiety, to an interpersonal encounter which omits expressions of affection. The same person may react to an affectionate relationship with intense sexual arousal.

Little research has investigated the role of cognitive learning in the development of childhood sexuality, except for studies of sources of sex information at various age levels (14, 47, 72). It would also be very useful to have research data about the nature and effects of sex misinformation upon erotic development. We do know that many parents teach children to associate their genitals and sexual activity with "dirtiness." Many parents also encourage a symbolic association of sexual matters with sickness, both physical and "emotional." Certainly, the traditional association of sexuality with sinfulness remains important in some families.

Parents attempt to structure the thinking of their children at the same time that they attempt to guide behavior. Even if parents clearly desire to do so, it is difficult to communicate accurate sex information geared to the child's age-level of comprehension (9, 10). Too much irrelevant detail may only confuse a child, while too much simplicity may underestimate the child's real ability to understand sexual matters. However, the difficulties of parents do not lie here as much as in their own anxieties about provoking a child's sexual curiosity and experimentation. (Parents, for example, can find adequate ways of "explaining" how a rocket is sent to Mars.) Many parents are also embarrassed about discussing sexual matters with children of the opposite sex. Fathers feel inadequate and anxious about discussing menstruation with daughters, and mothers feel similarly about discussing male sexual processes. When sex information is offered, it is usually too little and too late (47).

In addition, information which is considered "sex information" is almost always about reproductive sexuality. Rarely does "sex information," as conceived by parents (or schools), refer to matters of erotic pleasure, or even love relationships (47). These matters are viewed by parents as even more delicate, emotional and mysterious.

One aspect of parental control of sex information is particularly important to cognitive development. There is an absence of an adequate sexual language for children (80). American parents do not offer their children an adequate vocabulary to label and discuss genital parts, sex differences, sexual activities, and sensual feelings. This *linguistic deprivation* makes it very difficult for the child to express its curiosity and to understand its bodily feelings (3). Eventually, the child is forced to rely upon the subterranean language of the streets, learned from older playmates (14). The child quickly learns that the use of sex slang and "obscene" language will be punished by parents and other adults. Since that language becomes the only relevant language in which a child can express its sexuality, it is reserved for secretive use among playmates. Especially among boys, as they reach adolescence, "obscene" language becomes a code language for acceptance in the male peer group. Girls are much less likely, to learn and use such language, because it is permeated with connotations of male superiority and contempt for women. (For example, to "fuck" or "screw" a girl connotes a hostile act, which symbolizes male superiority. Girls do not "fuck" boys. They "make love" to them.) There has been little research on the effects of this subterranean sex language upon the cognitive development of sexual attitudes in children and adolescents. The use of sexual language may be one cause of the earlier erotic awakening in boys than girls.

The absence of an adequate vocabulary in any matter impedes thinking and communication. Sexual concerns are no different from any other aspect of human life in this respect (21). The problem of linguistic deprivation extends from childhood into adulthood. Many parents, as husbands and wives, find it very difficult to communicate with each other about their sexual feelings, desires and intentions. This is partly because adults also lack an adequate sexual vocabulary. The clinical sex vocabulary of science is foreign and quite awkward for everyday use. In contrast, the Anglo-Saxon vernacular ("vulgar") sex vocabulary is quite vague for delicate self-expression, in addition to being considered disreputable. Well-educated couples, who have open communication about their sexual relationship, doubtless find ways of fabricating a reasonably adequate sexual vocabulary. However, the deprivation of an adequate sexual language may account for the difficulties that lower-class parents have in communicating about sexual matters between husbands and wives and between parents and their children (14).

Perception

The meaning of a "sexual" stimulus (person, object, or event) is not the stimulus itself. Instead, human meaning is attributed to stimuli. Perception involves the brain's reception of stimulation, as well as the interpretation of its meaning (48). Stimuli which are interpreted as being "sexual" do not directly affect the nervous system through the body senses, mechanically triggering sexual arousal. In the human brain, the processes of perception ("seeing") and cognition ("understanding") are linked. We see with our brain as much as with our eyes. The brain attributes human meaning to the data of the senses, simultaneously as it processes those data.

Sexual stimuli are perceived as sexual only because erotic meanings are being attributed to them by the brain. This does not imply that perception involves conscious and deliberate judgments. Instead, most of the time, perception is a response to ingrained learning, and operates on a subconscious level of awareness.

The cognitive attribution of erotic meaning applies even to the perception of internal bodily sensations associated with physiological arousal. (Including, for example, genital throbbing, nervous restlessness, and increased heartbeat.) In isolation from external feedback information, bodily sensations are ambiguous. We must rely upon external informational cues to guide our understanding of our own internal feeling states (75). An ingenious laboratory experiment provided evidence for this principle (88). A sample of male subjects were asked to appraise and rate the attractiveness of several *Playboy* centerfold pictures. They were told that their heartbeats would be monitored and amplified as they viewed the pictures. Actually, what they heard was an amplification of false heartbeats. The experimenter wanted to test the effects of false feedback information, so he systematically increased and decreased the false heartbeats. This falsified information had a dramatic effect upon the subject's appraisal of the pictures. Those pictures which were accompanied by increased heartbeats were rated as more attractive by the subjects. This experiment demonstrates that emotional and sexual responses are not simple physiological reactions, detached from cognitive functioning. Even the sensations of sexual arousal are subject to varying cognitive interpretations and therefore varying perceptual experiences. Such sensations may occasion pleasure, anxiety or revulsion.

Compared with other animals, humans are capable of being sexually aroused by an unusually wide range of stimuli. This is a consequence of the human ability to attribute erotic meanings to all sorts of stimuli which have only a distant association with coitus. Erotic meanings may be attributed by some people, for example, to articles of clothing, particular body parts, special words, artistic creations and even certain foods.

Two levels of erotic meanings can be distinguished: 1) the cultural level and 2) the personal level. The cultural level refers to widely shared meanings, which have their source in the common cultural heritage of a society. Such erotic meanings are rooted in traditional beliefs and expectations about sexual stimuli. When individuals attribute erotic meaning to any sexual stimulus, they usually do so because of socially structured learning. The seductive mood music of our culture is not apt to seem erotic to natives of New Guinea, just as their cosmetic body scars would not be an erotic "turn-on" for us. There is also a personal level of erotic meanings which are a product of relatively unusual experiences and learnings within a society. Personal erotic meanings are much like personal preferences. Just as personal taste in food differs somewhat within a society, so do erotic tastes. However, it is an error to exaggerate the extent to which erotic meanings are personalized. Most people who share a culture share erotic tastes in common, just as they do their tastes in food.

Some examples will serve to illustrate the levels and types of erotic meanings. In American culture, lip kissing is primarily a symbolic expression of intimacy. It may also be considered a mild sensual pleasure. In some cultures the custom does not exist; instead, lip kissing is regarded as peculiar, vulgar, or amusingly novel. In American culture, oral-genital kissing used to be considered perverted and repulsive. These symbolic associations were a product of traditional sexual beliefs and values embedded in American culture. However, today a majority of Americans have redefined it as an expression of intimacy (37). Some people are sexually aroused by wearing the clothes of the opposite sex (transvestites). In our culture, as well as most others, such an erotic taste is an expression of very unusual, personal learnings. Similarly, many behavioral scientists believe that erotic responsiveness to the bodies of members of one's own sex is learned. Homosexual eroticism may be learned through unusual personal experience.

Even the nude body is not a sexual stimulus in itself. Erotic definitions of nudity are attributed to nude bodies as a consequence of people's social learning. In many societies in hot climates, people may wear little clothing, while in other places they may wear much clothing. Nudity and body modesty are a response to cultural expectations. Nude-bathing beaches are becoming fashionable in some places in the United States and Europe (13). On such beaches, public nudity is not regarded as an occasion for sexual arousal, except perhaps among nonparticipants. Research in nudist camps has found that various subtle customs serve to discourage people from attributing erotic meanings to public nudity (90). In public situations, sexual arousal in response to nudity can result in embarrassment, especially for men. Nudists and "skinny dippers" certainly continue to regard nudity as a stimulus for sexual arousal, but they learn to respond to it erotically in a situation of privacy.

In relation to the perception of erotic meanings, it is instructive to consider the great American "breast fetish" (38, 62). (A fetish involves sexual behavior which has become especially focused upon a particular object or body part, as an erotic symbol.) After his research on male sexuality, Kinsey concluded that there "is reason to believe that more males in our culture are psychically aroused by contemplation of the female breast than by the sight of the female genitalia (40)." Many American men believe that all women are sexually aroused by breast caressing, and that large-breasted women are more sexually responsive than are small-breasted women. (Neither is true.) At an early age, when sexual intercourse would evoke feelings of guilt and embarrassment, American teenagers commonly practice breast fondling as a substitute for genital contact. Breast fondling during petting reinforces the erotic significance of women's breasts. Yet, in many societies, women are publicly bare-chested without having to be concerned about evoking sexual arousal in men (87). In many societies, the female breast is not an erotic symbol, and breast fondling does not occur during sexual activity (17). In many societies, the female breast is a symbol of motherhood and maternal nurturance (unreplaced by bottle feeding). However, in American society, women who have breast-fed their babies in public have been arrested for public sexual indecency (11). The percentage of American mothers who breast-feed their infants is among the lowest in the world (11). It is clear that women's breasts are a sexual rather than a maternal symbol among Americans. In American culture, there has arisen a veritable breast cult composed of training bras, padded bras, bustline exercises and silicone treatments. Many young women suffer anxiety about their breast size and worry about their attractiveness to men (12).

Why is the female breast so important as an erotic symbol in American culture? Perhaps because the female breast is an obvious physical symbol of feminine identity. It has become a prestige symbol as well. Many Americans worry about the degree of their masculinity or femininity. In sharp contrast to increasing similarities between the sexes in behavior and clothing styles, women's breasts acknowledge their distinctiveness from men. Well-developed breasts symbolically reassure women of their feminine attractiveness. In a complementary way, men learn to be erotically attracted to that symbol of female sexuality, often confusing quantity with quality.

There is as yet no clear understanding of the psychological factors which influence perception, so that certain forms of stimulation come to be regarded as sexually arousing. Why are certain stimuli "seen" as erotic and others not perceived as such? Social learning obviously accounts for nature of perception, in general terms. However, more specific perceptual mechanisms are relevant. People learn certain psychological predispositions to "see" stimulation as being sexual. Such predispositions are technically known as a person's *perceptual set*. In other words, people learn to respond to particular "cues" in a social situation with a readiness for sexual arousal. The naked breasts of women are such a cue for many men. Yet, the meaning of cues are judged from their social context. Nudity, or even genital manipulation, is not generally defined as a cue for sexual arousal when it occurs in a doctor's office (15). A person's perceptual set operates within the context of the particular *definitions of the situation,* shared by participants in that situation. Nudity in a bedroom may be a cue for sexual arousal, if a married couple define the occasion as being appropriate. (They may not do so, and the occasion may not result in sexual arousal.) In contrast, the definition of the situation in nudist camps and public nudist beaches is such that nudity is not a cue for sexual arousal. The possibility always exists, of course, that participants may not share the same definition of the situation. A woman who invites a male friend to her apartment for a few drinks may find that he has a perceptual set to see the situation in terms of erotic meanings, rather than as an occasion for friendly conversation. In summary, sexual arousal occurs when a person attributes erotic meaning to a situation. Erotic responsiveness is necessary for sexual arousal to occur.

Erotic Response

Two basic dimensions of sexual arousal can be distinguished: 1) sexual response and 2) erotic response. Sexual response is indicated by such bodily changes as erection in men, genital lubrication in women, and increasing muscular tension in both sexes. Sexual response in the body follows a cycle of physiological changes from initial excitement through orgasm to bodily relaxation (54). Erotic responsiveness facilitates these bodily changes. Erotic response is a reaction to learning, and as a psychological phenomenon it should be distinguished from sexual response, which is biological. The two are closely interrelated, of course, whenever sexual arousal occurs. Nevertheless, there isn't always a consistent relationship between them.

Erotic response is a psychological readiness for sexual arousal. It occurs as a consequence of a person's attribution of erotic meaning to stimuli. Certain psychological reactions such as affection, confidence and curiosity can enhance sexual arousal. On the other hand, certain psychological reactions, such as guilt, disgust, anger or embarrassment can inhibit a person's erotic response and deaden sexual arousal. And, as just previously noted, some people attribute no erotic meaning to stimuli which other people find sexually arousing. In the end, human beings experience sexual arousal in response to what they learn. They are not "turned on" by biological "switches."

Two dimensions of erotic response as a readiness for sexual arousal can be identified. These are: 1) disinhibition, and 2) anticipation. Disinhibition is a form of relaxation, which occurs at the same time as the bodily

Diagram 1: The Social Psychology of Sexual Arousal

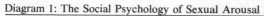

Diagram 1: The Social Psychology of Sexual Arousal

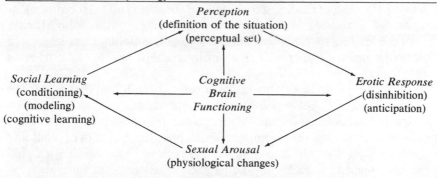

Perception
(definition of the situation)
(perceptual set)

Social Learning
(conditioning)
(modeling)
(cognitive learning)

*Cognitive
Brain
Functioning*

Erotic Response
(disinhibition)
(anticipation)

Sexual Arousal
(physiological changes)

The diagram above shows the interrelationships between the various factors relevant to the social psychology of sexual arousal.

nervousness of sexual arousal. Disinhibition lets down the barriers of social reserve. The disinhibited person relaxes worries about potential embarrassment, shame, guilt or distraction. That is what gives sexual activity its seemingly spontaneous quality. This relaxation response enables a receptivity to sensual stimulation, more than that which is usually possible in most ongoing everyday activities. Certain conditions, such as privacy, familiarity with partner and mutual affection, promote disinhibition for most people. Some people, in some situations, use alcohol to relax before sexual activity. Anticipation focuses attention upon sensual feelings and intensifies the buildup of bodily tension toward orgasm. It is the expectation that sexual activity will result in a pleasurable emotional state. Anticipation is intensified by such conditions as a short abstinence from sexual activity and variety in sexual activity. Anticipation is strengthened by past experiences of pleasure and weakened by displeasurable associations (50). In summary, both relaxation and tension are necessary aspects of erotic response.

SEXUAL FANTASY AS COGNITIVE PROCESS

Sexual fantasies provide an example par excellence of a cognitive-symbolic process which enhances sexual arousal. In the case of fantasies, cognitive stimulation is provided directly by brain functioning, although a chain of imagery may be evoked incidentally or deliberately by preceding environmental stimuli. The scientific investigation of daydreaming, sexual fantasies included, is still in its infancy. Research is finally being done with large samples of people who are not psychiatric cases. In the past, the almost singular reliance upon psychiatric case studies have distorted our understanding of this cognitive phenomenon. It is now becoming clear that sexual fantasies play a central role in sexual arousal. John Money, one of the leading specialists in human sexual functioning, has suggested that sexual fantasy is a crucial element in romantic and sexual attraction (58).

Daydreaming is an inborn cognitive capacity in children, first evidenced in their "make-believe" play. It may be encouraged or discouraged by parents and schools. The material environment of play toys is much less important than a social environment which provides a wealth of ideas and some privacy for children to play "make-believe." Research with children has found that such play helps their intellectual development by promoting their verbal ability, creative imagination, and ability to concentrate their attention (18, 70). Adults who were more frequent daydreamers during childhood are found to be more creative, imaginative and original thinkers (83). More research needs to be done; but at this point, at least, it seems clear that daydreaming is not a simple escape from frustrating experience, as has been the common assumption in the past. It also seems clear that certain kinds of learning enhance a person's capacity for daydreaming, while other kinds of learning may actively discourage the development of this cognitive process.

Sexual fantasies in daydreams are quite common for most people throughout their adult years. One research project investigated the daydreams of 375 men (23, 24). It found sexual fantasy to be the most common daydream content among men from ages seventeen to twenty-three, and second most common among men from ages twenty-four to sixty-five. After that age, sexual daydreams became less frequent. It has also been found that throughout the life cycle men's frequency of sexual daydreaming is closely correlated with their frequency of sexual activity. Men who are more sexually active also tend to have a more active sexual fantasy life than do men who are less sexually active (25). Sexual fantasy in daydreams may be self-induced during tedious tasks or just before falling asleep. Such flights of fantasy may also be a response to people encountered, advertisements, pornography, masturbation, or even sexual intercourse. In early adolescence, sexual fantasies may not be very explicitly sexual in content, instead focusing upon romantic seduction, kissing, hugging and petting (67). As age increases through the teenage years, the content becomes more sexually explicit and imaginative.

The evolution of sexual fantasies may be a response to the extent of sexual information (and misinformation) that becomes available to the imagination of a person. By late adolescence, or youth, many people have fantasies about socially forbidden sexual activities. Some young people feel needlessly guilty or worried about their sanity due to having such "dirty thoughts." Most of them, however, are less troubled in making the distinction between fantasy life and practical realities.

In recent years, some sex research has touched upon sexual fantasies while investigating other matters (16, 33, 37, 85). Such research reveals that the content of most sexual fantasies involves imagining past sexual experiences, sex with a beloved person, and sex with a stranger or acquaintance. Less common fantasies involve sexual activity with several partners, or sexual activity involving some degree of force. Least common are fantasies involving homosexual contact, physical harm, or public sexual exhibitionism.

A careful and systematic research investigation of sexual fantasies was carried out on a sample of 141 suburban housewives, none of whom were psychiatric patients (30, 31). The research investigated the sexual fantasies that these women experienced during sexual intercourse. The findings were surprising because they were contrary to psychoanalytic theories about women, which claim that only sexually frustrated women have sexual daydreams. Almost all the women reported having sexual fantasies during intercourse; 65 percent of them at least some of the time, and another 37 percent very frequently. The content of these daydreams is listed below, in decending order of their frequency of occurrence.

The Ten Most Common Sexual Fantasies of Women
(from Hariton, 1973; N = 141 women)

1. Thoughts of an imaginary lover enter my mind.
2. I imagine that I am being overpowered or forced to surrender.
3. I enjoy pretending that I am doing something wicked or forbidden.
4. I am in a different place like a car, motel, beach, woods, etc.
5. I relive a previous sexual experience.
6. I imagine myself delighting many men.
7. I imagine that I am observing myself or others having sex.
8. I pretend that I am another irresistibly sexy female.
9. I pretend that I struggle and resist before being aroused to surrender.
10. I daydream that I am being made love to by more than one man at a time.

Data from questionnaires and intensive interviews were submitted to extensive statistical analysis, so that conclusions could be drawn about the causes and effects of these sexual fantasies. The basic conclusion was that "the results indicated that general daydreaming frequency was associated with occurrence of fantasies during intercourse and that such fantasies were generally not related to sexual or marital difficulty, but rather with an enhancement of desire and pleasure (30)." In other words, women who daydreamed more frequently about other matters were also the ones more likely to daydream about sexual matters, and to use sexual fantasies to heighten their sexual arousal. One of the most important findings was that women who had positive thoughts about their husbands during sexual intercourse were just as likely to have sexual fantasies as were those women whose attitude toward their husbands were negative. Such findings have led investigators to question the assumption that sexual fantasies are an indication of psychological problems in women or in men. Sexual fantasies have long been regarded as dangerous and sinful in Western culture, perhaps due to traditional religious teachings about sexual thoughts.

It seems clear that sexual daydreams are similar in their causes, effects and purposes to nonsexual daydreams. Any single simplistic interpretation of the nature of sexual fantasies would be incorrect. Sexual fantasies may be a diversion from boredom; or they may serve to heighten the intensity of sexual pleasure. They may serve individuals as a rehearsal and extension of sexual possibilities; or they may be passing flights of entertaining imagination. Sexual fantasies may, for some troubled people, be a source of guilt, and for others a source of frustrated aspirations. Most importantly, the existence of the capacity for sexual fantasy may help to explain why so much of the human environment can become symbolically eroticized, in the absence of direct conditioning.

More systematic research about sexual fantasies is needed in order to better understand sexual attitudes and behavior. Such research can lead to a better understanding of psychological differences (and similarities) between the sexes. At this point, we already have some insight into male-female differences in sexual fantasy content (5). In general, it appears that the sexual fantasies common among men and women are those which are consistent with their differences in sex-role learning.

The sexual fantasies of men, contrasted with those of women, are usually more body-oriented, and neglect interpersonal relationships and emotional responses. In a sense, they are more genitally gymnastic, with few interpersonal preliminaries, like most of the pornography produced by men for men. Women's sexual fantasies usually give greater consideration to overall interpersonal relationships and emotional responses. They are less body-oriented, and many women's sexual fantasies are only indirectly sexual. In this relation, men's sexual fantasies tend to be much more visually detailed, in terms of imagination being focused upon women's body parts and genital activity. Women's fantasies very frequently provide few visual details of their fantasied partners but much more detail about their own imagined feeling states.

Another difference between male and female sexual fantasies reflects sex differences in socialization and role relations in a curious way. Many women have fantasies about being coerced, or forced, to engage in sexual activity, although almost always without any bodily harm imagined (tender coercion). Few men have fantasies of being forced to have sexual contact. Curiously, one study found that sexual-force fantasies are more likely to be imagined by women who have learned to be sexually assertive with men (30). Perhaps such fantasies serve to affirm women's sense of their (traditional) femininity (5). In women's "rape" fantasies, it is the power of a woman's physical attractiveness which causes men to lose control. An alternative interpretation may be that such women are simply more sexually self-confident and feel secure in such fantasy explorations (30). It should be noted, however, that the common existence of such coercion fantasies does not support the myth that many women actually desire to be raped and sexually abused (32). The private world of "make-believe" is one in which imaginary actors can be carefully controlled by the daydreamer. Most people are well aware of the distinctions between fantasy life and actual behavior.

An important research question concerns the relationship between sexual fantasy and socially condemned sexual behavior. Do fantasies of such behavior have the effect of increasing the likelihood of the actual behavior? Should such fantasies be regarded as symptoms of psychological problems? Unfortunately, little adequate research has been carried out on this matter.

It is known that sexual fantasies about group sex, homosexual contact, exhibitionism, sadistic (harming others) and masochistic (being harmed) practices are not particularly common. Yet, such fantasies are by no means rare. Indeed, such fantasies occur more frequently than do the socially condemned behavior which they portray. That provides a clue. Perhaps even fantasies about deviant sexual behavior may be only passing imaginary diversions, unless they are reinforced by actual life experience. One research project investigated the sexual fantasies of rapists, child molesters and homosexuals, as compared with a control group of men. As expected, homosexuals tended to have more homosexual fantasies and rapists tended to have more sadistic fantasies than did the control group. However, the investigators noted that they could not determine if the sexual fantasies were a contributing cause or a consequence of their sexual activities (26).

Daydreams about strongly condemned sexual activities, much like other sexual fantasies, may represent merely cognitive explorations of improbable happenings, prompted by nothing more than curiosity. At any rate, the research evidence which exists indicates that the contents of a person's fantasies (of any kind) are not particularly useful in predicting a person's actual behavior (42).

THE PSYCHOLOGY OF MALE AND FEMALE EROTIC RESPONSIVENESS

Erotic response refers to the psychological factors which enhance a person's sexual arousal. Recent research has found no clear-cut difference between men and women in their erotic responsiveness. Instead, all the erotic differences which exist between men and women are matters of statistical differences in modal frequencies. There is considerable overlap between males and females in any factor which may be discussed as a difference. Indeed, the research indicates an increasing convergence of male and female sexuality, especially among more recent generations of Americans and Europeans. In the future, it might become impossible to make any useful distinctions between men and women in erotic responsiveness. Any distinctions will become matters of individual differences. Even today, the differences in erotic response and sexual behavior are, perhaps, greater among males and among females in different social groups, such as ethnic groups, religions and social classes. In contrast to much speculation, no biological differences have been found that can account for any differences in erotic response between men and women. There is increasing agreement among sex researchers that male-female differences in erotic responsiveness are a consequence of differences in erotic socialization.

Most of the research on erotic response has been done since the late 1960s and there is not enough of it to allow any definitive conclusions. Many of these investigations have relied upon laboratory experiments in which relatively small and unrepresentative samples of volunteers are exposed to vicarious sexual stimulation. The stimuli usually consist of photographs, slides, movies, tapes of stories, or selections of readings in which explicit sexual activity is depicted. The laboratory research has proven to be very useful. Nevertheless, some caution must be maintained in appraising the findings drawn from such research. First of all, people's responses in laboratory conditions may differ considerably from those in actual interpersonal situations. In addition, most of the subjects in these experiments have been college students, so the findings may tell us very little about the responses of people who are older and not college-educated. Finally, past measurements of sexual arousal have usually had to rely upon self-reports. More recently, however, instruments have been developed to directly measure penile erection and vaginal swelling (33, 34). These are now being used in conjunction with self-reports of attitudes.

A variety of personality factors have been found to be associated with an enhancement or inhibition of erotic responsiveness. The most important of these include feelings of love, previous sexual experience and degree of sex guilt.

Feelings of love in response to an affectionate relationship is one of the most potent intensifiers of erotic responsiveness for men, as well as women. While it is true that more men than women are capable of responding with sexual arousal to a sexual relationship in which affection is absent, it is incorrect to suggest that men are erotically unaffected by feelings of love. An affectionate partner who enjoys sexual activity is probably the single most stimulating "stimulus condition" for the vast majority of people of both sexes. Men and women are about equally responsive to erotic stimuli in a romantic, affectionate context (33, 34, 78, 79, 82). An intensive study of the factors associated with orgasm in women found that a woman's feelings of love for her partner, and confidence in that love relationship, was the single factor which was most predictive of a woman's consistency in experiencing orgasm (16). Phrased negatively, a woman's lack of confidence in a love relationship was the factor found to be most predictive of problems in achieving orgasm. Unfortunately, similar studies have not yet turned attention to the relationship of affection with male orgasmic problems. While it may still be true that a context of affection is a necessary ingredient in the erotic responsiveness of more women than men, increasing numbers of young men associate love closely with sexual arousal. And, among many older men, feelings of being unloved by a marital partner may be an important source of early impotence.

There is some evidence that previously enjoyable participation in a sexual activity may serve to reinforce and strengthen erotic responsiveness to future involvement in that activity. Research with middle-aged and elderly couples has found that past enjoyment of sexual activity is the most important determinant of the maintenance of erotic responsiveness (68). In addition, one research project found that men and women who had more previous sexual experience were more sexually aroused by slides depicting various explicit sexual acts than were those subjects who had less sexual experience (27). Another research project using sexually explicit films had the same findings about sexual experience (63). Simple familiarity with a sexual activity may not be sufficient to reinforce erotic responsiveness. In social learning terms, participation in any activity must be emotionally enjoyable for the experience to strengthen a learned response. The meanings which people attribute to their experience are crucial. Prostitutes have considerable sexual experience, but they are usually erotically unresponsive to their clients (46).

The effects of sex guilt upon erotic responsiveness and sexual arousal have been a topic of frequent discussion and controversy but unfortunately little research until recently. Sex guilt may be described as a form of self-condemnation, which results in feelings of anxiety and disgust, when a person transgresses his or her personal standards of sexual conduct. Several investigations have found that college students who scored high in tests of sex guilt reported themselves as engaging in less socially condemned sexual behavior than did college students who scored low in sex guilt (1, 64). The high-guilt students were less likely to engage in masturbation, any form of heavy petting, or in premarital sexual intercourse. They gave moral reasons rather than practical ones for their abstinence, and also condemned cunnilingus and fellatio in any sexual relationship as being "abnormal." These findings confirm the hypothesis that the sexual behavior of high-guilt persons is much more self-restricted than is that of persons with low sex guilt. But what about erotic responsiveness and sexual arousal in high-guilt persons? Other research throws some light on this question. Studies of reactions to sexually explicit literature and films have found that both high and low sex guilt subjects respond with sexual arousal to such erotic stimulation (65). However, the subjects who were high in sex guilt responded with significantly greater feelings of guilt, disgust, and embarrassment, and with lower arousal. It is not known whether high sex guilt persons are erotically inhibited in marital sexual relations. It is most probable that variety in their marital sexual relations is severely inhibited, and limited to sexual intercourse in conventionally accepted positions. In summary, it would appear from the available research that high sex guilt does not extinguish erotic responsiveness, but it does result in unpleasant emotional states in response to unconventional sexual behavior.

Are women more likely than men to learn sex guilt, as is popularly believed? There is no direct evidence that this is so, but the indirect evidence strongly suggests that it is true. Experimental studies have shown that as many women as men react to sexually explicit photographs, films and literature with sexual arousal, but many more women have negative emotional feelings about it (33, 36, 63, 77, 78, 79, 82). Several of these studies have also found that more women than men react negatively to presentations of unconventional sexual practices, such as unusual intercourse positions and oral-genital caressing (63, 77). Research focusing upon actual sexual behavior has found that more women than men respond with guilt to masturbation and premarital intercourse (73). It should be noted with caution that many of the findings about negative emotions do not distinguish reactions of simple sex anxiety from those of sex guilt.

Kinsey came to the conclusion after his research that fewer women than men are erotically aroused via visual stimulation, as for example, by the sight of nudity in the opposite sex (41). Today, evidence about this conclusion is contradictory. Recently, a large sample of male and female college students were shown copies of either *Playboy* or *Playgirl*, and asked about their emotional responses to the contents (86). The reactions of the women indicated considerable ambivalence to photographs of male nudes, while the men were much more consistently pleased by the female photographs. While 75 percent of the men found the photographs to be sexually stimulating, only 25 percent of the women reported a similar reaction. Yet, much research appears to contradict assumptions about sex differences in visual erotic responsiveness. It has been found that men and women are about equally aroused sexually by much more explicit movies of people engaging in sexual activity (63, 76, 78). This is particularly true when such movies do not convey a contemptuous attitude toward women as does most pornography. It would appear that photographs of mere nudity are less stimulating for women (and perhaps, simple nudity itself), but that presentations of sexual activity do elicit women's sexual arousal. A resolution of this apparent contradiction may be that the social context of nudity is more relevant to the sexual arousal of women than men.

Since movies of interpersonal activity are equally arousing for both sexes, but that still photographs are less so for women, it may be that women can more easily relate to such a context as being more "real." Perhaps, also, the gradualness of movies functions to moderate sex anxiety in response to erotic stimulation (20). Abrupt sexual stimuli, having little association with interpersonal relationships, may more easily evoke sex anxiety among women.

If we shift the focus of attention to the erotic responsiveness of men, these differences in reaction to nudity may indicate that many men continue to be sexually aroused by stimuli which are relatively impersonal. The greater male responsiveness to impersonal contexts of erotic stimulation is revealed in a number of ways. Men's erotic fantasies, in contrast with those of women, are more likely to focus upon genital gymnastics than interpersonal relationships (5). Much pornography, which is made by men for men, illustrates such fantasy by giving disproportionate attention to genitals (rather than people) in action. Facial expressions, emotional reactions and interpersonal relationships are matters given little consideration (84). In actual sexual behavior, many men continue to be able to engage in petting or sexual intercourse without "loving" or even caring about their female partners.

The traditional male attitude toward sexuality has been that sex is basically a matter of physical functioning. This attitude is expressed in moralistic, hedonistic and scientific messages. It is curious, and indicative of the depth of change in the meaning of human sexuality that, in all these sexual matters, concern is shifting to a more interpersonal conception of sexuality, one more consistent with a symbolic interactionist perspective on human relationships.

THE NATURE OF SEXUAL DESIRE

In popular thought, the motivation for sexual behavior is often labeled an "instinct." Unfortunately, the popular meaning of this label is far from clear. Different people use it in different ways. Generally, it is intended to imply that the motive for sexual behavior is inborn and unlearned. It is meant to suggest that all people are born with some sort of predisposition to behave in complicated sexual ways. Also, the notion of a sexual instinct is often meant to suggest that familiar forms of sexual behavior are rooted in the biology of human beings. The implication is that human sexual behavior does not change over the ages, nor is it very different throughout the world. However, behavioral scientists today know that these presumptions are incorrect (7). This kind of thinking flows from a purely biological model of human sexuality.

It is useful to compare human sexual desire with hunger, in order to gain insight into the nature of sexual motivation. Hunger results from a definite bodily need. The need is for nutrient substances (proteins, carbohydrates, fats, vitamins, minerals) which enable the cells of the body to survive and reproduce. If a person is deprived of these nutrients, that person will die. No comparable situation exists in relation to sexual desire. If a person's sexual desire is deprived of gratification, no cell tissue is destroyed. People need not worry about death from sexual starvation. The many people who have trained themselves to live a celibate life such as monks, priests and nuns (Christian, Buddhist and Hindu) are a testimony of this simple reality. In addition, there is no conclusive evidence that such people suffer terrible psychological consequences. The bodily sexual need is quite unlike the bodily need for food, water, air or sleep.

However, there are some interesting similarities between sexual desire and hunger. A person's hunger may be inflated or diminished as a consequence of what they learn. People can rather easily learn to diet or overeat. Similarly, sexual desire may be inhibited or intensified in response to what a person learns. Eating certain socially condemned foods are regarded as "perversions," as are certain forms of sexual gratification.

The effects of abstinence upon level of sexual desire is not entirely clear. A short period of abstinence appears to increase sexual desire in most people who are predisposed to enjoy sexual activity. However, abstinence from sexual activity alone does not in itself always result in an increase in sexual desire (29). A crucial factor may be whether or not previous sexual activity has been experienced by a person as being pleasurable. In addition, the effects of long-term sexual abstinence may be quite different from short-term abstinence. There are many reports that long-term deprivation of sexual stimulation actually diminishes sexual desire, resulting in sexual apathy. (A similar effect is found in cases of long-term food starvation.) Reports of sexual apathy, due to long-term sexual abstinence, come from instances of people who are sexually isolated for long periods of time, such as in prisons or in remote military installations (53). It should also be noted with caution that much sexual stimulation among humans is indirect and in symbolic form. Indirect sexual stimulation encountered in conversation and the mass media may function to maintain a certain level of sexual desire, in the absence of direct sexual activity. This may account for relatively high levels of sexual desire among some people who have very infrequent sexual activity.

Sexual desire is often termed sexual "drive" by behavioral scientists. Thus they seek to classify sexual desire as one of the basic motives for a person's behavior. A drive is characterized by: 1) the arousal of bodily energy, 2) exerted in persistent behavior directed toward particular goals, which 3) become the focus of selective attention. Certainly, sexual desire exhibits these characteristics. Unfortunately, when the label sexual "drive" is used in conversation, it often implies the imagery of some kind of internal driving motor which propels the individual. (Freudian theory even suggests the existence of a special energy, "libido," which activates the motor.) The temptation is to think of sexual drive as a biological unit in personality, of varying strength, and having no links to environmental forces. Yet, sexual desire, or drive, is not a singular unit. It is a product of the interaction of sociocultural and psychological, as well as biological, forces. It is artificial, even if convenient, to envision sexual desire as a personality trait, apart from the interpersonal environment. It is traditional to regard sexual desire as a response to an intensely demanding biological need. However, in order to account for individual differences in sexual desire, we must consider the effects of learning and situational factors upon that desire.

Sexual desire is not a response to an intense bodily need. Instead, it is very easily molded by social forces in a society (19). Differences in level of sexual desire are found not only among individuals, but also among cultural groups. Anthropologists have found certain societies in which sexual desire is merely sufficient for reproductive purposes. One anthropologist studied an Irish village and found that any interest in sexual pleasure was consistently discouraged for both men and women (55). In that village, premarital and extramarital sexual contact are almost nonexistent. Marital intercourse is expected for the sake of childbearing, and is performed in a perfunctory manner which enables quick release for the husband. In contrast, other cultures encourage a constant preoccupation with sexual activity. Another anthropologist studied a society on a South Pacific island where premarital sexual activity begins during early adolescence (52). It assumes the character of competitive athletics for both sexes, aimed at achieving prestige by exhibiting the ability to sexually please the opposite sex. The ability of a boy to provide a girl with several orgasms night after night, as well as the ability of a girl to be very active during sexual intercourse are highly prized. Inadequate performance may occasion loss of self-esteem and village gossip, full of ridicule. After marriage, such ability continues to be esteemed by a couple and marital intercourse is quite frequent, even though frequency declines with age. In the Irish village, any amount of sexual desire is a cause for regret; while on the South Pacific island, insufficient desire is an embarrassment.

There is one question which constantly arises in considerations of male-female erotic differences: Are there differences in sexual desire between men and women?

On the average, American men are more sexually active than American women, as measured by their frequency of orgasm over the life-cycle (41). However, there is no evidence that any one particular underlying factor accounts for this difference. The most simple explanation is that, on the average, American men give higher value-priority to sexual activity, among diverse activities, than do American women. Women are likely to have more unpleasant associations with sexual activity: fears of pregnancy, feelings of being used rather than loved, feelings of being degraded and shamed by engaging in condemned practices, and lack of orgasmic relief in sexual intercourse. In addition, the erotic socialization of women, as compared with that of men, results in less self-confident sexual assertiveness and lower expectations for erotic pleasure in male-female relationships. Sexual satisfaction is more important to the self-esteem, and therefore more central to the self-concept of the average American male than female. Beginning at puberty, with warnings and fears of pregnancy, girls learn to regard sexual activity as being less important than do adolescent boys. Women learn to develop much more ambivalent attitudes towards sexual activity than the more purely enthusiastic attitudes of men (6). This becomes clear when we examine erotic socialization in American society.

There does not seem to be any biological factor which could help to account for the male-female difference in the valuation of sexual activity. Research on the physiology of sexual response indicates that men and women have equal capacities for enjoying erotic pleasure in sexual arousal (54). No differences in male and female genital sensitivity have yet been found. It is possible, as previously noted, that differences in genital anatomy (clitoris vs. penis) may enable men to be more easily aware of milder levels of sexual arousal (6). Yet, in most cases, past pleasurable experience probably enables women to learn to sense mild genital arousal when it occurs.

It should be noted that any male-female difference in sexual desire, as a value-priority, is not an absolute contrast. A high value-priority given to any activity is essentially a high level of interest in that activity. Studies of marital preferences for frequency of intercourse still find more husbands than wives reporting a higher level of preference (37). However, the situation is changing. There are increasing numbers of wives who report a higher preference level than do their husbands. One study of a national sample of men and women, for example, found that about 50 percent of husbands aged forty-five and older desired sexual intercourse more frequently, whereas about 25 percent of wives aged fifty-five and older reported the same desire for a higher frequency (37).

What effect, if any, does intensity of sexual desire have upon erotic responsiveness? There is no direct research on this question, partly due to the difficulties of defining and measuring "sexual desire." However, if high sexual desire can be taken to mean a high value-priority or interest in sexual activity, it is quite possible that high sexual desire enhances erotic responsiveness. It is likely that a high interest in sexual activity intensifies a person's anticipation, and thereby readiness for sexual arousal. The same reasoning can be applied to personal differences in interest in food. A high interest in eating makes people more responsive to the sight, smell and taste of food.

CONCLUSIONS

This paper has extended the theoretical work of Gagnon and Simon to a more micro-sociological level of analysis (19). Their symbolic interactionist interpretation of human sexuality has been used to link physiological factors with sociocultural factors in sexual arousal. Human sexuality is different from the sexuality of other animals, because a more powerful cerebral cortex influences physiological responses. The cerebral cortex accounts for the crucial role of cognitive learning, which is able to extend the individual's experience beyond the immediate environment. Such learning links abstract sociocultural erotic meanings to the physiology of sexual response. This paper has suggested the existence of social psychological mechanisms of erotic response, which are distinct from the psycho-physiological mechanisms of sexual response. Biological interpretations of sexual arousal, as well as those drawn from studies of animal behavior, generally neglect this particularly human dimension of human sexuality. Symbolic interactionist theory is particularly useful in understanding the "missing link" of erotic meanings in human sexual arousal.

*This chapter is an extension of a paper presented at 1976 annual meeting of the American Sociological Association. The material in this chapter has been developed from the author's book, *Human Sexuality in Personality and Society,* forthcoming from Prentice-Hall.

REFERENCES

1. Paul R. Abramson and Donald L. Mosher, "Development of a Measure of Negative Attitudes Toward Masturbation," *Journal of Consulting and Clinical Psychology* 43, no. 4 (August 1975): 485–490.
2. John Bancroft, *Deviant Sexual Behavior*. Oxford University Press, London, 1974.
3. Albert Bandura and Richard H. Walters, *Social Learning and Personality Development*. Holt, Rinehart and Winston, New York, 1963.
4. Lonnie Garfield Barbach, *For Yourself: The Fulfillment of Female Sexuality*. Doubleday, New York, 1975.
5. Andrew M. Barclay, "Sexual Fantasies in Men and Women." *Medical Aspects of Human Sexuality* 7, no. 5 (May 1973): 205, 209–211, 216.
6. Judith M. Bardwick, *Psychology of Women*. Harper and Row, New York, 1971.
7. Frank A. Beach, "The Descent of Instinct," *Psychological Review,* 62, no. 6 (November 1955): 401–410.
8. ———, "Its All in Your Mind," *Psychology Today,* (July 1969): 33–35, 60.
9. Anne C. Bernstein, "How Chidlren Learn About Sex and Birth," *Psychology Today* (January 1976): 31–35, 66
10. ——— and Philip A. Cowan, "Children's Concepts of How People Get Babies," *Child Development* 46 (March 1975), 77–91.
11. Datha Clapper Brack, "Social Forces, Feminism, and Breastfeeding." *Nursing Outlook* 23, no. 9 (September 1975): 556–561.
12. George Calden, Richard M. Lundy, and Richard J. Schlafer, "Sex Differences in Body Concepts," *Journal of Consulting Psychology* 23, no. 4 (1959): 378.
13. Bill Devall, "A Place in the Sun: An Ethnography of Some Pacific Coast Free Beaches," paper presented to the annual meeting of the American Sociological Association, August 1976.
14. James Elias and Paul Gebhard, "Sexuality and Sexual Learning in Childhood," *Phi Delta Kappan.* 50, no. 7 (March 1969): 401–405.
15. Joan Emerson, "Behavior in Private Places: Definitions of Reality in Gynecological Examination," in Hans Peter Dreitzel (ed.) *Recent Sociology,* No. 2. Macmillan, New York, 1970, 73–100.
16. Seymour Fisher, *The Female Orgasm*. Basic Books, New York, 1973.
17. Clellan S. Ford and Frank A. Beach, *Patterns of Sexual Behavior*. Harper & Row, New York, 1951.

18. Joan T. Freyberg, "Hold High the Cardboard Sword," *Psychology Today* (February 1975): 63–64.
19. John H. Gagnon and William Simon, *Sexual Conduct*. Aldine, Chicago, 1973.
20. Paul H. Gebhard, "Sex Differences in Sexual Response," *Archives of Sexual Behavior* 2, no. 3 (June 1973): 201–203.
21. Viktor Gecas and Roger Libby, "Sexual Behavior as Symbolic Interaction," *Journal of Sex Research* 12, no. 1 (February 1976): 33–49.
22. James H. Geer and Robert Fuhr, "Cognitive Factors in Sexual Arousal: The Role of Distraction," *Journal of Consulting and Clinical Psychology*. (April 1976): 238–243.
23. Leonard M. Giambra, "Daydreams: The Backburner of the Mind," *Psychology Today* (December 1974): 66–68.
24. ———, "Daydreaming Across the Life Span: Late Adolescent to Senior Citizen." *International Journal of Aging and Human Development*. 5, no. 2, (1974): 115–140.
25. ——— and Clyde E. Martin, "Sexual Daydreams and Quantitative Aspects of Sexual Activity: Some Relations for Males Across Adulthood," unpublished Research Report. Gerontology Research Center, National Institute on Aging, 1976.
26. Michael Goldstein, Harold S. Kant, and John J. Hartman, *Pornography and Social Deviance*. University of California Press, Berkeley, Calif., 1973.
27. William Griffitt, "Sexual Experience and Sexual Responsiveness: Sex Differences." *Archives of Sexual Behavior* 4, no. 5 (September 1975): 529–540.
28. David A. Hamburg and Donald T. Lunde, "Sex Hormones in the Development of Sex Differences in Human Behavior," in Eleanor E. Maccoby (ed.). *The Development of Sex Differences*. Stanford University Press, Stanford, Calif., 1966, 1–24.
29. Kenneth R. Hardy, "An Appetitional Theory of Sexual Motivation." *Psychological Review*. 71, no. 1 (January 1964): 1–18.
30. E. Barbara Hariton, "The Sexual Fantasies of Women," *Psychology Today* 6, no. 10 (March 1973): 39–44.
31. ———, "Women's Sexual Fantasies During Sexual Intercourse: Normative and Theoretical Implications," *Journal of Consulting and Clinical Psychology* 42, no. 3 (June 1974): 313–322.
32. Molly Haskell, "Rape Fantasy." *Ms.* (November 1976): 85–86, 93–98.
33. Julia R. Heiman, *Responses to Erotica: An Exploration of Human Sexual Arousal*. State University of New York at Stony Brook: April 1975, unpublished doctoral dissertation.
34. ———, "Women's Sexual Arousal," *Psychology Today* (April 1975): 91–94.
35. Donald E. Henson and H. B. Rubin, "Voluntary Control of Eroticism" *Journal of Applied Behavior Analysis* (Spring 1971): 37, 44.
36. James M. Herrell, "Sex Differences in Emotional Responses to 'Erotic Literature'," *Journal of Consulting and Clinical Psychology* 43, no. 6 (December 1975): 921.
37. Morton Hunt. *Sexual Behavior in the 1970s*. Dell, New York, 1974.
38. Clinton J. Jesser, "Reflections on Breast Attention," *Journal of Sex Research* 7, no. 1 (February 1971): 13–25.
39. Gilbert R. Kaats and Keith E. Davis, "The Social Psychology of Sexual Behavior," in Lawrence S. Wrightsman (ed.), *Social Psychology in the Seventies*. Wadsworth, Belmont, Calif., 1972, 549–580.
40. Alfred C. Kinsey, Wardell B. Pomeroy, and Clyde B. Martin, *Sexual Behavior in the Human Male*. Saunders, Philadelphia, 1948.
41. ———, ———, ———, and Paul H. Gebhard, *Sexual Behavior in the Human Female*, Saunders, Philadelphia, 1953.
42. Eric Klinger, *Structure and Functions of Fantasy*. John Wiley, New York, 1971.
43. Andrew Kopkind, "Middle America Takes Its Clothes Off," *New Times*. (August 20, 1976): 32, 34, 40.

44. Helena Kraemer, Heather B. Becker, J. Keith Brodie, Charles H. Doering, Rudolph H. Moos, and David A. Hamburg, "Orgasmic Frequency and Plasma Testosterone Levels in Normal Human Males." *Archives of Sexual Behavior* (March 1976): 125–132.

45. Ursula Laschet, "Antiandrogen in the Treatment of Sex Offenders: Mode of Action and Therapeutic Outcome," in Joseph Zubin and John Money (eds.), *Contemporary Sexual Behavior*. Johns Hopkins, Baltimore, 1973, 311–310.

46. Edwin M. Lemert, "Prostitution," in Edward Sagarin and Donal E. J. MacNamara (eds.), *Problems of Sexual Behavior*. Thomas Y. Crowell, New York, 1968, 68–109.

47. Robert A. Lewis, "Parents and Peers: Socialization Agents in the Coital Behavior of Young Adults," *Journal of Sex Research* (May 1973): 156–170.

48. Alfred R. Lindesmith, Anselm L. Strauss, and Norman K. Denzin, *Social Psychology*. Dryden Press, Hinsdale, Ill. 1975.

49. Norman M. Lobsenz, "Sex and the Senior Citizen," *The New York Times Magazine* (Jan. 20, 1974).

50. Frank A. Logan and Allan R. Wagner, *Punishment and Reward*. Allyn and Bacon, Boston, 1965.

51. William G. Luttge, "The Role of Gonadel Hormones in the Sexual Behavior of Rhesus Monkey and Human: A Literature Review," *Archives of Sexual Behavior* 1, no. 1 (1971): 61–88.

52. Donald S. Marshall, "Sexual Behavior in Mangaia," in Donald S. Marshall and Robert C. Suggs, (eds.), *Human Sexual Behavior*. Prentice-Hall, Englewood Cliffs, N.J., 1971, 103–162.

53. Clyde E. Martin, personal communication (1976).

54. William H. Masters and Virginia E. Johnson, *Human Sexual Response*. Little, Brown, Boston, 1966.

55. John C. Messenger, "Sex and Repression in an Irish Folk Community," in Donald S. Marshall and Robert C. Suggs (eds.), *Human Sexual Behavior*. Prentice-Hall, Englewood Cliffs, N.J., 1971, 3–37.

56. Walter Mischel, "Toward a Cognitive Social Learning Reconceptualization of Personality," *Psychological Review* (1973): 252–283.

57. John Money, "Adolescent Psychohormonal Development" *Southwestern Medicine*. 48, (1967): 182–186.

58. ———, "Role of Fantasy in Pair-Bonding and Erotic Performance," paper presented to the International Congress of Sexology (October 1976), Montreal.

59. ———, "Sex Hormones and Other Variables in Human Eroticism," in W. C. Young (ed.) *Sex and Internal Secretions*. (Baltimore: Williams and Wilkins), 1961, 1383–1400.

60. ——— and Anke A. Ehrhardt, *Man and Woman, Boy and Girl*. (Baltimore: Johns Hopkins University Press), 1972.

61. ——— and Paul A. Walker, "Psychosexual Development, Maternalism, Nonpromiscuity and Body Image in 15 Females with Precocious Puberty," *Archives of Sexual Behavior* 1, no. 1, (1971): 45–60.

62. Denton E. Morrison and Carlin Paige Holden, "The Burning Bra: The American Breast Fetish and Women's Liberation," in Marcello Truzzi (ed.) *Sociology for Pleasure*. Prentice-Hall, Englewood Cliffs, N.J. pp. 345–362.

63. Donald L. Mosher, "Sex Differences, Sex Experience, Sex Guilt and Explicitly Sexual Films," *Journal of Social Issues*. 29, no. 3, (1973): 95–112.

64. ———, "Sex Guilt and Premarital Sexual Experience in College Students," *Journal of Consulting and Clinical Psychology* 36, no. 1 (1971): 27–32.

65. ⸻ and Irene Greenberg, "Females' Affective Responses to Reading Erotic Litera-ture," *Journal of Consulting and Clinical Psychology* 33, no. 4 (1969): 472–477.
66. I. T. Nathanson, L. E. Town, and J. C. Aub, "Normal Excretion of Sex Hormones in Childhood," *Endocrinology* 28, (1941): 851–865.
67. John F. Oliven, *Clinical Sexuality*. J. B. Lippincott, Philadelphia, 1974.
68. Eric Pfeiffer and Glenn C. Davis, "Determinants of Sexual Behavior in Middle and Old Age, *Journal of the American Geriatrics Society*. (April 1972): 151–158.
69. Kenneth Plummer, *Sexual Stigma: An Interactionist Account*. Routledge and Kegan Paul, Boston, 1975.
70. Mary Ann S. Pulaski, "The Rich Rewards of Make Believe," *Psychology Today* (January 1974): 68–74.
71. Jan Raboch and L. Starka, "Reported Coital Activity of Men and Levels of Plasma Testosterone," *Archives of Sexual Behavior*. (December 1973): 309–315.
72. Glenn V. Ramsey, "The Sex Information of Younger Boys," *American Journal of Orthopsychiatry*, (April 1943): 347–352.
73. Ira L. Reiss, *The Social Context of Premarital Sexual Permissiveness*. Holt, Rinehart and Winston, New York, 1967.
74. Udall J. Salmon and Samuel H. Geist, "Effect of Androgen Upon Libido in Women." *Journal of Clinical Endocrinology* 3, (1943): 235–238.
75. Stanley Schachter and Jerome Singer, "Cognitive, Social and Physiological Determin-ants of Emotional State," *Psychological Review* 69, (1962): 379–399.
76. Gunter Schmidt, "Male-Female Differences in Sexual Arousal and Behavior During and After Exposure to Sexually Explicit Stimuli," *Archives of Sexual Behavior* (July 1975): 353–365.
77. ⸻ and Volkmar Sigusch, "Sex Differences in Response to Psychosexual Stimula-tion by Films and Slides." *Journal of Sex Research*. (November, 1970), 6, no. 4, 268–283.
78. ⸻ and ⸻, "Women's Sexual Arousal," in Joseph Zubin and John Money (eds.), *Contemporary Sexual Behavior*. Johns Hopkins, Baltimore, 1973, 117–144.
79. ⸻, ⸻, and Siegrid Schafer, "Responses to Reading Erotic Stories: Male-Female Differences." *Archives of Sexual Behavior* (June, 1973), 2, no. 3, 181–199.
80. Robert R. Sears, Eleanor E. Maccoby, and Harry Levin, *Patterns of Child-Rearing*. Harper & Row, New York, 1975.
81. Frank K. Shuttleworth, "A Biosocial and Developmental Theory of Male and Female Sexuality," *Marriage and Family Living* (May 1959), 163–170.
82. Volkmar Sigusch, Gunter Schmidt, Antje Reinfeld, and Ingeborg Wiedemann-Sutor, "Psychosexual Stimulation: Sex Differences," *Journal of Sex Research* (February 1970): 10–24.
83. Jerome L. Singer, *The Inner World of Daydreaming*, Harper & Row, New York, 1975.
84. Don Smith, "The Social Content of Pornography," *Journal of Communication*. 26, no. 1, (1976): 16–24.
85. Robert C. Sorensen, *Adolescent Sexuality in Contemporary America*. World Publishing Co., New York, 1972, 1973.
86. John Stauffer and Richard Frost, "Male and Female Interest in Sexually-Oriented Magazines," *Journal of Communication*. 26, no. 1 (1976): 25–30.
87. William N. Stephens, "A Cross-Cultural Study of Modesty and Obscenity," *Technical Report of the Commission on Obscenity and Pornography* IX. United States Govern-ment Printing Office: Washington, D.C., 1971, 405–451.
88. Stuart Valins, "Cognitive Effects of False Heart-Rate Feedback," *Journal of Personal-ity and Social Psychology* 4, no. 4, (1966): 400–408.

89. Sheldon E. Waxenberg, Marvin G. Drellich, and Arthur M. Sutherland, "The Role of Hormones in Human Behavior: Changes in Female Sexuality After Adrenalectomy," *Journal of Clinical Endocrinology* 19 (1959): 193–202.

90. Martin S. Weinberg, "Sexual Modesty, Social Meaning and the Nudist Camp," *Social Problems*. 7, (1965): 311–318.

THE SOCIAL CONSTRUCTION AND RECONSTRUCTION OF PHYSIOLOGICAL EVENTS: ACQUIRING THE PREGNANCY IDENTITY*

Rita Seiden Miller, BROOKLYN COLLEGE, CUNY

INTRODUCTION

This study was designed to examine the basic Meadian/Schutzian assertion that all identities are acquired through processes of social construction of reality which may be independent of "objective" reality. [Cf. Dreitzel (9), Mead (9), Shibutani (31), Berger and Luckmann (3), Holzner (15), Schultz (30)]. As Denzin (8) has noted:

> Man's environment does not consist of objects that carry intrinsic meaning. Social objects are constructs and not "self-existing entities with intrinsic natures." An object is "anything toward which action can be organized and it may be as physical as a chair or as imaginary as a ghost." Objects consist of any event that persons can designate in

Studies in Symbolic Interaction—Volume 1, 1978, pages 181–204.

a unitary fashion and organize action toward. The meaning of an object resides in the meanings that are brought to it and hence must be located in the interaction process [p. 261].

Within this framework, this paper focuses upon the *social construction and reconstruction of pregnancy*.[1] The emphasis is on how pregnant American women routinely acquire a pregnancy identity, become socially pregnant, and transform *physiological pregnancy* into *social pregnancy*.[2] *Physiological pregnancy* is defined solely by the presence of particular bodily conditions: a viable fetus and corresponding physiological patterns in the woman; *social pregnancy* is defined as the social identity that is attributed to a particular person who claims the right to that label (says, for example, "I am pregnant") or who is given that label by others (for example, "You must be pregnant").

From this perspective, social and physiological pregnancy may be viewed as separate phenomena which are only brought together by elaborate social effort that 1) creates the meaning of pregnancy as the appropriate signs appear, or 2) re-creates it as the perspective is acquired that allows for reassessment. The result of these efforts is to make social pregnancy *appear* to be inseparable from its physiological counterpart. But the emergence of social pregnancy is not a guaranteed event; since the social aspect and the physiological aspect *are* separable, it is possible for one to occur without the other. This separation of the physical from the social component suggests four different potential identities produced by the presence or absence of physiological and/or social pregnancy (see Figure 1).

Figure 1. Identities produced by presence/
absence of physiological and/or social
pregnancy

		Physiologically pregnant	
		Yes	No
	Yes	"Normal" Pregnancy	"False" Pregnancy
Socially pregnant			
	No	"Undiscovered" Pregnancy	"Non-Pregnancy"

"Normal pregnancy" and "nonpregnancy" fit the common-sense model of how physiological pregnancy is *in*separable from social pregnancy. In the two other cases, however, the two aspects of the identity are obviously separated: (A) *Pseudocyesis, "false pregnancy"* is, of course, the extreme case of social pregnancy without physical pregnancy. A popular medical handbook for lay readers describes it as follows:

> In its classic form pseudocyesis can include enlarged abdomen and breasts, a slight secretion of colostrum from the nipples, changes in the uterus and cervix, weight gain, the experience of fetal movement, failure to menstruate, and a conviction that the pregnancy is real (3).

In the everyday world, "false pregnancy" would be perceived as a misreading of the cues which supposedly inevitably link physiological and social pregnancy, rather than as evidence of the not inevitable connection between the social identity and the physiological fact. (B) *"Undiscovered pregnancy"*—physiological pregnancy without a social label—was reported in the local newspaper where this study was conducted:

Pregnancy was Big Surprise
Grand Forks, N.D. (AP)

> Told three months ago she was not pregnant, Mrs. Lee Baker thought she was having a kidney attack when she went into the emergency room of a Grand Forks hospital Sunday. Two hours later she gave birth to her first child, a 4½ pound boy.
> "I probably sound like the dumbest person on earth," she said [March 13, 1971].

Thus, the thesis of this paper is that special effort is exerted by society to insure that social and physiological pregnancy do occur simultaneously. The data presented below illustrate the initially problematic nature of the social meaning of physiological pregnancy, and the processes by which social pregnancy develops over time as a result of labeling and socializing experiences that provide the bases for social interpretations of physiological events.

DATA COLLECTION

The Sample
The data were collected by means of tape-recorded interviews with obstetric patients in a Midwestern university town. Several focused interviews were conducted with each of forty-nine women who were at various

stages of first-time pregnancy careers. The respondents were selected to represent the variety of social factors that were thought to influence reproductive careers: social class, early/late arrival for prenatal care, married/unmarried, fertility/infertility. A pool of sixty-four women was initially assembled: eleven could not be contacted by phone, letter, or house call. Of the fifty-three who were contacted, four refused to be interviewed. Thus, a total of forty-nine women—forty-seven pregnant women (two of whom started out as infertility patients) and two infertility patients (who remained such)—were interviewed. Forty-four of the forty-nine subjects were drawn from a university medical center obstetrics and gynecology clinic; thirty-three of them were regular fee-paying patients while eleven were "clinic" patients. The remaining five respondents were patients of a local physician who had a private practice in the town in which the medical center was located.[3]

Only medically normal women were included in the study. Those with medical complications were excluded in order to avoid adding variables that do not usually affect the normal pregnancy experience. First-time pregnant women were chosen because they were "naive" subjects in the sense that they had no experientially gained knowledge which would bias their interpretations. The infertility patients were included because their more intense and deliberate efforts were expected to add additional information about their motivational factors under more ordinary circumstances.

The demographic characteristics of the sample indicated that they were not unlike the general American childbearing population: They had a median age of twenty-two;[4] most had been married just over twelve months at the beginning of their pregnancies;[5] they had a somewhat lower rate of illegitimacy[6] and premarital pregnancies.[7] In terms of social class origins, the respondents also fit the median American pattern: the respondents' fathers were predominantly blue-collar workers,[8] had median earnings of $7,500, and had completed high school;[9] the respondents' mothers held jobs with less occupational prestige than those of the respondents' fathers (half were housewives; most of the remainder were office workers or nurses), and earned less money than their spouses. The respondents and their husbands' marriages also reflected this American mating gradient pattern—except that there had been some social mobility: many of the respondents had become, by dint of marriage, part of lower middle-class white-collar families.[10] Most of the sample had grown up in cities and suburbs in the United States, and were white and Protestant.[11]

In short, the typical respondent followed the normative pattern for primiparous American women: she was the same age, was having her first child at a similar point in her marriage, came from upper working-class origins to a lower-middle-class marriage, and was participating in a martial relationship which reflected status characteristics similar to those in her parents' and typical American marriages. Thus, while our subjects were not randomly drawn from the general U.S. population, they were not markedly atypical of that population in terms of the variables considered.

The Interviews

One hundred and seventeen interviews were conducted covering early, middle, and late pregnancy, postnatal, postmiscarriage phases, and infertility experiences. Sixty-five interviews conducted during the early and middle months of pregnancy (approximately through the sixth month) provided the data base for the discussion here—thirty-two were early-pregnancy interviews; thirty-three were from middle pregnancy. During the early-pregnancy interview (about one and one-half hours in length), data were collected on the respondents' social class background as well as on the pregnancy experience. Topics covered were: anticipatory socialization to pregnancy; general reactions to being pregnant—including first recognition of pregnancy; family planning practices; changes in self-image: physical appearance, marital and other relationships and interactions since pregnancy began; nature of anticipations about the infant; norms for appropriate childbearing age and number of children; attitudes toward adoption; influence of religion on reproductive behavior and attitudes toward pregnancy; the effect of voluntary group membership, work and career, relatives, and physicians on their pregnancy experience; the timing and target of pregnancy announcement; use of a physician early in pregnancy; and expectations for the remainder of the pregnancy career. The middle pregnancy interview (about 45 minutes in length) largely reviewed the areas discussed in the first interview. In addition, information was collected about physical and social events that typically occur during the fourth to six month—namely, "getting bigger," recognition of fetal movement, and the wearing of maternity clothes.[12]

RESULTS

Goffman (13, p. 128), Hughes (16, pp. 409–410), Becker (2, pp. 24, 102), Roth (27, pp. xviii, 115), and Davis (9) have all emphasized the importance of the concept of "career" for the study of social meaning and the process of organizing that meaning. Three aspects of the early social pregnancy career are readily identifiable: 1) Becoming physiologically pregnant, 2) becoming socially pregnant, and 3) becoming "really" pregnant.

1. Becoming Physiologically Pregnant:

Three patterns of entry into physiological pregnancy were found: true planners, sort-of planners, and nonplanners.[13] The *true planners* constituted thirty-four of the forty-nine respondents. They and/or their husbands had been using some contraceptive method and then stopped using it in order to become pregnant; or, they (along with their husbands) had chosen not to use contraception from the time of marriage because they wanted to get pregnant. All welcomed getting pregnant at that point. They typically described their situation as follows: "Yes, we planned this pregnancy. I stopped using birth control pills in October; getting pregnant any time after that was fine." Or, "We both wanted a baby so bad, I never used anything."

Eleven of the women in the sample were *sort-of planners*. The sort-of planners recognized the possibility that they might get pregnant from sexual activity with a husband or boyfriend; five used some contraception occasionally, while six just worried about not using any at all. The sort-of planners did not deliberately choose to get pregnant, but they also did not deliberately choose to avoid getting pregnant. They generally described themselves as "surprised" by their pregnancies. All regarded becoming pregnant as somewhat of a "problem." Typical self-characterizations were: "We sort of used foam; sometimes I used it, and sometimes I didn't." Or, "I sort-of used the rhythm method—I sort-of kept track of my cycle with the calendar."

The four *nonplanners* formed the smallest subgroup of respondents, but they provided invaluable insight into the process of acquiring the pregnancy identity. They and their husbands (or boyfriends) had in no way intended pregnancy; they had used "safe" contraception, or had reason to believe that they were infertile, or simply did not expect to become pregnant; none wanted to get pregnant at the time. This group was genuinely surprised by their pregnancies. Typical self-describing remarks were: "The doctor told me the I.U.D. was 'safe.'" Or, "We had been trying for several years and nothing happened; so we adopted kids—the doctor said it was very unlikely that I would get pregnant."

Not only did the ways in which the women in the sample gained entry into pregnancy careers vary in terms of intentionality, but the type of decision to become pregnant affected both how the women became socially pregnant and how they became "really" pregnant. That is, the mode of entrance into physiological pregnancy affected the process of becoming socially pregnant. As I will show in the next section, the women who became pregnant intentionally (true planners) anticipated the signs of pregnancy, recognized them almost immediately when they occurred, and took the least time in getting medical confirmation. Those women who happened into pregnancy (sort-of planners) anticipated the signs of pregnancy but did not recognize the symptoms immediately, so they delayed getting an official medical label for their condition. Those women who were truly surprised by pregnancy (nonplanners) did not anticipate the cues, did not recognize their meaning when they occurred, and went initially to a (nonobstetric) physician for diagnosis of "illness" rather than confirmation of pregnancy. The true and sort-of planners constructed their new identities as the "signs" occurred; the nonplanners *re*constructed their identities once their "illnesses" had been diagnosed as pregnancy—only in retrospect were they able to make "sense" of their identity "cues."

2. Becoming Socially Pregnant

The main thesis of this paper is that physiological events have no meaning until actors choose to ascribe meaning to them. In the everyday world, when a physical event is anticipated, it appears to have meaning without any apparent meaning-supplying effort on the part of the actors. For example, if everyone has nausea and headache from this year's flu epidemic, when I experience nausea and headache I *know* (apparently without interpretative interaction) that I have the flu. Similarly, I am positing that the "natural" discovery of pregnancy occurs because the physical signs that a woman experiences as "cues" are cues because she has located them quickly within a context of meaning-constructing activity that makes *social pregnancy* a highly plausible interpretation. For example, one of the respondents described her first steps in the awareness phase:

> Right after I forgot [to use] the diaphragm, I said: "I forgot the diaphragm." [My husband] says: "I know." I go, "Oh my goodness." I didn't even bother to get a pregnancy test . . . Getting to the doctor was more or less confirming something that we already knew. I just knew that I was pregnant by the time I saw [the doctor]. And we just kind of went at it—like, he didn't examine me first. We sat down and took down all this information, just like we'd already gotten a positive test back . . . and he asked how many weeks I thought I was and then went back and calculated dates.

Clearly, this women could have enacted the same scenario and not have been physiologically pregnant. No constellation of physical signs inevitably or invariably means anything or the same thing. Only by locating events in meaningful contexts do actors come to attribute common-sense obvious interpretations to these events.

In instances where events are unanticipated, this meaning-constructing activity is most visible. For example,

I was gettin' sick and throwin' up and scared—I didn't know what was wrong. My mom took me to the Emergency Room. They examined me and asked some questions, and they gave me a paper to go around to the obstetrics clinic. Then I realized I was probably pregnant.

Prior to seeing the physician, this woman could have interpreted her combination of "symptoms" as pregnancy—but instead she interpreted them as "illness."

Planning Types and the Construction and Reconstruction of Social Pregnancy

Nonanticipation or initial anticipation affected the social construction of the pregnancy identity for each of the three planner types.

The majority of true and sort-of planners anticipated their new identities and were able to interpret their symptoms "correctly"; a minority of trues and sort-ofs and most of the nonplanners did neither. While the nonplanners and the minority patterns from the other two types represent only a small proportion of the entire sample, the comparisons that follow underscore the truly social and taken-for-granted nature of acquiring a new identity.

Self-interpretation of physical cues. When respondents were asked how they knew that they were pregnant, they usually offered as evidence some change in their physical condition—absence of menstruation and/or variation in overall physical condition. But when the responses were examined, it was fairly obvious that it was the *interpretation* of the physical cue, not the physical cue itself, that triggered the change in identity. For example, one true planner noted:

I'd been "irregular" before, so just not having my period didn't really mean anything. But I really felt like I was pregnant even though I had not had any "typical" symptoms at all . . . [But] I was tired, and I just felt physically different. It wasn't anything I could pinpoint. I felt slow; and I've always had a lot of get-up-and-go. And I couldn't get a great deal accomplished in any day. And I would just work fast for two hours, and then I just could not do one more thing. I just had to quit, and then in a couple of hours I could go again.

Another true planner described the initial interpretation in these words:

. . . a lot of people around town here had the flu. And, of course, I got sick and I thought it was the flu—so I didn't pay no attention to it. I said, "Oh, it's just the flu." And then I was washing dishes—at that time I was working on the afternoon shift—so I told Mrs. H—, "You know, I've never had my period yet; and I'm just wondering if I'm pregnant, or am *(sic)* I just got the flu?" And she said, "Well, you might be pregnant." And I said, "I'll tell you what—I'll just give it a few days because it generally takes me 24 hours to get over it." Well, two or three days I tried to put it off or throw it off the best I know how. So finally I didn't get over it. And I got sick on a Friday, and one of the girls had to take me home. I just wanted to throw up and I couldn't hardly work. And it was on Friday—and Friday and Saturday is somethin' else in the café—you know what I mean—rush time; so anyway, they had to send me home; and then the next day I put up with it. Saturday, and then Sunday. And then, Monday, I made a point to get to the doctor . . . And the first doctor I saw was Dr. O-, I told Dr. O-, I says: "I haven't had my period," and I says: "I been sick for about a week. And I don't know if I'm pregnant or I don't know if I've got the flu." He says, "Well, you might have the flu." I says: "Well, I've got a few more days"—it was getting close to the last of the month—and, I said: "Well, I'll just wait." And finally he says: "Well, you might be pregnant." I just pretty near had to tell Dr. O- that I was pregnant. And so finally, I just went to Dr. H-, and sure enough I was right. I was.

All of the respondents reported knowing beforehand what the physiological signs of pregnancy were; but only the true and sort-of-planners (and not all of them) reported having recognized *at the time of occurrence* that the various physical happenings were *probable* cues to pregnancy identity. That is, "correct" self-interpretation was possible only when the actor was ready for the changes. One true planner commented:

I was pretty sure I was pregnant when I went to the doctor . . . based on the fact that I had been taking my temperature—and if the temperature plateaus early and doesn't come down for like fifteen days, that's an almost absolute positive proof of pregnancy. Also my breasts were larger. And, I started to feel a little queasy, you know, about fixing dinner. So I was pretty sure. And I had missed one period—almost two—so I was pretty sure when I went to the doctor.

In contrast, the nonplanners all experienced the same physiological changes but did *not* make the pregnancy interpretation. Rather, *after* receiving an official medical diagnosis, they *recalled* that they had had "typical" pregnancy symptoms. The retrospective relabeling of cues is emphasized because *all four* of the nonplanner women reported that at the time the early symptoms occurred they had thought that they were "sick," "had the flu," or "something was wrong." One nonplanner (who had thought she was "infertile") reconstructed the meaning of her early pregnancy symptoms as follows:

Remember when you came to see me the first time [when Dr. G- gave you my name as an infertility patient]? I apologized then for being sick—I said I thought I had the "flu." Well, I was *pregnant* then!

Even among the true and sort-of planners, "symptoms" did not always immediately have the proper framework in which to be interpreted. One true planner who also had been an infertility patient said:

> I didn't feel like I was pregnant . . . I didn't have a period but I have done that so many times before and gotten just the same story again [infertility, irregular menses, etc.]. But I had been having cramps off and on for a couple of weeks. Of course, [the doctor] was following me anyway [because of a history of menstrual problems] and he wanted to know what was going on. So I went and talked with him about it. And I told him I had been cramping but still I hadn't had a period . . . and he said, "Maybe you're pregnant." I said, "I never stopped to think about *that.*"

Another true planner said:

> I was having stomach pains; I thought it was "period pains—they usually start about a week ahead of time. Then one day I fainted while I was on the phone with J-[husband]. I didn't think about being pregnant. I just thought it was the heat, and me working so many hours. But J—had kind of figured I was [pregnant]. He had a feeling I was. He was the first who suspected I was. I was diagnosing all kinds of things there for a while. But he was right.

A sort-of planner attributed her "slow" recognition of symptoms to her reluctance to be pregnant; her ambivalence about the identity interfered with the adoption of a perspective that would have made "normal" pregnancy out of what she was experiencing:

> My parents had been here, and I hadn't been feeling well. So I went home with them, and mother thought I should go to the doctor. I hadn't had my period, so I went home, and saw the doctor and asked him if he could get it straightened [out]. He gave me just a—not a complete physical, but he thought I was pregnant and he would give me tests. He did that, and told me to call him back. And I did. That's when he told me I was pregnant . . . [My] first period was supposed to be September 4th, and I didn't have that one; and I didn't have the one in October . . . The thought [that I was pregnant] ran across my mind. But, when he told me I actually was—it just shocked me, because I had just put the thought out of my mind . . . [My mother] had her personal ideas, but I think she thought it was possible. But I had been sick with the flu just before my parents got here. That was in August—no, September. About the 24th maybe, I think that's when I got pregnant. Being sick, I didn't think anything about it; but I just kept having this nausea. It kept going on and on for about two weeks. And it was just getting ridiculous. I didn't feel well in the mornings. My sister and I talked about it; and, she suggested that I find out about it, saying I could be pregnant. I said, "Oh no! No!" When I came back home from my folks, I had had the tests and all, but I wanted all the

proof I could get. So I went to a doctor here and said: "I hope you aren't going to tell me I'm just sick." He said no—that I was pregnant.

In sum, all of the women cited similar physical signs for how they knew they were pregnant. Most of the true and sort-of planners made a pregnancy interpretation at about the time the "symptoms" appeared; some of the sort-of planners delayed their interpretations; the nonplanners made their recognitions retrospectively. Each of these modes of interpretation illustrates the principle of social construction and *re*construction of reality. Those who anticipated the changes and wanted to be pregnant had a perspective from which to make, and motivation for making a "common sense" interpretation of their experiences. Those who thought they might get pregnant, but were ambivalent about the possibility, possessed the perspective from which to make a pregnancy interpretation, but lacked the positive motivation for doing so; hence the "objective" reality often went unlabeled. Those who did not anticipate their identities recognized the meaning of physical changes only after they had been labeled as pregnant by others; the signs acquired a special meaning only after there was a special perspective in which to make sense of them—the nonplanner women did not understand what was taking place until pregnancy was "discovered" for them. Then, and only then, did they reconstruct their physical experiences as signs of pregnancy. Thus, rapid identification, slower recognition, and retrospective acknowledgment all necessitate meaning-making activities, motivation, and an organizing perspective if the same objective reality is to acquire a similar social identification.

Degree of reliance on others (husband, friends, relatives, physicians) for interpretation of physical symptoms. The women's social circles also participated in constructing pregnancy identities for them—with the pattern of entry into physiological pregnancy affecting the women's reliance on others for interpretation. Those who were reluctant to be pregnant or who were unprepared for a shift in identity were more reliant on others for interpretations than were those who were eager to be and prepared for the possibility of pregnancy. Figure 2 indicates the pattern of reliance on self- and others' interpretations.

The true planners made their own initial construction of their pregnancy identities, and then discussed the matter with husbands—physician confirmation came third; the identity was usually announced to (not debated with) friends last.[14] The sort-of planners relied heavily on friends, family, and co-workers for initial interpretation and labeling of their condition.[15] They had entered their careers with considerable ambivalence, and were unwilling to identify themselves with the new status. Most reported wondering aloud with friends about "what was the matter" or whether they

Figure 2.   Patterns of reliance on self and others' interpretations

TYPE OF PLANNER	PATTERN OF RELIANCE			
	Self primarily	Self & others	Others primarily	Others exclusively
True planner	Almost all ←→			
Sort-of-planner			Almost all: More than half here ←→	
Nonplanner				All

"might be pregnant." One sort-of planner described the typical sort-of planner pattern:

> My sister started asking me—she thought I was acting different—like I might be pregnant. That was in August—and I didn't get my period. That's when I first thought I was pregnant—after she started to ask questions and I didn't get my period. But I didn't get to the doctor till October or November—just kept putting it off. I don't think I was reluctant to go but I just—I don't know—I kept thinking I was going and then I'd do something else—or I'd forget about it.

In contrast, the nonplanners relied almost exclusively on "official" (physicians') interpretations of physical cues. They typically reported "not even having a hunch" that pregnancy was the root cause of their physical discomfort when it was first experienced. No discussion of possible pregnancy occurred with friends. As a result, three of the four women took atypical routes to medical diagnosis. One went to a family physician for "flu," one went to a hospital Emergency Room for treatment of vomiting and nausea, and a third went to a family physician to treat her delayed menstruation. The fourth woman's husband was a medical student with gynecological experience; because of his special expertise she was routed directly to her gynecologist. But even this fourth case confirms the central thesis. Only the husband, who had reason to use a particular perspective, made "proper" sense of his wife's condition.

Thus, most of the true and sort-of planners went directly to a gynecologist-obstetrician (the true planners went to the obstetrician earlier than the sort-of planners) for examination and confirmation only after tentative, unofficial diagnoses had been made. The nonplanners not only did not initially recognize what they later came to call typical pregnancy signs, but they regarded themselves as ill, and chose a general practioner-physician or general out-patient clinic for diagnosis and treatment of their illnesses. In fact, the nonplanners got to *some* doctor earliest of all the pregnant women because they felt "sick" and did not have a pregnancy interpretation to allay their concern. The result of first assuming a sick role was that the onset of social pregnancy coincided with medical diagnosis. In one case, even an initial diagnosis of pregnancy was not enough to make the new identity "stick": "Even after the doctor ran the Gravidex test a second time, my husband couldn't believe it!"

Once the physician replaced the sick role label with a pregnancy identification (and it was accepted), the women shifted to obstetric caretakers. Since awareness of the pregnancy identity had not been preceded by informal or tentative consideration of the possibility of pregnancy, after pregnancy was identified, the *nonplanners then* went out to the members of their social circles to discuss how getting pregnant could have happened and how they did not realize what the symptoms meant. That is, since the true and sort-of planners used their husbands, friends, and relatives as central sources of identification, the obstetrician became a confirmer (not a creator) of identity; but since the nonplanners used their social circle to make *retrospective* sense of what had happened, the physician became the initial creator of identity. The nonplanners use of a physician for treatment of illness (not pregnancy) symptoms, and their almost total reliance on medical identification makes the observer aware that the normal process of social identification is usually made invisible by its fast and unofficial nature.

In sum, whether the label initially comes from the woman herself, the woman and her social circle, or *only* from someone in the social circle (whether husband, friend, relative, or physician), all the respondents relied on interpretive behavior—their own or others—to make sense of their experience. That this meaning-construction happens so casually, and in such a routine, taken-for-granted manner, obscures the fact that it is happening at all. The nonplanners (and a minority of the other types) make the normal process stand out because they have been largely excluded from the speedy and informal (and therefore "invisible") aspects of the process: when pregnancy was not a plausible explanation of physical symptoms and no cue to the pregnancy identity was received informally, the medical labeler had to provide the meaning for the nonplanners. *Someone* has to apply an interpretive perspective for physiological pregnancy to become socially meaningful pregnancy.

Becoming "Really" Pregnant

After all the sources of initial recognition had been exploited and the women had begun to publicly label themselves as pregnant, even the true and sort-of planners had only a tentative attachment to their new identities. For example, ". . . it doesn't seem very real . . . it's on an intellectual level rather than an emotional "my baby!" kind of thing. . ." Or, "It doesn't seem like a reality in a way . . . I don't feel different, and I don't look different right now, so it's very hard . . . I am, but how do I know I am?"

Almost all of the true and sort-of planners regarded certain signs as vital for a more definite attachment to identity—these signs included both physical changes and changes in social interaction that they had expected the physical changes would precipitate. For example,

> Unless you really stop and think about it, that there's a person growing inside your body, you don't feel that close to it. I'm sure I will when it begins to move and I can really tell there's something there.

> I'm anxious to start showing so I just don't have to tell people.

> I wish I could have an x-ray and just see the baby, because it's still hard to believe. . . . Only when people talk about it, like sitting here right now, only then does it really seem real—I'm not just fat.

With minor variations, the true and sort-of planners only partially identified with their new status, even after that status was informally and formally recognized by others. They expected that the *further* development of physical signs and interaction patterns would assist them in making their new identities fully real.

The nonplanners expressed somewhat greater concern over not feeling that their new identity was real. These women seemed more inclined to feel that their pregnancies would not actually be real until they had further evidence in the form of marked body changes and clear signs of fetal movement.

> The baby part seems totally unreal. All I can think about is how tired I am, and how nauseated I am, and how I can't get things done like I used to . . . Before I got pregnant—when I wanted so much to get pregnant—I used to think a lot about what it meant, and I thought I knew. But now I don't really know what it means. . . . It may get better as I get bigger and begin to feel movement—and I guess I'll have a clearer sense of what's happening after it gets here—but sometimes I wonder.

Thus, the nonplanners needed even more *ex post facto* evidence in order to construct identities that fit their physiological changes.

Transforming this tentative sense of self into a definite identity became the respondents' focus of attention during the middle (second through sixth) months of pregnancy. Proofs or benchmarks for the "real" self were created out of natural signs and social encounters. Sources of evidence included illness symptoms and sick-role interactions, fetal movement, "getting bigger," wearing of maternity clothes, and continuing encounters with physicians.

Illness symptoms (nausea, vomiting, lassitude) became, through processes of social construction, confirming evidence of the pregnancy reality in two ways. First, nausea and vomiting were understood to be "normal" (even if unpleasant).

[I] always have a nasty taste in my mouth which wasn't always there [before] . . . I was real tired about the first few months or so. Up until a few weeks ago I always felt sick to my stomach—all pregnancy "things."

Thus, their occurrence confirmed that everything was on course—even for those who did not want that particular sign or who thought of it as something that happened to "weak" women.

It's like I expected it to be; and yet, it's a little different, too . . . Some people will say "Well, I have this problem," or "I had that problem, and "This went this way." And in that way it's kind of different. I wasn't really expecting any problems, but if it had happened I would have been prepared for it.

Second, based on the presence of nausea, vomiting and related discomforts, the respondents were granted exemption from regular obligations and allowed special privileges that were tied directly to acknowledgment that the woman was suffering pregnancy-related sickness. For example,

I've noticed [different] treatment especially at work. The orderlies we've got over there—every time I start to pick up something, they'll run over and say: "Oh don't do that, don't strain yourself." And, they'll do it for me. If I go to push a bed back to the operating room or something, they'll push the bed for me, and if I'm scrubbing in and start getting a little bit weak or something, whoever's circulating with me notices it right away, and brings me a stool to sit on. Our head nurse has been telling me not to do anything like that, and everybody's been asking me how I feel. And when I passed out there was about three or four people all wanting to take me out to a stretcher. And, they bring me ice for my head and they'll bring me something to drink. And everybody's just been really great about it. But in a way, they almost overdo it, because it's not gonna hurt me to lift a stool—you know, some of those little things; but they've been real nice about it. . . . They don't want anything to happen: they want to make sure that I do fine; and, that the baby's okay, you know; and, that I don't have any

problems—is the feeling that I get. And it's not just "Gee, I'm going to have a baby,"
it's just that "Well, you're a pregnant woman, you gotta be careful," you know.

Hence, it was not the occurrence of symptoms themselves, but what
people "made" of them, that contributed to the confirmation of the pregnancy identity.

Fetal movement also was transformed from a physiological occurrence
into a social event by interactional processes of meaning-making. First, it
was used to confirm the early tentative identity: "When I first felt the
baby move, it was really like the first step, you know, that it was really
something happening. Until then it was just something we talked about."
Second, questions about the basis for knowledge that fetal movement had
actually occurred and how to identify it, revealed that recognition of
movement was commonly described as "instinctive" or "naturally"
known—but that all of the respondents, when asked, could name sources
of this "instinctive" knowledge. Such as,

I think it was in November [that I first felt it move]. I can't really remember that far
. . . When I went to the doctor the first time he gave me a booklet about what to eat
and all—and, it said, when you get so far along it feels like a flutter in your stomach. So
that's what it was. I figured that's what it is, you know. There wasn't any question in
my mind: if you know you're pregnant you know what it is. I guess it was more or less
instinct how I could tell . . . I had asked my sisters about it. They told me it might be
like having heartburn or something moving and kicking.

I had been kind of expecting it. It started at about three and a half or four months. The
first time I felt it I thought it was my imagination, you know. After I felt it again, I knew
what it was . . . my mother-in-law had told me what to expect—and I asked around—
especially the girl across the street. She's got two kids.

Finally, this socially interpreted event was then given further social significance when physicians used it as the basis for estimating a more accurate due date.

"Getting bigger" was also a socially constructed benchmark for the
women themselves and their social circles. First, it was used as direct
confirmation of the pregnancy identity; but, at least as important, it precipitated others' pregnancy-oriented interactions which further focused
the respondents' attention on the reality of their new status.

[My husband] teases me about "growing" all the time. He calls me pot-bellied . . . I
just finally started showing last month—before that [my family] said: "She's not
pregnant—she's not pregnant," you know—that's when they started kidding me. Last
month they came up [and said]: "Well, I guess she *is* pregnant!"

Second, use of maternity clothes as a benchmark was related to the interpretation that the change in size/"getting bigger" was indeed a sign of *pregnancy*. Thus, maternity clothes were used not just as a rational solution to a need for larger-sized clothing, but simultaneously to reveal and conceal the new shape. The true planners and the nonplanners were most excited about using the new type of clothes; the sort-of planners were only warm toward the idea—and, were more mixed in their estimate of their importance. All seemed to understand the basic reality-conferring function of wearing a special uniform appropriate to a new status, and the fact that it drew other people's attention to their new identity—which, in turn, heightened their own sense of their new selves. For example,

> [My husband] loves for me to wear maternity clothes. He thinks I look so cute in them. I think he really just likes the idea of it . . . So, I had this new maternity blouse, and I went out last night. But, everybody said: "What are you doing? What are you trying to prove?" . . . Well, they just didn't know quite what to make of it. They just think I am awfully small—you know—to be pregnant and everything. But, if I wore regular clothes they wouldn't hardly notice it that much.

> The [maternity] outfits I have are "neat." I think it's ugly for your stomach to stick out. But with maternity clothes, there's just sort of a nice bulge there.

Finally, the medical encounters all reinforced the idea that "bigger" indicated normal progress, i.e., further social meaning of the future of the identity was constructed out of the evidence that the women were using to indicate that they were actually pregnant: "[When] I went to the doctor this time . . . he assured me that I'm the right size. My husband has been saying that I was too small."

Thus, change in physical appearance was given meaning as a confirmation of the pregnancy reality: by precipitating changes in interaction, by being covered by a uniform that was specifically intended for pregnancy (not just obesity), and by drawing the approving remarks of medical personnel who made projections about the future of the pregnancy career line on the basis of those changes.

In short, various signposts and interactional situations were utilized by the respondents to convert their lingering sense of unreality into a definite feeling of being "really" pregnant. By the end of the middle phase, pregnancy had become real to all of the respondents. Both they and the people around them recognized the reality of their pregnancy careers.

At this point (months six to nine), the subjects of this study were interested in understanding labor and delivery, wondered about their postpartum physical condition, and seriously considered new time and work schedules. The husbands of the respondents were reported to be anticipating their own postdelivery careers—replete with new obligations, responsibilities, rewards and identities. The fetus-to-baby's transition was, obviously, made in its behalf: serious debate about naming, sex preference, clothes, and living arrangements were undertaken with a degree of concentration that had been lacking previously. But, by and large, these transitions to postpregnancy statuses became the focus of attention only after the pregnancy reality had been established.

SUMMARY

The social construction (and reconstruction) of the pregnancy identity has been the focus of attention in this paper. Data from panel interviews with first-time pregnant women were analyzed to illustrate the ways in which a physiologically based identity was converted into a social identity. The data support the view that physical signs are transformed into evidence of social pregnancy through a typically speedy, informal, "invisible" process of social construction of meaning. The pregnant women tentatively recognized their new identities, but awaited further confirmation of their new status before they acknowledged their identities as fully "real."

IMPLICATIONS

While the preceding discussion of the creation of the pregnancy identity focused in detail on the process by which nonpathological physiological changes were perceived and incorporated into identity, the most striking general implications of the data concerns the *ongoing* nature of an individual's attachment to an identity.

Creating identity. For the most part, the range of sociological literature that falls within the labeling perspective [See Becker (2), Goffman (13), Lemert (18), Schur (29), etc.,] emphasizes the processes by which identity labels become attached. Once the labels are attached, it is generally assumed that the identity is *set.* For examples, in reference to deviance-in-general, Freidson (10) says:

> The actors do not seem to devote themselves to avoiding the behavior or even its label so much as to avoiding the punishment that the official or unofficial world demands for behavior. The career, by and large, is learning to enjoy the behavior, developing protective justification for it, and creating ways of avoiding punishment [p. 344].

Then, in regard to a particular type of deviant (being handicapped) label, he says: ". . . characteristically, the career consists in a progressive narrowing of alternatives until none but the deviant role remains" (p. 344). The presumption is that the "pigeonholing" period is a process; but, once the categorizing is accomplished, no further efforts are expended to maintain the identity.

However, it seems apparent from examining a nonpathological and more desirable career (such as pregnancy), that identities must be *upheld*—that new supporting evidence is constantly sought and integrated into the identity framework. For example, none of my respondents would have continued to view themselves as pregnant without the appearance of new, confirming evidence. One woman was labeled as "pregnant" through two steps: she missed her menstrual period, and the examining physician said she "could be" pregnant. But the negative results of pregnancy lab tests ended the identity to which she had begun to become attached. Another woman progressed through several more phases of the pregnancy career—but when new contradictory evidence (*not* getting bigger, *absence* of fetal movement) occurred, she gradually relinquished the pregnancy identity and redefined herself as a "miscarriage." Indeed, the process of becoming "really" pregnant rested on the continuous incorporation of additional data into the identity-making process—the women became "more" pregnant with positive lab tests, physical and interactional changes, new clothes, etc. Similarly, in other types of identity, people generally look for (or are faced with) continuing evidence that they may claim a label as theirs. If this were not the case, sudden changes in a single status (such as unemployment, widowhood, retirement) would not have such a significant impact on an individual's general sense of self. Blau (4) comments on the congruence between objective and subjective age:

> . . . All people age chronologically, but many maintain a stable identity and resist the social pressures to relinquish their middle-aged identity. By doing so they preserve a sense of sameness in themselves and confidence in the continuity of how they are perceived by the people they know and care about [p. 102].
>
> . . . . .
>
> The loss of the occupational role, the mainstay of one's identity—not age or physical changes—leads people to change their age identity and accept old age.
>
> When people of similar age are compared, those who are retired perceive themselves as old much more often than do their employed age peers [pp. 104–105].

While Blau does not document the transition period (having studied individuals only before and after retirement), I would argue that the actual retirement is probably only one piece (albeit a large one) in the gradual accumulation of evidence (children growing older, hair getting gray, physical changes, etc.) that a new status constitutes a "real" identity—and it is likely that the retired person (in contrast to the same age nonretiree) continues to look for additional evidence that confirms the correctness of his or her old-age identification.

Stabilizing identity. The ongoing process of maintaining an identity acquires a stable *appearance* because other events, data, etc., are incorporated into the framework that has been developed. For example, the women in my study had a tendency to explain changes in behavior in light of their pregnancy identity: "I get tired more easily since I got pregnant." When this woman was asked how she had learned that fatigue was related to pregnancy, she said: "I asked my doctor; he said so." Thus, the same evidence confirms the identity and is explained in terms of that identity. Using the identity to explain the evidence gives the label the appearance of an objective, independent reality. For an example in another context, Sagarin's (28) discussion of homosexual identity is of interest.

> The English language is constructed in such a way that we speak of people *being* certain things when all we know is that they *do* certain things. . . . The result is an imputed identity [Author's italics, p. 25].

"Coming out" (which is presumably based on the accumulation of evidence that one is homosexual) then becomes the identity framework which explains current behavior. By organizing a series of behaviors under a title (such as homosexual), one almost guarantees that future behaviors will be understood in the context of that title. By "coming out" publicly, of course, one involves others' awareness [Glaser and Strauss (12)] and further stabilizes the maintenance of the identity. Sagarin says:

> . . . "the sharing of some kind of essential character with others" tends to be self-perpetuating, especially when a person internalizes the notion of identity and says to himself, "That is what I am."
>
> . . . . .
>
> . . . There are . . . people who behave in a given manner, at various times of their lives, in some cases over an entire lifetime. The behavior is real, but the identity is an invention. It is an invention believed in so thoroughly by some people that they become what they were . . . tagged as being [p. 31].

Newspaper readers were given a glimpse of this process of identity stabilization when Renée Richards (a newly "come out" transsexual) competed in a women's singles tennis match. A former (male) opponent, acknowledging the male *and* female components of the new transsexual's identity, said,

"Her endurance is nowhere near what it was, and she doesn't move as well either. . . . Basically, Dick Raskind never played the power game as a man. But the motion of her serve has changed now, too. *I don't know whether it's because of the operation or what.*" . . . Dr. Richards *still* showed fluid left-hand ground strokes . . . that her former opponent recalled from their 35-and-over men's rivalry [italics added, Amdur (1), p. 5].

Here again, the evidence confirms the new identity and, at the same time, is explained in terms of the identity it confirms.

Reconstructing Identity.   While people are busy creating and stabilizing identities, they are also involved in reviewing old "data," and making it consistent with their new labels. People reconstruct their understanding of past events in order to align it with present identity. Freidson (10) points out that

This lay process of retrospective selection of evidence confirming the label . . . is similar to the process in some official agencies of building up a case history or dossier, observed Goffman [14]; it is not a process by which evidence disconfirming the label is sought out and weighed against that confirming the label, but rather one by which the confirming evidence alone is recorded [pp. 341–342].

For example, as reported earlier in this paper, one nonplanner reinterpreted her bout with "flu" as "really" pregnancy. The woman who experienced the miscarriage emphasized in a post-miscarriage interview the difficulties that her mother had had in pregnancy—events which had been glossed over in earlier interviews.

Accounts by reformed alcoholics usually have a similar component—past behavior comes to be understood as alcoholic behavior only after one has the identity framework in which to understand it:

Sometime that year, she crossed what alcoholics call "that invisible line"—the line only the individual can sense *in recollection*—into alcoholism [italics added; Robertson (26), p. 14].

Similarly, former spouses come to wonder what they ever saw in the other person; an individual who changes professions may explain it as something he or she always wanted to do; a homosexual may understand past attachments to males or disinterest in females as clear evidence (retrospectively) that he was "always" a homosexual [Reid (25)].

Thus, identities of all sorts are continually constructed and reconstructed through processes of social interpretation. Future research might fruitfully be conducted on the ways in which normal/nonpathological/nondeviant identities are established, stabilized, and reconstructed.

FOOTNOTES

*This is a revised version of a paper presented at the Midwest Sociological Society Meetings, Chicago, Illinois, April 1975. I would like to thank Ron Miller, James McCartney, Norman Denzin, and Scotty Embree for their comments. I would also like to acknowledge the thoughtful and gracious guidance provided by Edward W. Lehman and Caroline Persell for the dissertation upon which this paper is based.

1. For a discussion of the previous pregnancy literature that concentrates on "deviant," "pathological", and/or "problem" pregnancies see Miller (20).

2. See Freidson (10), especially pp. 205–206, for the original conceptualization of the relationship between the objective fact of a physiological condition and the social fact of that condition.

3. This additional source of subjects was used to attempt to control for biasing factors that might have existed in a sample chosen only from the medical center facility. As it turned out, there appeared to be little difference between the women from the private physician and the women from the medical center.

The resources to seek out pregnant women who did not make use of medical care were not available. It was believed by various informants that such women must have existed among the city's poor and among the poor of the surrounding rural areas since there was no publicly supported obstetrics clinic in the area except for the activities of the medical center.

4. Range for the sample was 15–35 years of age; 1960 Census data show that 70 percent of couples age 20–24 have at least one child. Census data for 1970 show that the median number of children born in the 15–24 ever-married age groups was .995; for the 25–35 ever-marrieds the figure was 2.3. [U.S. Bureau of the Census (33), p. 94; U.S. Bureau of the Census (32), p. 369].

5. Census figures for 1960 show that 25 percent of all births occur within the first year of marriage; 69 percent have occurred by the end of the second year [U.S. Bureau of the Census (33), p. 84].

6. Sample rate of illegitimacy was 4.3 percent compared to 8 percent nationally [see Winch (34), p. 194, for discussion of the problems in making this estimate].

7. Sample rate of premarital pregnancy was 6.4%; estimate for U.S. population is 20–35 percent [Coombs, *et al.* (6), p. 800].

8. Median occupational level for men in the United States is foremen, craftsmen, and kindred workers [U.S. Bureau of the Census (32), p. 375].

9. In the sample, income of the fathers of the respondents = $7500. National median income = $8,500. In the sample, median education for respondents' fathers = completed high school. Nationally, median education = 12.1 years.

10. Husbands of the women in the sample had more education, higher occupational status, but the same size incomes as the women's fathers. Median earning for the husbands and the respondents was about $2,500 each. When student-husband and housewives/student wives were excluded, husbands' incomes were similar to their fathers-in-law: $7,500; the respondents' income remained similar to what their mothers had earned: $2,500.

11. In this sample, 93.8 percent were raised in cities or suburbs; white = 87.7 percent, black = 4.1 percent, other = 8.2 percent. The U.S. population is 73 percent urban and 89 percent white [U.S. Bureau of the Census (32), pp. 1–258 (chart) and p. 382, Table 86].

In the sample, Protestant = 70 percent, Catholic = 20.4 percent, Jewish = 2.4 percent, other = 7.2 percent.

12. Data from the third set of interviews are not included here because this paper focuses on the process of acquisition of identity. For a complete discussion of all materials collected with the various interview guides see Miller (20).

13. Other researchers have suggested "types" of reproductive careers. For example,

Rainwater (23) described four patterns of contraceptive-usage that result (or do not result) in control of number and spacing of children: early, "do nothing", sporadic, and late 'desperate' users—but all of his subjects were women who had had at least one child; his focus was not on the development of the pregnancy career but on multiple-child-bearing and rearing as a career. The most frequently used typologies are the two-fold ones of planned-unplanned or wanted-unwanted—usually used interchangeably [see Pohlman (22) for a complete accounting of the research using those distinctions]. But, these typologies are usually focusing on the number of children desired, not on the pregnancies themselves.

14. The data also reveal social class variation in these stages. For discussion of the effect of socio-economic status on pregnancy career see Miller (20).

15. There were social class variations here; with blue-collar women more oriented to friends and family. Komarovsky (17) found similar patterns of reliance.

16. See Miller (20), pp. 324–329 for an extended discussion of this phase.

REFERENCES

1. Neil Amdur, "Dr. Richards Beats Miss Been in Tennis Week Open, 6–0, 6–2," *New York Times,* August 22, 1976, Sec. 5, pp. 1, 3.
2. Howard S. Becker, *Outsiders.* The Free Press, New York, 1963.
3. Peter Berger and Thomas Luckmann, *The Social Construction of Reality.* Doubleday, Garden City, N.Y., 1967.
4. Zena Smith Blau, *Old Age in a Changing Society.* Watts, New York, 1973.
5. Arthur Colman and Libby C. Colman, *Pregnancy: The Psychological Experience.* Herder, New York, 1971.
6. Lolagene C. Coombs, Ronald Freedman, Judith Friedman, and William F. Pratt, "Premarital Pregnancy and Status Before and After Marriage," *American Journal of Sociology* 75 (1970): 800–820.
7. Fred Davis, *Passage Through Crisis.* Bobbs-Merrill, Indianapolis, 1963.
8. Norman Denzin, "Symbolic Interaction and Ethnomethodology." *Understanding Everyday Life* (ed. Jack Douglas). Aldine, Chicago, 1970, pp. 261–286. A revised and shortened version of this essay appeared in 1969, *American Sociological Review,* 34 (1969): 922–934.
9. Hans Peter Dreitzel (ed.), *Recent Sociology, No. 2.* Macmillan, New York, 1970.
10. Eliot Freidson, *The Profession of Medicine.* Dodd, Mead, New York, 1970.
11. ———, "Disability as Deviance." (eds. Eliot Freidson and Judith Lorber), *Medical Men and Their Work.* Aldine, Chicago, 1972, pp. 330–352.
12. Barney G. Glaser and Anselm L. Strauss, "Awareness Contexts and Social Interaction," *American Sociological Review* 29 (1964): 669–678.
13. Erving Goffman, *Stigma.* Prentice-Hall, Englewood Cliffs, N.J., 1963.
14. ———, *Asylums.* Doubleday, Garden City, N.Y., 1961.
15. Burkart Holzner, *Reality Construction in Society.* Schenkman, Cambridge, Mass., 1968.
16. Everett C. Hughes, "Institutional Office and the Person," *American Journal of Sociology* 43 (1937): 404–413.
17. Mirra Komarovsky, *Blue-Collar Marriage.* Random House, New York, 1962.
18. Edwin M. Lemert, *Human Deviance, Social Problems, and Social Control,* Prentice Hall, Englewood Cliffs, N.J., 1967.
19. George Herbert Mead, *Mind, Self and Society.* Aldine, Chicago, 1934.
20. Rita Seiden Miller, "Pregnancy: The Social Construction of a Physiological Event," unpublished doctoral dissertation, New York University, 1973.

21. ——, American Sociological Association Section on Sex Roles, Washington, D.C., 1974. "The Social Aspects of Pregnancy: A Preliminary Bibliography."
22. Edward H. Pohlman, *Psychology of Birth Planning*. Cambridge, Mass.: Schenkman, 1969.
23. Lee Rainwater, *And the Poor Get Children*. Quadrangle, New York, 1967.
24. ——, *Family Design: Marital Sexuality, Family Planning and Family Limitation*. Aldine, Chicago, 1964.
25. John Reid, "The Best Little Boy in the World Has a Secret," *New York* magazine, May 7, 1973.
26. Nan Robertson, "The Young of A.A.: When Euphoria of Wine and Drugs is Gone," *New York Times*, August 2, 1976.
27. Julius Roth, *Timetables*. Bobbs-Merrill, Indianapolis, 1963.
28. Edward Sagarin, "The High Personal Cost of Wearing a Label," *Psychology Today* 9 (1976): 25–31.
29. Edwin Schur, *Labeling Deviant Behavior: Its Sociological Implications*. Harper & Row, New York, 1971.
30. Alfred Schutz, *On Phenomenology and Social Relations*. University of Chicago Press, 1970.
31. Tomatsu Shibutani, *Society and Personality*. Prentice-Hall, Englewood Cliffs, N.J., 1961.
32. U.S. Bureau of the Census, "General Social and Economic Characteristics, United States Summary," *Census of the Population*, 1970.
33. ——, "Subjects Reports," *Census of the Population*, 1960, Vol. II.
34. Robert F. Winch, *The Modern Family* (3d ed.) Holt, Reinhart and Winston, New York, 1971.

THE MEDITATION MOVEMENT: SYMBOLIC INTERACTIONISM AND SYNCHRONICITY

Richard Bibbee, MISSISSIPPI STATE UNIVERSITY

Julian B. Roebuck, MISSISSIPPI STATE UNIVERSITY

INTRODUCTION[1]

In this paper we are primarily interested in understanding the effect that the meditation movement has and is likely to have on society in the United States. Adherents to this movement purport to focus on the self, the transformation of the self, a reinterpretation of meaningful interaction with objects and others, and a re-evaluation of human relationships. Symbolic interactionism is utilized as a critical paradigm in the analysis of this macro-level phenomenon because we believe that it offers a better explanatory model for the construction and maintenance of this movement than any other sociological frame of reference (e.g., the conflict paradigm or structural functionalism). No sociological frame is com-

Studies in Symbolic Interaction—Volume 1, 1978, pages 205–240.

pletely adequate for the study of this novel social movement wherein doctrine does not appear to be causally related to adherents' behavior. For example, how can chanting a mantra (e.g., "OM") repeatedly for twenty minutes or gazing at a mandala (a geometric design) directly affect social relationships? Furthermore, many have charged that symbolic interactionism has "either ignored or renounced the idea of 'the unconscious' and has provided no explanatory principle in its place [Meltzer, *et al*. (56), p. 117]." Any paradigm employed to describe and/or explain the meditation movement must include some notion of the "mind" that extends beyond conscious rational thinking. Whether we label nonrational thinking the "unconscious" or what Huxley (32) termed the "mind-at-large," a concept including both nonrational and nonconscious behavior must be added to the symbolic interactionism paradigm if we are to adequately understand the meditation movement. Jung's (39) concept of "synchronicity," when combined with symbolic interactionism, appears to meet the aforementioned charge. We introduce it as a sensitizing concept into the paradigm of symbolic interactionism.

We reason that two types of logic must be utilized to adequately describe meditative effects: causality and synchronicity. The first is an objective (experimentally verifiable) logic of cause and effect which connects two or more events. The second is a "subjective" logic of cause and affect which connects two or more events by the meaning that is given to such relationships by any participant, regardless of whether these events appear to be causally connected. Rather than being experimentally verifiable, synchronistic connections must be experienced. Thus, if meditators believe, think or feel that chanting a mantra has a beneficial influence on the rest of their behavior, we must take them seriously if we are to understand them. Symbolic interactionists have always given recognition to W. I. Thomas's remark: "If men define situations as real, they are real in their consequences." We feel symbolic interactionism is ideally suited to handle the two logics of connection simultaneously: causality and synchronicity.

Several varieites of symbolic interactionism are extant [Meltzer, *et al*. (56)]: the Chicago School, the Iowa School, the dramaturgical approach, and ethnomethodology. Though there is still some dissensus on basic concepts such as the "self," we agree with Meltzer's observation that "each orientation accepts, to some degree, the methodological necessity of 'getting inside' the reality of the actor in an effort to understand this reality as the actor does." Our analysis draws from each variety of symbolic interactionism. Several questions are essential to our analysis: Does the widespread interest in meditation designate a social movement? Can symbolic interactionism be used to explain the meditation movement? Can symbolic interactionism be used to explain meaningful relationships which do not appear to be causal? Is the meditation movement just another form of self-help in an increasingly alienated society? What is the effect of the meditation movement on society?

THE MEDITATION MOVEMENT

A surprising number of Americans have developed an interest in some form of meditation. In a November 21, 1976, Gallop Poll, respondents were handed a card with the following question: "Which, if any, of these are you involved in or do you practice?" The results give a good idea of the widespread interest in introspective esoterica of which meditation is one example. The following was estimated: that 4 percent of the American people (six million) are in transcendental meditation (TM); 3 percent (five million) are in some form of yoga; 2 percent (three million) are in some form of charismatic movement; 2 percent consider themselves mystics; 1 percent (two million) are into some form of Eastern religion. Fully 22 percent of the population (thirty-two million) are actively engaged in some form of astrology, with 80 percent of the people knowing their birth sign. Most of those expressing these interests were young (eighteen to twenty-four years old), and well educated (college background). The data tell us two things. First, that the interest in meditation is widespread and, second, that this interest is extremely diversified,[2] including elements from astrology, mysticism, Eastern folklore, and yoga.

Social movements usually generate a great deal of literature, pro and con. Meditation is extremely hard to describe [Naranjo and Ornstein (59); Weil (75)], and the best illustrations come from those individuals who have actually tried it for extended periods of time [Bloomfield (10), Castanada (17), Maharishi (50, 51), Ornstein (60), Shainberg (68)]. The intellectual approaches to a description of meditation are just as varied as the content: theologians Kierkegaard (41), philosophers Krishnamurti (42); James (33); novelists Hesse (30), Huxley (32); psychiatrists Assagioli (2), Jung (35); psychologists Ornstein (61); medical practioners Benson (6); and scientists Brown (12), have all engaged in some form of descriptive analysis. Meditation literature seems to remain on the descriptive, how-to, level for individuals. Few have analyzed the sociological effects of meditation [with the exception of Schur (65)] or given any sociological explanations for the origin of this movement [with the exception of Lasch (43)]. Sociologists have long known that what may appear to be beneficial to the individual may be detrimental to society. Slater (70, 71) has certainly illustrated this paradox well, and when all is written, the meditation movement may turn out to be just another form of the pursuit of loneliness [Shainberg (68)].

Social movements usually generate some sort of structural foundation. There are hundreds of organizations which teach or use meditation as an integral part of their program (e.g., Maharishi International University, Theosophy, Rosicrucians, Astara, Arica, the Arcane School, and the School for Esoteric Studies). And there are hundreds of foundations devoted to studying the effect meditation has on man (e.g., Esalen, Academy of Parapsychology and Medicine, Higher Sense Perception Research Foundation, Institute for the Study of Consciousness, Institute for Noetic Sciences,[3] Kundalini Research Foundation, Psychical Research Foundation, and Psychosynthesis Foundation). The interest in meditation has even spawned a whole new branch of psychology: transpersonal psychology, which tries to include the spiritual dimensions of man as opposed to psychoanalysis, behaviorism, and humanistic psychology.

There are several typologies which could be used to describe the outstanding characteristics of any social movement. Blumer's [in McLaughlin (49)] distinction between general, specific, and expressive social movements is helpful. General social movements (as opposed to specific social movements) do not have a definite program nor a single goal for collective action. Collective action is often episodic and widely scattered and not intended to change the institutions of the social order or its objective character. However, general movements are structured, containing many organizations, ideologies, and spokesmen. They generate gradual and pervasive value changes in a general direction (e.g., the labor movement, the youth movement, the women's movement), often giving rise to specific social movements with a definite program pointed toward precise goals. The widespread interest in meditation designates a general social movement. It is also an expressive movement because it does not seek actual social change. Adherents to expressive movements turn their frustration and dissatisfaction with society inward, releasing tension not in terms of action, but rather in feelings (e.g., religious and fashion movements). The members of the meditation movement are preoccupied with self and self-analysis and exhibit an attitude of indifference toward a society to which they feel they no longer belong.

Symbolic interactionism is an ideal model for the analysis of general expressive social movements. The conflict paradigm seems best suited for an analysis of militant movements (reform, revolutionary and nationalistic, reactionary and revivalistic) and the consensus paradigm seems best suited for movements of withdrawal and revitalization (communitarian, cultic, millenarian, messianic). Symbolic interactionism seems best suited for analyzing the *general* characteristics[4] of transcendental movements (conversionistic, adventist, introversionist, agnostic) and movements of psychosensual escape (hedonistic, contraculture, collective identity quests).

Social movements generate certain mechanisms and means necessary for their development, and in this vein we utilize the following guideline for the rest of this section: the perception of a shared problem by large numbers of people; spokesmen and an organizational foundation; a pervasive ideology which is more easily believed in than understood; and some form of social impact.

Especially for the young, the immorality of the war in Vietnam, the Watergate affair, an ambivalence toward traditional values, and the increase in crime and lawlessness are thought to be the major causes of the interest in meditation. The meditation movement not only promises a solution to an individual's problems, but appears to offer very simple instructions on how this solution may be effected. Naranjo (59) believes that the major problem for modern man is that he is detached from the cultural forms of the past and dissatisfied with the results of technology. *Psychology Today* (April 1974), certainly a reflector of "the popular mind," holds that meditation is attractive to an alienated society because it transmits "the idea that everyone has a very important Self, which is somehow identical to God." Campbell (15, p. 37) sees the meditation movement as another form of the pervasive optimism of the American people, i.e., "an abiding belief in the salvation of individuals and the world." It has also been observed that meditation groups offer instant intimacy in a mobile society where primary relationships are structurally tenuous. None of these observations are adequate as explanations. Campbell, for instance, begs the question when he comments that, "the seeds of transcendence are native to this country." And sociologists know there is nothing "instant" about real intimacy [Simmel (69) pp. 325–330].

There are dozens of roshis, lamas, swamis, teen-age perfect masters, and middle-aged wise men who consider themselves to be the only real voice of the meditation movement. In order to simplify matters we have focused on the doctrines of the two most radical spokesmen (Oscar Ichazo of Arica, and Werner Erhard of EST–Erhard Seminars Training) and the most popular one (Mahesh Yogi Maharishi of TM). We can do no more than illustrate some of the general characteristics of the meditation movement by examining these doctrines.

In less than two years Arica has grown from a single center with fewer than a dozen people to centers in Los Angeles, San Francisco, and New York with a staff of over 250 teachers. Arica's founder is largely responsible for this success. Ichazo, who moved to this country from Arica, Chile, is attempting to train enough teachers in the Arica technique to save Western culture from what he considers to be certain death. To Ichazo, man has been corrupted "as a result of the fall in society [Keen (40)]." His program is designed to destroy all aspects of the "self" that are socially constructed: "the ego is false or distorted consciousness." To him, "we sense our basic unity with all life in our guts." Ichazo does not understand the entire process of socialization or that consciousness itself is a reflection of social interdependence. To teach that man's basic unity is a result of his animal body denies that man also has a mind, and that real unity can only be sought in society. The only importance that can be attached to the community is, "when people see others with their same ego fixation, they feel less alone and less serious about their hangups." And, "when a person feels a part of a community of fools or sinners he begins to realize that the pretentions of the ego are no longer necessary." This doctrine is clearly antiintellectual and antisocial.

Ichazo does not understand that the ego is a linguistic structure [Becker (4)] and should it be destroyed we could not even talk to one another. And yet Ichazo labels ego destruction as his program's primary goal: "When we are in perfect awareness we know nothing . . ." [Keen (40, p. 76)]. Ichazo is not a sociologist. He gives no "social programs" for bringing about this ego-less state, excluding how class, status, or party might hinder his "utopian" vision.

Adam Smith's (72) account of Arica, as a postgraduate, is most interesting. He quotes Ichazo as saying, "This school is the most important thing going on on the planet at this time." But as Smith makes clear, "Arica was developing something we used to call in the money business, limousine syndrome." As one teacher put it: "I can't be in *satori* on less than $1,000 a month." Arica, since its initial success, has been losing members. As Smith points out, many teachers and students find themselves in a Catch 22 situation: to communicate about the enlightenment achieved through the Arica technique you must use language, but language is a product of the ego which must be destroyed.

EST is such a concentration of social rudeness that after two weekends of "training" nothing else for the rest of your life could possibly be worse—so you automatically feel at ease about it. EST is specifically designed to make you wet your pants (it is even called "no-pee" therapy), vomit, freeze, sweat, take insults, and learn to be bored—and they charge you $250 to do it. Anyone who goes through this has to tell others it was enlightening or else his friends might think him insane. Indeed, the central message of EST is that what you do has no effect on anything else. You are a machine, what you do really does not matter, and no one cares for you. Acceptance of these themes enables one to face reality. Instead of calling reality itself into question the EST trainee is taught not to let it bother him—as if air and water pollution and the thousand or so cancer-causing chemicals in our food could be ignored. The person who dreamed up this concentrated exercise in contradictions rides in a chauffeured Mercedes, has a $48,000 salary, a valet and chef, and two wives—hardly the essence of mystical detachment!

Erhard believes that the biggest social fear is of being conned. There-fore (for their own good) he puts people through the biggest con they are ever likely to experience so they will no longer have this fear. As Litwak (47, p. 48) puts it, "Essentially the message of EST goes something like this: the mind imposes judgments on a neutral world. In reality there are no 'good' or 'bad' experiences." Erhard maintains that you can change nothing, so accept what is. Like many "put-ons," EST is very successful—making over $9.3 million last year alone.

The Mahesh Yogi Maharishi is the most popular spokesman in the meditation movement, and like most, he too is interested in the redemp-tion of mankind. TM has from the beginning been designed as a mass movement.[5] According to the "World Plan" there are to be 3,500 centers which will train the three and a half million teachers needed to reach the world's three and a half billion people. TM is *consciously* modern. The Maharishi even has his own engineering company, Veda Vision, which will be the center for a world-wide television network, the plans of which were sent to every national leader in the world. TM has over sixty fulltime employees at its World Plan Center in Los Angeles. There are several organizations teaching meditation which have their own university, but TM's is the largest. Maharishi International University consists of a 185-acre campus in Fairfield, Iowa, with approximately 600 students who will form the Vanguard of the World Plan. At present there are about 400 TM centers and more than 6,000 instructors. With six million already engaged in TM and about 30,000 new members joining each month, TM itself seems to be a social movement.[6]

TM is acceptable to a vast variety of people. New Jersey and New York, along with cities as diverse as Miami and Hartford, are offering high school courses in TM.[7] The National Institute of Mental Health (NIMH) has even given a $21,500 grant to train high school teachers in TM. There are at least seventeen other federally funded TM research projects, e.g., to study its effect on stress, and its rehabilitating effects on criminals and alcoholics. When both the Army and the U.S. Bureau of Prisons suggest that TM might serve as a means of coping with drug abuse, this is an indication that meditation as a technique of therapy and development has become an accepted practice.[8] After all, if such diverse people as Joe Namath, Governor Jerry Brown [Wills (76)], and Major General Frank Davis, commandant of the U.S. Army War College, do it, then surely it must be taken seriously! The news media have helped make TM popular and have been respectful rather than critical, partly because a great deal of the scientific community is taking it seriously [Bloomfield (10); Benson (6); Capra (16); Mitchell (58); Ornstein (60)]. *Newsweek,* for instance, calls the meditation movement "the consciousness revolution, a diffuse but culturally pervasive movement that may well turn out to be this century's version of Colonial America's Great Awakening (September 6, 1976:56)." One observer of the cultural barometer, Theodore Roszak, describes us as being on "the biggest introspective binge any society in history has undergone." The meditation movement is unique in terms of both size and quality.

The meditation movement seems to identify itself with everything. As a consequence, it has not developed a single coherent ideology. To illustrate, in TM, a form of mantra yoga, the individual must repeat a specific mantra over and over again for about a half hour twice a day. This exercise is supposed to bring enlightenment because the mantra can be identified with anything. As Naranjo (59, p. 5) observes: "My own exploration of meditation shows me that the essence of meditation . . . is the essence of doing anything in the right attitude." That is, "all life is meditation, and meditation is living." Rather than being a weakness, this type of ideology gives the meditation movement real strength, as it can appeal to people in all aspects of society.

Many critics have seen the impact the meditation movement is having on society as a new form of narcissism. Instead of deploring the isolated individual in a mobile technological society, the meditation movement reverses the emphasis and calls this very isolation the goal of spiritual enlightenment. Schur (65) has called this new form of "awareness" a trap which veils the real issues, i.e., if the individual in American society is in fact alienated, it is not a cure to accept and deify it. This is really a social illusion.[9] Instead of defining alienation negatively vis-à-vis society, the meditation movement defines it positively in terms of our deeper nature and its "detachment" from everything except godly purity. What this means is that you can be concerned for others but that you must not *take* on their problems or allow these problems to affect you. As Naranjo (59, p. 24) describes it: "True indifference is not indifferent. When the individual is able to remove his little ego (moral ideas included) from the course of his deeper nature, the melody played by the gods through his hollow reed is one of goodness and beauty . . ." How is this possible? How is it possible to really be *in* a social relationship but not be *of* it? It is this contradiction which we next explore.

MEDITATION AND SYMBOLIC INTERACTIONISM

We examine the meditation movement in terms of the tenets of symbolic interactionism, i.e., the position of each on self, objects, symbols and society. Regardless of the particular meditative techniques employed, the one thing that seems to tie them all together is a mental attitude [Naranjo (59, p. 8]: "meditation is concerned with the development of a *presence,* a modality of being, which may be expressed or developed in whatever situation the indiviudal may be involved." In this respect the meditator's definitions of the mind and self are not the definitions of the symbolic interactionist. As Naranjo (59, p. 13) explains, "the ordinary state of consciousness is one of not truly experiencing, of not being in contact with the world or self, and, to that extent, not only deprived of bliss but comparable to a non-being." This is opposite to the way a symbolic interactionist would describe reality and self. To meditators the true self is already there and all else—body, ordinary everyday life [Berger and Luckmann (7)], and especially society—are illusions. Symbolic interactionists view the mind as a process rather than a structure, and term the process of using symbols covertly "imaginative rehearsal." What they consider to be reality, meditators consider illusion and vice versa.

To Mead, the self is a social product that contains unique mental capacities such as using symbols to designate objects in the environment, mentally rehearsing alternative lines of action toward these objects, and inhibiting inappropriate action by selecting the proper line of overt action. When the individual does these things he develops a self, i.e., he can symbolically designate his own behavior and thinking as any other object in his environment. He can understand another self by taking the role of the other, i.e., another person ought to be thinking the same thing socially when he is in the same social position. Without the ability to role-take and imaginatively rehearse alternative lines of action, individuals could not socially coordinate themselves. Society is an ongoing process of fitting together interaction made possible through mutual interpretations, negotiations, evaluations, definitions, and lines of action.

Meditators take an entirely different view of the self. First, in Mead's terms, the "me" would be considered an illusion, something that must be destroyed in order for a person's "true self" to emerge. This "true self" is not something which can be developed, it is there at birth, and society obscures it through conditioned responses which do not let it come forth. The very word "meditation" means the center within us or the practice of knowing the "self" within. Basically there are three forms of meditation (the way of forms, the expressive way, and the negative way) each concerned with contacting the inner self [Naranjo (59)].

The "way of forms" is basically concentrative or absorptive meditation.[10] In absorptive meditation the individual confronts an "other" (e.g., the idea of God, a mandala, a mantra) upon which he focuses his mind and with which he hopes to identify. The nature of the meaning of these objects varies from that of the symbolic interactionist. Meditative objects have intrinsic meanings which evoke the same quality in the individual's "true self." Meaning is not a process but an intrinsic quality in the proper relationship of self and object. Focusing on such "universal objects" certainly negates spontaneity and interpretation, but such is the goal of this form of meditation, i.e., to identify the self with all past meaning. Crucial aspects of this form are centrality (around which all action flows, e.g., the lotus, cross, heart, or "OM"), order, regularity, and lawfulness (e.g., the union of opposites, yin-yang, night-day). What this type of meditation tries to do is concentrate the individual's attention upon the reflection of his self in the mirror of symbolism. Even the self can serve as such a symbol, for example, in the maxim "Know thyself." Thus, it is not the perception of the object but its intrinsic meaning which is of importance. Such a view differs from the way a symbolic interactionist conceives objects or meaning in relation to the self.

In the "expressive way" of meditation,[11] "the meditator seeks to become receptive to, and to identify with, himself, without the mirror device of the symbol [Naranjo (59, p. 11)]." In this type of meditation, the individual is expected to eliminate all forms of expectation, preconceptions, and predetermined courses of action. Spontaneously generated symbolic objects from the "formless depth" of our "true inner self" is the goal. All external symbolic patterns and objects are to be eliminated from conscious attention, including social relationships. Supposedly this elimination of all social patterns will not lead to chaos but to the expression of a definite structure that all men share. As Jung showed in the domain of visual fantasy, images become increasingly "collective" as the subject explores his presumably individual depth [Naranjo (59, p. 17)]. This type of innate similarity leading to some sort of universal connection between all men is foreign to symbolic interactionism.

The "negative way" of meditation is more directly opposed to the assumptions of symbolic interactionism than the former meditative techniques. In this type, the individual is neither focusing his attention outward, trying to identify with the intrinsic meaning of some symbolic object, nor does he focus his attention on the spontaneous meanings arising from that part of his self connected to all nature. Rather he attempts a total "self-emptying." This type of meditation asks the individual to withdraw from all forms of goal-directed behavior and both internal and external experience. Techniques in this type of meditation are designed to completely destroy what a symbolic interactionist would label as ordinary states of consciousness, especially the self and all mental concepts. Fasts, feats of self discipline, and other privations are designed to do away with all physical, emotional, and mental desires.

A very interesting similarity can be found between Zen's (the essence of the negative way) conception of self and Goffman's formulation (a polemic example from symbolic interactionism). According to Zen Buddhism there is no "self," and the only image that can convey the experience of attainment is sunyata, emptiness. Sunyata literally means "no-bottom" [Naranjo (59, p. 22)]. Just as one can infinitely divide any line segment into halves, so is the self endless. Goffman has illustrated his conception of self as an endless series of masks (persona) in which at bottom there is nothing but another mask. If these masks are each destroyed in a never-ending process of seeing through illusions, then one approaches what the Buddhists call nirvana (which means extinction). Only out of such emptyness can one find everything. Even though the disintegration of the ego must be done in solitude, it is supposedly only at this level that one can find the deepest solidarity with all mankind. Our stance here is that if the illusions a Buddhist addresses are primarily social, then why is the escape from illusion always individual? As Marx once observed, why not do away with those conditions which require illusions. Rather than destroying the symptom, why not eliminate the source?

Blumer (11) sets down the three postulates of symbolic interactionism: 1) "human beings act toward things on the basis of the meanings that the things have for them"; 2) "the meaning of such things is derived from, or arises out of, the social interaction that one has with one's fellows"; and 3) "these meanings are handled in, and modified through, an interpretative process used by the person in dealing with the things he encounters." Essential to these postulates is the concept of object, anything which can be symbolically referred to either physical, social, or abstract. To Blumer, as well as to each form of meditation, the most important object is the self. But, where Blumer designates the expectation structure (e.g., norms and values) as next in importance, a meditator would always label this structure illusion. Meditation doctrine is in partial agreement with Blumer's first and third postulates, but not with his second postulate. To Blumer, the quality of objects consists of the meanings that people attribute to them. Therefore, different people might attribute different meanings to the same object. For example, an artist's conception of a table would be different from that of a physicist. Different meanings arise from a different history of social interaction. Meanings come out of mutual symbolic indications, which make group life possible.

Meditator's meanings are changed by acts of reinterpretation. In EST, for instance, Werner Erhard teaches that the mind deceives you into reacting to an artificial reality. This reality can be altered by changing your interpretation of it. When you become "enlightened," then you become the sole author of your own emotions, ideas, and reactions. A key phrase in EST is, "I am the cause of my own world." EST converts learn to create an inner "space" into which each of them can retreat and immerse himself in his *own* consciousness [Woodward (77, p. 59)]. Even more to the point, love becomes "never having to tell someone else he's wrong." EST and those forms of meditation which take this position are socially irresponsible. In terms of Blumer's second postulate how can EST construct or even criticize meaningful social relationships, which can only be derived with others? For example, what do we do about Hitler or Watergate under these assumptions? Love, as EST defines it, is reduced to sheer meaningless if one cannot discriminate between Hitler's actions and the actions of a guru. Socially, we must intepret wrongful from rightful action. EST is filled with such contradictions. Another example illustrates the point. EST assumes that "What is, is," and at the same time the individual is seen as the sole cause of his own world. How can people believe that they must accept the world as it is and simultaneously make themselves responsible for everything that happens to them? This certainly negates Blumer's notion that social interaction, not the isolated individual, is responsible for the generation of meaning. As Woodward (77) concludes, EST graduates seem to be searching for a sudden transformation without moral cost or consequence. They learn not to share in the suffering of others, but to be emotionally detached. Naranjo (59, p. 8) observes that all forms of meditation try to create in the individual an attitude which "transforms whatever it touches" so that it "is not merely a *how to mediate* but a *how to be*." However, it is a *how to be* in separation from social interaction. In these terms meditation becomes a persistent effort to free oneself from all social encumbrances. This type of "freedom" is an illusion (Franks, 1976). Individuals may not be made solely responsible for their social position or their interpretation thereof. Socially, EST could never bring about meaningful change or deal adequately with conflict. As Woodward observes, the meditation movement persists because of the romantic notion that inner experience alone can transform reality and that anyone can fashion his life into a perfect work of art.

Schutz (66, p. 537) would certainly argue against the meditation movement at this juncture. As he observed, meaningful reality can only be overcome by resistance, either through working on objects or exerting effort on others. Dreams, for instance, where there is no directed effort, would be an illusion to Schutz. He would criticize adherents to the meditation movement for living in a phantasm (p. 555). Conscious life exhibits an indefinite number of different planes, ranging from the plane of action on one end to the plane of dream at the other. Each plane can be characterized by a specific tension in the consciousness of the individual. What is crucial here is that the plane determines the amount of conscious tension needed to deal with it, and not necessarily the individual. To Schutz, dreams represent a complete lack of interest in terms of life, while action represents our highest interest in meeting *reality* and its *requirements*. Therefore, "attention to life is the basic regulative principle of conscious life."

Attention to life must be a joint effort as sociology has always maintained. What symbolic interactionism tries to make clear is that those who participate or "work" together share in part the same reality. As Blumer (11, p. 22) puts it, "resistance gives the empirical world an obdurant character that is the mark of reality." As Becker (3, 4, 5) has observed, what we all have in common is our bodies. Each of us must "resist" it (e.g., we *all* must eat, that *is* a reality). The range of interpretative meaning is limited in this realm, as it is in terms of social relationships (i.e., the expectation structure), but, when we examine the "plane" of the individual's own mind the range of possible interpretations increases because resistance and conscious tension decrease. As Berger and Luckmann (7) define everyday reality, institutions are possible because we all can pretty much agree on the economy of doing and acting in certain ways. As we move away from this type of reality, agreement weakens because resistance weakens and there are more possibilities to discharge conscious tension. Meditation takes an opposite stance, i.e., it switches the order in which reality becomes meaningful—everyday life is less meaningful than the meditative life.[12] And, if a meditator changes his interpretation of everyday life, then he believes that everyday life will also change. But, as Blumer would caution, such change can only take place within a very limited range. That is, the actor can select, check, suspend, evaluate, construct, regroup, and even transform his action, but he can not *deny* everyday reality. One must always check his meanings in light of the situation in which he is placed and the direction of his action. Meditators do not take cognizance of the situation or the direction of *action*.

When Blumer (11, p. 12) states, "Nothing is more important than that objects in all categories can undergo change in their meaning," he never intended that a change would be so drastic as to reduce the object to a state of meaninglessness by defining it outside the limits of reality. Or, when he maintains that a person "acts toward himself and guides himself in his actions toward others on the basis of the kind of object he is to himself," he does not mean that the person would become detached from others, as the following statement implies: "the self-object emerges from the process of social interaction in which other people are defining a person to himself." Thus, Blumer and Mead would argue that the more people a person comes in contact with the greater is his potential for internal development. This is especially the case when significant others are somewhat diversified. In the meditation movement committed adherents associate with few people, most of whom are fellow sectarians. Their truly meaningful social contacts are with the "master" or guru. If the guru is perfect, then association with ordinary people must of necessity have little significance. This position translates into something like the following: "Only if the master likes me can I possibly like myself."

Further, in several sects the adherents are given special mantras which as objects are supposed to become more meaningful than any other association, including people.

When society is considered, meditators either tend to deny it or else they retreat into an artificially constructed society, where everyone shares a common esoteric understanding. Blumer (11) gives us good insight into monasteries and ashrams: "The meaning of objects for a person arises fundamentally out of the way they are defined to him by others with whom he interacts." The whole purpose of retreats, monasteries, or ashrams is to insure that the convert interacts with no one except persons of the same mind.[13] Thus, interaction with others is extremely limited and in some cases forbidden. As Blumer makes clear, "we see ourselves through the way in which others see or define us." This is certainly true of Zen monasteries.[14]

According to Shainberg (68), who went to the new Zen center in the Catskills, the largest most authentic Zen temple outside of Japan, "Zen meditation is always solitary, but as time goes on the solitude wants to be shared." How this contradiction is solved is never really made clear. Zen attempts to destroy the social aspect of the self. The practice constitutes an assault upon the self, and Zen monasteries are its ultimate weapons [Shainberg (68)]. As Blumer recognized, the environment includes only the objects that people recognize and know. But in a monastery there are few objects that the person comes in contact with. Shainberg terms this "the violence of just sitting." Symbolic interactionism can explain this situation. Because of the reflexive nature of the self the individual can treat himself and others as social objects. However, this process occurs *only* after the individual's self has been socially constructed. A person can be completely alone only after he has been in society. In such situations claustrophobia is common. What else?

Shainberg (68, p. 58) maintains that the people he knew came to Zen as a result of psychic desperation and disenchantment with other self-improvement fantasies, and that they displayed an intense interest in the doctrine's concreteness and simplicity. In short, these people's lives had been so decimated by the complexity of our technological society that they opted for the social desert of monastery life. The impact of Zen on convert's lives is revealed in this statement: "Zen is disinterested in solution and unenthusiastic, even bored with the idea of happiness." What *value* to society is a doctrine that is not interested in the solution of our most pressing social problems? Rather, Zen makes a religion out of isolation. Small groups of Zen converts will not disrupt society, but, should significant numbers take this position society may well disintegrate.

Very little is mentioned in the meditative disciplines about how spiritual evolution proceeds from a community base. Indeed, the only interpersonal techniques are some forms of tantric yoga, where a man and a woman engage in the sexual embrace and meditate to orgasm. The goal—that both participants' minds contain the exact same thoughts—is another form of individualism. Regarding these forms of yoga, a practitioner of another form was overhead to say: "What need have I for a woman? I am my own internal woman." Should large numbers of people take this latter viewpoint the human species could soon die out. Many types of meditation place restrictions on sexual intercourse, or at the very least emphasize a monogamous relationship where sex is used only for procreation [Fortune (23)]. Indeed, the sexual energies are to be transmuted into a "higher" form in the mind or "higher bodies" ("We never touch the higher planes save by fidelity" [Fortune (23)]. This energy is not used to communicate with other people, but with beings of a higher order, or with the higher parts of ourself ("Union upon the physical plane need not take place, and, in fact, will not take place while the life-forces are being used upon other levels. . . ," Fortune (23). It is believed by various schools of yoga that certain centers in the brain can be developed by meditating on various nerve plexuses in the body which are physical gates to "higher" forms of energy. Concentrations of these "higher" forms of energy (called chakras) stand "behind" or "above" these plexuses. The individual is trained to keep his chakras pure by not dissipating his sexual energies, by maintaining pure feelings and thoughts, and by not eating meat.[15]

MEDITATION AND SYNCHRONICITY

To understand the meditation movement we must address what Goffman (27, p. 13) has called the "organization of experience," recognizing that an individual's organization of experience (e.g., acceptance of what is meaningful and rejection of what seems meaningless) is somewhat different from the social organization of experience (e.g., the classification of knowledge in a library). Like Goffman, we must be concerned with how and why an individual meditator accepts certain concepts and what his criteria are for structuring them—a necessary prerequisite to understanding how meditators construct their reality. Often what seems to "fit together" and be understandable to one person may be labeled as madness by another. This is why we must take the actor's point of view, as best we can, recognizing we are always partial outsiders to most of his mental processes. However, we must also look for similarities in the organization of experience by many different individuals. This allows us to look at forms, structures, or "collective" patterns in the organization of experience. Historically, William James recognized "subworlds" (e.g., the natural sense world, the scientific world, the abstract world, mythology, the world of the madman); Schutz (66) noted "provinces of meaning"; Mead (54, pp. 342–354) recognized the objective reality of perspectives; Goffman (27) analyzes different patterns or "frames"; and Garfinkel (26) seeks the rules that generate a given kind of world.

As an analytic paradigm symbolic interactionism is crucial in understanding how an individual meditator organizes his experience (both internal and external). But, in the examination of similarities in the organization of experience by many different types of meditators (especially when they have no physical contact with one another, e.g., in history), another analytic perspective is needed. Such a perspective was first given systematic form by Jung (39), who called similarities in the organization of experience "synchronicity." We contend that symbolic interactionism and synchronicity may be combined in order to understand the effect that the interest in meditation is having on society.

In symbolic interactionism a crucial factor in the individual's organization of experience is the reaction of others to his behavior, commonly resulting in a consensus on values and their subsequent internalization via the medium of language (both body language, which often remains unconscious, and social language). Meditators try to reverse this process. They are convinced that, should they restructure what they have internalized, their external reality (both their behavior and other's behavior toward them) will also change.[16] For example, some forms of yoga hold that certain vowel sounds, spoken in an appropriate "frame of mind," can harmonize or transmute the reality which these sounds represent. Again, certain incantations and meditative states can, it is believed, change people's reactions toward the mediator. Butler (14) maintains that internal organization is directly connected to certain external forms of behavior. By restructuring the way in which he organizes his experience an individual is said to be able to bring about changes in the external world. Especially in absorptive meditation, an individual is supposed to focus his mind on a particular object (e.g., mandala) in order to identify with its intrinsic meaning. Such identification is said to automatically restructure an individual's system of organizing experience, thereby aligning him with the "natural" organization of the universe. Accomplishing this, everything in the meditator's environment changes in relation to him.

Symbolic interactionism can explain *how* certain concepts and social meanings arise from social interaction, but it has been criticized [Harrell (28)] for not adequately explaining *why* the individual accepts some of them as meaningful and rejects others in the socialization process. Conversely, a meditator can change certain internal states of mind and tell you *why* he wants to do so, but he cannot adequately explain *how,* if, or when certain external changes will follow. This latter perspective has been analyzed by Jung (39).

To Jung, devices such as mandalas and mantras are really "gates" into what might be called "the collective organization of experience." Gates into particularly meaningful aspects of the collective organization of experience Jung (37) called archetypes. Archetypes represent that part of the mind which all humans share as a species [Jung (37, p. 40)]. Because archetypes have been used over and over again by man, each time a person employs one, its collective meaning[17] is reinforced. Berger and Luckmann (1967) illustrate how social behavior is constellated into institutions. This organization of social behavior makes everyday life less problematic. Similarly, the organization of collective experience may be constellated into meaningful groupings called archetypes. The generation or activation of archetypes requires work and energy just as do the institutions of everyday reality [Jung (36)]. To illustrate, a library is really a physical imprint of the collective organization of experience of a particular society. Likewise, an archetype is a particular constellation of collective meaning, such as the paradigms of chemistry or sociology. Individuals "align" themselves by being socialized into particular paradigms the more they read and research them in the library. Meditators seek "socialization" into the "nobler areas" of collective meaning by identifying themselves with certain archetypes. For example, "mandala" is the Sanskrit word for circle, a "magic" circle which serves as the design for many Eastern temples and paintings. At the center of the mandala is God or divine energy, surrounded by a cloister with four portals usually leading into a "garden" and then on to the outer circle. A mandala, Jung would maintain, is an example of a collective symbolic pattern for a holy place. Naranjo (59) observes, "Not only is the process of deliberate identification with an archetype the bridge between meditation and worship and between meditation and art, but it is also at the basis of magical evocation." Indeed the meditator as magician attempts to bring into external reality the things he internally meditates upon [Butler (14, p. 30)].

In both the absorptive and expressive way of meditation the "name" of the object, image, symbol, deity, angel, or demon is crucial. However, it is not *how* the name is spoken but the state of mind of the individual who "speaks" it that acts as the key in unlocking the power behind the name. In other words, it is the meaning of the mantra that is essential, not its sound, and there are certain exercises before and after pronunciation[18] which are necessary to produce the proper state of mind. Naranjo (59) holds that the archetypal images which personify and summon up the forces, are models that direct these forces to their appropriate channels. Mystical experience in this regard is the experience of archetypes. For example, the lamb, dove, and fish all have a collective meaning for the Christian tradition. Butler (14) claims that the secrecy in genuine magical orders does not inhere in terms of secret words, handshakes, or symbols, but rather in the meaning derived from the way in which secret objects are combined in the ritualistic organization of experience. It is the ritualistic *pattern* which is the real object of secrecy.

Archetypes are diagrams of "pure" relationships (e.g., number),[19] i.e., they are not based on sensory properties (e.g., size, weight, hardness, color). The traditional symbol for yin-yang is seen in Figure 1. This is an example of a pure relationship: that the universe is cyclical, or the union of opposites, e.g., night and day, the ebb and flow of moon and ocean, male and female, positive and negative. By focusing the mind on images of pure relationship meditators believe they can "cause" external changes accordingly ["The more clearly the phantasy is built, the more clearly do you come into contact with the energy concerned," Butler (14, p. 41)]. To illustrate, we shall take an archetype from the Christian tradition: communion. When a Christian eats a wafer and drinks wine he symbolically partakes of the body and blood of Christ. This periodic ritual is intended to bring Christians closer to the force standing behind these symbols. Similarly, the redeemer, the cross, the baptism have collective meanings which have motivated people for 2,000 years to behave in certain ways. Since archetypes are collective patterns, "they actually behave as if they did not exist in yourself—you see them in your neighbors but not in yourself" [Jung (37, p. 50)]. However, when they are "constellated in larger social groups, the result is a public craze, a mental epidemic[20] . . ." This is another perspective from which to describe the meditation movement.

Archetypes can best be "understood by comparing them with historical parallels" [Jung (37)]. The fiery wheel is a sacred sun symbol in tantric yoga and refers on the micro-level to the manipura chakra near the abdo-

Figure 1.   The Yin-Yang symbol.

men. On the macro-level it is the ancient sun-wheel upon which the hero is crucified in sacrifice for the fertility of the earth. "The sun-wheel is an exceedingly archaic idea, perhaps the oldest religious idea there is" [Jung (37)]. Indeed, these symbolic wheels are found as far back as the Paleolithic Age, much earlier than when we find the real wheel invented in the Bronze Age. A cross is a four-armed wheel, so that the crucifix has from the beginning always had the same basic meaning: the hero and his sacrifice for mankind. "The hero motif is invariably accompanied by the dragon motif" [Jung (37, p. 100)]. Christ is always depicted as the champion who slays Satan, who always takes the form of a serpent. This is the collective language of man. As such it must be expressed in symbols readily available to all men, i.e., the symbols of nature [Douglas (20)]. This is also what we mean by a "pure" relationship, i.e., relationships that all men have the potential for understanding. For example, the serpent also represents the cerebro-spinal system, where at one end we have the "serpent power" of sexual energy (Kundalini) used for union with other mortals, and at the other end, the upraised serpent power used for union with the immortals, or mental beings. The serpent was always found in the crowns of Egyptian kings to depict their wisdom.

Archetypes are always representations of multidimensional concepts because pure relationships can be interpreted in so many different ways. The hero motif might refer to Hercules and the Hydra, Christ and Satan, or King Arthur and the Dragon. Entire cultures can be trapped on one level of meaning (e.g., Christianity) without understanding how other cultures (e.g., Greek mythology) can have a different understanding of the same relationship. Individuals are of necessity socialized into their "culture's" interpretation of a particular archetype.

Jung (39) maintains that there are at least two fundamentally different types of logical connection that man must deal with simultaneously if he is to fully explain relationships. The first one is the logic of causality and the second is the logic of meaning or synchronicity. In Jung's words, "events in general are related to one another on the one hand as causal chains, and on the other hand by a kind of *meaningful cross-connection*." It is well to add that Jung never expresses the view that one type of logic is more essential than the other. Both are of equal importance, and both are needed for the complete explanation of relationships.

In terms of causality, effects observed in the external environment are explained by logically linking them with specific previously occurring factors—factors that are said to have caused these effects. The techniques of meditation try to link up a series of factors in a causal manner: by sitting in a certain posture, taking a certain bodily stance (mudras), chanting a certain phrase, breathing in a certain manner, or by holding the correct mental, emotional, and spiritual attitude, the meditator believes he can change his character and the world around him. Causality, however, is inadequate as a complete explanation of the meditative experience for at least three reasons. First, meditative effects are often singular, i.e., they may occur only once. Causal explanations seem valid, as Lewin (46) argued, because through the experimental method certain effects can be reproduced by following certain logical procedures and sequentially linking up all the factors said to cause the effect. Thus, frequency and regularity are the hallmarks of the experimental method. Singular events, (e.g., a prophetic vision) which cannot be experimentally reproduced, are considered to be random.

Second, meditative effects are by definition multidimensional, i.e., they affect the body, the emotions and character, and the mind. As such, experimental validation, designed primarily for one-dimensional effects, is extremely difficult. As Jung (39) observed, "the experiment imposes limiting conditions on nature, for its aim is to force her to give answers to questions devised by man." If causality is only interpreted through the experimental design, this forces nature in all her multidimensional splendor to answer through a one-dimensional filter, preventing her from giving complete answers. Jung (39) certainly resembles a symbolic interactionist in this regard: "we need a method of inquiry which imposes the fewest possible conditions, or if possible no conditions at all, and then leaves nature to answer out of her fullness." And Blumer (11, p. 32) notes that present methodology offers no sanctions to such direct scrutiny of the empirical world. This is why synchronicity is important.

As Goffman (27) recognizes, "it is obvious that in most 'situations' many different things are happening simultaneously—things that are likely to have begun at different moments and may terminate dissynchronously." In order to understand how an individual organizes his experience we must proceed in a multidimensional manner rather than by combining one dimension at a time for analysis. This is certainly the case in the study of complex human behavior and the subsequent presentation of findings. We find ourselves agreeing with Goffman: "Often the complaint of the writer is that linear presentation constrains what is actually a circular affair, ideally requiring simultaneous introduction of terms." Synchronicity is a logical perspective which tries to deal with multidimensional effects, i.e., it attempts to explain how an individual connects many "provinces of meaning" "subworlds," or "frames" simultaneously.

Synchronicity, as does symbolic interactionism, begins with the individual's meanings, his interpretations of reality, and his conceptualization scheme and not those of the objective observer. All of our data must rest on the meditator's interpretation of what is happening to him, i.e., if meditators say they feel changed and/or if we can observe an associated physiological response (e.g., lowered blood pressure, a slower heartbeat, greater skin resistance), then we must accept the meditator's interpretation of experience. From both the synchronistic and interactionist perspectives, action is forged by the actor out of what he perceives, interprets, and judges. One must see the operating situation as the actor views it, perceive objects as the actor perceives them, and determine their meaning with regard to the meaning they have for the actor [Blumer (11)].

Finally, synchronicity enables us to explain the meaningful coincidence of "outer" and "inner" events that are not necessarily connected by causality. This logic is needed to adequately understand the meditative experience. Two examples will illustrate the point. As Franz explains synchronicity [in Jung (36, p. 226)], "if I bought a blue frock and, by mistake, the shop delivered a black one on the day one of my near relatives died, this would be a meaningful coincidence . . . it seems as if the underlying archetype is manifesting itself simultaneously in inner and external events."

One of the authors reports the following. During a dinner discussion of synchronicity with a Jungian psychiatrist from Cambridge, I suggested a walk along the Charles River and turned the conversation toward more romantic subjects. Right in the middle of our first kiss the bells in Harvard Square began ringing and both of us began laughing simultaneously. The meaning each of us gave to this simultaneous occurrence of events was the rockets and bells of true love. Continuing to walk and talk, we soon forgot this event. The next time we began to kiss, we heard a doorbell from a house across the street. Again we laughed, this time it was quite clear that we were experiencing "synchronicity." After this, we walked back to the car and just before we got in we decided to try again. Exactly as we began to kiss the bells of Harvard Square began ringing again, a full hour having passed. This sequence of events—the discussion of synchronicity and the three kisses which coincided exactly with the ringing of three bells—cannot be a question of cause and effect, but of a falling together in time, a kind of simultaneity [Jung (39)]. In the history of science we can also find many instances of simultaneous discoveries, e.g., Darwin's and A. R. Wallace's similar manuscripts on the theory of evolution. Working under the logic of causality, it is hard to see any connection between these illustrated events and it seems unlikely that they could be repeated for experimental verification. Causality, then, is not the only connecting principle in the organization of experience. Imputed meaning can also connect two events. In each of the illustrated events the same meaning was given by each participant at exactly the same time. In Schutz's (66) terms multiple realities are usually separate come together for a brief moment in time.

Many sociologists have begun this type of work. Simmel's (69) work on the pure forms of sociation, Weber's (74) ideal type, Schutz's (66) multiple realities, and Goffman's (27) frame analysis are attempts to explore constellations of meaningful human relationships. Jung's archetypes would fit into this tradition. As Harrell (28, p. 126) states, "The knowledge of relationships requires symbols but the fact that some relations are persistently described by man in time and space suggest that relations are not only symbolic events but real events as well." We suggest that synchronicity and symbolic interactionism are crucial in helping us to understand these relations.

MEDITATION AND SELF-HELP

Maslow (53) recognizes that human needs may be divided into three levels. The first level consists of physical needs (e.g., food, shelter, sex). The second level contains social needs (e.g., love, respect, status). The last level contains what he calls meta-needs (e.g., wisdom, truth, beauty), arising only in affluent societies that have already provided satisfaction on the two "lower" levels. In the East, where society did not furnish satisfaction for the first two-level needs, religious practices such as meditation offered an escape from these basic hungers. In order to critically assess the meditation movement we must determine whether meditation in the United States functions primarily as an escape mechanism from unfulfilled social and/or physical needs. It is unlikely that the poor in America, who seek social recognition for relief of physical needs, would find interest or solace in meditative escape. The meditation movement is primarily a middle-class phenomenon that offers escape and relief from social needs rather than satisfaction of meta-needs or an exploration, for its own sake, of the "higher" aspects of mind [Huxley (32)]. As such, the interest in meditation is part of an even larger self-help movement, e.g., transactional analysis [Berne (8)], gestalt therapy [Perls (62)], primal scream [Janov (34)], bioenergetics [Lowen (48)], psychosynthesis [Assagioli (2)], the Alexander (1) technique, nude marathons, rolfing, feldenkrias, and polarity therapy.

The self-help movement is concerned with enabling the individual to survive in a complex technological society. Most scientific interest generated by this movement, especially TM, has focused on physiological effects (e.g., does meditation reduce stress?). Such effects can be measured on machines and are subject to experimental replication. This is what makes biofeedback so important. Biofeedback machines measure differences in the brain's activity[21] and teach individuals to identify the corresponding internal state. This technique is completely technological in that biofeedback trainees are taught to respond to the reactions of a machine and not to those of people. This is not to say that biofeedback is not important in its own right or even that the technique cannot teach us a great deal about the relationship of the brain to every other system in a person's body.[22] However, when biofeedback is labeled as a cure-all, and elevated to a central place in the meditation movement, its effects on society could be detrimental. Replacing the reactions of others with machines that teach us to be peaceful is no different from using vibrators to help us achieve orgasm. For the individual the short-term effects may be beneficial,[23] but in the long run biofeedback is simply another form of machine dependence and not social reciprocity. To illustrate the point, biofeedback proponents argue that going into "alpha" (a turning-off of information processing) alleviates anxiety and hypertension and thus the need for tranquilizers, but this only replaces one form of external dependence (drugs) with another (a machine). It cannot be asserted that "alpha," a drowsy relaxed state (produced normally whenever the eyes are closed), is any closer to nirvana than sleep. As Dr. John Laragh, of the New York Hospital–Cornell Medical Center, observes, "I'm not sure that meditating has had any different effect on blood pressure than relaxing and sitting on a couch and reading a book." Also there is no "hard" evidence on the effect of prolonged alpha activity. If Weil (75) is correct, any type of prolonged brain activity can be dangerous to mental health.

Probably the single largest physiological factor in stimulating an interest in meditation is its effects on stress and anxiety. Benson (6) believes that the effects of stress and anxiety are resulting in the largest epidemic ever to attack mankind. Hypertension is directly responsible for hardening of the arteries, heart attacks, and strokes. These diseases, claimed by many to be primarily social in origin, account for more than 50 percent of all deaths in the United States each year. Benson attempts to demonstrate that social stress is directly responsible for hypertension, and that meditation is essential to the reduction of hypertension. Indeed, the beneficial effects of meditation (up to 20 percent less oxygen consumption, reduced respiratory and heart rate, the production of alpha-wave brain activity, reduced blood pressure, up to 100 percent increase in skin resistance—an indicator of anxiety and tension) are said to be more pronounced than the effects of sleep. Robert K. Wallace,[24] who took his doctorate in the physiology of meditation at UCLA, suggests that the meditative condition represents a fourth state of mind, in addition to waking, sleeping and dreaming.

To Benson (6) modern man is living in the most stressful times that the species has ever endured. And, it is not macro-level problems which plague us ("What psychological price do we pay in attempting to adjust to the knowledge that war or its imminence is with us everyday.") but rather everyday life itself ("We generally can't even solve the less earthshaking problems, such as being on time to work in a large, congested city.").

Benson's reason for the high disease rate associated with stress is the following: "Humans, like other animals, react in a predictable way to acute and chronic stressful situations, which trigger an inborn response that has been part of our physiologic make-up for perhaps millions of years." This reaction has been labeled the "fight-or-flight" response. In modern society these response patterns are socially inappropriate so man represses his behavior by discharging tension internally rather than externally. Benson suggests that meditation is becoming an absolutely necessary survival technique.

What is needed are programs designed to change a society which requires such drastic survival measures. The advocates of meditation, especially TM, do not mention this. Bloomfield (10, p. 12) even maintains that we must master stress rather than do away with it. This view seems inappropriate for several reasons. First, since not everyone *can* meditate, how then do we reduce their stress? Second, how can an individual master the stress of nuclear annihilation? Further, who would want to master this kind of stress at any rate? TM seems full of such unanswered questions and contradictions. At one place we find: "The technique of TM involves no effort to alter bodily or mental states or to analyze or control the mind." In another place we are told that anyone can master the body's natural response patterns: "a solution to the myriad problems of our society lies in the widespread application of a technique to psychophysiologically strengthen the individual and unfold his untapped resources" [Bloomfield (10)]: What are the individual's untapped resources supposed to unfold into? To be more conscious or calm about the contradictions in our society will not change them. The teachers of meditation rarely blame the overcrowding, pressure, and rush associated with industrial life but focus their attention on the individual's *reaction* to these things.[25] They maintain that if we change our reaction to these stressful circumstances we will no longer experience stress. But the reaction to stress is a normal physiological response which cannot be interrupted without causing some unbalance or overcompensation at another point of the body. It is not the individual's reaction which must be criticized but social conditions which elicited these reactions in the first place. How can we change our reaction to a poisonous atmosphere, unclean water, food additives, or noise? Ignoring these social conditions will not change them and may well kill us. This is exactly what Franks (24) would call false consciousness.

Librium and Valium (the anti-anxiety tranquilizers) are the number one prescriptions in the United States. Just as these drugs do not alleviate the *cause* of anxiety, neither will meditation. Meditation may eliminate our dependence on these drugs only to substitute itself as another form of dependence: "TM is the AM and PM." Becker (4) maintains that by controlling our natural physiological response to a vulgar society we only become more neurotic not less.

Bloomfield's (10) "social program" is stated thus: "Individual meditators inspire change in those around them," their "energy, optimism, acceptance and love catalyze positive feelings in others, including nonmeditators." Such statements are little more than romantic poetry. The early Christians expressed similar beliefs and feelings, but the lions found them as tasty as non-Christians. According to Bloomfield, social institutions are taking meditation seriously. Some corporations and governmental agencies consider the TM program to be the best personnel-enrichment program to date. If the structure of business is partly responsible for the high stress levels, then the structure should be changed—not the people within it. Everything that Bloomfield addresses (TM and Prison Reform, TM and Education, TM and Business) is either peripheral or completely irrelevant to the *structure* of most social problems, i.e., even if it were possible to teach every single member of society TM, this would not change its structure.

Ornstein (60) offers a credible physiological explanation as to why meditation seems to work to produce feelings of enjoyment and relaxation. TM, for instance, focuses the brain's attention on a single input—the mantra—which causes the brain to shut off after about twenty minutes in order to protect itself from overusing a single subroutine or nervous pathway. This shutdown phase leaves what Ornstein calls "pure" attention, where the brain is not focused on anything in particular but remains in a relative state of inactivity. When the brain begins to process information again (either external or internal) everything seems alive and fresh because the nerves are rested. Such periodic rest is crucial to mental, emotional, and physical health, and TM is very adept at helping the majority who try it achieve this restful state. However, TM is in error in labeling this state as being closer to God, or to fulfillment, or anything, except a state of nervous relaxation. Several critics have argued that an afternoon nap will produce similar results, without any elements of false consciousness, i.e., relaxation and a "blank" mind may be beneficial periodically for the individual, but only work and effort can solve social problems.

Prolonged meditation may be more dangerous than beneficial. Schwartz (67) proposes that Ornstein's (60) explanation of the connection between the right and left hemispheres of the brain (which specialize in their activities) may be crucial in determining the effects of meditation on bodily activity. To the extent that meditation promotes low arousal and self-reflective behavior typical of right-hemisphere processes, it increases spontaneity and creativity. At the other extreme, excessive meditation may hinder a person's logical, left-hemisphere processes. When meditators, after fourteen days of sensory deprivation, report seeing halos around fellow meditators' heads, we assume that this experience is somewhat different from that of mental patients who report seeing the same thing. Meditators are supposedly in control of themselves, bringing on this condition by their own devices: mental patients have little or no control over what they see. The image may be the same but the degree of control varies. However, Schwartz holds that the nervous system requires reasonably intense and varied external stimuli and that there is no evolutionary, ethological or biological predecessor for extensive meditation. Most importantly, some people with a predisposition toward mental illness may even worsen their condition through prolonged meditation.

Psychotherapy really started the self-help movement. There is a close relationship between meditation and psychotherapy, because both supposedly share the same goals: to help develop an individual's capacity to face reality, and to help develop his capacity for increased efficiency in life. However, there is a major difference between them in technique. Psychotherapy is primarily concerned with alleviating anxiety by focusing on, rearranging, and reinterpreting the *content* of the individual's character (i.e., it focuses on such things as dreams, slips of the tongue or pen, body language, past crises) with the intention being that the structure of the individual's personality will automatically be improved. Meditation is primarily concerned with improving the *structure* of personality, the aim being to automatically reorganize the content of character in a manner more conducive to a "meaningful life." Both techniques require long periods of time, a great amount of work, full attention, and, given the dismal record of psychotherapy, both seem to work equally well. Perhaps the issue is not a matter of whether either technique works but rather that the individual takes an active part in the control of his own life. At any rate, some hold that meditation in the long run will prove to be more beneficial than psychotherapy. Meditation concentrates on the positive aspects of the individual whereas psychotherapy dwells on the negative side. Further, it is claimed that meditation has a goal that psychotherapy lacks: to realize by firsthand experience one's position in the cosmos and to sense that one is so much a part of this cosmos that there can be no detachment or alienation from it [Le Shan (45)]. This is probably meditations' chief historical contribution, i.e., the feeling of connectedness, of a wholeness that is associated with an altered state of consciousness. Unfortunately there is no *program* that ensures we are all connected to the same thing.

It may be enlightening to view meditation as if it were a condition for producing "controlled" fantasies. The importance of fantasy in this regard has not been analyzed in any detail, with the exception of Jung (38, p. 165) who postulated that the less conscious control we have over our social relationships the more they are influenced by fantasies generated

from our unconscious mind. In meditation the person deals almost exclusively with his own fantasies, with two primary social effects: individuals
are trained to see social reality as they think it *ought* to be rather than the
way it is; collectively, meditators reinforce each other's fantasies, giving
the illusion that all social relationships can and ought to be like their own.
Also, there is real danger in contacting the unconscious mind[26] if the
person is not prepared to handle the "ego-alien" images which often flood
into consciousness during such meditative practices [Jung (37)]. To be
possessed *by* these visionary phenomena is exactly what has been called
psychosis: a failure of the ego to deal with the content of the unconscious.
Meditative states which resemble psychosis are often part of the "inner
journey" of some shaman, mystics, and artists. The Greeks often spoke
of the poet who was possessed by the Muses. Similar reports are found in
the lives of Socrates, Dante, Whitman, Swedenborg, Goethe, Heine, Bal-
zac, Emerson, James, Browning, and especially Blake (whose parents
were insightful enough not to label their son mad, but encouraged his
visions and provided private tutors for him). Bucke's (13) work illumi-
nates this point. The very word "genius" means to have a possessing
genie or a helping spirit. In fact, the practice of what Jung called "active
imagination" can be found in every culture at every point in time. What
seems to separate the madman from the shaman is that the latter protects
himself by going on his journeys to help others. The shaman does not go
for himself alone. Social relationships seem to provide psychic solidarity
just as they do moral solidarity [Durkheim (21)].

Erich Fromm (25) claims that no psychoanalyst can understand his
patients' problems without including the crucial dimension of morality.
To Fromm, the psychoanalyst deals with problems of the soul, the very
same problems that the philosopher and theologian have dealt with, i.e.,
instead of words like "sin," "god," and "wayward," the modern physician of the soul substitutes "alienation," "society," and "neuroses."
The prophets of old understood that no single sin or sinner could be
separated from society as a whole. Fromm would agree. According to
him, most people in our society are well adjusted because they have given
up the battle for independence sooner and more radically than have
neurotic persons. Speaking of the majority in modern society, Fromm
observes, "from the standpoint of 'adjustment' they are more sick than
the neurotic person from the standpoint of the realization of their aims as
human beings." In terms of the people who seek to help themselves
through meditation we must observe along with Freud that there are no
cures for unfulfilled individuals living in a loveless society. Freud tried to
cure neurotic symptoms, which made people unable to act, only to reunite
them with the common misery of all mankind. In other words, there are
no individual solutions to the common problems that plague us. Individual

solutions have gone under many names, e.g., wealth, baptism, and conversion, education, psychoanalysis, and now meditation. Several thinkers have adequately assessed this problem, e.g., C. Wright Mills (57) and Marx. That is, society itself must be transformed.

MEDITATION AND SOCIETY

Our critique focuses on the social effects of the meditation movement not its effects on particular individuals. It is our contention that most adherents seek relief from social needs rather than an expansion or exploration of their "inner" capacities. As such, they are not really meditating, at least not as Jung would define it (i.e., the experience of archetypes). Repeating a mantra, in and of itself, is not a meaningful experience, and such an exercise is unlikely to transform an individual's character, let alone the structure of society.

The meditation movement lacks a genuine social purpose and implies that somehow human beings can act and interact within a social and moral vacuum [Schur (65)]. Lasch (43) maintains that Americans do not wish just to forget the horrors of the recent past, but their entire collective identity. This loss of historical continuity, a sense of connectedness with the past and hopes for a brighter future, encourages a pervasive ideology of individual survival and the satisfaction of immediate needs. Hougan (31) concludes that all critics of present-day society agree there is no meaningful future. And the Club of Rome [Meadows (55)] argues that attempts to solve the world's major social problems must be worked at collectively and simultaneously, i.e., single solutions to each problem (e.g., pollution, overpopulation, malnutrition, inflation) by individual nations will no longer meet global problems. Perceptive scholars recognize that global solutions are impossible to attain given the present economic and political structure which dominates the world. As generation after generation lives with threat of poverty, alienation, rising crime (especially in government), class and race conflict, and nuclear annihilation, what else is left except hedonism? Indeed, personal crises (let alone national and international ones) are so widespread and frequent that they must be considered political issues [Hougan (31)]

Societies generate the type of social movements they deserve. The core belief of the meditation movement is that we live entirely in the present. Unlike other movements concerned with transcendental values, the meditation movement neglects collective salvation in favor of individual survival. Thus, such a movement is incapable of addressing itself to or solving complex structural problems. Even on the individual level symptoms are treated rather than causes. For people suffering from inner emptiness and loneliness, meditation offers "panaceas" that only worsen their problems. Retreating into one's self cannot make full what is empty to begin with. The self can only be filled by connection with others. In this light, meditation doctrine is the exact opposite of what is required. To illustrate, if a man cannot find a meaningful relationship with a woman, isolation and spiritual masturbation are not the solution. The answer lies in the creation of new relationships, enabling the self to grow through the reactions of others. Yet, meditation tenets teach us to love ourselves and not to depend on others. Narcissism, reflecting a fragmented society, gave rise to this movement in the first place—a movement that exacerbates what it intends to solve by individualizing problems instead of examining the social conditions underlying them. An agglomeration of self-centered, present-oriented individuals is not a society, but such would be the impossible outcome if the majority were to follow the dictates of the meditation movement.

According to Hougan (31), Lasch (43), and Schur (65), narcissism gave rise to the meditation movement and reflects the moral climate of contemporary society. Narcissism is more than a metaphorical term for self-absorption; it designates a real condition pervading social life. Sexual relations are a good barometer of the emotional health of a society. The recent trend toward promiscuity is not just an experience of more freedom, but sheer hedonism, and an avoidance of close intimate ties that traditionally serve to give people insight into themselves. One of the key tenets in symbolic interactionism is that our relationships with others give us direct insight into how our self is formed. If we cannot form consistent intimate ties with others, then we can be sure that the resulting self-images are not integrated. Social fragmentation coexists with schizophrenia [Becker (4)]. The meditation movement does not address this issue on a social level. If all of us are narcissistic and actually feel there is no one worth relating to, then society must be called into question and not the individual.

The narcissist is chronically bored and restlessly in search of instant intimacy. When doubt arises, he fantasizes an ideal and represses his resentment and rage at a world which does not present clear plans of action. Narcissistic fantasizing makes stable self-clarification difficult because the narcissist seeks to live in a world of his own creation with little input from others. If interaction with others is defined as worthless, then it is very difficult for the narcissist to form intimate relationships. The symbolic interactionist would immediately realize that the narcissist's attempt to view himself as his own significant other is absurd.

In a society where great emphasis is placed on youth, beauty, periodically obsolescent social relationships (e.g., renewable marriage contracts), consumption of materials rather than social exploration, optimism in the face of hazardous dilemmas; and, where few heroic role models obtain [Becker (4)], pervasive narcissism will prevail. As Lasch (43) notes, "Every age develops its own peculiar forms of pathology, which express in exaggerated form its underlying character structure." Early capitalism, with its acquisitiveness, work devotion, and sexual repression, produced hysteria and obsessional neuroses which gave rise to psychoanalysis. Later capitalism, with its massive material production and its devotion to profit and wealth instead of people, has produced narcissism and precipitated the development of the meditation movement. The result of all of this is a fragmented society, within which, out of necessity, many individuals futilely look to their own self for satisfaction—a better orgasm (the promise of bioenergetics), a sense of exhilaration (yoga), and a mystical vision or two (guided fantasy). There is no lasting social value in any of this. As Lasch (43) saw, "It is the world view of the resigned."

Sociologists have recognized an irrational core in most ideologies that purport to "transcend" social institutions. As Marx contended, if people attribute to hypothetical causes characteristics which must remain social, they lose their ability to rationally solve social problems. As Hofstadter (30, pp. 174–177) concludes, Americans historically have often preferred to speak of destiny rather than face reality. To illustrate, Blavatsky (1947), the founder of Theosophy, admits that her *Secret Doctrine* is revealed truth and contains all the "masters" can give out in this century. Such thinking is really a blatant form of spiritual Darwinism [Fortune (22), Plummer (63)], wherein we are all evolving toward "cosmic" perfection. Should we interfere in someone else's "lessons," given under divine supervision, we only hinder their "progress." Under such a doctrine, we are not responsible for others socially or spiritually.

Social problems require social solutions. No amount of meditation can solve economic inequality and unemployment, a legal and political system which plays class favorites, racism, sexism, and government fraud. Contacting the "inner self" will not cause conflict and discontent to disappear—but will erode further our sense of social responsibility. As Schur (65) concludes, "When problems transcend the personal or interpersonal levels, so too must the solutions."

The ideology of the meditation movement completely ignores social class. However, as Schur (65, p. 7) observes, "Only a leisure class can afford to devote so much time, energy, and money to self-exploration." The cost of EST, for instance, would completely wreck the workingman's budget. The meditation movement addresses itself to the "problems" of a leisure class not to the poor. For the poor the problem is not whether one should eat meat, but just eating. One of the central tenets of the meditation movement is that "we are all just human beings." Schur (65, p. 182) believes that the self-preoccupation of the middle class "while their less fortunate fellow Americans struggle and starve is criminal." This narcissistic ideology is more dangerous than meditative activities. Such thinking could bring to a halt whatever prospects there still may be for structural change. The massive power structures that dominate American life and which create most social problems are hardening (e.g., multinationals and big banks). Fragile institutions, for example, the family, that give us our sense of community, are becoming increasingly tenuous. The meditation movement is not the solution to these types of problems.

It is not enough simply to repeat a sound over and over for twenty minutes twice daily and think that an inconsistent and distorted mirror image endured over many years will be consequently clarified. If such is the case on the individual level how much further removed is meditation from the solution of social problems? Life is more than just feeling good and being less anxious, it is inherently political.

The ideology of the meditation movement never tells us exactly what constitutes the real self. If anything, the "inner" self is defined negatively by focusing on what it is not. The individual is admonished never to play the social game, i.e., social roles. The interactionist would maintain that we can never be anything except what our roles make us and what we make of them. Social roles constitute nexi within the interactional network. With them we develop, express, and maintain a self that cannot be considered illusionary. Meditation doctrine takes no cognizance of the fact that even the guru plays a social role.

The meditation movement disdains formal credentials. Its gurus and disciples are frequently without training in any discipline, occupation, or trade—let alone training in social analysis. Yet many of the movements graduates see themselves as qualified in dealing with psychological and social problems, and some of them set up their own centers to teach self-development, etc. With each succession of new centers the substance of the original doctrine degenerates [Schur (65)]. Neither psychological nor social problems can be handled effectively by amateurs. There are no cookbook solutions or shortcuts to societal or personal transformation. Yet thousands of books "some . . . are quite simple-minded, and it is easy to make fun of them" [Schur (65)] are bought by millions of people in an attempt to seek self-help. This is false consciousness. The books themselves are designed to preclude either serious self-analysis or social analysis. As the *New York Times Book Review* ("Book Ends," May 18, 1975:53) summarizes the basic rules in achieving success for such books: "Keep it simple and practical, don't induce any unsettling introspection; be positive (life is full of problems but they can all be solved); touch a nerve."

CONCLUSION

This paper has made several contributions to the symbolic interactionism paradigm. First, we have demonstrated that symbolic interactionism can be used for critical analyses. Second, we have demonstrated that it can be used to examine macro-level phenomena. Finally, we have added a sensitizing concept—synchronicity—which we feel is fruitful in helping us to understand how and why individuals attribute meaning to relationships which appear not to be causally connected.

FOOTNOTES

1. We wish to express our thanks to Daniel Dotter, a Ph.D. candidate, for his critical reading and able assistance in the preparation of this paper.

2. According to one *Newsweek* estimate there are over 8,000 different meditative techniques and ideologies.

3. Edgar Mitchell (1975:20), the former astronaut and founder of this institute, states: "As I survey the challenge facing humanity today, I see only one answer: *a transformation of consciousness.*" As Mitchell sees it, science, in its present technological form, cannot deal with the problems of man's self-centeredness, which to him is the root of all present problems.

4. We fully realize that all of these paradigms are needed for a complete analysis of each type of movement. We only intend this analytic separation as a device for isolating general traits.

5. The bureaucracy of TM is astounding: it includes the Spiritual Regeneration Movement, the Students' International Meditation Society which is on more than one hundred college campuses, the International Meditation Society, and the American Foundation for the Science of Creative Intelligence.

6. TM is an extremely lucrative business, charging $45 for students, $75 for adults, $125 for a family, and $1,100 for the twelve-week course to become an instructor.

7. The legislatures of Illinois and Connecticut have even passed resolutions thanking the Maharishi for bringing TM to the United States.

8. There are over sixty corporations, including AT&T, General Foods, and Blue Cross/ Blue Shield of Chicago, which are offering courses in TM to improve employee efficiency.

9. It is very beneficial to look at those who have been in the meditation movement for some time to see if their beliefs can be sustained. Mike Murphy, the founder of Esalen, admits that he "mistook the initiation experience for the path."

10. An example of absorptive meditation is TM. This type of meditation stresses the sense organs (e.g., the use of incense or music) and action (e.g., mudras or Tai Chi Chuan). To illustrate, hatha yoga concentrates on breathing in an effort to increase physical vitality, kundalini yoga concentrates on the psychic nerve forces of the body, and yantra yoga concentrates on the power of geometrical forms (mandalas).

11. To illustrate, laya yoga meditates on the powers of the mind, bhakti yoga meditates on the powers of love, raja yoga meditates on the powers of discrimination, and samadhi yoga meditates on states of ecstasy.

12. Naranjo (59, p. 9) describes exactly what we mean. "Just as we do not see the stars in daylight, but only in the absence of the sun, we may never taste the subtle essence of meditation in the daylight of ordinary activity in all its complexity. That essence may be

revealed when we have suspended everything else but *us*, our presence, our attitude, beyond any activity or the lack of it.''

13. As Jung (36), Marcuse (52), Reich (64), and Weil (75) have noted, a total emphasis on a single form of consciousness can produce mentally unbalanced and incompetent people.

14. There are literally hundreds of Zen groups, dozens of communes, and two full-time monasteries in the United States.

15. In one form of esoterica called Summit University, males and females are not even allowed to touch one another. The following statement is from the University catalog [Summit Lighthouse (73)].

Summit University was founded by Gautama Buddha to prepare students of the ascended masters for the initiations of Lord Maitreya. The purpose of the University is to teach disciples of the masters scientific methods for discovering reality, defining identity, balancing karma, and knowing the True Self of all.

The curriculum, based on five 12-week quarters, is under the direction of the World Teachers, Jesus and Kuthumi. Classes are taught by the ascended masters through their appointed representative Elizabeth Claire Prophet with the assistance of qualified instructors. All of the courses are based on the unfoldment of the Christ consciousness through the mastery of the seven rays.

In this university the chakras are purified and all rejoice in the knowledge of the "divine plan." Why this perfect knowledge, and their perfect initiates are not known all over the world by now is not explained.

16. We quote Butler (14, p. 31) at length in this regard as he describes how meditation works for the individual.

He may not, except indirectly, work upon the outer world, but he can directly alter and remould his own subjective world, and this will cause him to come into such new relationships with the outer world, that he finds it shaping itself in accordance with his new point of view, since these deeper aspects of himself, are part of the corresponding depths of the collective unconscious of the race, and of the universal consciousness.

17. We quote Naranjo (59, p. 15) at length in this regard.

. . . typical meditation objects partake in the quality of becoming more rather than less after repeated contemplations . . . the cross . . . the Star of David . . . the rose . . . the lotus, have not persisted as objects of meditation on the basis of tradition alone but on the grounds of a special virtue, a built-in appropriateness and richness, which meditators have discovered again and again throughout the centuries. Being symbols created by a higher state of consciousness, they evoke their source and always lead the meditator beyond his ordinary state of mind, a beyondness that is the meditator's deepest self, and the presence of which is the very heart of meditation.

18. The School for Esoteric Studies maintains that pronunciation of the mantra should never be verbal but remain entirely a sound in the mind.

19. Jung maintained that the next breakthrough in the science of man would be in the application of mathematics to the psyche.

20. As one magician, Butler (14, pp. 57–58) has described it,

When two or three or many people gather together in one place to perform certain actions, to think along certain lines, and to experience emotional influences, there is built up, in connection with that group, what may be termed a composite group-consciousness, wherein the emotional and mental forces of all the members of the group are temporarily united in what is known in occultism as a group-thought form . . .

21. Basically there are four types of electrical activity generated by the brain [Chase (18)], all of them falling within 0-40 cycles/second. Delta (0-4 cycles/second) and theta (4-7 cycles/second) activity only occur in extremely deep sleep when a person is weary and not dreaming. Alpha (7-12 cycles/second) activity represents the electrical waves produced when the visual cortex is not processing visual information, i.e., alpha waves are generally produced whenever a person's eyes are closed. They can be produced with the eyes open by unfocusing them, as is taught in meditation when a person gazes at a mandala. Beta (15-30 cycles/second) activity represents wakefulness such as problem solving, sorting and filing incoming data, worrying, and the retrieval of memory data. This type of activity is also produced during intense dreaming.

22. It has been less than ten years since it was scientifically demonstrated that the visceral processes could be brought under conscious control, e.g., lowering blood pressure and heart activity. As Chase (18) observes: ". . . we now know that the brain can actually learn to control its own pattern of activity."

23. Biofeedback may be extremely useful in conditioning epileptic patients to identify and reduce the electrical activity responsible for their attacks. Also, it seems possible to teach patients with Parkinson's disease to turn off the neuron which is misfiring and causing their tremors. Other beneficial research is the control of artificial limbs by the person's own nerves and brain.

24. Wallace is now president of MIU.

25. There are several studies which claim that meditators can take more stress without serious illness than non-meditators. Our response is so what! Who wants to learn how to take more stress? Coleman (19, p. 86) reports on an experiment in which meditators and non-meditators watched a movie depicting bloody industrial accidents. "This pattern of greater initial arousal and faster recovery showed up in expeienced meditators whether or not they had meditated before the movie began. . . . Rapid recovery from stress is a typical trait of meditators."

26. Naranjo (59, pp. 121–124) does an excellent job in reporting on such experiences.

REFERENCES

1. F. Matthias Alexander, *The Resurrection of the Body*. Delta, New York, 1969.
2. Roberto Assagioli, *Psychosynthesis*. Viking Press, New York, 1971.
3. Ernest Becker, *The Structure of Evil*. Free Press, New York, 1968.
4. ———, *The Birth and Death of Meaning*. Free Press, New York, 1971.
5. ———, *The Denial of Death*. Free Press, New York, 1973.
6. Herbert Benson, *The Relaxation Response*. Morrow, New York, 1975.
7. Peter Berger and Thomas Luckmann, *The Social Construction of Reality*. Doubleday-Anchor, New York, 1967.
8. Eric Berne, *Games People Play*. Grove Press, New York, 1964.
9. Madame Helena P. Blavatsky, *The Secret Doctrine* vols. I and II. The Theosophy Co., Los Angeles, 1947.
10. H. H. Bloomfield, *et. al. TM: Discovering Inner Energy and Overcoming Stress*. Dell, New York, 1975.
11. Herbert Blumer, *Symbolic Interactionism: Perspective and Method*. Prentice-Hall, Englewood Cliffs, N.J., 1969.

12. Barbara B. Brown, *New Mind, New Body—Biofeedback: New Directions for the Mind.* Harper & Row, New York, 1974.
13. Richard M. Bucke, *Cosmic Consciousness.* E. P. Dutton, New York, 1966.
14. W. E. Butler, *The Magician: His Training and Work.* Wilshire Book Co., North Hollywood Calif., 1973.
15. Colin Campbell, "Transcendence Is as American as Ralph Waldo Emerson," *Psychology Today* (April 1974): 37–38.
16. Fritjof Capra, *The Tao of Physics.* Shambala Publishers, Los Angeles, 1975.
17. Carlos Castanada, *Don Juan Trilogy.* Simon and Schuster, New York, 1974.
18. Michael H. Chase, "The Matriculating Brain," *Psychology Today* (June 1973): 82–86.
19. Daniel Coleman, "Meditation Helps Break the Stress Spiral," *Psychology Today* (February 1976): 82–93.
20. Mary Douglas, *Natural Symbols.* Vintage, New York, 1973.
21. Emile Durkheim, *The Division of Labor in Society.* Free Press, New York, 1964.
22. Dion Fortune, *The Cosmic Doctrine.* Helios, London, 1966.
23. ———, *Esoteric Philosophy of Love and Marriage.* Samuel Weiser, New York, 1974.
24. David D. Franks, "Social Power, Role-Taking, and the Structure of Imperceptiveness: Toward a Redefinition of False Consciousness," *The Annals of Phenomenological Sociology,* vol. 1 (1976): 93–111.
25. Erich Fromm, *Psychoanalysis and Religion.* Bantam, New York, 1972.
26. Harold Garfinkel, *Studies in Ethnomethodology.* Prentice-Hall, Englewood Cliffs, N.J., 1967.
27. Erving Goffman, *Frame Analysis.* Harper Colophon, New York, 1974.
28. Bill Harrell, "Symbols, Perception, and Meaning," *Sociological Theory: Inquiries and Paradigms,* Llewelyn Gross (ed.). Harper and Row, New York, 1967, pp. 104–27.
29. Hermann Hesse, *Siddhartha.* Bantam, New York, 1974.
30. Richard Hofstadter, *The Paranoid Style in American Politics.* Vintage, New York, 1967.
31. James Hougan, *Decadence: Radical Nostalgia, Narcissism, and Decline in the Seventies.* William Morrow, New York, 1976.
32. Aldous Huxley, *The Doors of Perception.* Harper and Row, New York, 1954.
33. William James, *Varieties of Religious Experience: A Study in Human Nature.* Mentor, New York, 1958.
34. Arthur Janov, *The Primal Scream.* Dell, New York, 1970.
35. C. W. Jung, *The Undiscovered Self.* Mentor, New York, 1958.
36. ———, *Man and His Symbols.* Dell, New York, 1964.
37. ———, *Analytical Psychology.* Vintage, New York, 1968.
38. ———, *The Portable Jung.* Viking Press, New York, 1971.
39. ———, *Synchronicity.* Princeton University Press, Princeton, N.J., 1973.
40. Sam Keen, "Oscar Ichazo and the Arica Institute," *Psychology Today* (July 1973): 66–72.
41. Soren Kierkegaard, *The Sickness Unto Death.* Doubleday-Anchor, New York, 1954.
42. J. Krishnamurti, *The Only Revolution.* Harper and Row, New York, 1970.
43. Christopher Lasch, "The Narcissist Society," *New York Review of Books* (September 30, 1976): 5–13.
44. ———, "Planned Obsolescence," *New York Review of Books* (October 28, 1976): 7–10.
45. Lawrence LeShan, "The Case of Meditation," *Saturday Review* (February 22, 1975): 26–27.
46. Kurt Lewin, "Aristotelian and Galileian Modes of Thought," in *A Dynamic Theory of Personality.* McGraw-Hill, New York, 1935.
47. Leo Litwak, "Pay Attention, Turkeys/Est's Formula for Success," *New York Times Magazine.* (May 2, 1976): 44–60.

48. Alexander Lowen, *Bioenergetics*. Coward, McCann and Geoghegan, New York, 1975.
49. Barry McLaughlin (ed.), *Studies in Social Movements*. Free Press, New York, 1969.
50. Mahesh Yogi Maharishi, *Transcendental Meditation*. Plume Books, New York, 1975.
51. ———, *Meditation of Mahesh Yogi Maharishi*. Bantam, Des Plaines, Ill., 1975.
52. Herbert Marcuse, *One Dimensional Man*. Beacon Press, Boston, 1964.
53. Abraham Maslow, *The Farther Reaches of Human Nature*. Viking Press, New York, 1971.
54. George Herbert Mead, *George Herbert Mead on Social Psychology*, Anselm Strauss (ed.). University of Chicago Press, 1964.
55. Dennis Meadows, *the Limits to Growth*. Mentor, New York, 1972.
56. Bernard, Meltzer, *et al. Symbolic Interactionism: Genesis, Varieties and Criticism*. Routledge and Kegan Paul, Boston, 1975.
57. C. Wright Mills, *The Sociological Imagination*. Oxford University Press, New York, 1971.
58. Edgar Mitchell, "Outer Space to Inner Space: An Astronaut's Odyssey," *Saturday Review* (February 22, 1975): 20–21.
59. Claudio Naranjo and Robert Ornstein, *On the Psychology of Meditation*. Viking Press, New York, 1971.
60. Robert Ornstein, *The Psychology of Consciousness*. W. H. Freeman, San Francisco, 1972.
61. ———, *the Nature of Human Consciousness*. W. H. Freeman, San Francisco, 1973.
62. Frederick Perls, *et. al., Gestalt Therapy*. Dell, New York, 1951.
63. Gordon L. Plummer, *The Mathematics of the Cosmic Mind*. Theosophical Publishing House, Wheaton, Ill., 1970.
64. Wilhelm Reich, *The Function of the Orgasm*. Meridian Books, New York, 1970.
65. Edwin Schur, *the Awareness Trap: Self-Absorption Instead of Social Change*. Quadrangle, New York, 1976.
66. Alfred Schutz, "On Multiple Realities," *Philosophical and Phenomenological Research* 5 (1945): 533–575.
67. Gary Schwartz, "Tm Relaxes Some People and Makes Them Feel Better," *Psychology Today* (April 1974): 39–44.
68. Lawrence Shainberg, "The Violence of Just Sitting," *New York Times Magazine* (October 10, 1976): 16–71.
69. Georg Simmel, *The Sociology of Georg Simmel*, Kurt Wolff (trans.). Free Press, New York, 1964.
70. Philip Slater, *Earthwalk*. Bantam, New York, 1974.
71. ———, *The Pursuit of Loneliness*. Beacon Press, Boston, 1976.
72. Adam Smith, "Alumni Notes—Altered States U," *Psychology Today* (July 1973): 75–79.
73. Summit Lighthouse, *Teachings on the Path of Enlightenment*. Summit Lighthouse Publishing, Colorado Springs, Col., 1975.
74. Max Weber, *The Methodology of the Social Sciences*. Free Press, New York, 1949.
75. Andrew Weil, *The Natural Mind*. Houghton Mifflin, Boston, 1972.
76. Garry Wills, *"The Real Jerry Brown: Anti-Papa Politics,"* New York Review of Books (June 10, 1976): 12–16.
77. Kenneth Woodward, "Getting Your Head Together," *Newsweek* (September 6, 1976): 56–62.

BODIES AND SELVES: NOTES ON A FUNDAMENTAL DILEMMA IN DEMOGRAPHY*

David R. Maines, CENTER FOR THE STUDY OF HEALTH

SERVICES, YALE UNIVERSITY

A photograph showing Secretary of State Henry Kissinger entering his office followed by Secretary of State-designate Cyrus Vance appeared on the December 16, 1976, front page of *The New York Times*. It was a human-interest approach to the serious business of political transition, and at first glance it was really quite an ordinary picture. As a symbolic interactionist interested in demography, however, I viewed that photograph selectively, in terms of a particular perspective containing a vocabulary capable of describing what was going on in the situation depicted by it. It represented two bodies roughly in the same place, but one body was associated with an out-migrating identity (Kissinger) and the other body was associated with an in-migrating identity (Vance). To the trained demographer, this may seem to be a curious way of talking about migration. But that usage expresses precisely one of the major contentions of this essay; namely, that however one wishes to define migration, *iden-*

Studies in Symbolic Interaction—Volume 1, 1978, pages 241–265.

tities migrate every bit as much as bodies. I will further argue that demography ignores identities, and consequently fails to investigate that which is particularly social about human beings. Put another way, even at his hardest glance, the trained demographer would only have seen two bodies in the photograph. The identities of Kissinger and Vance would have been left to the realm of social psychology.

Demography and symbolic interactionism traditionally have not shared a common arena of discourse, and I do not propose to solve or even identify all the features and problems of their potential overlap. Rather, this will be an exploratory essay and analysis of demographic processes from the standpoint of symbolic interactionism.[1] I will selectively focus on issues of migration, because it is an area of demography where symbolic interactionism can clearly make a contribution as well as accounting for most of the demographic changes in a population [Bogue (5, p. 752)]. I therefore am concerned with an area of both substantive and conceptual relevance.

My aims are at once simple and complex. I hope to make certain broad distinctions concerning human migration, but the demographer may well become impatient with my discussion, because in pursuit of those distinctions I may violate certain canons of professional demography. The distinctions fall within the boundaries of a proper sociology, however, and once comprehended, have the potential for leading to a vocabulary and perspective on demographic processes heretofore missing in the standard approach to demography. My approach rests on an analytic and to some extent substantive distinction between *bodies*—the physical fact of human existence, and *identities*—social categories through which people may be located and given meaning in some organizational context. If one does not concur with that distinction, much of this essay will make little sense; if one does concur, however, then it may make some sense and perhaps even open up new avenues of thought and research. Pushed to an extreme, of course, the distinction commits the fallacy of mind-body dualism.[2] I do not wish to push it that far. I merely wish to suggest that through its use a new and interesting way of thinking about demography is created which has much to do with social behavior.

My argument is that demographers fail the sociological mandate to examine social conduct insofar as in their work they count, measure, and discuss bodies rather than identities. A casual examination of any number of demography texts or monographs [e.g., Beshers (3); Smith and Zopf (44); Bogue (5); Wrong (59); Davis (7); Thomas (53)] will show that migration is thought of in terms of physical movement, and that population growth and decline is considered as the relative adding and subtracting of bodies in a population. Even historical demography in which considerations of identities might be expected to appear, it is "birth, death and marriage rates [which] form the basic descriptive language . . ." [Wrigley, 58, p. 12]. While this observation is accurate, however, the demographic practice of conceptualizing people as mere bodies is so commonplace that it is hardly earth shattering. A substantial part of the reason for this practice, of course, is methodological in nature since it is easier to count bodies than it is to count identities. This is because our bodies tend to follow at least some of the laws of physics whereas our identities do not. Our bodies cannot be in more than one place at a time, nor can two bodies occupy the same space at any given time. This, however, is not necessarily true for our identities. Each of us has many identities, and it therefore can be said that there always are more identities in a specified geographical area than there are bodies.[3] This is a critical point, because it is identities as much or more than bodies which mobilize social interaction [McCall and Simmons (26, pp. 82–88)]—a point typically overlooked by demographers. Moreover, it creates the circumstances for a number of micro-ecological problems such as enacting certain identities which are appropriate for given "space expectations" [Ball, (2)]. Over and above this, however, I want to argue that the proliferation of identities presents the demographer with a wide range of empirical and conceptual puzzles. Consider for a moment the implications involved in the birth of the first child to a couple. This, of course, is an everyday occurrence, and is the very "stuff" of demography. Upon knowing about that birth, the demographer will accurately add one new person to the population, but he will be accurate only insofar as he regards that child as a physical object. Were he to regard the child as a social object, he would observe that, with the birth of the body, multiple new identities are introduced into the population—father, mother, son or daughter, cousin, aunt, uncle, niece or nephew, grandmother, grandfather, grandchild, and perhaps bastard. It is true that these family identities exist as consensual objects prior to birth, and in that sense are merely appropriated, but the point is that nearly a dozen identities and even more identity relationships now function to redefine previous relationships or bring new ones into existence. The individuals involved must now deal with one another in new ways. Thus, one new body gives rise to many new identities. Consider, on the other hand, what happens if that child grows up and then dies at, say, age twenty. The demographer will subtract one person from the population; but, again, because of the failure to see people as social objects, he will overlook the fact that *the deceased person's identity remains in the population.* Friends and relatives remember the person, take him into account, talk about him, mourn him, and sometimes even celebrate his birthday. In this sense, it is clear that such identities continue to have an impact upon social relationships involving the living.

Based on the terminology and the manner in which I have accounted for this illustrative instance, there are two hypotheses which can be immediately suggested. The estimates of the amount of population increase made by trained demographers will always be smaller and will be seen as occurring at a slower rate when based on bodies than similar demographic estimates based on identities. Estimates of population decline, however, will be larger and seen as occurring at a faster rate than would be otherwise if members of the population were regarded as social objects rather than physical objects. Thus, purely in quantitative terms, there are rather dramatic consequences to be derived from demography's *asocial* approach to social behavior. The implications for demography's capacity to depict the nature of social organization are even more complex; however, I shall not comment on that topic until toward the end of this essay. I shall simply note here that a whole series of questions are raised concerning differential rates of increase and decrease between bodies and identities, the kinds of social structures that produce those rates, the properties and mechanisms involved in the migration of bodies compared to the migration of identities, and the entire mosaic of relationships between the two.

In reflecting on some of these questions, I first will briefly discuss demography and migration, and will pay particular attention to claims made by demographers concerning the social nature of demography. Then I will discuss six categories of possible relationships between bodies and identities, with the last four constituting an initial attempt to analyze identity and body migration within the same conceptual framework. Finally, the last section will be devoted to a general discussion of social organization and demography in terms of the substantive claims made in the body of the paper.

DEMOGRAPHY AND THE BODY-IDENTITY DILEMMA

The importance of demographic analysis for our understanding of society cannot be denied. We must know about population density and fluctuations, age and sex ratios, rates of fertility and mortality, as well as associated social characteristics if we are to round out our conceptions of social systems. A knowledge of age distributions, for example, helps in understanding the dependence of educational institutions on community structure, and it is easier to understand the existence of profitable prostitution enterprises by observing sex ratios favoring males. Others, however, have depicted the importance of demography more efficiently than I. Shibutani and Kwan (41), for instance, state that "A social system is geared to a particular demographic balance" (p. 346), and Hawley (18) asserts that "demographic structure contains the possibilities and sets the limits of organized group life" (p. 78). While some of us might quarrel over the precision of these assessments, I think there should be no debating the point that demography yields a class of information which, once having been applied, results in greater insight and understanding of problems under investigation.

Sociologists have found greater relevance for their concerns in areas considered by social demography, however, than in those dealt with by population studies or formal demography. I see no purpose in dwelling on the differences between these areas here,[4] except to note that the extent to which demography has become sociological has occurred in the area of social demography. Resting at the base of demography, however, is a collective sentiment asserting the inevitable social nature of its subject matter. Peterson (38) reminds us that "Demography . . . denotes a subject matter that impinges on our everyday life in a variety of ways" (p. 11); Wrong (59), in his discussion of migration, notes that "migration is a distinctively human activity" (p. 82) and that it "always occurs in a distinctive social and cultural context from which it cannot be separated" (p. 83); and Bogue somewhat arrogantly claims that "demography enjoys a very enviable status among the social sciences: it interacts freely with all and finds itself incompatible with none" (p. 5). These statements, of course, can relate to a wide range of human activities, including the fact that age is a social construct, that fertility is a consequence of sexual intercourse, and that migration involves a highly subjective component (all of which, by the way, demographers tend to ignore); and that population density, growth and decline, fertility and mortality, migration and other demographic phenomena are associated with social factors such as industrialization and urbanization, medical knowledge and technology, public welfare programs, family size and structure, occupational structure, and other areas of sociological concern. It is this latter kind of analysis that constitutes the domain of social demography and represents the area of greatest interpenetration between demography and sociology.

Even in this vigorous and sophisticated practice in demographic analysis, however, there is fostered a basically *asocial* conception and imagery of human conduct. My reason for saying this, of course, rests on the observation that demographers have not addressed and consequently have not solved the body-identity dilemma. One has only to read any analysis of migration to realize that it is the geographical location of the body that defines whether or not migration has taken place. There are abundant discussions among demographers concerning this very point, but answers to the question of what constitutes migration are typically framed in terms of two other factors: distance and permanence. Even here, though, there is not a great deal of consensus. Everett Lee (22) defines migration simply as a permanent or semipermanent change of residence, while Bogue (5) defines it as "the movement of people from one residence to another"(p. 752), and Mangalam and Schwarzweller (27) confine it to collectivities which have moved on a relatively permanent basis resulting in some degree of interactional change for the migrants. Additional qualifying factors are included in other definitions [Bogue (5, pp. 756–758) discusses some of these factors], but the one thing they all have in common is that migration is defined as the movement of the body from one geographical area to another. The closest one finds any consideration of identity is in terms of motives for migration, but these considerations are masked in positivistic and psychologistic terms and distinctions. Taft and Robbins (51) for example, state that "Like all human behavior, migration is rooted subjectively in psychological drives; objectively in conditions which stimulate those drives" (p. 3).

Thus, we have an imagery of human migration involving the movement of a body propelled by psychological needs and drives in a trajectory defined by the objective circumstances of social structure. It is an imagery based on an assumption of utilitarianism in that migration is seen as taking place in order to satisfy individual needs; on an assumption of man as a passive recipient of biological, physical, and social forces; and to a more limited extent on an assumption of rationality which is apparent not only in push-pull theories but in Stouffer's (48) theory of intervening opportunities. This is not to say that there is no appeal in some demographic perspectives on migration. Rather it is to suggest that the imagery of migration processes offered to us by demographers rejects as insignificant the very feature which Robert Park pointed to a half century ago as that which makes us uniquely human; namely, the possession of *the reflexive self*. It is that very self which provides the symbolic nature to human conduct; and it is ironic that without that symbolic component, i.e., the capacity to transform environments and then respond to those transformations, demographers would have no claim at all to the social nature of the demography. Yet migration is seen merely as a "demographic response" [e.g., Sly (42)] rather than as a process, and in that insistence together with the mechanistic imagery of man and society, demography shows itself as not really embracing a fully social perspective.

As already implied, I maintain that the social component of human migration can be effectively discussed in terms of identity. My perspective on identity corresponds closely to that of Stone (45) and Strauss (49). Stone notes that the term identity "established *what* and *where* the person is in social terms" (45, p. 93), and in the sense that it refers to one's being situated in a matrix of social relations, it can be seen as a dimension of social organization. Further, identity, or the person's meaning, is always negotiated to some degree through others' acts of *placing* us in some social category as well as our *announcing* to others those categories in which we see ourselves or in which we wish to be placed. Strauss emphasizes naming as an act of placement, noting, for example, that "to name is not only to indicate; it is to identity an object as some kind of object" (53, p. 19). Identity, therefore, can be seen as a structural concept insofar as it refers to our location in a social world, and as a processual concept insofar as that location is defined in terms of ongoing processes of identification.

As James, Cooley and Simmel each pointed out, however, we have as many identities as we have group affiliations, with the only minimal requirement for such affiliation being that others place us or take us into account when forming their conduct. Thus, considerations of social worlds are introduced into the identity equation, and it becomes evident that we can be placed in an identity about which we are unaware or we can seek to establish an identity in which no one will place us.

It is in this sense of identity, identification, and multiple group affiliation, then, that I wish to offer a more fundamentally sociological view of migration which fully takes into account the reflexive self and its social organizational component. The problem to be addressed, therefore, concerns relationships between bodies and identities in the migration process. This problem can be seen as taking on at least two dimensions. The first dimension pertains to body-identity isomorphism, or the extent to which they occur together; and the second pertains to the dimension of sequencing, or the extent to which one precedes the other in the migration process. In discussing these dimensions, I will make liberal use of materials from research reports, books, the public media, and personal observation in an attempt to demonstrate the possible variations in these dimensions. First I will consider matters of the polar extremes in body-identity relationships.

BODIES WITHOUT IDENTITIES AND IDENTITIES WITHOUT BODIES

Before entering into this discussion of polar extremes of body-identity relationships, I should make it clear that I am fully aware of the fact that the existence of bodies tends to put identities into play. This is the basic justification for the use of the variable of "co-presence" in studies of interaction as well as the disciplined inquiry into face-to-face encounters, whether defined by the work of Goffman or that of Bales. But if I am to support the argument that identities as well as bodies are capable of migrating, I must first establish that they can occur apart. That is, I must present some evidence that one is not necessarily dependent upon the other. Thus, in this section, I will attempt to show that (a) there can be bodies without identities and (b) identities without bodies.

Bodies Without Identities.

Of the two polar extremes, the demonstration of this class of phenomena will be the more difficult. We are a naming or identity-conferring species, and seem compelled by our very social nature to identify things. As such, there are few bodies in a population existing without any meaningful or defined relationship to the social order. This is a sort of negative evidence supporting my earlier contentions regarding the proliferation of identities in society. There are a few examples, however, of bodies without identities or whose only identification is based on the fact that they can't otherwise be socially placed. Disasters frequently produce these bodies, such as the 1976 Colorado flood where people who had been washed downstream couldn't be identified. The eventual response of rescue teams when locating these bodies was to set up some administrative apparatus through which families might be able to claim the bodies of relatives; and in the act of claiming, the identity was established. If not claimed, however, the body remained unidentified and thus had no known relationship to the social order other than that of flood victim.

Arlington National Cemetery is full of bodies whose only identities are those of former soldiers. There are two thousand nameless bodies from the Civil War, 167 bodies from the explosion of the U.S.S. *Maine* in Havana Harbor in 1898, and 250 who died at Guadalcanal in 1945 when an ammunition ship blew up. The only thing we know about these bodies is that they were of American soldiers, but since they are nameless, they cannot be related to networks of human association, and in that sense can't be located in society.

Finally, I might mention the discipline of Archaeology, whose business it is to find bodily remains and then reconstruct identities (e.g., age, sex, and status identities) through the process of reconstructing the social organization of past societies [Wiley and Phillips (56).] Archaeology, in this way, is devoted to the systematic creation of identities. A fundamental conflict arises, however, between Indian groups and archaeologists. At the center of that conflict is the Indians' contention that burial remains constitute real identities. Thus, a rather clear-cut division of interests is defined in terms of the body-identity dimension.

It is interesting and I think instructive to observe the difficulty in trying to think of bodies without identities. In the very strictest terms, we simply can't do it, because we eventually confer upon the body the identity of "unidentified person." Once the body is placed in that identity, of course, it can be accordingly handled by the state. These otherwise unidentified bodies, however, were in some way enmeshed in the social order when they were alive; the problem now is that we know nothing about that involvement. In other words, we cannot name the body, and as Dewey and Bentley (10) would have argued, we therefore cannot know it.[5]

Identities Without Bodies.

It is infinitely easier to think of instances in which there are identities existing in a society without a corresponding body. Of course, to argue that many of these identities once were associated with bodies is correct but sociologically moot. The point is that these identities are socially real and we can act toward them just as meaningfully as we do other identities. George Washington, for instance, recently was promoted to the rank of five-star general, and Robert E. Lee was pardoned for his role in the secession of the South. There also is the Catholic Church which, in addition to recently reconsidering the excommunication of Martin Luther, has created literally thousands of new identities through conferring sainthood on former Catholic priests [George and George (12)]. And then there is the case noted by W. Lloyd Warner in the *Yankee City Series* in which the body of a person who was a member of an upwardly mobile family was moved to a new gravesite in a higher-status location of the cemetery. This process of identity creation is of course quite common, and transcends the reconstructive acts of individuals. Institutions and organized collectivities such as the discipline of History are often intimately involved in this process. For instance, Captain Bligh has a new identity these days because revisionist historians are now seeing him not only as a good naval officer but as one of the more compassionate in the 18th Century British Navy. Even communities can undergo identity reconstruction. The federal government and Kinderhook, New York are now attempting to "rehabilitate" the identity of Martin Van Buren, his house (Lindenwald), and the community by attempting to confer on them the same kind of luster associated with Monticello and Mount Vernon. Communal identities, moreover, can persist beyond the life of bodies in a community. For years, Turkey has imported fungicide-treated seeds for agricultural purposes. Because villagers, especially children, consumed these seeds, however, between 1955 and 1960 there were many villages that didn't have any children in them between the ages of two and five [Peters (37)]. Yet the poisoned children's identities remained, and minimally, the age category persisted in these villages.

To take this kind of thinking one step further, I should like to note instances in which identities without bodies have had a degree of impact on existing social organizational arrangements. One such instance has occurred in Norwich, Connecticut, where Benedict Arnold was born 225 years ago. Although his body has long ceased to exist, his identity is very much alive, and has caused the residents of Norwich a considerable amount of trouble. The problem was what to do with his identity in the bicentennial year of 1976. Was he to be honored as a famous figure in the Revolutionary War or dishonored as a traitor? The residents of the community were passionately split into factions concerning Arnold's identity, the city council has debated the issue, and even the mayor's job came into jeopardy.

Another instance involves Arlington National Cemetery and the tombs of the unknown soldiers. All the ceremony and military ritual surrounding the tombs for World War I and World War II are now being similarly invested in the tomb of the unknown soldier for the Vietnam War. The only difference is that there isn't a body in that tomb! The more advanced medical evacuation techniques and the nature of the war itself (there was little artillary used) has served to preserve the identities of the dead. So there is yet no body, but at the tomb there is an identity completely legitimized and financed by Congress and guarded by the military merely waiting for a body.

A somewhat related problem has existed in White Plains, New York, for the last forty years. Different historical interest groups and politicians have been debating furiously over where George Washington actually planned the battle of White Plains—in the Miller House or the Purdy House. The debate is over where the body was at the time. His identity, however, is mobile, residing in either house depending upon who is rendering the account of Washington's activities.

Finally, there is ancestor worship, which is one of the most interesting examples of all concerning how past identities can mobilize collective action. This practice revolves around identities without bodies, and permeates and influences authority and status systems as well as functioning as a mechanism of social control. E. Adamson Hoebel (19) writes that:

> Most Plains Indians and the Navahos abandon any house in which a person has died. The ghost haunts the house and disturbs the inhabitants. Navahos, therefore, take a seriously ill patient who is about to die outdoors in order to save the house, or they rush him to the Navaho Service Hospital, which is already inhabited by ghosts. The Arizona desert is dotted with hogans abandoned because a death has occurred within (p. 483).

Ghost fear has been a real hindrance for the Indian Service's efforts to provide modern housing on some reservations. In some northern Plains areas, though, a sort of compromise between ancestor worship and modern technology has been achieved. Fumigation of the house has been accepted as an effective antidote to ghosts. In any case, it is clear that ancestor worship is widespread, and that it has a tremendous effect on existing patterns of social organization. These effects include types of human sacrifice, the structuring of lineage and clan organization, house construction, and economic competition [Hoebel (19, pp. 483–485)].

So, from these examples, it should be clear that bodies and identities need not necessarily depend upon one another nor is there any *necessary* relationship. One can occur without the other, with the more frequent pattern being that of identities existing without bodies. Thus, for any social science to focus on or confine its methods and analysis only to bodies is a serious self-imposed limitation.

ANALYTIC FRAMEWORK FOR UNDERSTANDING RELATIONSHIPS BETWEEN BODIES AND IDENTITIES

The potential for such polarity is a necessary circumstance for my discussion of migration, and as may be recalled, I will advocate and attempt to support the view that identities as well as bodies are capable of migration. Operationally, I will regard an identity as having migrated whenever it is taken into account in the activities of others not in the same geographical area or when a person identifies with a group, social world or other person in another geographical area. To a limited extent, the territorial dimension is still present in identity migration, but the critical factors involve processes of identification, the involvement of people in multiple social worlds, and the degree of meaning attached to different aspects of a person's life organization.

Before attempting a systematic presentation of these notions, however, I will try to illustrate what I mean by identity migration. Consider the well-documented pattern of youth migrating out of rural areas into urban areas. This migration pattern has been related to restricted job opportunities and the influence of mass media, and results in an altered age structure of many rural communities [Taylor and Jones (52)]. In this instance, however, I would argue that there is a phase involving the out-migration of an identity which precedes the out-migration of the body. That is, before the person physically relocates, there first is a period of identification with the urban area. This process has usually fallen under the rubric of anticipatory socialization, and correctly so, but its implications for migration processes have not yet been worked out. I maintain that in this process of identification, a person physically located in a rural area can be effectively "located" in social terms in an urban area. He can think in terms of urban expectations, conceive of himself in urban terms, adopt an inner city argot and the like, and in this sense, identification can well exceed mere wishful thinking. It may even involve certain concrete associations with urban dwellers, and may function to significantly realign his relationships with other rural youth.

I suspect that this is a general process found in any instance of voluntary migration insofar as the person anticipates the move, symbolically places himself in the future, and then responds to or takes into account social situations to be found in that future. It is not necessarily the case for involuntary migration. For instance, during World War I, when Polish citizens were relocated from their homes to concentration camps in Germany, the pattern was reversed. Using the body-identity distinction, we can say that those relocations consisted of the migration of the body preceding the migration of the identity. Significant social selves remained in Poland with family, friends, jobs, and other involvements, and the physically relocated Poles had to adjust to situated identities forced upon them by an unknown future [May (28, pp. 710–739)].

We therefore have instances in which bodies and identities can precede one another in the migration process. The remaining portion of this section of the essay will be devoted to the analysis of four possible relationships between bodies and identities. These relationships bound the limits of practical possibilities, and are presented in the following table, which consists of two variables—bodies and identities—each capable of migrating or not migrating.[6]

Identities	*Bodies*	
	Migrated	Doesn't Migrate
Migrated	A. Body migrates, identity migrates	B. Body doesn't migrate, identity migrates
Doesn't migrate	C. Body migrates, identity doesn't migrate	D. Body doesn't migrate, identity doesn't migrate

This attempt at conceptualizing body and identity migration should be regarded only as an orienting perspective. At times, the cells merge into one another, and since their boundaries are not fixed, it becomes difficult to account for all the variation. The purpose of the table is to represent the center of four analytic categories rather than to chart their exact shape. Each cell representing a particular body-identity relationship, therefore, will be discussed in order.

1. *Bodies and Identities Both Migrate.* In terms of residential migration, this cell would be illustrated by a person or family who wants to change residence, plans on it, has the resources to do it, and then actually

moves to a desired area. It might be thought of as "ideal migration," and is the type probably presumed by most studies of migration. Even in this ideal condition, however, there can be certain elements of discontinuity. One such element stems from the fact of home ownership and the chance of doubling one's financial responsibilities if one home is not sold before the new one is purchased. Buying one house and selling another can be tricky and usually involves a number of risks, particularly if the proceeds from the sale of the first house are to be used for the purchase of the second. Real estate specialists indicate that the most important element is good timing. If timing is off, a number of contingencies can enter the picture, such as changing market conditions and values, the necessity of negotiating loans having high rates of interest, and unforeseen home-inspection reports. While these are mostly financial and market problems, there is a substantial social psychological element present as well. In the terms I'm using, owning two homes involves not only the ownership per se, but having unwanted identities with respect to those houses. A wanted identity has migrated to the new house, but that process is colored by an unwanted identity which is caught up in the other house. The past won't let go. This case properly belongs in the discussion of a future cell, however, to which I will attend shortly.

2. *Body Doesn't Migrate but the Identity Migrates.* In terms of residential change, this case would involve those who want to move to a new residence in another area, who think about it, plan and save for it, and who might even have a house picked out, but who don't make that change or can't make it. This instance represents a form of fantasy in the sense that the person is significantly future-oriented and perhaps even has a substantial investment of self in that future, but there is no hope or likelihood of the body's migrating. We might say that the body hasn't yet caught up with the migrant identity.

There are quite a number of examples from across the spectrum of social life in which identities migrate before bodies migrate. Mandy Rice-Davies is primarily identified in terms of her involvement in the 1963 Profumo sex scandal in England. This involvement created an exceedingly sticky identity for her, and it puts her in the position of constantly trying to prove what she's not. In a 1976 interview with *The New York Times,* she stated that "My reputation has always preceded me. My problem was learning how to deal with it." That problem, of course, was a widely disseminated identity which merely had to wait for her body in order to be activated.

A similar process has occurred with Julius Erving, the professional basketball player. Erving had been a charter member of the American Basketball Association in the 1960s, and had led the New York Nets to two ABA titles. His name and body were soundly associated with New

York City. He had a contract dispute with the Nets in the fall of 1976, however, and was sold to the Philadelphia 76ers. Tony Kornheiser, a *Times* reporter, writes:

> He had been a Philadelphia 76er less than one day and already the word had spread, saturating the city with feverish expectation of what he would do, what he could do. Local newspapers had bannered his acquisition across their front pages. Local radio and television stations had announced it with bulletins on their news reports. Local cab drivers had all but canonized him to their fares. His reputation as basketball's greatest natural resource had preceded him (October 23, 1976).

Not only had his identity effectively migrated prior to the migration of his body, but before he had left for Philadelphia, Net fans were requesting refunds for their season tickets in anticipation of Erving's body following his identity.

Think also of transitions of political office. One has only to see the front pages of newspapers before January 20, 1977, to see articles involving state decisions being made by President-elect Jimmy Carter. The datelines are Washington, D.C., but Carter is in Plains, Georgia! We hear very little about President Ford except that he has put his house up for sale. In other words, Carter's identity has migrated to Washington while his body is in Plains; and Ford's body is in Washington while his identity has out-migrated elsewhere. This interesting process is dramatized in subheadlines such as "Carter Begins to Look and Act Presidential, While White House Aides Turn to Playfulness." But the process is a common one. Eisenhower was largely dormant in 1960 while national attention shifted to President-elect Kennedy, and in 1968 President Johnson stayed in Texas while Richard Nixon dominated the news from his headquarters at the Hotel Pierre in New York. The process, moreover, involves entire families. Amy Carter's identity has been effectively placed in Washington through her enrollment in the Thaddeus Stevens School, and this placement has had a major impact on the school's operation.[7]

One last example involves organizations. Many halfway houses or homes for the retarded meet tremendous community resistance. This is a common occurrence, and has taken place in Yonkers, New York. The hostility of the community was directed not at the retarded themselves— they haven't even moved in yet—but at the identities of those patients. Their identities have already in-migrated, and have mobilized considerable community pressure against them.

3. *Body Migrates, but the Identity Doesn't Migrate.* This relationship can be illustrated by people who relocate to another residence but who really don't want to. It can involve a certain form of nostalgia since there

may still be strong attachments to the former residence, and thus the problem here is one of the identity having to catch up with the migrant body.[8]

This problem is a chronic one for the wives of corporation executives [Warner (55)]. It is so chronic and in some cases so personally devastating that these wives frequently establish organizations designed to provide identities otherwise missing. One such helping organization is in Westport, Connecticut, and is called "New Neighbors." It has nearly 500 members, while Old Greenwich, which covers only three square miles, has a similar organization with 150 members. These moves can occur so frequently that some families, having moved out of a particular community, find themselves moving back a few years later. But the move back is the same as moving to still a different community. "Everyone I knew here was gone when I got back," said one Westport wife, while another stated that "It's hell when you move a lot. I've seen women who refuse to unpack the crates, they're so unhappy."

There are many other instances in which identities lag behind migrant bodies. For example, organized crime leaders can still control criminal activities in various neighborhoods or cities even though they may be in prison; but probably the best information comes from accounts of immigration. Oscar Handlin's *The Uprooted* (16) is among the best and most vivid of these accounts. Immigrants to the United States typically maintain strong identifications with their native countries, which usually affects their patterns of behavior in the United States. In 1860, for instance, the Irish who had settled here sent back nearly five million dollars to those they had left behind in Ireland. Crises or disasters such as war or famine frequently mobilize increased contributions, but the point to be made is that these contributions rest on a continued connectedness with the native country. Furthermore, the former country is symbolically transformed by the immigrants.

> As the passing years widened the distance, the land the immigrants had left acquired charm and beauty. Present problems blurred those they had left unsolved behind; and in the haze of memory it seemed to these people they had formerly been free of present dissatisfactions. It was as if the Old World became a great mirror into which they looked to see right all that was wrong with the New. The landscape was prettier, the neighbors more friendly, and religion more efficacious; in the frequent crises when they reached the limits of their capacities, the wistful reflection came: *This would not have happened there* [Handlin (16, pp. 260–261)] (emphasis in original).

But sometimes the present pulls harder than the past. "In every real contact the grandeur of the village faded. . . ," Handlin writes (16, p.

262). When looking at a photograph of the village church, it was clear that
"This indeed was the church, but it had not been remembered so; and the
depressing contrast took some of the joy out of remembering" (p. 262).
Handlin further notes that

> Both impressions were true, but irreconcilable. The mental image and the paper rep-
> resentation did not jibe because the one had been formed out of the standards and
> values of the Old Country while the other was viewed in the light of standards of the
> New (p. 263).

They had, in other words, become Americans, and having become so,
they were no longer villagers.[9]

4. *Neither Body nor Identity Migrates*.   What we are referring to here,
of course, is immobility, and depending upon one's sentiment, it can be
either "ideal immobility" or a rut. It is illustrated by those who do not
want to move and don't. They stay where they are. Identities can remain
with bodies even in spite of compelling circumstances tending to separate
them. For instance, there was a rash of muggings of the elderly in New
York City during 1976. One couple, each individual having been mugged
twice, who do not go out of their apartment after five o'clock in the
afternoon and when they do go out do so only in groups, refuse to leave
their neighborhood because that is where their lifelong friends are. They
have an open invitation to move in with their son and family who live in a
Long Island suburb, but they refuse the invitation because, as one of them
said, "we'd just wither away and die out there." In other words, their
bodies would be safe with their son's family, but there would be a deadly
lack of identification. So the couple stays in Brooklyn where bodily risks
are high but where also they are immersed in a significant social structure
of sentiment and identification.

The immobility of bodies and identities, however, is mobilized through
the function of mechanisms other than long-term residence. Neighborhood associations, such as the Fish-Bay Association in the north Bronx,
often have the same effect. While much of the Bronx is socially eroding,
the Fish-Bay section has shown signs of functional integration of the past
few years. There are few muggings, local businessmen are staying in the
neighborhood, it has a healthy local credit union, the streets and
sidewalks are clean, voter turnouts are heavy, and there is a collective
concern for one another. Much of this is due to the efforts of Linton
Cummings, the president of the association, who, rather than moving his
family out of the neighborhood, elected to invest in it. Now there is ample
reason to stay, not only because it is a "good" neighborhood, but because
he has a substantial portion of his social self invested in it.

There are many other examples which could be included as illustrations of these four basic variations of body-identity relationships in the migration process. My purpose, however, is not to be exhaustive but rather to be suggestive of a kind of social behavior having relevance for our better understanding of society.

MIGRATION, SOCIAL ORGANIZATION, AND PROCESS

I would think that the substance of this kind of analysis would be commonplace for the trained sociologist, although the particular use of the term "migration" might seem a bit odd. It doesn't seem to have penetrated the thought and practices of demography, however. I think it is clear from the illustrative materials I've cited that identities need not bear any absolute relationship to bodies. Certainly it can be said that identities tug at our bodies. We change residence, but identities enmeshed in social relationships pull us back to previous geographical area; or they pull us forward, tugging at our bodies to follow them into new social relationships. But it really is even more complex than that. For heuristic purposes, I have discussed identities for the most part using the singular term "identity." We have many identities, however, and in considering matters of migration, it therefore becomes important to determine which identities accompany the body, which ones precede it, which ones lag behind, and which ones are created in the overall process. The body is really only a crude indicator of the "location" of our identities, all of which may be in various and different phases of mobility or immobility. Our identities, in other words, can be thought of as being in different phased relationships to our bodies depending upon the distribution of meaning in social relationships, differential enmeshment in social worlds, the degree of activity in our various lines of communication, and the strengths of the identification processes which underly all of it.

It is ironic that some of the theoretical statements made by demographers, in contrast to their methodological practices, at least in principle come close to this view. I have in mind Bogue's (5) assertion that

> Ultimately, all migration (if it is voluntary) results from a subjective response to two subjectively perceived and subjectively interpreted socio-economic environments—the one presently occupied and another one that is a possible alternative (1, p. 754).[10]

Even though a similar statement can be found in Mangalam and Schwarzweller (27), this view is rarely expressed in studies of migration much less incorporated into research designs. The more usual case is to find some discussion of "psychological factors" associated with migration [e.g., Peterson (38, pp. 271–275)], which simply affirms the psychologistic perspective demographers take when dealing with matters of identity. Bogue's subjectivism is entirely internalistic, and consequently bears no relationship to social organization. Also, Miller's (33) investigation of decision making, family orientation, and migration, which takes as its starting point Back's (1) argument that as society becomes more fluid social psychological approaches to demography become more appropriate, is premised essentially on an individualistic portrayal of identity. This kind of individualistic and subjectivistic analysis of migration is based on a fundamentally atomistic conception of society, and clearly indicates the lack of a sociologically responsible conception of social organization. In contrast, Killian (21) has suggested a viable perspective on migration, identity, and social organization in his study of adjustments of Southern whites to Northern urban areas, but for the most part demographers present us with an imagery of man as one buffeted about by a series of external forces and internal needs.[11]

What is overlooked is the interpenetration of society and the person which was implied by Park and Burgess (35) a half century ago. They state that "There are no social forces which are not at the same time forces lodged in individuals, deriving their energy from individuals, and operating in and through individuals" (p. 451). The possibility of demography adopting such a perspective, however, is severely limited so long as humans are defined in physical terms. The social component of human conduct in demography, as noted previously, is constituted purely in the quantitative dimensions of replacement and movement of members of society, with membership operationally defined in physical not social terms [Wallace (54, pp. 18–20)]. Perhaps it is this notion of membership which lies at the base of demography's problem with the body-identity dilemma. Anselm Strauss (50) has written that "the constitution of any human group is a symbolic, not a physical fact" (p. 149). That is, mere geographical or biological proximity is not sufficient for group membership as demographers seem to think. Rather, it is the common symbolization—the mutual conceiving of being together or occupying common territory—that gives rise to groups. Membership involves much more than mere "joining," and to regard it in this way ignores people's allegiances as well as the nature and quality of those allegiances. Thus, membership boundaries and criteria often are confusing; they overlap, change, and even are differentially regarded by people of different perspectives. There is nothing eternally fixed about these boundaries.

Considerations of membership are intimately related to migration, but they cannot be confined to formal membership in the sense of holding office or being a member of a residential neighborhood. They must include degrees of allegiance [Strauss (50, p. 150)]. Robert Park (34) pointed out in 1926 that if all social relations could be reduced to relations of space, the logic of the physical sciences could be applied, and "social phenomena would be reduced to the elementary movements of individuals" [Park (34)]. This is not appropriate, however, because as Dewey (9) has argued, and Park notes so well, society and group membership exist in and through communication processes which not only give society its form but which involves a transformation of those who communicate. Park brilliantly brought together the seemingly disparate elements of physical distance, geography, population, and the self into a perspective in which he used the term "moral order" to refer to the organization of sentiment and relationships between identities and the societal factors shaping those relationships. What he managed to accomplish, of course, was the incorporation of the notion of social process into considerations of these matters.[12] In terms of the body-identity distinction, this view leads to a conceptualization of migration as a process which both links and transforms two systems of social organization. It leads us further not to observe the fact of bodily migration and then to inquire into its causes or correlations, but to focus on the social organization of migration processes and to inquire into the kinds of social structures which mobilize different types of migration.

This point of view rests on a conceptualization of human beings as social objects [Mead (30)] and society as the organization of identities [Cooley (6); Znaniecki (61)].[13] In a sense, it is based on a classical view of society and the person. Simmel has written that "Man does not end with the limits of his body or the area comprising his immediate activity" [Simmel, in Wolff (57, p. 419)], just as a city extends in social terms beyond its physical limits. There is a transcendence here—one which allows everyone to have a little bit of New York City as well as Marion, Indiana, in them—which is grounded in the very processes of identification, communication, and multiple group affiliation suggested in this essay as essential for achieving a more sociologically proper view of demography and migration. It is not at all mystical, as some of my demographer friends have accused it of being, but a logical extension of implications derived from the facts of social existence. Communities can have identities to which residents are deeply loyal [Firey (11)], and the urban area, which Strauss (49, p. 59) sees as a "complex related set of symbolized areas", contains many locales which because of that symbolization attract a wide variety of people. These communal identities at times seem even to exist independently of the residents. Ossining, New York, has been in a process of flight from an identity for decades. In the early 1900s, it was known as Sing Sing, New York. The prison there took on the name of Sing Sing, however, so the community changed its name to Ossining. A few years ago, the prison changed its name to the Ossining Correctional Facility, which in effect puts the community right back where it started. Now, real estate brokers, in advertising Ossining houses for sale, refer to those properties as a "Croton commute" in reference to the express train station stop at the adjacent community of Croton-on-Hudson. Perhaps advertising, or generically the intentioned ways in which we talk about things, is another critical dimension of identity migration and proliferation. Certainly the you-can-be-young-too message of mass media advertisement produces an age identification distribution which differs from the distribution of chronological age. Activities such as these, in addition to any number of social movements (feminists, racial, political, etc.), function to alter the identity structure of a society, and results in changing identity densities or identity clusterings of different areas.

Of course, demographers traditionally have studied population density, i.e., the number of bodies per square mile in a given geographical area, but they have overlooked identity density. Identity density results from the fact that identities "imply not merely personal histories but also social histories" [Strauss (50, p. 164)], and thus it is a dimension of social organization which impacts on the very structure of social action. Some cultures cannot engage in certain organized acts because of the lack of a specified degree of identity density. The Stones (46), for instance, note that the Sanema Indians cannot play a game of baseball because the relevant identities do not exist in that culture; furthermore, they estimate, perhaps metaphorically, that if they did exist, the Sanema would double their identity population. Identity density, therefore, is crucial for understanding social action, and we can even hypothesize certain body-identity relationships in terms of that dimension. When identity density is high, for instance, the out-migration of bodies will have little impact on a sociocultural area; but when identity density is low, the out-migration of bodies will have a greater impact. New York City is an example of a city which has been undergoing a process of body out-migration for years but which still maintains an identity because of high identity density. Even industries which move to other cities, such as the recent relocation of Time-Life, Inc., from New York to Alexandria, Virginia, do not in themselves affect the degree of identity density. The identification persists. Yet, when an industry relocates from a company town, the community suffers not only in economic terms but in terms of community identity loss. Identity density, therefore, must be seen as a factor relevant for the analysis of the social organization of migration.

One other factor involved in the process of identity and body migration is what Gerson (14) calls "commitment organization" or patterns of participation which limit the extent of participation in other settings or situations. The point to be made here is that those elements which commit our bodies are not necessarily those which commit our identities. Some kinds of occupations, for instance, tend to lock us into patterns of mobility or immobility. Corporation managers and assistant professors find themselves involved in patterns of committed migration, while store owners and farmers find themselves involved in patterns of committed nonmigration. But the mobile may dream of immobility (assistant professors wanting to be promoted) and the immobile may dream of mobility (such as my neighbor who unsuccessfully tries to escape the demands of his hardware store). Furthermore, there is the career dimension of this commitment process. When, for example, do children become a committing factor? Or the spouse's job? Children enmeshed in peer networks can result in parents with immobile bodies but mobile identities, while two-career families must continually negotiate migrating occupational identities [Rapoport and Rapoport (39); Holmstrom (20)]. It frequently boils down to an exceedingly complex juggling act. The migrant identity of one person can limit the nonmigrant body of the other, or the nonmigrant identity can constrain the bodily migration of the other. The degree of interpersonal involvement and identification has a lot to do with the various combinations possible. Lopata (24) has shown that less-educated women have fewer identity problems when their husbands die, because "they communicate with the mate less; his entrance into and exit from their lives does not require conscious reformulation of their own identities and location in the constructed world" (p. 416). In somewhat different terms, less-educated women's identities do not "migrate" with their husbands' dead bodies because the extent of identification was relatively low. There is in a sense less density in their relationships.

This kind of analysis could be extended, and indeed it must be if the ideas presented here are to eventually constitute an alternative to the existing analytic status of demography. But I feel that, in sum, I may have accomplished the limited tasks I set out for myself at the beginning of this essay. I have attempted to demonstrate a source of sociological inadequacy in demography through the use of the perspective of symbolic interactionism. That perspective dictated a conception of humans as social objects, which logically led to the use of the body-identity distinction. I then suggested a number of possible relationships between bodies and identities in the migration process, and sought to empirically illustrate those relationships. Finally, I made some suggestions concerning social organization, migration, and the process of identity and body migration. This last section has not been intended as a fully developed theory of migration, but as indicative of some of its components. In my judgment, the minimal requirements of such a theory are the accounting of how social structures create mobile and immobile bodies and identities, the relationship that identity density has to migration, and the overall organization of commitment structures which rest at the base of the social organization of migration. The virtue of such thought would be to direct attention away from conceiving of migration simply as the geographical relocation of a person's body and toward a perspective that respects the complex nature of social experience. It is through such thought that demography may be able to exceed its current ability to merely indicate surface parameters of ongoing social processes.

FOOTNOTES

*Shorter versions of this paper were read at the Symposium on Symbolic Interactionism and Social Structure, University of Missouri, April 1976, and as part of the Upsala College Faculty Lecture Series, December 1976. I am especially grateful for the helpful comments of Gregory Stone, Elihu Gerson, Sue Gerson, and Marvin Scott.

1. The standard works explicating this perspective include Rose (40), Blumer (4), Strauss (50), Stone and Farberman (47), and more recently, Meltzer, *et al.* (31).

2. Wylie's (60) extensive examination of methodological approaches to the study of identity and self-concepts includes a discussion of approaches which do or do not violate the fallacy of mind-body dualism. Gerson (13) provides a lucid argument against the dichotomy expressed in terms of the community-individual distinction, and offers an appealing alternative.

3. This assertion is implicit in the Meadian perspective. Gregory P. Stone, who is fond of saying, "There are always more identities in a room than there are bodies," however, brought it to my attention some years ago in the terms in which I'm using it here.

4. The distinctions are discussed rather extensively, however, by Davis (8), Hauser (17), Peterson (38) and Bogue (5).

5. To Dewey and Bentley (10), naming is a kind of social conduct. "We take names always as namings: as living behaviors in an evolving world of men and things" (p. 90). The relevance of naming behavior to identities and social worlds is shown in their statement that "Naming does things. It states. To state, it must both conjoin and disjoin, identify as distinct and identify as connected. If the animal drinks, there must be liquid to drink. To name the drinking without providing for the drinker and the liquid drunk is unprofitable except as a preliminary stage in the search. Naming selects, discriminates, identifies, locates, orders, arranges, systematizes" (p. 133).

6. There is some similarity between the distinctions made in this table and Gouldner's (15) distinction between locals and cosmopolitans. Cells A and D tend to be locals and cells B and C tend to be cosmopolitans. In this sense, migration refers less to geography than it does to social worlds.

7. The transforming capacities of in-migrating identities is indicated in a December 13, 1976, article in *The New York Times,* five weeks before Carter took office. The principal of the Thaddeus Stevens School reported that she has been receiving ten to fifteen calls per day from parents who want to send their children to the "now famous school." Many were suburban parents who were willing to pay $1,000 a year tuition for the "privilege of busing their children downtown to rub shoulders with the President's daughter." Not long before, the school was nearly closed because of the lack of students.

8. This represents a modification of the process of anticipatory socialization in that the temporal frame of reference is in the past rather than in the future. Lipset and Gordon (23) use the term "retrospective orientation" to refer to the retaining of "value systems of a past

membership group" (p. 496), and on the basis of their investigations of union membership, suggest that the distinction is worthwhile and warranted. This notion also lies at the center of Mead's approach to the whole topic of process. He points out that the present "builds out at both limits," toward the past and the future, and that "the immediate position of the moving body is conditioned by that which preceded it" (29, p. 236). Process therefore involves not only a reconstruction of the meaning of the past but a temporal sequencing of acts which help shape future acts. Fred Davis (7) has presented an intriguing analysis of nostalgia using this very perspective.

9. In a personal communication, Stanford Lyman indicates that this general process also occurs with Chinese immigrants. The analytic dimensions relevant to points made in this essay, however, are even more precise. Chinese identities are lodged in local clan lineages and language subgroupings. These identities were carried with Chinese immigrants to the United States, a large proportion of whom were male heads of households who were committed to bringing over their families at a later date. Many of these men couldn't afford to send for their families, however, and when they died, they almost universally were shipped back to China for burial in the local villages. This constituted a symbolic act of family and community fidelity. Even here, though, there often wasn't enough money to pay for the shipment of the body back to China. So, they were in effect kept in "storage" in the United States until financial resources were available. Vancouver, British Columbia, has a large mausoleum containing such bodies. The point is that their identities, which were defined in terms of Chinese social organization, never really left China, while their bodies, having migrated to the United States, were destined to at least symbolically return to the "location" of their identities. Some of this process is discussed in Chapters 1 and 2 of Lyman's (25) *Chinese Americans*.

10. It also is ironic that this statement is completely compatible with ethnomethodology. Reality is seen in both as internalistic rather than transacted with others. See Perinbanayagam (36) for a discussion of this point.

11. See Blumer [(4, pp. 78–89)] for an elaborate criticism of this view.

12. See Gerson (13) for a recent discussion of urban space and social process which in many respects refines Park's position.

13. Similar views can be found in Merton (32) and in Scott (43). Scott is especially explicit, and argues that social organization is the organization of information.

REFERENCES

1. Kurt Back, "New Frontiers in Demography and Social Psychology," *Demography* 4 (February 1967): 90–97.
2. Donald Ball, *Micro-ecology*. Bobb-Merrill, Indianapolis, 1973.
3. James Beshers, *Population Processes in Social Systems*. The Free Press, New York, 1967.
4. Herbert Blumer, *Symbolic Interactionism*. Prentice-Hall, Englewood Cliffs, N.J., 1969.
5. Donald Bogue, *Principles of Demography*. Wiley, New York, 1969.
6. Charles H. Cooley, *Social Organization*. Scribner's, New York, 1909.
7. Fred Davis, "Nostalgia as a Mode of Consciousness," presented at the Third Annual Meeting of the Society for the Study of Symbolic Interaction, New York, August 1976.
8. Kingsley Davis, "The Sociology of Demographic Behavior," pp. 309–333 in Robert Merton, Leonard Broom, and Leonard Cottrell, Jr. (eds.) *Sociology Today*. Harper and Row, New York, 1959.
9. John Dewey, *Experience and Nature*. Open Court, Chicago, 1925.

10. —— and Arthur Bently, *Knowing and the Known*. Beacon Press, Boston, 1949.
11. Walter Firey, *Land Use in Central Boston*. Harvard University Press, Cambridge, Mass., 1947.
12. Katherine George and Charles George, "Roman Catholic Sainthood and Social Status," pp. 394–401 in Reinhard Bendix and Seymour Martin Lipset (eds.), *Class, Status, and Power*. New York: The Free Press, New York, 1966.
13. Elihu Gerson, "Commitment Management and Urban Morphology," paper presented at the Annual Meetings of the American Sociological Association, Montreal, Canada, August 1974.
14. ——, "On 'Quality of Life,'" *American Sociological Review* 41 (October 1976): 793–806.
15. Alvin Gouldner, "Cosmopolitans and Locals: Toward an Analysis of Latent Social Roles-I," *Administrative Science Quarterly* 2 (1957): 381–306.
16. Oscar Handlin, *The Uprooted*. Grossett and Dunlap, New York, 1951.
17. Phillip Hauser, "Demography in Relation to Sociology," *American Journal of Sociology* 65 (September 1959): 169–173.
18. Amos Hawley, *Human Ecology*, Ronald Press, New York, 1950.
19. E. Adamson Hoebel, *Anthropology*. McGraw-Hill, New York, 1966.
20. Lynda Holmstrom, *The Two-Career Family*. Schenkman, Cambridge, Mass., 1972.
21. Lewis Killian, "The Adjustment of Southern White Migrants to Northern Urban Norms," *Social Forces* 32 (October 1953): 66–71.
22. Everett Lee, "A Theory of Migration, *Demography* 3 (February 1966): 47–57.
23. Seymour Martin Lipset and Joan Gordon, "Mobility and Trade Union Membership," pp. 491–500 in Reinhard Bendix and Seymour Martin Lipset (eds.), *Class, Status, and Power*. The Free Press, Glencoe, Ill., 1953.
24. Helena Z. Lopata, "Self-Identity in Marriage and Widowhood," *Sociological Quarterly* 14 (Summer 1973): 407–418.
25. Stanford Lyman, *Chinese Americans*. Random House, New York, 1974.
26. George McCall and J. L. Simmons, *Identities and Interaction*. The Free Press, New York, 1966.
27. J. J. Mangalam and Harry K. Schwarzweller, "Some Theoretical Guidelines Toward a Sociology of Migration," *International Migration Review* 4 (Spring 1970): 5–20.
28. Arthur May, *A History of Civilization*. Scribner's, New York, 1956.
29. George Herbert Mead, "The Nature of the Past," pp. 235–242 in John Coss (ed.), *Essays in Honor of John Dewey*, Holt, New York, 1929.
30. ——, *Mind, Self and Society*. University of Chicago Press, 1934.
31. Bernard Meltzer, John Petras, and Larry Reynolds, *Symbolic Interactionism*. Routledge and Kegan Paul, Boston, 1975.
32. Robert Merton, *Social Theory and Social Structure*. The Free Press, New York, 1957.
33. Sheila Miller, "Family Life Cycle, Extended Family Orientations, and Economic Aspirations as Factors in the Propensity to Migrate," *Sociological Quarterly* 17 (Summer 1976): 323–335.
34. Robert Park, "The Urban Community as a Spatial Pattern and a Moral Order," 1926, reprinted in Ralph Turner (ed.), *Robert Park on Social Control and Collective Behavior*. University of Chicago Press, 1967, pp. 55–68.
35. —— and Ernest Burgess, *Introduction to the Science of Sociology*. University of Chicago Press, 1921.
36. Robert Perinbanayagam, "The Significance of Others in the Thought of Alfred Schutz, G. H. Mead, and C. H. Cooley," *Sociological Quarterly* 16 (Autumn 1975): 500–521.
37. Henry Peters, "Hexachlorobenzene Poisoning in Turkey," *Federation Proceedings* 35 (1976): 2400–2403.

38. William Peterson, *Population*. Macmillan, New York, 1969.
39. Rhona Rapoport, and Robert Rapoport, *Dual-Career Families*. Penguin Books, Baltimore, 1971.
40. Arnold Rose (ed.), *Human Behavior and Social Processes*. Houghton Mifflin, Boston, 1962.
41. Tamotsu Shibutani and Kian Kwan, *Ethnic Stratification,* Macmillan, New York, 1965.
42. David Sly, "Migration and the Ecological Complex," *American Sociological Review* 37 (October 1972): 615–628.
43. Marvin Scott, *The Racing Game*. Aldine, Chicago, 1968.
44. T. Lynn Smith and Paul E. Zopf, *Demography: Principles and Methods*. F. A. Davis, Philadelphia, 1970.
45. Gregory P. Stone, "Appearance of the Self," pp. 86–118 in Arnold Rose (ed.), *Human Behavior and Social Processes*. Houghton Mifflin, Boston, 1962.
46. Gregory Stone and Gladys Stone, "Ritual as Game: Playing to Become a Sanema," *Quest* 26 (Summer 1976): 28–47.
47. ———— and Harvey Farberman, *Social Psychology Through Symbolic Interaction*. Xerox, Waltham, Mass., 1970.
48. Samuel Stouffer, "Intervening Opportunities: A Theory Relating Mobility and Distance," *American Sociological Review* 5 (1940): 845–867.
49. Anselm Strauss, *Images of the American City*. The Free Press, Glencoe, Ill., 1961.
50. ————, *Mirrors and Masks*. The Sociology Press, San Francisco, 1969.
51. Donald Taft and Richard Robbins, *International Migrations*. Ronald Press, New York, 1955.
52. Lee Taylor and Arthur Jones, *Rural Life and Urbanized Society*. Oxford University Press, New York, 1964.
53. Dorothy Swaine Thomas, *Social and Economic Aspects of Swedish Population Movements, 1750–1933*. Macmillan, New York, 1941.
54. Walter Wallace (ed.), *Sociological Theory*. Aldine, Chicago, 1969.
55. W. Lloyd Warner, "Successful Wives of Successful Executives," *Harvard Business Review* 34 (March–April 1956): 122–134.
56. Gordon Wiley and Philip Phillips, *Method and Theory in American Archaeology*. University of Chicago Press, 1958.
57. Kurt Wolff, *The Sociology of Georg Simmel*. The Free Press, New York, 1950.
58. E. A. Wrigley, *Population and History*. McGraw-Hill, New York, 1969.
59. Dennis Wrong, *Population and Society*. Random House, New York, 1967.
60. Ruth Wylie, *The Self-Concept*. University of Nebraska Press, Lincoln, 1974.
61. Florian Znaniecki, *Social Relations and Social Roles: The Unfinished Sociology*. Chandler, San Francisco, 1965.

TYRANNY*

Dan E. Miller, UNIVERSITY OF DAYTON

Marion W. Weiland, WICHITA STATE UNIVERSITY

Carl J. Couch, UNIVERSITY OF IOWA

The dominant concern in political sociology is the nature and degree of power and control present in a society. The prevailing analyses of asymmetric control[1] generally fall under one of the following rubrics: autocracy, despotism, dictatorship, totalitarian rule, and, less often, tyranny. The recurring weakness of this literature lies in the analytic focus and standpoint taken. By stressing static properties most analyses inadequately account for how such extreme forms of control are possible—how the relationship is produced and maintained by the participants.

A review of the literature reveals that most analyses of tyrannic autocracy focus on structural descriptions, manifest and latent functions of this form of control, the tyrannic personality, or specific cultural features in an attempt to account for the phenomenon.[2] However, some studies do

Studies in Symbolic Interaction—Volume, 1978, pages 267–288.

focus on the relationship between the ruler and the ruled [Simmel (35); Dallin and Breshlauer (6); Jaszi and Lewis (20); Wittfogel (38)]. Even when these latter studies focus on properties of relationships, they do not specify generic processes of tyrannic control and rule.

This paper attends to five closely interrelated topics. First, symmetric and asymmetric interaction patterns are contrasted.[3] Second, a distinction is made between tyrannic and paternalistic autocracy. Third, the dimensions of tyrannic interaction are specified. Fourth, the discussion is extended from simple (dyads, triads) to complex social networks. Finally, some consequences of tyrannic control are presented.

When people form tyrannic relations, the form of interaction is extremely asymmetric, nearly a pure form of superordinate-subordinate sociation [Simmel (35)]. In such relations no constraints are placed on the superordinates that in any way limit how they manage the behavior of the subordinates. The only requirement for the maintenance of the relationship is that subordinates attend to and comply with the directives of the tyrant. Consequently, the superordinate's behavior in a tyrannic relation is not comparable to the dictator's behavior which is circumscribed by law. Nor is the subordinate's compliance within a tyrannic relation comparable to that which is engendered by communal solidarity (ideological hegemony).[4] The behavior of a dictator is temporally and circumstantially constrained by law, whereas the tyrant's is not. Compliance with a context of communal solidarity is based upon the acceptance of the community's ideology, whereas compliance within a tyrannic relationship is based upon the anticipation of punishment or reward.

THEORETICAL CONTEXT

It is axiomatic that human beings are born into, live within, are molded by and continually construct a symbolic-behavioral communications context. As people go about their day-to-day lives they continually construct, modify, maintain and terminate temporal and spatial networks of interaction [Mead (28)]. They do this in a variety of forms, from dyadic sociability [Siimmel (35)], to hierarchically constructed asymmetric relations (bureaucracies, governments, etc.), to mass communications [Innis (19)]. Society, then, is only what its participants make it. All social relations, no matter how complex, are the coordinated activities, expressed ideas, and hardware-constructed, employed and destroyed within interaction networks. These interaction networks and their products continually evolve and change. Persons involve themselves in existing networks, develop new ones, and initiate new courses of action within these. They are confronted with problems, probe the unknown and develop different plans of action. They let old associations terminate or take a less involved form, and force existing networks to change. Change is generic. Stasis is problematic and can only be managed in a rather simple form of association where participants are held strictly accountable for a narrow range of behavior.

Interaction networks are not permanently structured. Once a pattern of interaction has been constructed other forms can be coordinated. A duly elected democratic elite conceivably could construct tyranny. Further, within interaction networks various patterns of interaction and combinations of them can be detected. For example solidary interaction[5] can be produced within an autocratic context. The relationship between master and slave is basically antagonistic and autocratic. Yet, the parties may cooperate and construct elementary solidarity when dealing with a common problem from a shared standpoint [Elkins (7); Genovese (11)].

SYMMETRY

Before the dimensions of tyranny are considered, a fundamental distinction needs to be made between symmetric and asymmetric (complementary) interaction patterns. "Symmetrical interaction, then, is characterized by equality and the minimization of difference, while complementary interaction is based on the maximization of difference" [Watzlwick *et al.* (36)]. Symmetric interaction patterns refer to those interaction networks jointly constructed by the participants and are mutually negotiable. Here, all parties involved can initiate new courses of action, build off previous acts with some change introduced, negotiate topics, offer new identities, construct shared or antagonistic standpoints, interrupt, or joke.

Varying from slight to extreme on a continuum, asymmetric interaction refers to the imposition of one party's will on another [Weiland (37)]. To accomplish this it is necessary that one party control the elements of coordianted action [Miller *et al.* (29)]. Such imposition would involve controlling the following: structural availability, attention, responsiveness, and identity negotiation. In extreme asymmetric interaction one party must also control the initiation of and sequencing of new courses of action and the standpoints taken by the participants. By controlling these interaction processes the superordinate controls the relationship. Consequently subordinate parties must comply, attempt to change the relationship, depart or withdraw.

AUTOCRACY

Autocratic relations can be produced in either a paternalistic or tyrannic form. They are not inherently destructive of the subordinate who is treated as an object [Weiland (37)]. Paternalistic autocracy refers to those asymmetric patterns of interaction where the behavior of the subordinate is controlled without the explicit consent of the subordinate. Paternalistic autocratic activities are those that protect and support the subordinate. Adults generally restrain children from running into traffic. Indeed, such paternalistic social activities are necessary for the survival of infants. Paternalistic interaction allows for the potential (future) initiation of new courses of interaction by the subordinate. They are so structured by the superordinates to allow growth; eventually the emergence of self-directed behavior destroys the asymmetric interaction context. As children acquire the knowledge, ability and opportunity to act autonomously they become less dependent on parents. Paternalistic interaction promotes the breaching of asymmetric interaction and subsequent parting or the renegotiation of the relationship in a more symmetric form.

Parents deliberately structure interaction games with children which allow the children to initiate new courses of action within a context controlled by the parents.[6] In order for autonomous activity to evolve within a paternalistic context the parent must be responsive to the child's effort to initiate a sequence of action. If the parent maintains control of the initiatory acts and the subsequent emergence of social activity, then autonomy will not evolve. The child will not learn to think and act independently.

Tyrannic interaction patterns prevent the subordinate from achieving autonomy, whereas paternalistic autocratic interaction often facilitates the development of autonomy. Nonetheless, in both patterns the subordinate is dependent on the superordinate.[7] Though all social interaction involves surrendering autonomy, in autocratic relations the surrendering of autonomy is grossly asymmetric. When a tyrannic relationship is imposed it is usually with the intention of producing patterns that make the initiation of new courses of action by the subordinate impossible. When tyranny has been successfully imposed, there is no potential for the subordinate to act in an independent fashion. The dependency of the tyrannic relationship is based on fear of the consequences of noncompliance. The dependency of the paternalistic relationship is based on uncertainty, lack of knowledge of how to cope independently, or acceptance of the pattern.

Whether tyrannic or paternalistic, "if relations between parent and infant remained purely autocratic, the infant would never acquire a mind or self" different from that imposed by the superordinate in the autocratic relationship [Weiland (37)]. In fact, in some situations tyrannic activities are commonly instituted to control and even destroy the mind and self of others [McHugh (25); Kogon (22); Schein (34)]. Such relationships are intentionally structured to maximize the probability of total compliance on the part of the subordinate. When successfully constructed, tyrannic interaction involves one person acting in a manner that destroys the other's ability to exercise intentionality [Hintz and Couch (18)]. It makes the subordinate a responder who becomes incapable of initiating a coordinated course of action. The superordinate acts largely or solely on the basis of his own desires and interests and is concerned with the other only as an instrument to facilitate the intended result.

The predator-prey relationship is the quintessential tyrannic form of interaction. The person who pulls a gun and commands, "Your money or your life" is behaving in a tyrannic manner. He is attempting to construct a relationship wherein we completely subordinate our will and behavior to his directives. As victims we can only prevent him from constructing (imposing) a tyrannic form of interaction by denying the threat.

The construction of sustained tyrannic relationships requires more than a single sequence of acts. Moreover, those wishing to construct a complex set of tyrannic relationships must stop short of killing all the subordinates. The successful construction of tyrannic relationships requires that the person initiating the interaction successfully commands the attention of others, have the threat acknowledged by the subsequent subordination of others to the standpoint and directives of the emerging tyrant. In extreme cases, torture or killing is employed to entice subordination by indicating to those attending that the threat is indeed serious, that the superordinate can and will probably carry out the threat. Consequently any future for the subordinate depends upon correct and immediate compliance to the directive.

DIMENSIONS OF TYRANNIC AUTOCRACY

The construction of a course of joined behavior requires that the participants can and do attend to each other, respond to each other's behavior, and generate congruent identities [Miller *et al.* (29)]. If the course of joined behavior is to achieve any degree of complexity the participants must share a symbol system—they must be able to produce shared understanding. If they are to construct and maintain a relationship they must employ vocabularies and standpoints consistent with the relationship. Conversely, inappropriate identities, vocabularies, and standpoints must be excluded. In all instances of joined behavior, ranging from the simplest to the most complex, those constructing it must be able to generate an imaginative completion of their efforts. They must be able to imagine at least some possible consequences of their behavior within the context of the relationship.

Availability

The construction and continuation of tyrannic relations requires that the participants are reciprocally but asymmetrically available to each other. At least from time to time each must be part of the other's perceptual field. Within a tyrannic relation the superordinate controls the availability of both himself and the subordinate. If the superordinate is as available to the subordinate as the subordinate is to the superordinate a tyrannic relation cannot be maintained.

Tyrannic relations are commonly constructed by the more powerful impinging upon or threatening to impinge upon the less powerful on a tactile level, e.g., punishment or torture. However, tyrannic relations may be mutually constructed, as when a mercenary soldier sells his services to a director for a negotiated payment. And it may be constructed by a person seeking out another to surrender his autonomy and making himself available to the other to be used by the other as an instrument.

The continuation of a tyrannic relationship over any period of time usually requires that the superordinate be capable of impinging upon the subordinate on the tactile level without the subordinate's being able to reciprocate, or to control knowledge that is critical to the welfare of the subordinate. If masters are to retain their superordinate position vis-à-vis their slaves it is necessary that the means of physical coercion and knowledge relevant to the slaves' wellbeing be vested in the master and kept from the slaves. If each has equal access to means of physical coercion and knowledge slaves would discontinue making themselves available or would renegotiate the context.

One of the difficulties of a tyrannic superordinate is that he must control his own availability while at the same time assuring the availability of his subordinates. One of the tactics for exercising this control is to act through mediators, e.g., the overseers who act on the behalf of the master toward the slaves. Reciprocally, the master is only available to the slaves after the subordinate has requested contact through a mediator, and then only when the master desires to make himself available.

Even when the superordinate controls the powers of coercion and knowledge of alternatives it is possible for subordinates to refuse to relate, to deny availability of self, to the tyrant. The Christians and Stoics of the Roman Empire often refused to make themselves available to their would-be tyrants as instruments. They developed a philosophy that denied the significance of earthly life, which served them well in their refusal to be active participants in the tyranny that encompassed them. With respect to stoicism, Jaszi and Lewis (20) correctly comment, "such an attitude could scarcely give support to any form of resistance; on the other hand, it could give little support to the dignity of rulers." When the subordinates refuse to make themselves available as subjects of the tyrant, the tyrant has only the alternative of treating them as objects, e.g., throwing them to the lions, or ignoring them. There can be no relationship, no exploitation, no extraction of value if the would-be subordinates refuse to submit to the will of the tyrant.

In general, tyrannic relationships include clear and unambiguous specification of how and when the subordinate may approach the superordinate and the denial of the right of the subordinate to cast claims of availability on the superordinate maintains the right to dismiss the subordinate whenever he chooses.

Attending and Surveillance

As with all instances of coordinated activity, the production of joined behavior by a tyrant and his subordinate requires that they at least intermittently attend to one another. To maintain the relationship it is necessary that the superordinate be capable of monitoring the activities of the subordinate when he wishes to or needs to while at the same time minimizing the opportunity of the subordinate to keep the superordinate under surveillance.

As persons construct sequences of joined activity, each attends to the other and in the process acquires information about the other. To prevent the subordinate from acquiring information about the superordinate that he might use to threaten the asymmetrical relationship, it is necessary for the superordinate to carefully control the opportunity of the subordinate to monitor him. Consequently, the appearance of the superordinate before the subordinate is restricted and minimized. Ideally, the tyrant provides no more information to the subordinate than that required for the subordinate to act as instructed.

Reciprocally, the continuation of the relationship requires that the superordinate attend to the subordinate either directly or indirectly in order to acquire any information about the subordinate's behavior that constitutes a threat to the relationship. Specifically, he must be able to monitor any activity of the subordinate that might be a prelude to revolt or withdrawal.

When the tyrant successfully controls the opportunities of the subordinate to monitor his behavior it places the subordinate in a bind. When the subordinate has only limited opportunity to monitor the behavior of the superordinate, it is difficult for him to accurately anticipate his desires, yet at the same time if the subordinate is to achieve rewards and avoid punishment he must be able to attend and comply with the wishes and desires of the tyrant. Some tyrants add to the difficulty by behaving in a capricious manner from time to time. Such behavior operates to assure that subordinates will attend closely whenever they can thereby be maximally available yet be incapable of predicting the behavior of the tyrant.

The successful imposition of asymmetrical monitoring frees the superordinate so that he can plan the future for both. Unless the tyrant can with some degree of success program the future for both himself and his subordinate he will have difficulty in maintaining the relationship. Reciprocally, to the degree the subordinate can avoid being monitored by the tyrant he can exercise control of his own behavior. Slaves routinely hide from their masters, and masters routinely attempt to inhibit the opportunity of their slaves to hide.

Responsiveness

The tyrant takes into account the action and intentions of the subordinate and is responsive to them. However, the responsiveness is not the mutual responsiveness that is present in the construction of a solidary course of joined action. Rather, the responsiveness is similar to the responsiveness of the predator to prey. The tyrant adjusts his action to that of the subordinate only to assure the continuation of the relationship. He may be responsive to the behavior of the subordinate by inflicting punishment whenever he detects any deviation. The superordinate is responsive to the behavior of the subordinate but not to the subordinate's desires.

In contrast, the subordinate must continually be responsive to the desires of the subordinate. He attempts to note the future line of action desired of him and organizes his own behavior in an effort to fulfill those desires.

The reciprocal responsiveness between the tyrant and subordinate is not unlike that between the assembly line and the assembly-line worker. The successful production of a product on an assembly line requires that the worker be highly attentive to and responsive to the movement of the assembly line, while the assembly line is completely unresponsive to the intentions and desires of the worker. A difference is that a worker on an assembly line can usually anticipate with great accuracy the future behavior of the assembly line.

Within tyrannic relations the participants reciprocally respond to each other but they do not construct mutual responsiveness. They do not respond simultaneously in a similar fashion toward each other or toward a shared focus. Rather they respond differentially with the tyrant in control of the sequencing of the responsiveness. The tyrant initiates and the subordinate responds. To the extent that the subordinate initiates and the superordinate responds, the tyrannic relation has been eroded.

The tyrant's responsiveness is based upon both his planned activity as well as the immediate activity of the subordinate. But the superordinate's response to the subordinate's ongoing behavior is organized to assure that the subordinate acts in a manner desired by the superordinate. The subordinate's responsiveness is limited to immediate ongoing activity of the superordinate.

Congruent Identities

The complementary identities present within a tyrannic relation are those of the director and the complier. The superordinate commands the attention and responsiveness of the subordinate and suggests or dictates a line of future action for the subordinate, and the subordinate attends to and is responsive to the suggestions and directives of the superordinate. In the extreme case the interaction is so structured that the subordinate cannot initiate any new lines of action. Consequently, the subordinate is completely devoid of autonomy. Any expression of autonomy by the subordinate is often inimical to survival for the subordinate. The superordinate commands and the subordinate complies. No other acts are called for. Once the command is complied with another directive may be issued or the subordinate makes himself available and waits for future directives.

The construction of an enduring tyrannic relationship requires that once a given command-compliance sequence is completed the superordinate has the floor to elicit either another command or to terminate the immediate interaction until the services of the subordinate are desired again.

The continuation of a tyrannic relationship requires that the subordinate not be allowed to issue any insertions between the command and the compliance. The subordinate must not be allowed to ask, "Why do you want me to do that?"[8] The toleration of insertions would be to allow the subordinate to think, to concern himself about the future. He must respond as an instrument. When a button is pushed, he responds.

The construction of complex command-compliance sequences that endure is difficult. Typically, it is accomplished by the tyrant from time to time exercising coercion and then the threat of coercion.[9] Even so the establishment of complex tyrannic relationships requires that both the tyrant and the subordinate be trained to play their parts. Boot camp in the marine corps is largely organized to train subordinates to be effective compliers. Those who cannot or will not assume the identity of compliers are punished, and if the punishment does not result in compliance the person is dismissed from the unit. The ideal subordinate within a tyrannic relationship is mindless. He will do whatever he is instructed to do by his superordinate.

Yet, the construction of complementary identities within a tyrannic relationship requires that the participants be able to produce shared understanding. The subordinate must be able to understand what is desired, act as instructed, yet not to think about it. Consequently, one of the features of tyrannic relationships is that the instructions and commands are simple and concise. If the information conveyed by the superordinate about the future is more complex than is necessary for compliance, it provides a basis for the subordinate to begin thinking about the future he is helping to construct and may lead to noncompliance.

The maintenance of the complementary identities of director-complier is facilitated if the complier cannot anticipate forthcoming commands. The assembly-line worker must align his behavior with the machine. However, he is not in a tyrannic relationship, for he can predict with accuracy. When the subordinate can accurately anticipate the behavior of the superordinate he can to an extent organize his own action. Even if he cannot control or influence the behavior of the superordinate, he can organize his response to the superordinate in a manner which is most beneficial to himself. The subordinate can then ingratiate through impression management [Goffman (13)] and gain some power in the situation.

Further if the subordinate can accurately predict the behavior of the superordinate he may daydream, as assembly-line workers do, and think about affairs not part of the immediate situation. He can then develop a mind capable of reflexive behavior, and this may become more difficult to control. On the other hand, if he cannot anticipate the behavior of the superordinate at all, then his behavior will tend to become mindless in due time and he will be totally controlled by the superordinate.

The more tyrannic the relationship, the less the emphasis on consistency and the greater the emphasis on the maintenance of the form, i.e., the directive-compliance sequences. Superordinates attend to the behavior of the subordinates primarily to check the nextness and consistency of the compliance. Paradoxically, inconsistent demands require more attending and greater responsiveness by the subordinates. Thus, making it more difficult for the subordinate to ingratiate himself or to engage in impression management. The subordinate can only attend, accept the cast identities, and comply.

Within tyrannic relationships there is little potential for the development of a shared standpoint. The primary focus of attention of each is the behavior of the other. If there is the development of a shared standpoint it is typically that of the subordinate taking on the standpoint of the superordinate. This certainly seems to have occurred in some instances in the Nazi concentration camps, where the inmates assumed the standpoint and concerns of their guards [Bettelheim (2)]. However, for the most part, within tyrannic relations not only is there a clear and unambiguous differentiation of functional identities, there is also a clear differentiation of interests and concerns.

Objectives

The construction of units of joined activity by any two persons requires that to some degree they have a shared focus [Miller, *et al.* (29)]. To cooperate, whether to carry on a conversation or to lift a log, requires that to some extent they attend to something in common. In much of human life, as persons construct joined behavior, they are acting to some extent to achieve a social objective. To act toward a social objective they may act in a highly similar manner or even take identical lines of action, e.g., lifting a log together; or they may take highly differentiated lines of action toward a common focus, e.g., one person drives the car while the other pushed in an effort to free the car from the mud hole. In such instances both participants are attempting to achieve a shared social objective.

Tyrannic behavior differs from such instances of joined behavior in that there is no shared social objective. In the extreme, all that is present is complementary individual objectives.[10] The objective of the tyrant is usually a much longer range than that of the subordinate. The tyrant may be concerned with conquering a nation while the subordinate is concerned primarily, if not almost entirely, with personal survival.

However, for them to act together they must share a focus, but the focus is provided by the tyrant. It is the tyrant who specifies what will be acted toward and what will be done. The tyrant selects from the external world what both he and the subordinate will attend to and act toward. Successful completion of the acts results in the tyrant's achieving his objective and may result in the subordinate receiving some reward for his participation.

Within a tyrannic relationship only a contingent future is constructed, not a shared one. Further the future of the subordinate is in the hands of the superordinate. If the tyrant becomes incapable of controlling both his own future and that of the subordinate, the relationship will deteriorate. To the extent that the subordinate can negotiate and control his own future he has moved the relationship from a tyrannic one to one of mutual construction.

Tyrannic relations create conditions wherein the subordinate is extremely present-oriented; he attends almost entirely to the ongoing acts of the superordinate. Thus, it is difficult for him to project any long-range future. In extreme cases the subordinate may project no future line of activity other than that of continually attending to the behavior of the superordinate and attempting to derive a method from the madness. Any other behavior may be seen as a breach of the relationship and lead to dire consequences.

Reg Murphy, the former editor of the *Atlanta Constitution,* noted that when he was captive of political kidnappers he never attended to a distant future. Rather, he attended to the immediate behavior of the tyrants and continually tried to understand their position and anticipate their acts in order to make the sequences more fluid, thus minimizing any interpretation on the part of the tyrants that he was attempting to breach the relationship. Murphy's position, correctly taken, was that any future for him was contingent on total, immediate, and correct compliance to the directives of the tyrants.

COMPLEX SOCIAL NETWORKS

Tyrannic interaction can only be totally maintained in co-present contexts. The superordinate must be able to enforce the threat of coercion, given noncompliance by the subordinate. Superordinates must be able to touch subordinates [Leichty (23)]. Consequently, those who would establish a tyrannic regime within a large social system, e.g., a nation, are confronted with many problems.

At the minimum, the superordinate must be able to monitor the behavior of large numbers to check their compliant behavior and be perceived to be able to carry out contingent threats for noncompliance while at the same time directing their behavior. The tyrant must do this while at the same time remain relatively inaccessible to the subordinates. He must maintain control over the behavior of the subordinates while minimizing the potential for retaliation. Tactics that are commonly used to maintain complex tyrannic networks include: 1) presenting alternative relationships from emerging and thereby making all dependent on the tyrannic relationship, 2) restricting the movement of the subordinates so that they cannot withdraw from the relationship, and 3) keeping them ignorant so that they cannot anticipate future courses of action.

Compliance can be produced through involvement in mass media relations [Couch (5)]. Compliance can occur if the subordinates have access to the focus of attention (the medium and the message), if they understand it and if they understand the consequences of compliance and noncompliance. An order may be conveyed by the media that a curfew is in effect. Then if persons do not comply with the curfew order, some may be shot and that event made public.

Mediated directive-compliance sequences can be facilitated if the tyrants use agents provocateurs, informants, or if the subordinates believes the tyrant uses such devices.[11] The electronics explosion has produced highly sophisticated surveillance and accounting technology which allow a minimum number of people to check on the compliant behavior of others.[12] Such surveillance and occasional random terror would allow for large-scale tyrannic control with the necessary dimensions of tactile contact included. Such systems were the focus of interest of Orwell's *1984* and Bradbury's *Fahrenheit 451*.

For a tyrant of a large social unit to maintain the surveillance necessary to acquire information about the compliance, sentiments, and thoughts of the subordinates, it is necessary to use spies and informants. However, to obtain the necessary information in this manner is to place trust in some of one's subordinates, a risky endeavor; or, to maintain a tyrannic relationship with those acquiring the information, which will tend to render them incompetent to exercise the initiative necessary to do their job well.

Public appearances of tyrants are carefully orchestrated. They must be managed in a way that does not allow the subordinates to achieve information that may be useful in avoiding tyrannic interaction, or in plotting the overthrow of the tyranny. However, there is an additional reason for the careful orchestration of public appearances, namely, an effort to demonstrate to all that the tyrant is competent and of value and therefore deserves support. In many instances compliance has been generated in part on the basis that the tyrant is more capable of programming the future than anyone else. When it is possible to generate support in this fashion, then compliance may come not so much from fear of threats from the tyrant and his cohort, but from attempts to avoid negative sanctions from one's peers. The construction of compliance in this fashion is not unlike the compliance elicited by some mass advertising. One is to use a particular deodorant and mouthwash to inhibit the possibility of offending those with a refined olfactory sense.

While tyrants must achieve compliance, the activity necessary to maintain the relationship simultaneosuly tends to elicit responses that inhibit sustained compliance. Most subordinates dislike participating in sustained interaction with the tyrant and attempt to minimize their availability to him, a condition that can be partly rectified by punishment for failure to be available.

Perhaps of even greater importance is that fact that tyrannic relationships tend to destroy all relationships and persons become disembedded with each other. Much of the stability of our day-to-day behavior is derived from our embeddedness in a wide range of relationships. When these are destroyed or inhibited, a source of our personal stability is destroyed. Erratic and bizarre behavior become more common and we get "them ole anomie blues." Atomized individuals are not particularly predictable or reliable.

One procedure tyrants use to overcome this difficulty is the random use of terror. The perfection of this sytem was one of the essential keys for the construction and continuation of the Roman Empire. The Romans had the practice of killing every tenth person of rebellious units *(decimatio)*. Few complex tyrannic systems have systematically incorporated the idea of randomness in the exercise of coercive forces. Although in many, such as the systems constructed in Nazi Germany and in the Soviet Union under Stalin, the exercise of terror probably appeared to be fairly random from the point of view of the subordinates. In these cases even those close to the seats of power were often unable to predict the exercise of coercive responses, as Hitler's murder of Roehm and his cohorts indicate. Such a procedure operates to produce both compliance and informants.

Whether random terror, or terror directed to those who indicate any degree of opposition or independent thought and action, concern is generated among the subordinates to exert attention and control over fellow subordinates to prevent the unleashing of random coercion. Subordinates then become accountable to each other as well as to the tyrant. Subordinate concern is then directed to any behavior which may unleash a coercive response. Such a situation enhances the tendency for subordinates to be responders only—docile compliance. This culture, prevalent in Nazi Germany and Stalinist U.S.S.R., inhibits any overt planning for alternative courses of action. The successful tyrant minimizes concern for any future except that framed by the tyrant.

An individual cannot establish and maintain a complex social network built on tyrannic relationships without assistance. The tyrant must have lieutenants. In many instances the lieutenants avail themselves to the superordinate for personal gain, an exchange relationship. Mercenaries, bodyguards to the local mafiosi and some of the followers of the tyrants of ancient Greece take the job for purely economic reasons. Many subsequently find that they are in no way insulated from the coercive acts of the tyrant they have served.

In many cases willful participation in a tyrannic system is very much like making a deal on the market. The participants—the tyrant and those he employs—size each other up and attempt to make the best bargain possible. Tyrannic relations provide good training for the marketplace, and vice versa. In both, the participants are primarily self-centered as opposed to other- or collectivity-centered. Both inhibit the participants from becoming embedded in each other's lives and consequently in the likelihood of altruistic acts. They differ in that within the exchange relationship each person willingly enters the transaction and each is free to leave it at any moment. As a result, there is a basic equality inherent to exchange relationships. Each is dependent upon the other for the successful completion of the act.

The initiation and support of tyranny is not always done with hedonistic intentions. Many participate in the effort to establish a tyrannic system because they see it as a necessary step to extracting themselves from a chaotic or repressive situation. Many of those who aided in the overthrow of the Czar, many early supporters of Hitler, and many of the followers of the ancient Greek tyrants did so with paternalistic and humanitarian intentions. The early communist practitioners explicitly developed a rationale for the exercise of tyrannical procedures through the dictatorship of the proletariat. Lenin and others recognized that the introjection of a tyrannic system was an effective means for tearing persons from their embeddedness in the old system of relationships and ideology which would thereby make them more amenable to the new and more perfect system. A temporary tyranny was regarded as a necessary step in the movement of utopia. Paternalistic rationalizations for the use of tyranny was used by the Romans, the British Empire, and recently by the Canadian government when they instituted a garrison state and tyrannic rule during the political strife in Quebec in October 1970. This strategy is clearly described by Machiavelli in *The Prince*.

The maintenance of tyranny requires constant suspicion among the subordinates; subordinates must not be allowed to develop trust. The presence of and the belief in the presence of spies and informants operates to inhibit the development of trust among the subordinates. Without surveillance and the suspicion thereby generated, subordinates could easily become aware of their common sentiments toward the tyrant. If they could trust each other they might well develop solidary concerted action to alter the form of the relationship between themselves and the tyrant.

The secrecy surrounding the planning of the tyrants also operates to make concerted actions by subordinates difficult. Tyrants frequently rationalize that they cannot reveal their organization or plans to the public because to do so would threaten the continuation of the system. This knowledge would allow subordinates to anticipate the future and make plans to breach the relationship. Tyrants aver that secrecy and lack of knowledge must be maintained because incompetent subordiantes might use the knowledge "unwisely." This practice continually produces incompetent and ignorant subordiantes. American slaves had to remain subordinate since they were forced to be ignorant, incompetent, and illiterate in most worldly matters [Elkins (7)].

Nixon attempted to cloak his behavior in secrecy with the rationale that to make it public would be to the detriment of the nation. Nixon, like Hitler, Stalin, and many other tyrants attempted to develop the rationale that outsiders were like children and must be kept uninformed for their own good. To the extent that tyrants are successful in getting others to accept this rationale, it enhances the maintenance of tyranny and consequent incompetent and ignorant subordinates.

A consequence of secrecy[13] is that only tyrants and their lieutenants can participate in the planning and initiation of future courses of action. Tyrants keep private what should be public—the knowledge and competence needed for planning and carrying out the future of a community. Subordinates in this system can only participate by serving as instruments for the ruling elite.

By monopolizing knowledge and the formal and informal diffusion of knowledge superordinates act to insure the continuation of both their special position and the relationship. Without knowledge of the relevant operations of the system, or knowledge of alternative social forms, the subordinates can do little other than accept the current situation.

The secrecy surrounding tyrannic elite also inhibits the possibility of tyrants' being held accountable for their actions. Tyrants assume total responsibility for the system, but are accountable to no one. After Hitler had his friend Roehm and several hundred other members of his private army murdered, he justified it by stating, "In that hour I was responsible for the fate of the German nation, therefore the supreme court of the German people during these twenty-four hours consisted of me" [Jaszi and Lewis (20)]. Similar rationalizations were offered for the establishment of secret police forces and strategic weapons and tactics squads (SWAT) in the United States in the 1950s and 60s.

Tyranny, then, is essentially lawless. For law is a set of, if not publicly agreed upon rules that remain relatively constant, at least a set of publicly announced rules. To the extent that written law enters the field of action, it allows persons to anticipate the consequences of their action based on past standards. Even when the laws are highly discriminatory, e.g., there is one set of laws for the nobles and another set for commoners, it allows for all to anticipate with some accuracy. With the presence of written law, superordinates become accountable to its guidelines. To the extent that the ruler subordinates himself to the law and/or is subordinated to it by others, it prevents the development of tyrannic relations. Many dictators, kings, and others have behaved in a tyrannic fashion by ignoring the law. When they can get away with it they are transforming lawful relations into tyrannic ones.

CONSEQUENCES

Tyrannic social relationships destroy humans by inhibiting the possibility for people to develop solidarity with others and hold others, including superordinates, accountable for their actions. In solidary and accountable relations the participants are respected by others as having a will, an autonomous standpoint. Furthermore, in these interaction forms the intentions of others are taken into account and respected in the construction of complex social acts. Through mutual and solidary interaction people become embedded in each other's lives and concern, and understanding and tolerance can emerge. Through participating in accountable relations people acquire a standpoint of personal and social responsibility which guides their actions. Tyrannic relations prohibit the development of these dimensions and destroy them if they have been present.

Paradoxically, one consequence of tyranny is that while constructed to prohibit anarchy, it frequently engenders anarchy. By atomizing citizens and generating a primary concern with self and self-preservation, tyrannic interaction and enduring tyrannic relationships create a context of violent individual acts in a spiraling effect where more tyranny is needed to control people's behavior. The more tyrannic the relationships, the more anarchistic acts generated. The development of reciprocating terrorism in Northern Ireland and many ghettos in the United States point this out all too clearly.

As Mead (28) noted, an act on our part tends to call out in the other the same incipient act. The response elicited by tyrannic acts tends to be a tyrannic one. In short, it tends to elicit a condition of war upon all, including especially tyrannic acts toward the tyrant.

Any given tyrannic system is a relatively fragile relationship. Those who are intimate with the inner circle are well aware that if they can successfully manipulate certain events they can replace the one currently in power without having to deal subsequently with a large body of loyal and outraged followers. Those who are not part of the inner circle are usually indifferent and given the opportunity will migrate. When conflict occurs between the established tyrant and those attempting to replace him, because of their lack of embeddedness in other relationships most of them will attempt to present a neutral stance until one side gains advantage, whereupon subordiates will align with the emerging winner.

Tyrants are well aware of the reactions elicited by tyrannic rule; they quickly surround themselves with guards. To rule through terror is to live in terror. The bodyguards and other protective devices are employed in the attempt to keep the terror out, but as the walls of protection are made up in part at least of other human beings it is fragile protection at best. If they live long enough they usually advise their sons to trust no one, not even their brothers. And the history of tyrants suggests that it is sound advice. Furthermore, due to the widespread egoism common within most tyrannic systems, the tyrant knows or at least suspects that each member of his protective unit is available to the highest bidder, provided, of course, that they can either sell themselves without the tyrant's knowing about it or are able to remove themselves from the tyrant's reaches.

While efforts to do the tyrant in and to replace him are relatively common, popular widespread rebellion to change the system is difficult to generate. It is extremely difficult for the subordinates to organize them-selves effectively in the effort to destroy the system. Their concern with informers and spies severely inhibits such action. Most are too frightened to coordinate their action with others [Marx (27)]. About the only way an alternative social system can be constructed is for the subordinates to establish an underground network. But as most tyrants are aware of this, they maintain elaborate surveillance systems to inhibit such a develop-ment. In the recent past the United States government has spent a great deal of time and effort in the extended surveillance of supposed radical groups.

Within tyrannic relationships it is impossible for the participants to develop a unified code of ethics or morality. The development of such principles requires that participants jointly orient themselves to a shared objective and develop shared standpoints and plans of action toward that objective. It is possible for the elite of tyrannic relationships to develop a code of ethics among themselves. Slave owners in the United States developed a code of conduct among themselves about the "rightness" of slavery [Elkins (7); Genovese (11)]. However, masters and slaves seldom construct a solidary morality to justify the relationship. The structured antagonism prevents this.

Since tyranny inhibits the development of solidarity, consensual moral-ity, and commitments to future courses of action and fosters erratic be-havior, subordinates must be either kept under close surveillance or di-verted. Entertainment, sporting events, and discount prices divert their energy and keep them occupied, and inhibit their becoming reflective about the system. In the process they become Stepford wives. Such a hedonistic, simple-minded standpoint is a frequent consequence of par-ticipating in enduring tyrannic relationships.

Despite efforts to spy on, control and divert subordinates, justifications for the alteration of the tyrannic relations are frequently generated. Most of these justifications assess the tyrant as personally responsible for the destruction of traditional ethics and ways of life. When Nixon was de-posed he was personally blamed. The incipient tyranny was treated as a personality characteristic. By seating a new leader, the tyranny was seen as destroyed. This type of rationalization and action based on it was what allowed a succession of tyrants over a period of centuries in the Roman Empire.

A tyrannic system can be transformed into a more stable form by chang-ing it into a set of authoritarian relationships. The authoritarian system differs by incorporating elements of law. It thereby makes the behavior of the ruler more predictable. The tyrant who restrains himself or is re-strained by others to act in a lawful manner transforms tyranny into authoritarianism. When elements of law are maintained, subordinates can anticipate future courses of action and organize their own behavior accordingly. A degree of solidarity among subordinates and superordinates can develop regarding the morality and maintenance of the status quo.

CONCLUSION

Established law and independent subunits within the larger society are the antithesis to tyrannic social relations. The framers of the Constitution of the United States attempted to establish a set of laws and social relationships that would make it impossible for a tyrannic system to emerge. The system of checks and balances in the Constitution explicitly sets up a complex set of relations which makes the ruler accountable to and in part compliant to representatives of public constituencies. By creating a division of authority, a system of communication independent of the authority system (a free press), the practice of trial by peers, the practice of the right to be directly confronted by one's accusers and access to information contained in the indictment against the accused, and the prohibition of the accused person's testifying against himself, it is difficult to establish a complex tyranny.

Public oaths of office also operate to inhibit the construction of tyrannies. When a person fails to act as he has committed himself to, others, if they have the power, can hold him accountable for his public commitment. Of course, such oaths do not guarantee that a person will in fact behave in a like manner, but they do make it more likely [Weiland (37)]. In contrast, oaths of personal loyalty facilitate the construction of tyranny. During the Nazi period, the German generals were required to make a personal and public commitment to Hitler. This oath appears to have operated to inhibit the German generals from revolting against Hitler [Jazsi and Lewis (20)].

Despite the numerous safeguards against tyrannic rule in the United States Constitution, recent Presidents have used secrecy, inaccessibility, illegal coercion and widespread surveillance. This strongly suggests that elements of tyrannic relations are present and operative in the political system of the United States. The solution to the problem will not be found by replacing persons. The solution can only come by a thorough examination of extant relationships that allow persons to initiate such activity.

It is a sad commentary on humanity, but the history of complex societies suggests that many of them were constructed in large part on the basis of complex tyrannic relationships. However, to endure, it seems necessary that large elements of other social forms have to be present.

Many evolve into authoritarian social relations, such as constitutional dictatorships or monarchies where the ruling elite are constrained by law. This appears to be a necessary evolution if the social system constructed by tyranny is to endure.

While the focus of this paper has been primarily on features of large-scale tyrannic relationships, it must be recognized that tyrannic elements still abound in many of our day-to-day relationships. The teacher who gives a difficult multiple-guess examination, grades on the basis of a normal curve, and refuses to all the students to have access to their own examinations subsequently constructs a minor tyranny. Perhaps a thorough study of tyrannic relationships and their consequences will allow us to remove them from our day-to-day experiences. It appears to be a social objective worth working toward.

FOOTNOTES

*This paper was read at the Symbolic Interaction Symposium on Social Structure held in Columbia, Missouri, April, 1976. We would like to thank Robert Hintz, Gregory Stone, Peter Hall, Steve Brickey, Nick Tavuchis, Charles Axelrod, and Eve Finnbogason for comments on an earlier draft of this paper.

1. Asymmetric social interaction (relations) is a concept derived from Watzlawick, et al. (36) conceptualization of complementary social relations; relationships where in one party has more control over the flow of interaction and the nature of the relationship than do other parties. This concept is similar to Simmel's (35) notion of superordinate-subordinate relations. The terms are used interchangably.

2. Friedrich (9), Friedrich and Brzezinski (10), Hinton (17), Moore (30), McKinney (26), Arendt (1), and Neuman (31).

3. Tyrannic autocracy (tyranny) denotes the nearly pure form of asymmetric social relationships. Asymmetric social relations suggest a continuum ranging from totally symmetric interaction to totally asymmetric interaction. Tyranny has traditionally been conceptualized as an extreme form of control. We agree.

4. See Sallach (32) on ideological hegemony. Goffman (13a), Haney, et al. (16), Friedrich (9), and Hinton (17) all provide evidence of the construction of shared standpoints among subordinates in highly asymmetric relations.

5. Glenda Sehested notes that solidary interaction involves the construction of parallel (common) identities, a shared standpoint, a common focus of attention and concerted parallel action.

6. Haley (14) calls this process "metacomplementarity." The superordinate specifies the context of the unfolding interaction, but allows the subordinate to control the development of the interaction within the parameters of the context. Thus, it may appear that children are in control, but they are not. Similarly, wives may let husbands glow in the illusion of proper decision making, when in fact the wife has controlled the process.

7. Dependency can be based on many things. Subordinate dependence on the tyrant is generally based on fear (coercion). Paternalistic dependence may be based on uncertainty, incompetence, or perceived chaos. The point must be stressed that the dependency is reciprocal [Emerson (8)]; superordinates are dependent on the behavior of the subordinates.

8. The tyrant is almost totally responsible, but accountable to no one, least of all to his subordinates. He must monitor the development of the act but remain aloof and inaccessible to the claims of subordinates.

9. A notable exception would be those who voluntarily submit to sado-masochistic sexual practices for relatively short periods of time.

10. Though the participants of tyrannic interaction produce no shared future, they do produce a contingent future based on reciprocal dependence to achieve different objectives. The subordinate's objective is existence—any future. The superordinate's objective is some hedonistic benefit.

11. Marx (27) notes the effectiveness of agents provocateurs and informants in the inhibition of alternative social relationships.

12. Recent congressional hearings have revealed the degree to which American citizens are monitored by sophisticated surveillance equipment. Such public knowledge may inhibit future noncompliant behavior thus enhancing stability of current relationships, if subordinates assume surveillance and fear coercive accountability.

13. Secrecy refers to what Glaser and Strauss (12) called closed awareness context. One party is aware of what is transpiring, whereas the other party is unaware.

REFERENCES

1. Hannah Arendt, *The Origins of Totalitarianism*. Merridien Books, New York, 1958.
2. Bruno Bettelheim, *The Informed Heart*. The Free Press, Glencoe, Ill., 1960.
3. Herbert Blumer, *Symbolic Interactionism: Perspective and Method*. Prentice-Hall, Englewood Cliffs, N.J., 1969.
4. Carl J. Couch, Dimensions of Association in Collective Behavior Episodes," *Sociometry* 33 (1970): 457–471.
5. ——, "Mediated communication," in C. J. Couch and R. Hintz (eds.), *Constructing Social Life*. Stipes, Champaign, Ill., 1975.
6. Alexander Dallin and George Breshlaur, *Political Terror in Communist Systems*. Stanford University Press, Stanford, Calif., 1970.
7. Stanley Elkins, *Slavery*. University of Chicago Press, 1959.
8. Robert M. Emerson, "Power-dependence Relations," *American Sociological Review* 27 (1962): 31–41.
9. Carl Friedrich, *Totalitarianism*. Harvard University Press, Cambridge, Mass., 1954.
10. —— and Zbigniew Brzezinski, *Totalitarianism, Dictatorship and Autocracy*. Harvard University Press, Cambridge, Mass., 1956.
11. Eugene Genovese, *Roll, Jordan, Roll*. Random House, New York, 1974.
12. Barney Glasser and Anselm Strauss, "Awareness Contents in Social Interaction," in G. Stone and H. Farberman (eds.), *Social Psychology Through Symbolic Interaction*. Xerox, Waltham, Mass., 1969.
13. Erving Goffman, *The Presentation of Self in Everyday Life*. Doubleday, Garden City, N.Y., 1959.
13a. ——, *Asylums*. Doubleday, Garden City, N.Y., 1961.
14. Jay Haley, "An International Description of Hypnosis," in Don D. Jackson (ed.), *Communication, Family and Marriage—Human Communication*, Vol. I. Science and Behavioral Books, Palo Alto, Calif., 1968.
15. Peter M. Hall, "A Symbolic Interactionist Analysis of Politics," *Sociological Inquiry* 42 (1972): 83–95.

16. Craig Haney, Curtiss Banks, and Philip Zimbardo, "Interpersonal Dynamics in a Simulated Prison," in D. Steffensmeier and R. Terry (eds.), *Examining Deviance Experimentally*. Alfred, Port Washington, N.Y., 1975.

17. William Hinton, *Fanshen*. Monthly Review Press, New York, 1967.

18. Robert Hintz and Carl J. Couch, "Time, Intention and Social Behavior," in C. Couch and R. Hintz (eds.), *Constructing Social Life*. Stipes, Champaign, Ill., 1975.

19. Harold A. Innis, *The Bias of Communication*. University of Toronto Press, 1950.

20. Oscar Jaszi and John Lewis, *Against the Tyrant*. The Free Press, New York, 1957.

21. Arthur Koestler, *Darkness at Noon*. Signet, New York, 1948.

22. Eugen Kogon, *Theory and Practice of Hell*. Berkley, New York, 1960.

23. Marilyn Leichty, "Sensory Modes . . . and the Universe of Touch," in C. Couch and R. Hintz (eds.), *Constructing Social Life*. Stipes, Champaign, Ill., 1975.

24. Robert Jay Lifton, *Thought Reform and the Psychology of Totalism*. W. W. Norton, New York, 1961.

25. Peter McHugh, "Social disintegration as a requisite for resocialization," in G. Stone and H. Farberman (eds.), *Social Psychology Through Symbolic Interaction*. Xerox, Waltham, Mass., 1970.

26. David McKinney, *The Authoritarian Personality Studies*. Mouton, The Hague, 1973.

27. Gary Marx, "Agents Provocateurs and Informants: Some Neglected Characteristics of Social Movements," *American Journal of Sociology* 80 (September 1974): 402–442.

28. George Herbert Mead, *Mind, Self, and Society*. University of Chicago Press, 1934.

29. Dan Miller, Robert Hintz, and Carl J. Couch, "The structure and elements of openings," *Sociological Quarterly* 16 (Autumn 1975): 479–499.

30. Barrington Moore, *Social Origins of Dictatorship and Democracy: Lord and Peasant in the Making of the New World*. Beacon Press, Boston, 1966.

31. Franz Neuman, *The Democratic and Authoritarian State*. The Free Press, New York, 1957.

32. David Sallach, "Class Domination and Ideological Hegemony," *Sociological Quarterly* 15 (Winter 1974): 38–50.

33. Thomas Scheff, "Negotiating Reality: Notes on Power in the Assessment of Responsibility," *Social Problems* 16 (Summer 1968): 3–17.

34. Edgar Schein, *Coercive Persuasion*. W. W. Norton, New York, 1961.

35. Georg Simmel, *The Sociology of Georg Simmel*, Kurt Wolff (tr. and ed.), The Free Press, New York, 1950.

36. Paul Watzlawick, Janet Beavin, and Don D. Jackson, *Pragmatics of Human Communication*. W. W. Norton, New York, 1967.

37. Marion Weiland, "Forms of social relations," in C. Couch and R. Hintz (eds.), *Constructing Social Life*. Stipes, Champaign, Ill., 1975.

38. Karl A. Wittfogel, *Oriental Despotism: A Comparative Study of Total Power*. Yale University Press, New Haven, Conn., 1959.

THE SOCIOLOGY OF
FEMALE ARTISTS

Michal McCall, CASE WESTERN RESERVE UNIVERSITY

Thirty years ago, Hughes (15) discussed the career contingencies and status dilemmas of "marginal men" in occupations and professions. Occupational marginality results from contradictions between occupational status, as formally determined, and the auxiliary characteristics expected of incumbents, such as racial and sex status (p. 144). According to Hughes: ". . . in spite of American heterogeneity, this remains a white, Anglo-Saxon, male, Protestant culture in many respects. These are expected characteristics for many favored positions (p. 146). Among the favored positions are prestigeful professions like medicine, the law, and academic science. Women are marginal in these professions becasue of the contradiction between their professional and sex statuses" (p. 142).

Hughes thus anticipated by thirty years the theoretical concerns and

Studies in Symbolic Interaction—Volume 1, 1978, pages 289–318.

research results of a growing sociological literature, which includes studies of female lawyers [Epstein (7); White (28)]; female physicians [Lopate (18)]; female scientists and engineers [Mattfield and Van Aken (21); Cole and Cole (6)]; and academic women [Bernard (3), Simon et al. (26]. These and other studies of females' careers in predominately male professions have shown that women are indeed marginal persons who face the career contingencies, i.e., deviant careers—and the status dilemmas, i.e., isolation from professional colleagues—detailed by Hughes.

Female visual artists are "marginal men" in the predominately male art world, and there is evidence that they have faced special career contingencies and status dilemmas as a result [Whitesel (30); Rosenberg & Fliegel (24); White and White (29); Harris (12)]. However, female visual artists represent a unique instance of professional marginality. Hughes was concerned with the causes and consequences of marginality in occupations and professions with formal membership criteria, i.e., training credentials, formal certification, or employment. He explained that marginal individuals, who are indisputably members of such occupations and professions because they meet the formal criteria, nevertheless seem unauthentic to colleagues and clients and, thus, unworthy of colleagueship and occupational license because they lack the auxiliary characteristics expected of members. Artistic status is determined processually, not formally by means of training credentials, formal certification, or employment. Thus, the problem of professional marginality for female artists is not merely to seem like "real" artists, but to be considered artists at all.

During twelve months[1] of participant observation in the St. Louis art world, I gathered data on the artistic status of a sample of thirty-four female painters, sculptors, and printmakers. The research methods included respondent interviews; informant interviews with male and female artists, dealers, curators, and collectors; and participation, direct observation, and document analysis. The sample of respondents included women with graduate fine-arts degrees and art-faculty positions, as well as women without art degrees or with undergraduate and graduate degrees in fine art, art history, and art education, who were unemployed or employed as commercial and freelance artists and private and public school art teachers. All respondents were self-designated artists.[2]

Only those respondents (N=6) whose professional artistic status was like that of most[3] male St. Louis artists—female art-faculty members having MFA degrees—could be considered "marginal men" in Hughes's sense. The other five types of female artists represented in the sample had varying and nonpreferred occupational statuses, as well as deviant sex status. Each type lacked one or more of the determinants of artistic status and faced special career contingencies and status dilemmas as a result.

After describing the rules for determining artistic status, I will discuss the differences in artistic status among four types of female St. Louis artists and the particular career contingencies and status dilemmas of each type.

ART AND ARTISTS

Individuals are accorded artistic status in art worlds—ongoing, multi-situated social acts in which collective activity is organized and mediated by changing artistic conventions. The social objects of art worlds are art.

In George Herbert Mead's original sense, things are converted to objects through acts. A tomato (a thing) becomes nutrition (an object) by being *treated* as that object (eaten) [G. McCall and Simmons (19)]. Rectangles of canvas which have been stretched over wooden frames and painted on (things) become art (social object) by being *treated* as art in art worlds (social acts).

Treating things as art requires more or less complicated divisions of labor [M. McCall (20)]. To be art, a thing must look like art; lend itself to being discussed as art; be presented as art by and to persons who will regard it as art, and in places where art is presented; and be bought and sold in the way that art is, by persons who buy and sell art [Levine (17), Christopherson (5)]. The division of labor, or shape of particular art worlds differs through time and space [M. McCall (20)]. In art markets like the dominant New York City art world and its satellites in Chicago and Los Angeles, art is sold by dealers, exhibited in commercial dealers' galleries and museums, purchased by museums and collectors, and discussed by critics and art historians [Levine (17), Christopherson (5), Plagens (23)]. These activities may be allocated to other individuals and collectivities in nonmarket art worlds, as indeed they are in St. Louis [M. McCall (20)].

Artists are those members of art worlds who make art. Not only do artists produce the things that are converted to art; each artist is ultimately responsible for making sure that his things are treated as art. To be an artist, the individual must produce a thing that is capable of being treated as art, and he must protect his art by deciding how and by whom it shall be handled. In Becker's terms, individuals achieve artistic status for themselves and art status for their things by successfully manipulating current conventions of artmaking and presentation [Becker (2)]. Disagreements arise when other individuals and collectivities in an art world are unwilling to treat the artist's things as the kind of social object he intends them to be. These other individuals and collectivities are willing to treat the artist's things as art if they consider him "serious" and "dedicated."

THE DETERMINANTS OF ARTISTIC STATUS

Seriousness is the most important determinant of artistic status. An artist is considered "serious" if he intends that the things he makes shall be considered Art. The artist signals his intent by conforming to current artistic conventions, that is, by making things that look as art is expected to look and by presenting them in the way that art is presented. If it is apparent to others in the art world that the individual makes things to express his unique artistic vision, and that he expects his things to be treated as art, then he is taken seriously as an artist, no matter how bizarre the things he makes appear to people outside the art world. If this is not apparent, the things cannot be considered art, and the individual who makes them is not taken seriously as an artist.

Talent and skill would seem to be basic determinants of artistic status, but in fine-art worlds[4] the ability to render is a determining characteristic only insofar as it is necessary to the artist's purpose, which is to make art. If artistic talents and skills are used for other purposes—decoration or self-expression, for example, or if they are unnecessary to the artist's particular purpose—abstraction, for example, then they are irrelevant as determinants of artistic status. When they discuss one another as artists and express judgments of one another's work, artists seldom speak of how "good" the work is, or how "talented" the individual; rather, they speak of seriousness and dedication. One female St. Louis respondent, a young MFA with a faculty position, summarized the rules for determining artistic status.

> I wouldn't say how good a piece of work is or what is better—if it's serious. If it's dilettante work, it's bad work. But if it's serious, then I could only say whether I liked it and whether it's in vogue now. Maybe how well it's done, technically. But even that has to do with what the painter is trying to do—if he is trying to do a realistic piece of work and can't draw a hand, then it's a bad painting. But if he is doing something impressionistic, it doesn't matter if the faces look like a kid drew them.

The second determinant of artistic status is "dedication," which refers to an individual's willingness to keep producing things about which he is serious as the primary life activity. Dedication implies a commitment to continued productivity. Further, it implies a determination to continue making art even in the absence of recognition, which might make art work self-supporting, and even when art work can only be done in spare time. Griff (11) described the situation faced by beginning male artists, and explained why so few are "dedicated."

> As the student nears the end of his academic training he becomes anxious over what he will do when he graduates. . . . Eventually . . . each must find a source of steady

income. Some will find work in the post office or in stores and will paint in the evenings or on weekends. A prolonged seige of this work is disheartening, especially when the individual realizes that he may have to do this for many years—that is, until he is recognized—or that he may have to work at whatever he is doing for the rest of his life. In the end, most return to art in secondary ways—some as art educators and many as commercial artists (p. 153).

Artistic status is not determined by professional training or degree certification, since neither is required. Artists are trained in professional schools, in universities and colleges, in private classes, as apprentices, or not at all. The romantic belief in "untutored genius" is still prevalent [Nochlin (22)], and many artists and art educators do not believe that art can or should be taught [Kelly (16)]. Others agree that formal training may be valuable, while denying that it is necessary [Holden (14)]. Colleges and universities and most professional art schools offer degrees, but degrees are optional in some art schools, and a few prestigious art schools do not grant degrees at all [Holden (14, p. 268)].

Both the Bachelor of Fine Arts and the Master of Fine Arts degrees are considered professional degrees since they are awarded only to fine arts studio majors; art education and art history majors may earn BA, MA, and Ph.D. degrees. The MFA is the highest degree awarded to fine arts studio majors, and the requirement for most art faculty positions [Hausman and Ryan (13)].

Although neither determines artistic status, both degrees are credentials which help establish the individual's claims to seriousness and dedication. Indeed, individuals trained as artists are serious almost by definition; they have learned to make things that look like art and to treat the things they make as art is treated. In art school, students are socialized in the conventions of art making and presentation—formally, in art history courses, and informally, by watching them applied and used [Strauss (27), Griff (10, 11)]. The BFA is evidence of seriousness. The advanced degree is presumptive evidence of dedication as well, simply because degrees are not required of individuals who make art.

Artistic status is not determined by employment, either. Unlike individuals who are lawyers because they practice law or those who are secretaries or sales clerks because they are employed as secretaries or sales clerks, individuals needn't have art jobs to be artists. The ideal is a kind of self-employment in which the artist earns a living selling the art he makes, but very few artists attain this ideal; [Griff (10) estimated that only about a dozen artists in this country supported themselves in this way according to your conventions, most have other jobs].

Art faculty positions are not required for the attainment of artistic status, but they are important credentials nevertheless. Employment on an art school faculty presumes seriousness and implies dedication, too, since it means earning a living as an artist, if not earning a living making and selling art. In St. Louis, MFA degrees and art faculty positions were especially important credentials, since the St. Louis art world is a marginal art market, primarily organized around art schools and their faculties [M. McCall (20)].

THE STATUS OF FEMALE ARTISTS

Female visual artists are not expected to be serious and dedicated, simply because they are not men. A dedicated artist intends to make art for a living, or failing that, not to let earning a living interfere with making art. Males are expected to earn a living in our society; females are not. Women are rewarded for "ladylike accomplishment" in the arts [Nochlin (22)]. Females are allowed to have "artistic hobbies," and are not expected to have "serious" intentions, because they lack male sex status. Even serious women are considered less dedicated if they rely on a husband's financial support.

For men, art work requires sacrifices: a willingness to forgo the ordinary economic and status rewards of work, and the risk of being treated as deviant. No man, it is assumed, would seek artistic status unless he *were* serious and dedicated.

The artistic status of women, and the degree of their marginality, depends on *whether* they are serious and dedicated, and whether their credentials, their things, and their decisions about how their things shall be treated reflect seriousness and dedication. Among the six types of female visual artists in St. Louis[5] were four types representing various combinations of seriousness, dedication, and credentials: BFA mothers who were serious but not dedicated; semi-picture painters, who were dedicated but not serious; nonfaculty MFA's, who were serious and dedicated, but lacked the credential of faculty employment; and MFA faculty members, who were both serious and dedicated and to whom artistic status was accorded by women of all the other types.

TYPE I: BFA MOTHERS—SERIOUS BUT NOT DEDICATED (N=6)

Female BFA's are not expected to be dedicated. They are expected to use the skills they acquire in art school for self-expression or to encourage self-expression in their children; and to use the "serious" art standards and conventions they learn to enhance the "cultural" life of their families, and, perhaps eventually, to collect art.

Female BFA's can prove their dedication by going to graduate school or by going to New York to "paint and starve." The women in this group had proved their own lack of dedication by getting married, having children, and becoming unproductive. As students, these women learned that a choice between art and motherhood was expected of them. However, they all believed they could have avoided that choice if others in the art world had not perceived their marriages and pregnancies as choices already made. In other words, these women felt they had not given up art so much as they had been given up on. For example, one BFA mother said:

> I remember having a lot of free-floating anxiety while I was in school, knowing I could never be a painter because I could never live like Picasso. I still thought I could do both, though. I can still remember having the distinct feeling that I was being marked off the list when I got pregnant—that my old teachers were simply marking me off the list—that I no longer counted. I think they forgave me my first child, but when I was pregnant with the second, that was when I felt them marking me off. I would run into this one teacher that I dearly loved and he would never ask me what (painting) I was doing. He'd only ask "How's the family?" I'd try to tell him about what (work) I was doing, but he would refuse to comment. He wouldn't even answer when I asked if he'd like to see my work and comment on it, and he wouldn't say whether he thought I should go to graduate school.

Although these women had not continued to produce art work and did not consider themselves professional artists, they were serious. They knew and conformed to the standards and conventions of the art world when they did art work, but making things was neither a full-time activity nor fully work.

For almost three years, the six BFA mothers had been members of a drawing group that met once a week. Both the kind of work they did and the infrequency with which they did it are indicative of their lack of professional artistic status. Drawing is not considered real art work but, rather, preparation for art work. No art school offers a major in drawing, for example, even though drawing is an important part of art school curricula [Holden (14)]. Drawings are considered preliminary drafts or visual records of ideas. Once famous as a painter or sculptor, an individual's drawings are treated as art, but few artists specialize in drawing. Indeed, there is no noun formed from the verb to draw; artists call themselves painters, weavers, sculptors, and so on, but no one can call himself a "drawer."

Drawing, or perhaps more accurately, sketching, is a hobby activity for many nonartists. Other St. Louis female artists did not consider the BFA mothers to be "hobbyists," however. More often they were referred to as "amateurs" or "amateurs with some professional training." The term "hobbyist" was usually applied to women who were neither serious nor dedicated. One MFA faculty member called these women "essentially students," and one female informant, a recent BFA who had drawn with the group, suggested the same thing in describing her experiences:

> I love the drawing group. It's like they're teaching themselves and each other. Like, last time, we were working with this male model. (One woman) said she loved Greek sculpture and then they asked him to assume a "Greek sculpture pose" and then to keep shifting his feet so they could see what happened to his body, you know? It was like something you'd get in school only better, because it grew out of the group. It wasn't something imposed by *a* teacher.

Drawing is often a side-involvement[6] of art students, as it sometimes was for these women at meetings of a female artists' organization they belonged to. One female nonfaculty MFA said:

> I went to an art high school and that was what we did then. We'd have a party and then we'd all just sit around sketching each other. I think of it as a very "high school" thing to do, but I suppose it's a stage everyone goes through. I just happened to go through it in high school.

Since producing art things was a side-involvement in their lives, it is not surprising that BFA mothers produced drawings when they did work. Drawing is serious work and dedicated artists do this when they cannot be fully involved in making art. One BFA mother explained that "You can draw even when you can't paint." It requires less time to finish a drawing and less equipment and space, makes less mess, and requires less concentration. Female artists of all types reported that they could draw when their children were young, even if they couldn't paint. One MFA painter did a series of drawings one summer when her children were home from school all day. However, these were finished drawings and she treated them as art. The BFA mothers treated their drawings as student work.

Drawings are finished products and not rehearsals when they are framed, signed and dated, and hung on the wall (Howard S. Becker, unpublished). BFA mothers did not frame their drawings or hang them on the walls in their homes. At one drawing group meeting I attended, they discussed the necessity of dating their work, but they admitted to one another that they seldom did that. A female informant of this type described another way of announcing seriousness: starting each drawing on a clean sheet of good paper.

> My husband always made me buy more and better supplies than I was willing to admit I needed. I wasn't willing to define myself as being that serious, I guess. And he would always tell me to draw on a clean piece of paper so that if it was good, I'd really have something.

The BFA mothers drew on newsprint or student sketch pads. However, one woman kept a few sheets of expensive, watermarked paper to use for long model poses or when she "felt a good one coming on."

The BFA mothers saw themselves and one another as others saw them—as students ready to become dedicated as well as serious. One said:

> Being a professional artist, which is what I'm trying to be now, means working every day on your art. Even if it's only a short time every day or even if it's only thinking about what you will do the next day you have time to work. I've been just working once a week, drawing with the group. But full time work is something more than regular once-a-week work. It's a different attitude than working when you feel like it or when you have time. The real trouble with the drawing group—at least for me—is that . . . we've really come a long way with it, doing it once a week. We've polished up old skills and gotten the feeling that we *can* work, after all. And we've gotten our sense of ourselves as artists back. But it can't go further, at least for me, just doing it once a week. I find that I'm getting good ideas, ideas that I want to develop. But I can't, just working once a week.

Position in the Art Enterprise: Status Dilemmas

Some of these women were natives of St. Louis; others had been permanent residents since they graduated from art school there. They had contacts in the St. Louis art world that amateurs and students would not ordinarily have, and so their position in the St. Louis art world was better than their lack of dedication would indicate. In one case they made use of a local contact to arrange a group exhibition of their drawings in a gallery whose averaged prestige rating by twenty respondents was "very good."[7] This was the first exhibition for these women, and it is unusual for artists without credentials to have a first show in so prestigious a place. Indeed, artists do not expect to have shows at all until they have produced a body of serious work—that is, unless they are dedicated [Chamberlain (4)].

These women faced various difficulties in gathering the resources necessary to making serious and dedicated art because they had not yet achieved artistic status by proving their seriousness and dedication. One BFA mother explained the difficulty in getting art supplies:

> Yes, it's a problem getting supplies. You can't work if you have to worry about spending money for supplies. But I can't get a discount at the art stores. You have to be either a faculty member or a professional artist—one who has exhibited. I complained to the manager of one store, but that's their policy.

BFA mothers also had difficulty providing themselves with time and space in which to work. All respondents agreed that professional art work requires its own, separate space, but finding room to begin working, in homes where the space was already assigned to other ongoing activities, was problematic.

The most difficult to provide resource, in St. Louis, for these women, was an art "scene." One BFA mother said:

> There is no scene here. There's nowhere to go and just hang out with other artists—to talk about work. Of course, the poets hang out at (place). But how can I get a babysit-ter just to hang out?

A "scene"—exhibitions of contemporary art in museums and galleries, new ideas, and other artists to talk to—are crucial for serious artists, as Geldzahler (8) pointed out in describing the New York City art world, ". . . the true school for the young artist, once he has gained the confi-dence and passionate certainty to know that he wants to be a painter or sculptor, is the ferment and activity of the center, its multiplicity of styles and its complex traditions."

Their difficulty in finding a scene made it harder for BFA mothers to find their own artistic vision, the serious and dedicated expression of which is the prerequisite of professional artistic status. As one female informant said:

> When you get out (of school) you have all this knowledge but you really haven't found the statement you want to make. You flounder for a while. They always told us, when we were students, that you should do the work for its own sake, that the joy was in the doing. But you have to find your own statement before you can enjoy doing the work for its own sake. And that's a really hard thing to do. Even with all that training, and especially all that skill, you still have to flounder while you decide what it is you want to do.

Assessments of the St. Louis Art World

These women were most likely of all types of female artists to express negative assessments of the serious art world in St. Louis. Indeed, the striking differences between their negative expressions and the generally positive expressions of female MFA's first suggested to me the broader differences among types of female artists. All respondents and informants expressed negative assessments of the St. Louis Art Museum, but BFA mothers were especially critical. One said:

> It's the sticks. They don't even own a (work by a local male artist) and the Walker in Minneapolis has one. Their attitude is showing regional things of historical interest—

like Bingham—but not contemporary art and certainly not local art. And they don't have a big contemporary art collection.

Indeed, the BFA mothers' criticisms of St. Louis as a place to work centered on the Museum and its policy of infrequently exhibiting contemporary art. Perhaps their greater need to see the work of other artists, in order to find their own statements, explains their relatively more negative assessments.

TYPE II: SEMI-PICTURE PAINTERS—DEDICATED BUT NOT SERIOUS (N=5)

Female artists of this type intended to make art, but they were not taken seriously because they did not conform to the serious art world's conventions of artmaking and presentation. One woman was trained in an art school but chose not to conform to the conventions she had learned. The other four women had not learned the conventions of the art world in which they sought to achieve artistic status: two were trained in art education and two others had no formal training.

Although they did not use the term "dedicated," these women could be characterized in that way. They had not chosen between art work and motherhood; all five women had children, some of preschool age, but all five worked full-time at artmaking. One respondent, trained as an art teacher and the mother of two school-age children, said:

> I work everyday from nine in the morning, sometimes until five o'clock—even though the children come home at three. I feel awful if I don't work every day. It's like a compulsion. I even work on the weekends. Of course, if we have big plans on the weekend I don't work, but otherwise I do. I guess it's selfish, but I'd rather do my own work than teach.

Another woman explained that she had made an effort not to let motherhood and artmaking conflict.

> Actually I've worked more since my child was born than I did before. But since I had him so late, I felt that the only way to handle motherhood at all was to do my own work, too. So I've had a babysitting arrangement all along. I only work about twenty hours a week, but I'm very organized about it. While he's with the babysitter I don't do anything but work. Nothing interferes.

The semi-picture painters were also dedicated to showing and selling their work. Unlike BFA mothers, who felt they were not ready or not

interested in exhibiting, or MFA faculty members, whose positions locally were so secure that they were asked to exhibit, the semi-picture
painters actively looked for places to show. For example, one Type II
respondent had been co-owner of a gallery at one time; she said, "We
wanted a place to show our own work and it sounded like fun." Another
woman in this group told of visiting the same gallery owner again and
again until he agreed to show her work. "I had to beg him to take a few
things. Then they sold so fast he couldn't get enough."

Indeed, it might be said that these women were more dedicated to
"working the system" than any others. For example, one known but
seldom used tactic for getting work into a musueum collection is to donate
it. In her book, *The Artist's Guide to His Market,* Betty Chamberlain (4)
recommended the practice, pointing out that museums are less exclusive
when they aren't asked to pay for art. One woman in this group had
donated work to the St. Louis Art Museum. She said:

> I just figured that was the only way I'd get into the museum. I mean, I just went around
> telling everyone that I was going to be in the museum and that the only way *my* work
> would ever be in a museum was to give it away.

In his analysis of career timetables, Roth (25) showed how TB patients
worked the system by demanding timetables; patients tried to chart their
own recovery progress by questioning other patients and then using the
progress of others as benchmarks to measure their own. Although I expected that artists consciously compared their own career progress to that
of others, the only respondent who reported similar behavior was one
semi-picture painter. She said:

> I know this sounds awful but I decided to ask for a show at (gallery where she shows
> regularly) because I knew so-and-so had asked for a show there and got it and my work
> is better than his. I also talked to (another dealer) once about having a show there
> because I knew he was looking at (another artist's) work and she's nothing but an
> amateur.

Some other St. Louis female artists were equally dedicated to exhibiting their work—notably the nonfaculty MFA's—but there was an important difference, which pointed up the semi-picture painter's lack of seriousness. Serious artists, in managing the treatment of their things, decide
what they can do *for* the work; nonserious artists try to decide what they
can do *with* the work. The difference is between the reverence accorded
to a semi-sacred Art object and the matter-of-factness displayed by
businessmen selling products.

The semi-picture painters also differed from the three types of serious female artists in the way they sold their work. Serious artists are as careful about what they sell and to whom as they are about what they exhibit, and where; no work is sold if it would devalue the other things the artist produces. One MFA faculty member recounted her experiences selling work as an undergraduate student.

> When I was a junior I needed some money so I bundled up some of my drawings and went to New York. I'd leave one here and sell one there (at different galleries). First of all, I know I was ripped off on the ones I sold to dealers because I don't even know how much they sold for and I probably didn't get as much as I should have. But I *really* regret it because those things were very decorative and now they're out there with my name on them. People told me I would regret it, not to do it, but I went ahead and sold them.

Conversely, art objects are not exhibited under conditions which might affect their (sale) value. The local dealer of one female MFA said:

> The painting I was going to enter in (the regional competition) was sold and so I'm going to send another. That one was going to a good collection locally and the terms of the sale were that it would be delivered in the same condition it was in when they bought it. I didn't want to risk anything happening to it in the mail or at the show, and have (the artist) lose a sale. So I'm sending the (another) painting instead.

Semi-picture painters' decisions about where to show were influenced by their interest in selling, as well, but in slightly different ways. For example, these women might exhibit in a place they considered far from ideal, if it was a promising place to sell art work. One respondent of this type described a decision she made not to exhibit.

> They asked me to have a show at the Medical Center. I went to look at the space and I decided not to. Maybe it was a mistake not to and maybe I was wrong, but it was dark and the gallery was right outside the Coffee Shop and I didn't want my things to hang there. I understand it's a good place to sell and lots of people would see the work who might not otherwise see it. But they take a 20–30 percent commission and that would be one thing if it were a good space, and it would be another if the space was bad but it was a free show. But here it would cost me money and it wasn't a good space. So I said no.

Furthermore, unlike the serious artists who considered everything they exhibited or sold to be equally valuable (and if a painting wasn't "quite right yet" it was not exhibited or sold until it was right), Type II women were willing to match the quality of individual pieces of their work to the prestige of the place where it was sold and exhibited. One woman said:

> I have to decide what to do with each of my things. Some things will sell well at the (art) fairs and others I take there even though I know they won't sell all too well. Others are better for my one-man shows—the far-out stuff you'd have to sell to collectors rather than to people who just want to decorate their living rooms.

Their interest in the decorative quality—the prettiness of the things they made, was one thing that set the semi-picture painters off from serious artists. According to current conventions of artmaking, art exists for no other reason than to express the unique vision of the artist, to make a statement; things made for other purposes cannot be converted to art [Wolfe (31)]. Therefore, things made to be decorative—and by extension, decorative things—cannot be serious art, and the persons who make them cannot be serious artists. Most of the semi-picture painters did not conform to this convention because they did not know of it. One woman described the way her work changed as she learned the conventions of the serious art world.

> That was when I really made the breakthrough, when I really found my statement. I was always serious about my work, but I was trying to do things I didn't know how to do.

Another woman, a BFA mother, spoke of the change in the same woman's work.

> An artist uses color to create an illusion. That was what happened to (her). Her new work is fantastic because she does use color to create an illusion. In her earlier work, she just did design and it was not interesting, merely pretty. She thought she was doing something abstract and creating an illusion, but she wasn't.

One semi-picture painter defended her own work as being "simply not in the mainstream of avant-garde art." Another said she wanted to "make pretty things as well as making a statement, although I know you're supposed to want your things to be ugly."

Although the decorative qualities of their things signaled their lack of seriousness to others in the art world, it was their failure to conform to the conventions of presentation which really separated these women from serious artists. Art history contains examples of Art which expresses a "decorative vision"; one is the work of Matisse. But things that are not treated as art cannot be converted to art. Some differences in presentation practices between the semi-picture painters and other types of female artists have aleady been discussed. Perhaps the most striking difference has not been mentioned: every woman of this type had exhibited and sold work at local art fairs; no women of the three serious types said that she would even consider showing or selling work at an art fair.

For many reasons, art fairs are defined as unsuitable surroundings for art objects. Art fairs are outdoors and art must at all times be protected from the elements. The carnival atmosphere is not sufficiently serious. There is not enough space for properly serious presentation, and in any case, a semi-sacred Art object does not belong on a snowfence. Customers browse at art fairs instead of giving each thing proper attention. Buyers are seeking decorations for their homes rather than art for their collections. Sales are often anonymous and artists do not know where their objects will be housed. The conditions and terms of sale are not sufficiently restrained and discreet—folding chairs, cardtables and cashboxes cannot replace proper lighting, white-painted walls, and large checks; and the appearance (if not the reality) of mutual protection of interests lent by four solid walls and a permanent address is missing when everyone knows these tents will be folded and taken away in two days.

The semi-picture painters had also exhibited their work in movie theatres, hospitals, synagogues, and shopping centers. All of these were considered places not to exhibit art by the three types of serious female artists in St. Louis. For their part, the semi-picture painters were not convinced that the serious artists' standards and conventions of presentation were valid. One said:

> Some of the women (I know) are such
> snobs about where they will show. They
> would never show at a bank. They would
> never show at a shopping center. In
> fact, they would never show *most* places.

Assessment by Others

A further reason for shunning art fairs, according to serious St. Louis artists, was that they were sponsored and directed by local art associations. The individuals who belonged to these groups—and all the semi-picture painters belonged or had belonged—were labeled "Sunday painters," "Little Old Ladies," "hobbyists," and "sidewalk painters," and their work was often called "schlock." In short, serious artists did not take art association members or their work seriously. Neither was the St.

Louis Artists' Guild taken seriously, and the juried exhibitions it sponsored where shunned like art fairs. All of the semi-picture painters were also members or planned to become members of the Artists' Guild; all of them had exhibited work in the Guild's juried exhibitions.

Mobility

Although they retained ties to the art associations and the Artists' Guild, the semi-picture painters were upwardly mobile in the sense that they also belonged to the Community of Women Artists, a membership organization for serious female artists. The following remarks, by an MFA faculty member, explain how these nonserious artists were recruited into a serious artists' group.

> As part of the community service that the [art school] expects, I've gone to the meetings of these art associations and demonstrated [techniques]. The people in these groups are essentially Sunday painters. And some of them are very happy with their hobbies. Others start out as hobbyists and they join the art associations—its easy to find out about them because they are listed in the newspapers—and then they get pretty good and hear about other kinds of work, they quit the art associations and join CWA. They like to be around us. They feel they are stimulated by us and they are learning something. That's why they like to be in CWA, I'm sure.

Indeed, upward mobility in the serious art world is possible—for things, if not for people. Once things are treated as art, the possibility exists that they will be converted to art. In cities as small as St. Louis, the resources of artmaking, sometimes including personnel, are shared by the serious art world and others [M. McCall (20)]. Members of art school faculties sometimes juried the Art Guild's exhibitions; and the newspaper art critics sometimes awarded prizes at art fairs. Some dealers and gallery directors made a practice of "scouting" the art fairs for "new talent." One semi-picture painter was "discovered" at an art fair by the director of an important art gallery. She was given a show in the gallery and her things were art, at least for the duration of the exhibition. The possibility existed that they would continue to be treated as art, i.e., shown in places where art was exhibited, reviewed by the critics who talked about art, and purchased by art collectors. Two other semi-picture painters had begun to exhibit in places whose average prestige rating was "good" or "very good," but for the most part these women exhibited in places whose average respondent ratings were so low that they could be characterized as "professionally irrelevant" or "damaging."

Self-Assessments and Assessments of St. Louis

These dedicated but nonserious female artists did not refer to themselves as "hobbyists," "Sunday painters" or "schlock" artists. They considered themselves professional artists. The credentials they offered to support their claims differed, depending upon their formal training. The three women who had art degrees (although two were BA's in art education) pointed out that they were trained artists. These three and the other two without formal training defined "professional artists" as individuals who work full-time at making art and who exhibit their art work. And, on these criteria, they qualified as professionals.

On the whole, these women made the most positive statements about St. Louis, among all types of St. Louis female artists. One mentioned the St. Louis Art Museum's indifferent response to local artists, but another talked about what a good "little" museum it was. Perhaps their lack of experience in other local art worlds—none had worked regularly in any other city, and their meager knowledge about serious art worlds—none read the national art magazines, for example—made comparison difficult for them. Indeed, from their perspective there was no cause for complaint: they worked full-time at artmaking, they exhibited regularly in places they considered satisfactory, their works sold well, they did not need to see other serious contemporary work, and they were not looking for professional dealers.

TYPE III: NONFACULTY MFA'S—SERIOUS AND DEDICATED, BUT ISOLATED (N=5)

Although these women were both serious and dedicated, and had prestigious MFA degree credentials, they lacked the credential indicative of full artistic status in the St. Louis art world—faculty employment. Without it, they faced isolation, skepticism on the part of others in the art world regarding their dedication, and greater difficulty in arranging treatment as art for their things.

All three types of serious female artists felt isolated, to some extent, and all believed that their isolation, as women, was greater than that of male artists. One nonfaculty MFA made the following typical remarks:

> Of course art is an isolated occupation anyway. But I think its harder for women. Artists work alone, but they have to have contacts, and I think its harder for women to make contacts.

Female art faculty members reported isolation from male colleagues much like that of other academic women [Bernard (3), Epstein (7), Cole and Cole (6)], and St. Louis' marginal position nationally [M. McCall (20)] resulted in greater isolation for both male and female St. Louis artists. However, nonfaculty MFA's and BFA mothers lacked the routinized contacts with other local artists (however unsatisfactory) and nonlocal artists, that the art schools provided for faculty and students. Furthermore, for faculty and students, the art schools were the locale of the St. Louis art world. As one BFA mother said, when I asked how an artist would "get in" to the St. Louis art world:

> If you were a man, you'd be in, because you'd have a job [faculty position]. A woman could join the museum, join already existing groups or start one, get a dealer or gallery to show her stuff, or do the social thing—make friends.

Another possibility was to seek affiliation with an art school. Two women had established local contacts while they earned MFA's at a local art school. One said:

> Getting the MFA was a good way to meet people. And it got me working everyday from nine until three instead of from noon to three, which is what I had done before.

The other woman with a local MFA degree said:

> It's easy to become isolated here if you don't teach. But you can meet people if you just make an effort. Fortunately, I made a lot of friends during graduate school. They let me know whenever there's a lecture I should go to and I always hire their graduate students as assistants when I need help with (the technical aspects of) my work.

One woman made local contacts through her husband who was an art faculty member. The other two had applied for art faculty positions, but most of their local contacts were provided by membership in the Community of Women Artists. One said:

> Now that the women's group is viable (CWA), women artists coming into St. Louis can hook into that. I'd never tried to join an art scene before we moved here and I didn't know how. But the first thing that happened to me was that I ran into a friend from New York who had a friend who was organizing this women's group and she put my name on the list. And that was the way I got into the scene—entirely through the women's group. I even met my dealer that way, because she was a member, too, at first. Without CWA I would probably still be painting in the closet.

And the other woman said:

> I owe them so much. I got so much out of that group. I met people and it helped raise
> my consciousness. I don't need it so much now, but I support it because it helped me
> so much.

All five nonfaculty MFA's worked at artmaking full-time; indeed, without the demands of teaching and faculty committee work, and without the knowledge that even if they didn't produce art every day, they would still be artists because they were employed as artists, nonfaculty MFA's probably spent more time making art than MFA faculty members did. The two women with preschool children hired babysitters and housekeepers so that they could work every day. In short, Type III artists were dedicated, but their dedication was sometimes questioned by other serious artists because they were not earning their livings as art faculty members and so their dedication was not made public. One MFA faculty member stated the problem faced by Type III female artists, in explaining why one nonfaculty MFA left St. Louis to take a teaching job.

> She's married to a *very* rich man who's only too happy to support her "hobby". But
> she wants to be self-supporting—or at least to support her artwork. She says she won't
> feel grownup until she does. You have to have your head really straight to be able to do
> serious work if you aren't self-supporting.

Selling art is a solution to this problem. It not only provides an income, it proves to self and others that art work is an occupation, and not an avocation. With one exception, the nonfaculty MFA's were the serious female artists most interested in selling work. The BFA mothers were pleased with an occasional sale to friends. One said:

> It isn't possible to support yourself selling art in St. Louis. But I would like to sell some
> things. Just as a kind of proof that I'm an artist. So I could say I earned something
> when my husband teases me. I didn't used to want to sell anything, but now that I have
> a body of drawings, I could imagine selling some. Maybe one or two. For ten dollars or
> so. I'd like to see them in other people's homes.

The female faculty members were interested in exhibiting their work, but they didn't expect to sell it in St. Louis, and were willing to have it handled by dealers who didn't "sell." One said, "My St. Louis dealer isn't a real dealer in the way my Chicago dealer is—a dealer in the New York sense. He doesn't 'deal.' I've never sold anything through him."

This woman had an arrangement with the dealer for ten years and seemed perfectly happy to continue with it. Another MFA faculty member said: "Selling is nice, but I care more about having a dealer than having him sell. Anyway, my dealer doesn't sell that many of my things."

Two other female faculty members also said they had never sold work through St. Louis dealers; one was a member of a cooperative gallery and the other two did not have dealers.

The four nonfaculty MFA's, on the other hand, chose dealers who would sell their work; indeed, two were handled by private dealers without galleries, who only sold and did not exhibit the work. The other nonfaculty MFA with a dealer said:

> I don't know if she'll actually give me a show, but she took some of my things to sell. That's why you need a dealer. I certainly couldn't *sell* anything. And its much easier and nicer to have (my dealer) do the selling and handling. All I have to do is deliver the work and she does all the rest. And she is doing a good job of selling my things.

Two nonfaculty MFA's with private dealers sold regularly; one sold enough to support herself. For these women, selling work was an ongoing concern. One said:

> My dealer has been much more attentive lately, now that the things are really moving. I can make as much money selling art these days as I could [working]. I think I'm ready to explore the New York market now. That's where the big collectors are. In St. Louis it's very circular and dead-end. You just sell one painting to each person in a small circle of people who know your work. To get into the big collector's thing—selling work to people who collect it—for that, you have to have a New York dealer.

Along with the lack of public recognition of their dedication, nonfaculty MFA's had greater difficulty arranging to have their work treated as art by others in the St. Louis art world. Without public credentials, they were at a disadvantage in negotiating serious treatment for their things. If the prestige of places they had exhibited in can be considered a measure, faculty artists had been somewhat more successful than nonfaculty MFA's. Table I shows the numbers of female MFA faculty members and nonfaculty MFA's who had ever exhibited in each of the galleries with average respondent ratings of "excellent" or "very good." In general, more faculty members had exhibited in prestigious places, and the only respondents who had exhibited in the most prestigious places were faculty members.

Both nonfaculty MFA's and MFA faculty members were aware that nonteachers had greater difficulty in showing work in serious places. One Type III woman said:

Table 1. Number of Faculty and Nonfaculty Respondents Exhibiting in or Handled by "Excellent" and "Very Good" Galleries

Places	Faculty	Nonfaculty
"Excellent"		
Art Museum Invitational Exhibitions	1	—
Loretto-Hilton	2	—
Mid-America Show	2	2
Steinberg Hall	3	2
Bobbie Okun Gallery	—	1
"Very Good"		
Terry Moore Gallery	2	1
Martin Schweig Gallery	1	—
Emclen Gallery	3	—
Nancy Singer Gallery	1	1
Meremac Community College	1	1
Florissant Valley Community College	2	—
Mark Twain South County Bank	3	1

Ideally, artists shouldn't have to teach. They should be able to support themselves selling work if they're any good. But practically, the only way to get shown and known in St. Louis is to be on a faculty. If you asked anyone—if I asked you—to name five St. Louis artists, they'd all be on faculties and mostly men. But then most artists on faculties here *are* men.

And one female faculty member said:

You *have* to have a faculty job in St. Louis in order to be serious. That's not true in New York—there, you could get a job as a secretary at the Met or a maid to Claes Oldenburg or a garbage person. But here you have to be on a faculty. Otherwise, there's not enough of a scene.

The same woman went on to say, of one nonfaculty MFA: "She does really good work and she's not unserious. She was lucky, though, that she rose above not having a [faculty] job. She got recognized in spite of it."

The nonfaculty MFA's had, for the most part, overcome their lack of public credentials. Certainly those women had been more successful than any other category of female St. Louis artists, except faculty members. One way they saw to it that their things were taken seriously, despite their lack of faculty credentials, was by upholding conventions of presentation that were more serious than local standards demanded. An interesting example of this was the attitude of nonfaculty MFA's toward showing at "the bank." Banks usually rank with public libraries and churches as places for exhibiting work—i.e., they rank low. In St. Louis, however, one bank was considered a very prestigious place to exhibit serious art. One faculty member said:

This man has really been a local patron. He's bought a lot of local work, including mine. Ordinarily you don't show at banks—unless its his bank. The sequence of places to show in St. Louis is: first the colleges, then his bank, then the Loretto-Hilton, and then the Museum. The *big* step is when you go from colleges to his bank.

Three of the five respondents with faculty positions had shown at this bank and none of the five had refused to exhibit work there. Only one nonfaculty MFA, a woman who went to graduate school locally and retained close work and social ties with several faculty members, had shown at the bank. The other nonfaculty MFA's said they would not consider showing there because serious work is never shown at banks; two nonfaculty MFA's had refused invitations to exhibit at the bank.

Artistic Status and Assessments of St. Louis

The female artists in this category, with one exception, were very positive in their assessments of the St. Louis art world. These women traveled to New York regularly to visit galleries and museums, but they had no quarrel with St. Louis Art Museum or with local dealers; they were simply aware that the bigger museums, collections, and dealers were in New York. They liked St. Louis because they had worked productively there. St. Louis was considered a nice place to live and work, even though New York was the place to exhibit and sell.

These women were aware of their marginal position, and spoke of the negative label sometimes applied to them by faculty artists—"suburban housewife." However, they considered themselves dedicated, serious artists, as indeed they were by every criterion except faculty employment.

A DEVIANT CASE

The experiences of one other nonteaching MFA show the importance of local differences in conventions of presentation and the effects of failure to conform. This woman's work conformed to current artmaking standards and conventions, and she had prestigious credentials. But she exhibited regularly at the St. Louis Artists' Guild, a place where "Little Old Ladies" and "Sunday painters" exhibited work that was not taken seriously. As a result, this woman was not taken seriously by other serious female artists; indeed, she was called a "suburban housewife" by a semi-picture painter. She had come to St. Louis from another city where she had conformed to local conventions of presentation by exhibiting in the local Artists' Guild gallery; in that city she was taken seriously and was quite successful in achieving artistic status. The same decisions about where to show her work made artistic status nearly impossible for her in St. Louis.

TYPE IV: FACULTY MFA'S—SERIOUS AND DEDICATED (N=6)

Type IV female artists were the best known and most successful in St. Louis. These women had the best credentials, both graduate degrees and employment on art school faculties, and no respondent questioned their dedication or seriousness.

Of the six women in this category, only one had a discontinuous work history. The others had been employed on art school faculties continuously since leaving graduate school, except, in one case, for a short period as a commercial artist. Three of the six women had children, but none had stopped doing art work or teaching when their children were of preschool age. In short, these not only appeared to be, but were, dedicated women. They compared favorably with women in other professions, in their continuity of employment [Lopate (18), Astin (1), Epstein (7), Ginzberg et al. (9)]. Furthermore, their work histories were not unlike typical male work histories in art. Art school teaching has not required a career commitment from artists; part-time, intermittent teaching has been and still is more available to artists than to scientists, for example. An examination of the careers of forty-nine successful New York artists,[8] showed that whereas most—twenty-five—had been on art faculties at some time during their careers, only five had taught continuously.

St. Louis and Assessment of St. Louis

Because the St. Louis art world was not a major art market, but centered around the art schools, it was easier for women on art faculties, than for other female artists, to exhibit work. One said:

> In some cities you have to have a dealer but in St. Louis it isn't necessary. People's work can be seen in important shows at [art school] galleries and in the faculty shows. So they can be seen without local dealers. In some cities the art-buying public circulates around the dealers, but not here. In St. Louis, the art-buying public can go to the universities to find work.

Two of the five most prestigious places to show art work in St. Louis (average ratings of one, by twenty respondents) were galleries on campuses which had art schools. The women on those faculties were thus assured of showing in prestigious places once a year, in the annual exhibitions of faculty work.

Furthermore, it was not necessary for faculty artists to have dealers to sell work because they were not dependent upon sales for a livelihood. Nevertheless, three of the five Type IV women had local dealers. And, unlike all but one nonfaculty MFA, these women had asked dealers to handle their work, rather than waiting to be asked. One MFA faculty member explained how difficult it is for most artists to "go around to the dealers."

> The women who have told you they don't want to sell or don't want to exhibit seriously are afraid. That's a defense. It *is* awful to have to do that ego-risking thing of asking someone to show your work or handle it. But if you are serious, you do get tough.

Three of the six women had local dealers and dealers in other cities as well; one had only a local dealer, and two had no dealer.

For some of these women, especially the ones with out-of-town dealers or New York exhibitions, St. Louis was a nice place to live and work; they considered their jobs secure bases from which to seek further success nationally.

> I'll stay here because I have really good studio space and also because I have a job here. And neither of those would be so easy to find in New York. The rent is so high—$250–300 a month for studios I understand—and the cost of living. Unless you found a teaching job you'd have to work all the time at some job just to support yourself. And that wouldn't leave time to do much [art] work. Teaching jobs are really scarce right now.

Others felt that it was necessary to live in New York in order to "make it"; for these women, St. Louis, with its marginal art market, was not a good locale for artmaking.

> St. Louis artists don't cry over their colors. I do. And in New York they do. I really want to go to New York—I even went there and tried to rent loft space. But then I thought what an easy place St. Louis is to live in. Maybe if I got a good teaching job, I'd stay. Besides, I know who's who now. Like I know the [names collector] and I could never expect to know the Rockefellers or the Sculls like that. But [my professor] says it's hard to deal through the mail. So I don't know.

One especially well-known woman suggested St. Louis artists should organize to bring St. Louis art to national attention, instead of seeking individual success nationally, in the absence of a major local art market.

The men on (faculty) are elitists. They are too oriented to New York. They consider this a second rate place to be and they won't have anything to do with it. They won't exhibit locally or have much to do with other artists. They have no sense of community, except [one of the men]. It *is* a second-rate place to be but you still need an art community to work in. And we could have that even if the institutions—the museum and dealers and collectors—are second-rate. There are a few good things happening, like the Community of Women Artists. And something one of the men started, which was to ask people to come to his studio once a week to work. That's one thing St. Louis really needs—someplace where out-of-town dealers can go and see the work of several artists together.

Assessments by Others and Selves

Because all of these women shared the definitions of others in the art world, that professional artists are serious and dedicated, they defined themselves as professionals. And they were defined that way by all other categories of female artists. One serious female artist said of one female faculty member: "She is a professional by anyone's definition. She has an MFA and she's on a faculty. She exhibits locally and she has a dealer out of town. But I don't like her work." That this was said by a serious respondent about the work of another, who was nevertheless considered completely serious, dedicated and even professional, and that it was not said by any serious respondent about the work of any woman in the other two categories of serious female artists, points up the importance of credentials, seriousness, and dedication over judgments of worth in determining success in art worlds.

Marginality

Even though female artists employed on art school faculties were more successful than other serious female artists in St. Louis, women were marginal members of art faculties; they were a small minority of both full- and part-time members of the three largest St. Louis art faculties. Indeed, women were a slightly smaller minority of faculty members in St. Louis, where the art world was organized around art schools, than they were in a larger national sample that included artists working in art worlds organized as art markets. In a sample of 164 American college and university art departments, 79.5 percent of the full-time faculty was male and 20.5 percent female [White & White (29)]. Only 17 percent of the fulltime faculty members of the three largest St. Louis art schools were women; 83 percent were men (Table 2). Furthermore, many of these women taught fashion or interior design or commercial art, rather than fine art, and so were not considered artists by others in the local art world. Two of three female full-time members and all four of the female part-time members of the Washington University art faculty taught design. One of the four women on the Meremac Community College art faculty taught commer-

Table 2.   Percentages of Males and Females with Full-time and Part-time
            Faculty Positions at the Three Largest St. Louis Art Schools

	Washington University		Florissant Valley Community College		Meremac Community College	
Full-time	(percent)		(percent)		(percent)	
Male	89	(N = 24)	89	(N = 8)	67	(N = 8)
Female	11	(N = 3)	11	(N = 1)	33	(N = 4)
Total	100	(N = 27)	100	(N = 9)	100	(N = 12)
Part-time						
Male	67	(N = 8)	80	(N = 16)	100	(N = 10)
Female	33	(N = 4)	20	(N = 4)	0	(N = 0)
Total	100	(N = 12)	100	(N = 20)	100	(N = 10)

cial art. The only female with a fulltime art faculty position at Florissant Valley Community College taught studio courses.[9]

Sex differences in the academic rank of St. Louis art faculty members were also consistent with differences nationally. Four of ten instructors (40 percent) and two of four assistant professors (50 percent) on the Washington University faculty were women, but all of the six associate professors were men and only one of eleven full professors was a woman.[10] In the national sample of 164 art departments, 12 percent of full professors and 17.9 percent of associate professors were women; 22.5 percent of assistant professors and 30.2 percent of instructors were women [White and White (29)].

Female art faculty members had also been less successful than male faculty members in arranging exhibitions of their work in prestigious galleries and the local Museum. Six local artists had exhibited in two-person shows at the St. Louis Art Museum; in each show one exhibiting artist was male and one female. All three males who had exhibited were art faculty members, but only one of the three females was an art faculty member. In general, female St. Louis artists exhibited in one and two person gallery shows less often than men and in less prestigious galleries.

Although less isolated from male colleagues than were BFA mothers and nonfaculty MFA's, MFA faculty members nevertheless perceived their marginal status. Five of the six reported having to accept part-time or irregular faculty positions, several felt that they would have been members of more prestigious art faculties but for their sex status, and three reported instances of overt discrimination in the hiring practices of art schools. Their segregation in less prestigious specialties and the career contingencies they faced—lesser professional success and slower achievement of fulltime faculty status—were instances of their marginal

Table 3. Percentage of Male and Female Artists Exhibiting in
Twenty-One St. Louis Galleries

	Excellent Galleries		Very Good Galleries		Good Galleries		All Places	
	(percent)		(percent)		(percent)		(percent)	
Male	88	(N = 7)	76	(N = 29)	45	(N = 24)	62	(N = 60)
Female	12	(N = 1)	24	(N = 9)	55	(N = 29)	38	(N = 39)
Total	100	(N = 8)	100	(N = 38)	100	(N = 53)	100	(N = 99)

status. These women were "marginal men" in their profession, as Hughes defined that term, even though theirs was the most secure artistic status among all types of female St. Louis artists.

SUMMARY

The preceding comparisons of four types of St. Louis female artists demonstrate some ways that differences in seriousness and dedication affect females' success in achieving artistic status. Comparisons between three types of serious female artists—BFA mothers, nonfaculty MFA's, and MFA faculty members—and one type of nonserious female artists— semi-picture painters—demonstrate the effects of seriousness. Unless an artist conforms to the art world's current conventions of artmaking and presentation, she cannot be serious and she will not be taken seriously, no matter how dedicated she is. Without knowing, or conforming to, the conventions of presentation, the artist will not be able to arrange serious treatment for her things, and things not treated as art are not art. Likewise, an artist who does not know, or does not choose to conform to, current conventions of artmaking—especially the conventions which specify how art looks—is not taken seriously. Indeed, such an artist *is* not serious by definition; a serious artist intends to make art—i.e., to make things which *do* conform to current conventions of artmaking.

Comparisons among the three types of serious female artists demonstrate the importance of dedication and of credentials to achievement of artistic status. BFA mothers, who were serious but not dedicated, were not accorded artistic status by other serious female artists; at best, they were considered to be serious students. Acquiring the resources, including equipment and supplies, for artmaking was also problematic for these women. Finding and justifying the use of space and time resources in homes and lives already dedicated to other activities was especially difficult. Nor could they exhibit and sell work in order to acquire these resources, because their own lack of dedication meant that they did not have bodies of work to exhibit or sell. Even supplies were more expensive, since art-supply stores did not allow a professional discount to BFA mothers.

Although female MFA faculty members differed from nonfaculty MFA's only in having the credential of faculty status, they were more successful than nonfaculty MFA's in arranging serious treatment for their work and achieving artistic status for themselves. All categories of serious female artists accorded artistic status to MFA faculty members, but they did not always accord artistic status to BFA mothers and nonfaculty MFA's in return. In addition, acquiring colleagial resources was problematic for nonfaculty MFA's. They were isolated from male and female colleagues without the routinized contacts or the credential of faculty membership.

While a purely structural position would predict that female artists lack the auxiliary characteristics necessary for full occupational status in fine art worlds, the case study of thirty-four female artists in the St. Louis fine art world has shown that women were differentially successful in achieving artistic status. The interrelated processes of seriousness and dedication—commitments central to achievement in predominately male art worlds—when confirmed by conformance with the conventions of that world, mediate the structural effects of such auxiliary characteristics as sex itself. Persons failing to sustain, maintain, or succeed in defining themselves as serious, dedicated participants conforming to the normalized conventions of that world will differentially fail in their attempts to achieve artistic status. Accordingly, it is proposed that a thoroughly grounded sociology of art worlds and art objects must be concerned with the actual experiences, relationships, and definitions of those persons who are accorded or attempt to achieve the status of artist.

FOOTNOTES

1. I conducted field work from June 1974 through May 1975.

2. All were members or former members of the Community of Women Artists, a voluntary association.

3. Only one well-known male artist in St. Louis had never been an art faculty member.

4. Elsewhere I have discussed other visual art worlds with their own cultures and structures. Commercial art worlds and what I have called picture-painting art worlds may exist independently of, or symbiotically with, fine art worlds in various locales, as they did in St. Louis [M. McCall (20)].

5. I have not discussed two types of St. Louis female artists—Old Style (N=2) and Art as Self Expression (N=4) and two deviant cases here. They are discussed in M. McCall (20).

6. My usage here follows Goffman's, who defined a side-involvement as "an activity that an individual can carry on . . . without threatening or confusing simultaneous maintenance of a main involvement" [E. Goffman (9a), p. 43].

7. Twenty female respondents assigned prestige ratings to forty-three galleries and other exhibition spaces in St. Louis. A rating of 1 was high, and the lowest rating was 5; galleries unknown to a respondent were assigned ratings of 6. The ratings were averaged across respondents for each space. I labeled those spaces whose average rating was 1—1.99 "excellent"; those with average ratings of 2—2.99 "very good"; and those with average ratings of 3 to 3.99 "good." Spaces with average ratings of 4 to 4.99 were labeled "irrelevant," and those with average ratings of 5 or more, "damaging."

8. The work of these forty-three artists was chosen for an exhibition at the Metropolitan Museum of Art in New York City, entitled "American Paintings and Sculpture: 1940–1970" [Geldzahler (8)]. Career data were gathered from *Who's Who in American Art,* Jacques Cattel Press, 1973.

9. Data on the specialties of four female part-time members of that faculty are missing.

10. Data on the academic rank of artists on the two Junior College faculties are missing.

REFERENCES

1. Helen S. Astin, *The Woman Doctorate in America.* Russell Sage, New York, 1967.
2. Howard S. Becker, "Art as collective action," *American Sociological Review* 39 (December 1974): 767–776.
3. Jessie S. Bernard, *Academic Women.* Pennsylvania State University Press, University Park, Pa., 1964.
4. Betty Chamberlain, *The Artist's Guide to His Market.* Watson Guptill, New York, 1970.
5. Richard Christopherson, "Making Art with Machines: Photography's Institutional Inadequacies," *Urban Life and Culture* 3 (April 1974): 3–34.
6. Jonathan R. Cole and Stephen Cole, *Social Stratification in Science.* University of Chicago Press, 1973.
7. Cynthia Fuchs Epstein, *Woman's Place: Options and Limits in Professional Careers.* University of California Press, Berkeley, 1970.
8. Henry Geldzahler, *New York Painting and Sculpture: 1940–1970.* E. P. Dutton, New York, 1969.
9. Eli Ginzberg and Alice M. Yohalem, *Educated American Women: Self-portraits.* Columbia University Press, New York, 1966.
9a. E. Goffman, *Behavior in Public Places.* Free Press, New York, 1963.
10. Mason Griff, "The Recruitment of the Artist," pp. 63–94 in Robert N. Wilson (ed.), *The Arts in Society.* Prentice Hall, Englewood Cliffs, N.J., 1964.
11. ———, "The Recruitment and Socialization of Artists," pp. 145–158 in Milton C. Albrecht, James H. Barnett, and Mason Griff (eds.), *The Sociology of Art and Literature.* Praeger, New York, 1970.
12. Ann Sutherland Harris, "Women in College Art Departments and Museums," *Art Journal* 32 (Summer 1973): 417–419.
13. Jerome J. Hausman and Sister Joanne Ryan, "Degree Requirements for Art Faculty: Appointments, Promotion, Tenure," *Art Journal* 32 (Winter 1972): 179–181.
14. Donald Holden, *Art Career Guide.* Watson-Guptill, New York, 1973.
15. Everett C. Hughes, "Dilemmas and Contradictions of Status," pp. 141–150 in Everett C. Hughes (collected papers), *The Sociological Eye.* Aldine, Chicago, 1945.

16. Rob Roy Kelly, "Art in the American University: Fact or Facade?" *Art Journal* 32 (Winter 1972): 26–30.
17. Edward M. Levine, "Chicago's Art World: The Influence of Status Interests on Its Social and Distribution Systems," *Urban Life and Culture* 1 (October 1972): 293–323.
18. Carole Lopate, *Women in Medicine*. John Hopkins Press, Baltimore, Md., 1968.
19. George J. McCall and Jerry L. Simmons, *Identities and Interactions*. Free Press, New York, 1966.
20. Michal McCall, The Sociology of Female Artist: A Study of Female Painters, Sculptors, and Printmakers, unpublished Ph.D. dissertation. University of Illinois, 1975.
21. Jacquelyn A. Mattfield and Carol G. Van Aken (eds.), *Women and the Scientific Professions*. MIT Press, Cambridge, Mass., 1965.
22. Linda Nochlin, "Why Have There Been No Great Women Artists?" pp. 1–39 in Thomas B. Hess and Elizabeth C. Baker (eds.), *Art and Sexual Politics*. Collier Books, New York, 1973.
23. Peter Plagens, "Plagens Los Angeles," *The Art Gallery Magazine* 18 (April 1965): 18–19.
24. Bernard Rosenberg and Norris Fliegel, *The Vanguard Artist: Portrait and Self-Portrait*. Quadrangle, New York, 1965.
25. Julius Roth, *Timetables*. Bobbs-Merrill, Indianapolis, 1963.
26. Rita James Simon, Shirley Merritt Clark, and Kathleen Galway, "The Woman Ph.D.: A Recent Profile," *Social Problems* 15 (Fall 1967): 221–236.
27. Anselm Strauss, "The Art School and Its Students: A Study and Interpretation," pp. 159–177 in Milton C. Albrecht, James H. Barnett, and Mason Griff (eds.), *The Sociology of Art and Literature*. Praeger, New York, 1970.
28. James T. White, "Women in the Law," pp. 647–659 in Athena Theodore (ed.), *The Professional Woman*. Schenkman, Cambridge, Mass., 1971.
29. Leons White and Barbara Erlich White, "Survey on the Status of Women in Colleges Art Departments," *Art Journal* 32 (Summer 1973): 420–422.
30. Lita Whitesel, "Women as Art Students, Teachers, and Artists," *Art Education* 28 (March 1975): 22–26.
31. Tom Wolfe, "The Painted Word," *Harpers* (April 1975): 57–92.

THE USE OF IMPROVISATION AND MODULATION IN NATURAL TALK: AN ALTERNATIVE APPROACH TO CONVERSATIONAL ANALYSIS[1]

Reyes Ramos, UNIVERSITY OF CALIFORNIA – SAN DIEGO

Abstract. The musical concepts of improvisation and modulation are recommended for the study of natural conversation. A conversation is analyzed to show that a conversation can be seen as an extemporaneous composition produced by persons practicing the art of improvisation, and that conversants, like musical composers, make topic changes within extemporaneous compositions by using a procedure analogous to the modulation process used in music composition. Finally, it is suggested conversants tie in the ways they structure and manage conversations with the ways they structure and manage their routine activities in general.

In our everyday world, two sounds are ubiquitous; conversation and music. Sociologists have found both to be subjects of interest. Consequently there is a literature on natural talk [Gumperz and Hymes (10)] and one on the different aspects of musicians' lives [Becker (2, 3, 4);

Studies in Symbolic Interaction—Volume 1, 1978, pages 319–337.

Nanry (15)]. However, music theory and conversation theory have not been linked in studies done by sociologists.[2]

In this paper I will propose the use of two musical concepts, improvisation and modulation, to study natural talk.[3] In so doing, I will view conversants as improvisers, conversations as extemporaneous compositions, and topic changes within a conversation as modulations. Thus, I suggest that conversations can be seen as extemporaneous compositions analogous to the compositions produced by musicians when they improvise jazz, a contemporary form of improvisation, and that the process conversants use to make topic changes within a conversation can be seen as being analogous to the modulation process musical composers use to make key changes within a musical composition.

To illustrate the value of using the concepts of improvisation and modulation for conversational analysis, I present as data a short conversation between two college students and an interview with each conversant. I use the interview as a methodological device to do two things: first, to learn what each conversant was taking into account and using to structure and manage the conversation in the manner in which he did, and secondly, to have another aspect of the conversation so that I could compare the conversation with what was not audible, visible, or available to anyone listening to the conversation.

A discussion on how the data were collected is given with the presentation of the data in the body of the paper. I do this to show the relationship between the methodology I use and the conclusions I reach about conversants. Also, I do it to suggest that researchers document their data collection procedures in a concrete way, even when they are using the data for illustrative purposes.

To appreciate the relevance of using the concepts of improvisation and modulation for conversation analysis, it is important first to present the data and then to examine them in terms of the two musical concepts. To this end, I present first the conversation between Joe and Fred and the interview I had with each about their conversation.

A CONVERSATION BETWEEN JOE AND FRED

Fred was an undergraduate and a student in one of my classes. One day after lunch, Fred and I were sitting together discussing his term paper. Another student named Joe, who I assumed was a friend of Fred's, came to our table and began to talk with Fred. I wrote down what they said. I did it with the hopes of interviewing them separately at some later time.[4]

Figure 1

JOE	FRED
How are ya?	
	Great!
Haven't seen you for some time. Two quarters?	
	Something like that.
How's the little wife?	
	Rolling with the punches, rolling with the punches, you know how it is.
Yeah.	
	I remember when Ginny [Joe's wife] got uptight when you stayed out playing poker half the night. You guys still playing every Friday night?
	James still cleaning everybody?
Hmmm.	
No,	
	Some hell'va player.
he's won a few. Hasn't been coming lately. He and Harold have something going.	
No, no, nothing like that.	
	They're gay!
	Oh, didn't think so. They're pretty straight. I'm amazed they spend Friday nights away from the books.
They're pretty straight, straightest persons ever. June [Fred's wife] is pretty straight.	
	World is full of straight people and those who go around straightening others.
Yeah.	
	This is Professor Ramos, who is straightening out my term paper.
Oh, I didn't know I was interrupting anything. Listen, we'll just talk later. Give a call, say hello to June.	
	Right, right.

This conversation, if taken as it appears, only reveals what was said. It does not reveal what each conversant took into account when he said particular things in the conversation. Therefore, if we are to learn how conversants structure and manage a conversation and how conversants fit their conversations into some process which they create to manage their routine affairs, we need to probe further to learn about those things which are not said in a conversation, but which are taken into account by conversants.[5] To accomplish this, I interviewed each conversant.

INTERVIEWS WITH CONVERSANTS

After Joe left, I asked Fred if I could discuss his conversation with Joe. He agreed, but was somewhat reluctant because he could not see any value in talking about a "short and irrelevant" conversation. However, in spite of his doubt, Fred talked about it. In so doing, he revealed to me how he structured and managed the conversation to conceal information from Joe.

FRED: Look, there was nothing to it. He came, we talked, and he left.
RAMOS: Yeah, right, but, ah, I wrote a few notes. . . .
FRED: You wrote it down!
RAMOS: I didn't think you'd mind.
FRED: I don't, but isn't it a waste of time?
RAMOS: Probably, but I'm interested in conversations.
FRED: You heard it and you wrote it down. So what else is there?
RAMOS: I don't know. That's what I want to find out. Like, for example, what did you think
              when you saw Joe coming this way. I took the expression on your face as a cue you
              knew and expected Joe to come over.
FRED: Yeah, you see, I saw him and sorta hoped he'd wave and go on his way. I didn't
              want to talk with him, but he came over. As he got here [to the table] I kept
              thinking, Wonder if he knows?
RAMOS: Why did you think that?
FRED: See, Joe's from my hometown. You know, the high school hero, the good kid down
              the street. His parents know my wife's parents and my parents. He was elected the
              kid most likely to succeed. He really should've been elected the big gossip. He's a
              real blabbermouth. Personally, he's a pain in the ass.
RAMOS: He's a blabbermouth? [I was not sure about the connection between Joe's being a
              blabbermouth and Fred's wanting to avoid him.]
FRED: [He noticed that I did not appear as if I understood.] I kept wondering if he knew I
              was separated from my wife. I wasn't about to tell him if he didn't. Did you know
              about that? [His being separated.]
RAMOS: [I shook no with my head.]
FRED: Thought everyone did; seems that way. Oh well, when he came up and said, "How
              are ya? Haven't seen you, etcetera, etcetera," I kept thinking, Oh God. Why me?

He'll tell everybody [back home]! Then when he said, "How's the little wife?" I flipped. I couldn't tell if he knew or not and I assumed he didn't. At least I was going to play it that way. So I thought, God! If he doesn't know, I'm not gonna tell'm. He'll tell Ginny [Joe's wife], she'll tell her parents, they'll tell ours, then the shit'll fly. Gotta talk about some'm else. his troubles.

You know, I was searching for something to talk about. You know, how a lot of things go through your head when you're in a bind and you can't seem to think. Well, the only thing that kept popping into my head was the trouble he got into with his wife. You know, that's all I could think about. I guess because the last time I saw him that was the big thing with them. So I switched the subject to that, so we'd get away from my hassles and talk about poker playing.

RAMOS: Okay, what happened, ah, what did you think when he mentioned your wife's name?

FRED: I thought I'd gotten off into talking about poker and the other guys when he surprised me with that. At that point, I thought, He doesn't seem to give up. He knows. No, he's too dumb to be crafty, be cool. You know, I got carried away. I don't want him spreading this news around. But I caught myself, you know how your head goes wild and you eventually control it. That's when I sorta smiled at him and you, and figured I'd bring you into the conversation. With that I thought I'd change the conversation to a more permanent topic, you know, something we couldn't get off of as easily. I guess I used you. For a minute I didn't think he would leave. Did you? He finally left.

After we finished discussing the conversation, I told Fred I wanted to interview Joe in the same fashion I had interviewed him. He agreed to help me, even though he still could not see the relevance of what I was trying to do. He got Joe's telephone number for me and I called him. I explained what I wanted to do and he agreed to come to my office the following afternoon.

Interviewing Joe was difficult. He was too curious about why I wanted to interview him about his conversation with Fred. Consequently, every time I asked a question about why he had asked something about Fred's wife he wanted to know if anything was wrong with her. Every time he did this I had to engage in a few topic changes (or what I call smooth modulations) to keep from revealing Fred's secret. Besides trying to keep from revealing Fred's secret, I also had to promise Joe I would not discuss our interview with Fred. Below is part of the interview with Joe.

RAMOS: What were your thoughts when you saw us and decided to come over?

JOE: Nothing really, just, Should I say hello? You know, we're old high school friends.

RAMOS: How did you know what you were going to talk about? I mean, ah, how did you select your subject of conversation?

JOE: [Puzzled look.]

RAMOS: You know, you asked about the little wife.

JOE: What about her? Is there anything wrong?

RAMOS: I've never met her [gulp! There goes the secret.] I mean, the asking about her part
        of the greeting, or. . . .
JOE: Well no, I mean, ah, can you promise not to mention this to Fred? I'm flunking out.
        It's embarrassing. You know, I was the big hero in high school and Fred was a
        "nobody" and now he's making it here and I'm not. It's a put-down for me. So
        when I said."Two quarters," I thought school. The lights came on, you know.
        Then I thought, He'll ask about school. That's when I asked about the little wife.
        What did I say?
RAMOS: How's the little wife?
JOE: Right, and we started talking about poker and the poker group, James and Harold
        and all that. All along I kept thinking, Don't ask me. Because I didn't want to talk
        about my grades and all that. You know how it is.
RAMOS: No, I mean how is it with you?
JOE: You know, when you're preoccupied with something, it's always on your mind.
        Being near the end of the spring quarter, I'm preoccupied with grades and staying
        in school. Right?
RAMOS: Right.
JOE: Anyway, everything was okay until he brought up the subject. I think he men-
        tioned books because James and Harold study a lot. That's when I thought, Shit
        You know, I thought his talking about James and Harold would naturally lead to
        the usual question, "And how are you doing in school?" Then when I asked about
        June. I wanted to get the hell away from the subject of school, you know. She's
        straight arrow. Her family's very religious. Don't think they wanted her to marry
        Fred. They hassled him a lot. He's kind of immature, a great guy in ways, but
        immature.
RAMOS: How about when I was introduced? That dealt with school.
JOE: Yeah, but that also was my way out. Notice how we ended the conversation? Did
        you notice how I talked real fast there at the end before I left? I didn't give anyone
        a chance to talk, boom, boom, boom, and I left.

As can be seen, Joe also had a hidden side to the conversation. His was
as interesting as Fred's. While Fred wanted to keep Joe from knowing
about his separation from his wife, Joe wanted to keep Fred from learning
about his being on the verge of flunking out of school. He found it embarrassing to reveal that he, the high school hero, the one most likely to
succeed, was flunking out, while Fred, who was a "nobody" in high
school, was doing very well in the university. Therefore, every time the
subject of school came up in the conversation, Joe tried to change it to
something else.

AN ALTERNATIVE VIEW

By contrasting Joe and Fred's conversation with what they had to say
about it in their interview, we can see that there is more to conversations
than "meets the ear." As can be seen, Joe and Fred are not only con-

cerned with exchanging words during their conversation. They appear to be more concerned with structuring and managing the conversation in terms of other aspects in their lives, because they do not treat their conversation as a separate entity. They see it as being very much a part of the coping strategies they develop to manage their routine affairs in general, which tend to transcend the here and now of the individual conversations they have in the course of a day.[6]

Surprisingly, in the literature on natural talk, researchers have not studied the linkages conversants make between the conversations they have and the broader social context in which they operate. In practically all studies, researchers focus upon the internal structure of conversations. Consequently, attention is given to such things as the following: conversational openings and closings, the conversational sequencing which follows a particular conversational opening, and the ways in which conversants take turns speaking [(Jefferson, (11); Sack, (16, 17); Schegloff, (18, 19, 20)]. These internal features of conversations are interesting and useful. However, by focusing upon them, researchers do not provide an analytical framework broad enough to study my data (i.e., how a conversant ties in the ways he structures and manages a conversation with the ways he structures and manages his routine affairs in general). Therefore, I have had to develop an alternative framework to analyze my data, and it is based on the two musical concepts, improvisation and modulation.

IMPROVISATION

As stated earlier, the concepts of improvisation and modulation have not been used for conversational analysis, or for that matter, sociological analysis. Therefore, it is important to define them and to discuss briefly their particular use in music, while simultaneously delineating their value for conversational analysis.[7] Improvisation is defined as ". . . the art of performing music spontaneously, without the aid of manuscript, sketches, or memory" (*The Harvard Dictionary of Music,* 1969, p. 404). Implied in this dictionary definition, as well as in most lay persons' understanding of the term, is the idea that improvisation is an activity which requires no forethought or academic preparation. This definition, however, is oversimplified and greatly distorts the complexities of doing jazz improvisation.[8]

Improvising jazz is the art of extemporaneous composition. Jazz musicians, in composing extemporaneously, abide by the same rules of composition used by any other composer. There is little difference in the seriousness of composing on paper at a desk and of composing extemporaneously on a bandstand. The difference that can exist between the two types of composition is in terms of the manner and place in which it is done and in terms of the opportunity to correct mistakes. The person composing on paper has the chance to make corrections while the jazz improviser does not have that opportunity.

In improvising jazz, a musician must know what he is doing. He must know the general framework on which he bases his improvisation, which includes the following features of a composition or tune: the length, the thematic and harmonic structure, the length of the different sections of the tune, the tonality of the tune, and whether or not there are any temporary modulations to other keys. Moreover, he must know the chord progression on which the tune is based and the emotional quality or mood of the tune [Coker, (5) pp.4]. The jazz musician, then, develops harmonic,hrhythmic, and thematic strategies to weave into an ongoing process the motif or idea he is going to express.

If one were to listen to a jazz band play a given composition, he would first hear a theme introduced by the entire group. Theneach of several players would take a turn improvising upon that theme, while the others backed him up with an accompaniment. As he improvises, the musician must draw upon his knowledge of the tune they are playing: what he plays will have a relationship with what the others play and may even have a relationship to another piece they have played together at another time. For example, the entire jazz band may introduce the tune in the first segment of the piece. Following this introduction, the trumpet player, then the saxophonist, the drummer, and the pianist each take a turn improvising on the tune. The piece is concluded with the recapitulation of the theme, again played by the entire group.[9]

In conversational analysis, this aspect of taking turns is commonly referred to as either turn taking or sequencing, while in jazz improvisation it is called trading twos, fours, or eights. The numbers refer to the number of measures that are to be played by each member of a group. For example, when jazz musicians are trading fours, each musician improvises on the four measures which follow the four which were just performed. Jazz musicians do this until everyone in the group has had a chance to perform, or until it is decided to end the tune or move on to some other compositional form.

Besides knowing the musical requirements for doing improvisation, the musician also takes into account the qualitative features of his fellow performers and the audience, and makes what he considers the appropriate adjustments. In this respect, the musician and the conversant improviser are the same. Thus, when people come together to talk they have a sense of why it is they have come together and the specific and the possible range of topics they might talk about. That is, conversants, like musicians, have a sense of the thematic and harmonic structure on which they are going to base their improvisation (i.e., talk). Conversants usually know when they are talking out of "tune" and when and why the course of the conversation needs to be changed. (I will discuss topic changing in relation to the musical concept of modulation.) However, the point is that conversants are improvisers and they improvise in much the same way musicians do.

Within an entire piece, the improvisation that each musician produces can be seen either as a complete composition which stands by itself, or as part of a larger composition. Individual conversations can be described in the same way: a conversation can be seen as complete in itself, and also as talk which is part of a larger process. Thus an individual conversation can have a beginning, middle, and an ending, and can be taken to be complete, while at the same time the conversation can be taken to be a completed section which fits into a larger process or composition. For example, when two acquaintances meet and talk, their conversation seems to be a complete whole. However, what they say to each other also has a relationship to things they have said to each other in the past. In this sense, the immediate conversation is part of an ongoing whole of past and future conversations between the conversants.[10]

MODULATION

In music theory, the term modulation means the change of key or keys within a composition. Modulation is the passing from one tonality to another by means of a regular melodic or chord progression (*American Heritage Dictionary*, 1969, p. 844). Four functions of a modulation in a musical composition are to intensify harmonic motion, to underscore dramatic change, to produce contrasts of mood and color, and to emphasize structural divisions [Siegmeister (22, pp. 37–50)]. For a composer, then, the process of modulation is an expressive and structural device. It provides him with a means of unparallelled power for the achievement of emotional, psychological, and dramatic contrasts (p. 37).

The conversant, like the musical composer, makes use of a device similar to modulation to change topics within a conversation. In so doing, he can influence the direction of the conversation in much the same way that a musical composer orchestrates the internal structure of a composition. Furthermore, conversants usually make use of the process of modulation to change topics for one of two reasons, either to conceal or to reveal. Why this is done will be explored more fully when I return to Joe and Fred's conversation.

Basically, there are two types of modulation, abrupt and smooth. An abrupt modulation is exactly what the term implies: an abrupt change of key takes place without any structural preparation for the change within the composition. The abrupt change of key is usually noticed by the listener as well as by the performer of the composition.

The opposite is true in a smooth modulation. The change of key is structurally prepared. The change occurs gradually, and it is generally not noticed until the new key is well established. The smooth modulation process is usually accomplished in four stages, and they are as follows: the establishment of the home key, the use of a pivot chord, the entry into the new key, and the establishment of the new key.

The first and fourth stages of the process are the same and are necessary for both smooth and abrupt modulations. There must be a home key from which to modulate and it must be well established from the beginning of the composition, at least before the change takes place. This is accomplished by a chord progression in which there is sufficient dwelling on the primary chords in order to identify the key. For an abrupt modulation, the second stage, the use of a pivot chord, is not necessary. However, it is necessary for a smooth modulation. Several things can be said about the pivot chord: it belongs to both keys of a modulation, it serves as a link between the two keys, and it leads strongly to the dominant chord of the new key. Sometimes several pivot chords are used in a smooth modulation. The following is an example of chords which can function as pivot chords between the keys of C and G.

Two of the chords in the key of C are the I (one) chord, which is based on the tonality of C, and the V (five) chord. They are written in this way:

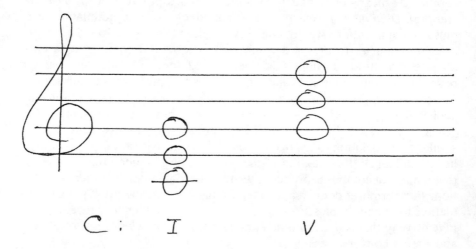

The I and V chords in the key of G are written in this way:

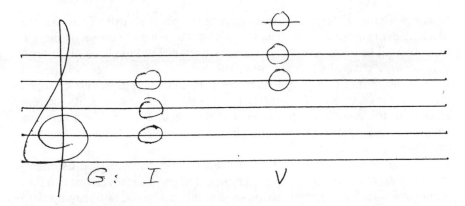

Notice that the I chord in the key of G is the same as the V chord in the key of C. When listening to this chord, the listener would not necessarily know which key it is in. Similarly, the IV chord in G is the same as the I chord in C.

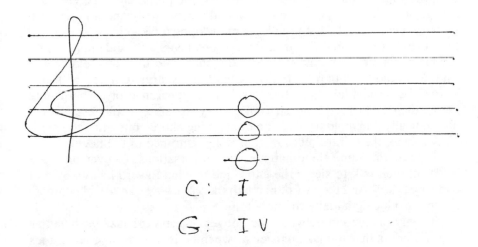

Those chords which can be found in two keys, such as the C-I and the G-IV, or the C-V and the G-I, are used as pivot chords. When a pivot chord is played, the listener does not know which key the chord is being played in and whether or not the key has changed or is about to be changed.

This uncertainty tends to be the case for the listener because the pivot chords are embedded in what is called a modulating sequence which is made up of modulating phrases. Moreover, the modulating phrases contain the melodic line of the composition and the melodic line generally consists of pivot notes which form part of the pivot chords. Thus, for the listener, everything that he hears is within the normal course of the old tonality until he discovers there has been a change of key. This discovery, if it occurs, generally comes after the new key is well established. I suggest this sort of thing happens to conversants when topics are changed during a conversation. This tends to happen when conversants are engrossed in the conversation and do not realize that their co-conversants have switched topics on them until later in the conversation when the new topic is well established.

Although there is a qualitative difference between a musical listener's and a conversant's response to the change, I suggest a conversant can find it embarrassing for different reasons to reveal that he did not keep up with the conversation. Therefore, on most occasions conversants accept the change without demanding directly that they return to the original topic. Sometimes a new topic can be an opportunity for all the conversants concerned.[11]

The third stage of the modulating process is the entry into the new key. In an abrupt modulation the entrance is not prepared, whereas in a smooth modulation it is. The entrance is done gradually and it is signaled by the appearance of what is called a modulating tone which is embedded in a modulation chord. The modulating tone bears an accidental characteristic of the new key and it signals the entry into the key melodically. That is, in modulating from a key without any sharps to a key with one sharp, the accidental characteristics is the appearance of a sharp note before the new key with one sharp in its key signature is fully established harmonically and melodically. The modulating chord containing the modulating tone, then, introduces the harmonic entrance of the new key.

I suggest the same thing happens in conversations. Conversants use words in their talk to signal the entry and moving toward a new topic of conversation.[12] And they work in much the same way as musical composers to introduce gradually the new topic.

The only distinction between the conversant and the jazz musician as improvisers is that the jazz musician, when he is improvising jazz, does not change keys privately. That is, any change in key is known and expected by the other musicians who are part of the musical group. I suggest this is not the case in most conversations. A conversant changes topics, in most cases, without telling the other conversants. He does this by using the smooth modulation process, and he uses this process either to conceal or reveal something. And, certainly, in doing so the conversant can control the conversation or at the very least influence its direction. I further suggest that in this sense, the conversant is more like the composers of written compositions than jazz musicians. The conversant withholds information or gives partial information in much the same way that a composer withholds certain aspects of the composition until it fits in with his idea of what is to go on.

This last aspect of conversant's use of information needs further discussion. I suggest that while managing and structuring a conversation to mesh with other strategies for coping with the problematic features of everyday life, conversants use four types of interpretive knowledge to make sense of what they are doing. Conversants continually use background knowledge which consists of past experiences that conversants may or may not share; foregoing knowledge, which consists of what a person knows, is categorically relevant for the duration of a particular setting; emergent ground knowledge consists of the topics or contents of a conversation that unfold in the process of interaction. Finally, there is the use of transcendent ground knowledge which consists of the potential topics which might be considered relevant and useful in some future point in the course of the conversation or some later conversation [Kjolseth, (12)].

I suggest that the process of using the four types of interpretive knowledge to make sense out of what is going on is synonymous with the art of composing extemporaneously. As conversants compose, they link what they are doing within the conversation with what they know about the larger world in which they operate. Moreover, I suggest that the modulating process within a conversation is the tie or link conversants make between the larger society in which each respective conversant operates and the conversation being produced. This aspect is seen in the interviews in which we can read what the conversants are saying and thinking throughout the conversation.

Finally, I do not wish to imply that conversants never change topics without notifying each other, because they do. As the reader might guess, the abrupt change in topic is analogous to abrupt modulations in music. However, I am more concerned here with smooth modulations than with abrupt modulations in natural conversation. Therefore, abrupt modulations and their use in natural conversation will not be addressed directly.

DISCUSSION

I have discussed in a general fashion how the musical concepts, improvisation and modulation, may be useful for conversational analysis. Now I will use them to discuss my data, and thus show in a concrete fashion their utility for conversational analysis. Consider Figure 2 in which the conversations between Joe and Fred is combined with the interview data and in which the pivots the conversants use to change the subject and the direction of the conversation are pointed out.

Figure 2

(Interview data) JOE'S THOUGHTS	JOE	FRED	(Interview data) FRED'S THOUGHTS
Should say hello.	How are ya?		Wonder if he knows?
	Haven't seen you for some time, Two quarters?	Great!	Oh God,
He'll ask me about school.	How's the little wife?		Why me? He'll tell everybody back home.
		Something like that.	God! If he doesn't know, I'm not telling 'm [about the separation from his wife]. He'll tell Ginny [his wife], she'll tell her parents, they'll tell ours, then shit'll fly. Gotta talk about some'm else, his trouble.
		Rolling with the punches, rolling with the punches, you know how it is. I remember when Ginny got uptight when you stayed out playing poker half the night. *[PIVOT]*	
	Yeah.	You guys still playing every Friday night? James still cleaning out everybody? Some hell'va player. *[NEW TOPIC]*	
Don't ask me.	Hmmm.		
	No, he's won a few. Hasn't been coming lately. He and Harold have		

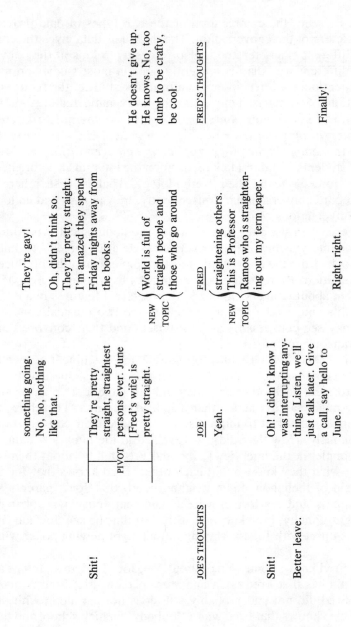

As can be seen, the combination of the two types of data provides a broader picture of the conversation. The interview data gives the conversation a different character and it also forces us to look at the conversation in a different way than is presently done in most studies on natural talk. As mentioned earlier, in most natural talk studies, the focus is on a conversation's internal structure (or the systematic features of talk's structure), and not on how *conversants create the internal structure of a conversation in terms of their respective practical circumstances which they have to manage in the process of doing their everyday lives.* I suggest that most students of natural talk focus upon the internal structure because they are "forced" to by their methodology. That is, researchers only seem to record conversations. Consequently, they always end up looking only at conversations.

However, when we alter or widen our methodological procedures to include the interviewing of the conversants, we are "forced" to shift our primary focus from the conversation to the conversants, the producers of the conversation. By making the conversant the primary focus, we then have to talk about conversations and their internal features in a different way. To this end, I recommend the use of the two musical concepts so that we may see conversants as improvisers and their conversations as extemporaneous compositions.

To be more specific, let's turn to Figure 2 and examine it as an extemporaneous composition produced by two improvisers. Joe and Fred did not plan to meet each other and they did not have a set plan or idea of what they might say to one another if indeed they met. Therefore, when they did meet, they had to improvise or compose their conversation extemporaneously. How they did it is revealed in the interview data.

For example, in the interviews, Joe and Fred tell us about themselves and about what they know about each other. Fred knows that Joe is the local gossip of their hometown neighborhood, that Joe's parents know Fred's parents and his former wife's, and that Joe plays poker every Friday night. Finally, Fred knows that the last time he saw Joe and Ginny, Ginny was upset with Joe for staying out all night playing poker with the boys.

Just as Fred knows some things about Joe, Joe also knows things about Fred. He knows that Fred is an immature person, that Fred is married, and that Fred did not and probably still does not get along with his in-laws. Joe also knows that Fred was a "nobody" in high school and that he is doing quite well in the university now.

In addition, in the interviews, each tells us that they have something to conceal from each other. Joe wants to hide from Fred the fact that he is flunking out of the university, while Fred wants to hide from Joe that he is separated from his wife.

All of what they know about themselves and about each other constitutes' the social knowledge they use to interpret how they are to structure and manage (i.e., compose extemporaneously) their conversation in terms of what they know about the broader social context in which they operate. Thus, each time the subject of school or wife is brought up (or thought by Joe and Fred that they are about to be brought up), Joe and Fred change the subject and direction of the conversation. And they do it to each other's respective disadvantage.

I suggest that Joe and Fred change the subject of the conversation by using the smooth modulation model described above. As they improvise (talk) Joe and Fred put into their extemporaneous composition words and phrases that they use as pivot points to modulate smoothly into another subject of conversation. For example, Fred uses the phrase "rolling with the punches," and the subject of Ginny getting uptight as pivot points in the modulating progression which changes the subject from talking about his wife to talking about poker playing. Both use the word "straight" as a pivot point to change the subject. Joe uses it to get to the subject of Fred's wife and away from the subject of school, and Fred uses it to introduce me and to get away from talking about his wife. And as can be seen from the two interviews, each uses the introduction of the professor as a means to terminate the conversation on a smooth and at an appropriate point.

By discussing Joe and Fred's conversation in the above ways, I have shown that an analytical framework based on the musical concepts of improvisation and modulation is possible for conversational analysis. I have done it by contrasting a conversation with what the conversants had to say about their conversation. In so doing, I have shown the following:

1. Conversants can be seen as improvisers.
2. Conversations can be seen as extemporaneous compositions produced by improvisers using four types of interpretive knowledge to make sense of what they are doing.
3. Conversations as extemporaneous compositions can be seen as standing by themselves as complete entities, as well as parts of a larger process (i.e., coping strategies) people create to manage their routine affairs.
4. The modulation sequences conversants (improvisers) use in their extemporaneous compositions (conversations) to change topics and direction of conversation can be seen as the linkages conversants make between the ways they structure and manage a conversation and the ways, stucture and manage the other activities they create to manage everyday life.

In conclusion, I suggest that to record and analyze only what people say to one another and not discover what people are taking into account while talking is to overlook why people talk with one another in the ways they do, and to miss how people create their coping strategies for managing everyday life.

FOOTNOTES

1. I wish to thank the following people for their helpful comments: Aaron V. Cicourel, Hugh Mehan, Edward Rose, and Bennetta Jules-Rosette. A summary of this paper appeared in *Sociolinguistics Newsletter,* Fall 1976.

2. Weber (1958) is the only possible exception. He used music theory to compare Western with Eastern music. However, he did not use musical concepts as sociological concepts in their own right.

3. This paper, and another one in which I used the same two concepts to provide a more concrete way to do depth interviewing, form part of a larger work now entitled *Rewriting the Social Scale: Music Theory as Sociological Theory.*

4. Although I wrote (very fast and in my "shorthand") most of the conversation as it occurred, I filled in the few gaps that existed in my version of the conversation when Fred and I discussed it. I write down conversations as a matter of habit, and this conversation was not taken down with the idea that I was going to use it in a paper. I am using it now because it is the best of all the conversations I have and because I had good and immediate access to the conversants.

5. When I say, "What conversants take into account," I mean that social knowledge which consists of what is going on during the conversation, as well as the social knowledge the conversant has about different aspects of the broader social context in which he operates.

6. I wish to point out here, as I do in more detail in a subsequent paper ("Movidas: Strategems in Mexican American Society"), that presentation management [Goffman (6–9)] like individual conversations tend to transcend the here and now of the immediate social context in which they occur. This is the case because presentation management (as specified by Goffman) and conversations are the same thing.

7. This discussion on the two musical concepts is written for the layman. Anyone looking for a more detailed discussion should consult a book on music theory.

8. For an excellent discussion on the complexities of jazz improvisation, see Gunter Schuller's piece on Sonny Rollins (21), and Jerry Coker's book (5).

9. I have outlined a standard way in which most jazz groups organize a performance. I do not wish to imply that all jazz groups perform in the manner outlined, because they do not.

10. Schegloff and Sacks (18) allude to something like this in their paper on "Opening Up Closings." However, they only discuss the opening up of a conversational closing in terms of the internal features of the conversation and not in terms of what the conversants, independent of each other, might be doing when they are "opening up a closing."

11. I suggest that the process by which persons turn the topic changes during a conversation into opportunities is the same as the process by which persons manage encounters. And I suggest that looking at presentation management in the way I have specified can be a more fruitful way of learning what takes place when people manage each other during their encounters.

12. I suggest that the person who is most likely to be first aware of the signal and the entry into a new topic is the person doing the modulating.

REFERENCES

1. W. Apel (ed.), *The Harvard Dictionary of Music*. Harvard University Press, Cambridge, Mass., 1969.
2. H. S. Becker, "The Professional Dance Musician and His Audience," *American Journal of Sociology* 57 (1951): 136–144.
3. ———, "Some Contingencies of the Professional Dance Musician's Career," *Social Problems* 3 (July 1955): 17–28.
4. ———, "The Culture and Career of the Dance Musician," pp. 65–98 in Charles Nanry (ed.), *American Music: From Storyville to Woodstock*. Transaction Books, New Brunswick, N.J., 1972.
5. J. Coker, *Improvising Jazz*. Prentice-Hall, Englewood Cliffs, N.J., 1964.
6. E. Goffman, *The Presentation of Self in Everyday Life*. Doubleday, Garden City, N.Y., 1959.
7. ———, *Behavior in Public Places*. The Free Press, New York, 1963.
8. ———, *Interaction Ritual: Essays on Face-to-Face Behavior*. Aldine, Chicago, 1967.
9. ———, *Relations in Public: Microstudies of the Public Order*. Basic Books, New York, 1971.
10. J. J. Gumperz and Dell Hymes (eds.), *Directions in Sociolinguistics*. Holt, Rinehart & Winston, New York, 1972.
11. G. Jefferson, "Side Sequences," in David N. Sudnow (ed.), *Studies in Social Interaction*. The Free Press, New York, 1972.
12. R. Kjolseth, "Making Sense: Natural Language and Shared Knowledge in Understanding," in Joshua A. Fishman (ed.), *Advances in the Sociology of Language*. Mouton, The Hague, 1971.
13. A. Marrian and Raymond Mack, "The Jazz Community," *Social Forces* 38 (March 1960): 211–222.
14. W. Morris (ed.), *The American Heritage Dictionary*. American Heritage Publishing Co., Inc., and Houghton Mifflin Co., Boston, 1969.
15. C. Nanry (ed.), *American Music: From Storyville to Woodstock*. Transaction Books, New Brunswick, N.J., 1972.
16. H. Sacks, "An Initial Investigation of the Usability of Conversational Materials for doing Sociology," in David N. Sudnow (ed.) *Studies in Social Interaction*. The Free Press, New York, 1972.
17. ———, "On the Analyzability of Stories by Children," in J. J. Gumperz and Dell Hymes (ed.), *Directions in Sociolinguistics*. Holt, Rinehart & Winston, New York, 1972.
18. E. A. Schegloff, "Sequencing in Conversational Openings," *American Anthropologist* 70 (June 1968): 1075–1095.
19. ———, "Notes on a Conversational Practice: Formulating Place," in David N. Sudnow (ed.) *Studies in Social Interaction*. The Free Press, New York, 1972.
20. ——— and Harvey Sacks, "Opening Up Closings," *Semiotica* 8 (1973): 289–327.
21. G. Schuller, "Sonny Rollins and Thematic Improvising," in Martin Williams (ed.) *Jazz Panorama*. Collier Books, New York, 1964.
22. E. Siegmeister, *Harmony and Melody*. Wadsworth Publishing Co., Belmont, Calif., 1965.
23. R. Stebbin, "The Theory of the Jazz Community," *Sociological Quarterly* 9 (June 1968): 461–494.
24. M. Weber, *The Rational and Social Foundations of Music*. Translated and edited by Don Martindale, *et al.* Southern Illinois University Press, Carbondale, 1958.

STUDIES IN SYMBOLIC INTERACTION

Volume 2.   Spring 1979   Cloth   Approx. 350 pages   Institutions $25.00
ISBN NUMBER: 0-89232-105-9   Individuals $12.50

CONTENTS:

A 10 percent discount will be granted on all institutional standing orders placed directly with the publisher. Standing orders will be filled automatically upon publication and will continue until cancelled. Please indicate which volume Standing Order is to begin with.

 **JAI PRESS INC.**

P.O. Box 1285
321 Greenwich Avenue
Greenwich, Connecticut 06830

(203) 661-7602   Cable Address: JAIPUBL.

RESEARCH IN SOCIOLOGY OF KNOWLEDGE, SCIENCES AND ART

An Annual Compilation of Research

Series Editor: Robert Alun Jones, Department of Sociology,
University of Illinois.

The essays in this annual series consist of original research done in the fields of the sociology of knowledge, science, and art. As the contents of the first volume suggest, the focus of the series will be explicitly interdisciplinary, including contributions from philosophers and historians as well as sociologists, and extending to the philosophy of science and history of ideas as well as sociology. A number of theoretical and methodological perspectives, as well as nationalities, will be represented. The series will also serve as the vehicle for essays of a length or content inappropriate to more conventional scientific journals.

Volume 1.   Published 1978   Cloth   304 pages   Institutions $25.00
ISBN NUMBER: 0-89232-026-5   Individuals $12.50

CONTENTS:

A 10 percent discount will be granted on all institutional standing orders placed directly with the publisher. Standing orders will be filled automatically upon publication and will continue until cancelled. Please indicate which volume Standing Order is to begin with.

 JAI PRESS INC.

P.O. Box 1285
321 Greenwich Avenue
Greenwich, Connecticut 06830

(203) 661-7602   Cable Address: JAIPUBL.

OTHER SERIES OF INTEREST FROM JAI PRESS INC.

Consulting Editor for Sociology: Rita J. Simon, Director, Program in Law and Society, University of Illinois

ADVANCES IN LAW AND PSYCHOLOGY
Series Editor: Robert L. Sprague, Director, Institute for Child Behavior and Development, University of Illinois

COMPARATIVE STUDIES IN SOCIOLOGY
Series Editor: Richard F. Tomasson, University of New Mexico

POLITICAL POWER AND SOCIAL THEORY
Series Editor: Maurice Zeitlin, University of California—Los Angeles

RESEARCH IN COMMUNITY AND MENTAL HEALTH
Series Editor: Roberta G. Simmons, University of Minnesota

RESEARCH IN ECONOMIC ANTHROPOLOGY
Series Editor: George Dalton, Northwestern University

RESEARCH IN LAW AND ECONOMICS
Series Editor: Richard O. Zerbe, Jr., SMT Program, University of Washington

RESEARCH IN LAW AND SOCIOLOGY
Series Editor: Rita J. Simon, Director, Program in Law and Society, University of Illinois

RESEARCH IN ORGANIZATIONAL BEHAVIOR
Series Editors: Barry M. Staw, Graduate School of Management, Northwestern University and Larry L. Cummings, Graduate School of Business, University of Wisconsin

RESEARCH IN RACE AND ETHNIC RELATIONS
Series Editors: Cora B. Marrett, University of Wisconsin, and Cheryl Leggon, University of Illinois, Chicago Circle

RESEARCH IN SOCIAL MOVEMENTS, CONFLICTS AND CHANGE
Series Editor: Louis Kriesberg, Syracuse University

RESEARCH IN SOCIAL PROBLEMS AND PUBLIC POLICY
Series Editor: Michael Lewis, University of Massachusetts

RESEARCH IN SOCIAL STRATIFICATION AND MOBILITY
Series Editor: Donald J. Treiman, University of California—Los Angeles

RESEARCH IN SOCIOLOGY OF EDUCATION AND SOCIALIZATION
Series Editor: Alan C. Kerckhoff, Duke University

OTHER SERIES OF INTEREST FROM JAI PRESS INC.

Consulting Editor for Sociology: Rita J. Simon, Director, Program in Law and Society, University of Illinois

RESEARCH IN SOCIOLOGY OF KNOWLEDGE, SCIENCES AND ART
Series Editor: Robert Alun Jones, University of Illinois

RESEARCH IN THE INTERWEAVE OF SOCIAL ROLES: Women and Men
Series Editor: Helena Z. Lopata, Center for the Comparative Study of Social Roles, Loyola University of Chicago

RESEARCH IN THE SOCIOLOGY OF HEALTH CARE
Series Editor: Julius A. Roth, University of California — Davis

STUDIES IN SYMBOLIC INTERACTION
Series Editor: Norman K. Denzin, University of Illinois

ALL VOLUMES IN THESE ANNUAL SERIES ARE AVAILABLE AT INSTITUTIONAL AND INDIVIDUAL SUBSCRIPTION RATES.

PLEASE WRITE FOR DETAILED BROCHURES ON EACH SERIES

A 10 percent discount will be granted on all institutional standing orders placed directly with the publisher. Standing orders will be filled automatically upon publication and will continue until cancelled. Please indicate with which volume standing order is to begin.

 JAI PRESS INC.
P.O. Box 1285
321 Greenwich Avenue
Greenwich, Connecticut 06830
(203) 661–7602   Cable Address: JAIPUBL.

RESEARCH IN SOCIAL PROBLEMS AND PUBLIC POLICY
An Annual Compilation of Research
Series Editor: Michael Lewis, Department of Sociology,
University of Massachusetts, Amherst.

Research in Social Problems and Public Policy presents original analyses of contemporary social issues and the policy responses they elicit. It is informed by an editorial philosophy which holds that the value of sociology must ultimately be measured by its power to provide an analytic basis for maximizing human serviceability in society. Each contribution will be selected because it breaks new ground and promises to provide fresh premises for policy discource. On the assumption that the nature of the problem to be studied should determine the method of its study, the papers appearing in this annual series will represent a variety of analytic approaches extant in contemporary society.

Volume 1.   Spring 1979   Approx. 350 pages
ISBN NUMBER: 0-89232-068-0

TOPICS COVERED: Deinstitutionalization, Resource Scarcity, Ethics as a Social Issue, Race Relations, Anti-Feminism, Adoption Policies, Etiologies of Criminal Deviance, Urban Affairs, The Sociology of Special People, The Pathological Implications of Crowding, Planning in Rural America.

PARTIAL LIST OF CONTRIBUTORS: Bernard Beck, Northwestern University; Robert Leik, University of Minnesota; Myron Glazer, Smith College; Lewis Killian, University of Massachusetts; Margaret Anderson, University of Delaware; Howard Alstein, University of Maryland, and Rita Simon, University of Illinois; Michael Lewis and Anthony Harris, University of Massachusetts; Sylvia Fava, City University of New York; Bernard Farber, Arizona State University; Harvey Choldin, University of Illinois; Robert Cook, free-lance sociologist; Rosalie Genovese, Cornell University.

A 10 percent discount will be granted on all institutional standing orders placed directly with the publisher. Standing orders will be filled automatically upon publication and will continue until cancelled. Please indicate which volume Standing Order is to begin with.

 JAI PRESS INC.
P.O. Box 1285
321 Greenwich Avenue
Greenwich, Connecticut 06830

(203) 661-7602   Cable Address: JAIPUBL.